Songs
of
Blood
and
Sword

Songs
of
Blood
and
Sword

A DAUGHTER'S MEMOIR

FATIMA BHUTTO

NATION
BOOKS

NEW YORK

Copyright © 2010 by Fatima Bhutto
Published in the United States by Nation Books,
A Member of the Perseus Books Group
116 East 16th Street, 8th Floor
New York, NY 10003

Nation Books is a co-publishing venture of the Nation Institute
and the Perseus Books Group
Published in Great Britain by Jonathan Cape, Random House

Books published by Nation Books are available at special discounts
for bulk purchases in the United States by corporations, institutions, and
other organizations. For more information, please contact the Special Markets
Department at the Perseus Books Group, 2300 Chestnut Street, Suite 200,
Philadelphia, PA 19103, or call (800) 810-4145, ext. 5000, or
e-mail special.markets@perseusbooks.com.

A CIP catalog record for this book is available from the Library of Congress.
LCCN: 2010925718
ISBN: 978-1-56858-632-8
British ISBN: 0780224087537

10 9 8 7 6 5 4 3 2 1

For my Joonam, Nusrat, who is always with me
And my mother Ghinwa
for giving me life

THE BHUTTOS OF LARKANA

Taken from a family tree commissioned by Zulfikar Ali Bhutto
and kept in 70 Clifton

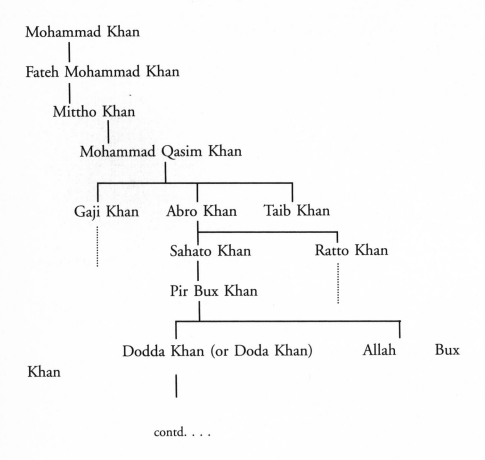

Mohammad Khan

Fateh Mohammad Khan

Mittho Khan

Mohammad Qasim Khan

Gaji Khan   Abro Khan   Taib Khan

Sahato Khan   Ratto Khan

Pir Bux Khan

Dodda Khan (or Doda Khan)   Allah   Bux

Khan

contd. . . .

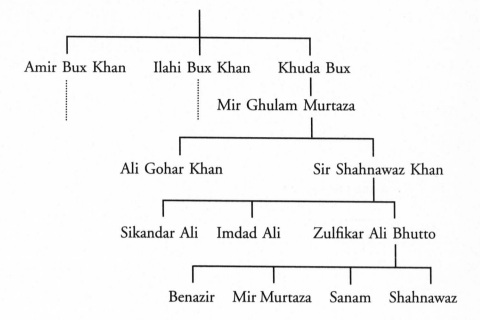

شعر بی نام

بر سینه ات نشست
زخم عمیق و کاری دشمن

اما
تو ایستاده نیفتادی
این رسم توست که ایستاده بمیری
در تو ترانه های خنجر و خون
در تو پرندگان مهاجر
در تو سرود فتح
این گونه
چشم های تو روشن
هرگز نبوده است

Poem of the Unknown

On your breast lay
the deep scar of your enemy
but you standing cypress did not fall
it is your way to die.

In you nestles songs of blood and sword
in you the migrating birds
in you the anthem of victory
Your eyes have never been so bright.

KHOSROW GOLSURKHI (Executed 1972)

Preface

12 November 2008

It is almost eleven at night in Karachi. From my bedroom in 70 Clifton I can hear the constant hum of traffic. I'm used to the sound now; it has become the soundtrack to my writing and thinking here. But now there are sirens too. Ambulances, or maybe politicians, driving around the city blaring out announcements of their arrival. Heavily armed elite guards, mainly Rangers toting Kalashnikovs, accompany them. Sometimes, there's gunfire. More often than not, it's a staccato burst and it sounds far away. It's not the wedding season in Karachi, when macho males take to the streets and spray the sky with bullets. It's not New Year's Eve, traditionally boisterous and often peppered with gunfire to mark the start of the New Year. This is the new Karachi. But we've seen it all before.

Fourteen years ago I missed weeks of school because of the violence that had taken hold of our city. I remember going to sleep hearing the hum of bullets nearby. I remember picking up the newspapers the next morning and seeing the previous night's body count. It was a dangerous city then, my Karachi. The Sindhi PPP government launched a genocidal strike, called Operation Clean-Up, against the ethnic Muhajirs who form the bulk of the MQM political party. The MQM began to hit back. They formed their own death squads and the sound of their revenge became aggressively familiar too.

There were moments, when I was younger, when it scared me to be here in Karachi, in this house. I used to shiver in the dead of summer nights, begging myself to sleep and praying that I might push past the fear of the violence and the spectres of the dead that surrounded me and my city. But one night I heard the mynah birds outside my window crowing at five in the morning. After that I would wait to hear them, these dark, rough birds, and I would fall asleep as they reassured me with their raven song that we had defeated the night once more. I made my peace with 70 Clifton and with this city when I realized that the sounds of the mynah birds would not follow me elsewhere and that I would miss them should I pack my bags and head somewhere far away

But that was a long time ago. We haven't lived like this in over a decade. We haven't been this afraid in a long time.

After the PPP government fell in 1996, on the heel of more violence, we had a few years of calm in Karachi as Nawaz Sharif, the leader of the sometimes opposition sometimes ruling party, the Pakistan Muslim League, blundered through his own second term. It was quiet then. We went to school, took our tests, ate our watery lunch at the school cafeteria, and came home safely.

After the Musharraf coup and the advent of the war on terror, we saw violence rear its head in our city again. The times and methods of terror had changed in the sleepy interim period; violence shifted its course and mutated, growing stronger until it became an unrecognizable strain of what we once knew intimately. This time they weren't gunmen. Instead, they were suicide bombers and they tended to strike fast-food outlets and crowded malls designed like traditional bazaars. When they were feeling particularly aggrieved, they attacked embassies. But we Karachiites, so schooled in survival, knew which ones to avoid. We avoided driving past the American consulate. We didn't drive very close to the British high commission either. And we ordered take-away when we were feeling peckish.

The electricity just went off, blinking out in between the typing of these words. The lights go out all the time now; this is the fifth time the power has been cut today. It's worse outside the city, though. A friend recently returned from the interior told me today that in central Sindh villagers are lucky to get two hours electricity a day, if any at all. Autumn in Sindh, oddly enough, is one of the hottest periods of the year. Rarely, on good days, my friend explained, four hours worth of electricity might reach the poorest houses across the province. There is, fortunately, a generator in my house so I sit in the darkness listening to the restless sound of Karachi's errant traffic, chaotically composed of cars, trucks, amped-up motorcycles carrying families of four or more and auto rickshaws, as I wait by the glow of my laptop for the generator to whirr into life. Its frenzied sound overpowers everything. It's like a mosquito buzzing in my ear as I write.

Electricity prices under this new PPP government have soared. The Karachi Electrical Supply Company, one of the most corrupt organizations in this country, has always been appalling – no matter whether you're at home or not your electricity bill is always the same. You pay phenomenal changes and then sit in darkness for most of the year. The poor, who don't have generators, subsist in darkness. Pakistan recently missed its millennium goal of eradicating polio, still rife in our country, because the state could not guarantee the proper refrigeration of the vaccines. Corruption is as simple as that. This winter, Karachi traders have decided not to pay their KESC bills in protest over the latest blackouts. They've been on the streets every day this week, burning their electricity bills in Saddar, the city's commercial centre; burning tyres in Malir, a poor Baloch neighbourhood near the airport; and protesting outside local press clubs and business centres. India has just launched a moon mission and we can't even light up the streets. We are a nuclear-armed state that cannot run refrigerators.

But back to the violence. We've had a record number of suicide bombings in the past year, topping Iraq and Afghanistan at various points. Suicide bombers have grown plucky now; they are no longer targeting infidel Western food outlets or foreign embassies. Now they strike on main roads, outside office buildings, police stations and army barracks; they direct their vengeance against the government and those politicians, back in office, who have promised us to a foreign power.

For several months, unmanned American Predator drones have

been flying over Northern Pakistan in what feels like daily missions. Local newspapers report the strikes that kill scores of people with disheartening ease. They say the 'operations' were 'successful'. Our newspapers, which are now so heavily censored that my column, which I wrote for two years, has been halted because the democratic government of Pakistan does not tolerate criticism – especially not internally – are shallow empty shells of what newspapers ought to be. They never say exactly what they mean – that a 'successful' drone mission means people were killed, often as they slept. Sometimes, they tell us that the dead were militants. Sometimes they tell us they were Al Qaeda operatives. Other times, they say they were part of the burgeoning Pakistani Taliban. They're never civilians. There are never mistakes; the drones remove the possibility of human error. This is terrorist hunting, American-style. Dead women and children killed in their schools and fields are 'human shields', young boys armed with only blackboard slates in their local madrassahs, since they have no government schools to attend, are future *jihadis*, it is inconceivable that anything less than the hysterical is possible.

We are a country that has enthusiastically fought the war on terror against our own people for the last seven years. But never before have we allowed a foreign country, American or otherwise, to carry out strikes on our own soil. It's unheard of. Never before have we allowed machines to fly through our skies and kill our citizens for free, as if life here costs nothing and can be swiftly cancelled out if the political will is strong enough.

Pakistan is being spoken of now, as if the transition happened quietly, almost secretly, as the third front in this war: Afghanistan, Iraq and now Pakistan. Robert Fisk was on Al Jazeera – a channel still officially banned in Pakistan, the ban circumvented by wily cable operators – saying the excitement over the recent global financial meltdown has been used to cover the fact that Pakistan is the world's new battleground. The American vice-presidential candidates, in their debate, both said Pakistan represents more danger than Iran. Barack Obama has said, if need be, America will bomb us. But they already have.

Tonight, as I write this, the BBC is reporting that a US missile strike in North Waziristan has killed eight schoolchildren. Two missiles, fired from yet another drone, hit the school this morning. The school was near a supposed Taliban commander's house. The Pakistani Army issued a classic *we're investigating this* response. The United States has said nothing. This is how wars are fought now. The new President of Pakistan has hungrily asked for drone technology for himself; he needs it, he says, to fight Pakistan. The new parliament has vowed vigorously to continue to help America, and its allies, the Pakistani Army, to launch successful operations against the terrorists. Or militants. Or Al Qaeda. Or schoolchildren, if they happen to get in the way.

Bodies, mutilated corpses bearing the signs of torture, have started turning up again in Karachi, on the outskirts of the city, in jute sacks. The newspapers, sedated, merely note this. Man found on a highway, cause of death body riddled with bullets, killer unknown – the victim had been shot to death. End of story. There is nothing new about this. Recently, I met the German consul general; he had come to say goodbye – he was retiring from his post and leaving Pakistan. I mentioned the resurgence of tortured bodies and roadside burials, mentioned that there was a time when this happened before. He told me his office had reports of sixty such deaths. Sixty such sacks since the new government took over in February, not even a year ago. I asked him what the timing meant to him. He shrugged and nibbled on some more goodbye cake. 'I'm retiring,' he laughed.

Political opponents of the PPP, not necessarily very active or interesting ones, have left the country. They're waiting out their time in Dubai or London. Those who stayed have missed the opportunity to lounge in exile and have been dealt a different sort of banishment. The former provincial representative of Larkana, a rotund, thuggish fellow, who belonged to an anti-PPP pro-Musharraf party, has been in jail since he lost the February elections. The charge levelled against him is that he plotted to kill the President's sister, a housewife turned politician. His lawyers have quit. No one will defend him. Another opposition member, a currently elected

7

member of parliament and former Chief Minister of Sindh who belongs to the same passé pro-Musharraf party, was physically beaten in the middle of the assembly. The Home Minister, a wealthy business associate of the new President turned politician, came on television after the public beating his party associates had carried out and said, ghoulishly, 'I'm a doctor, we've just treated a sick man.* If he is not careful, he will receive more of our medicine.' The Information Minister of the PPP – who also happens to be a former Karachi socialite and journalist as well as being the Minister of Health and an advisor to the President – said in August, ahead of the new President's debut, that her party 'never indulges in the politics of revenge'. It was telling that such a statement had to be made; they're prostesting too much, thought those of us who have suffered under these political demagogues. But that's how the business of politics is done now.

How have we come to this state of affairs? The journey goes back a long way, before my father was murdered.

Four years ago I set out to trace my father's life. I opened dusty boxes filled with newspaper clippings, letters, diaries and official documents kept and collected by various members of the family over a forty-year period. I unearthed my father's old school bag, kept in its own dusty box, and racked my memory for names of college friends and classmates, cold-calling people whose names sounded familiar and writing long letters to addresses that I hoped were still valid. The search for my father's past took me across Pakistan, from our Karachi home to the peaks of the Frontier province and the lush plains of

---

* The Home Minister is a doctor, businessman, politician, was once in the supposed running for the chairmanship of the Pakistan Cricket Board and is an old chum of the President. He has been charged, at various points in time, with the crimes of fraud and murder. His wife, a doctor, businesswoman, politician and old chum of the President, is the speaker of the assembly.

Punjab. I travelled across Europe and America, searching out lost loves and old acquaintances, all connected in the web of my father's youth. Interviews were conducted in person, by email, and on the telephone. Photographs were scanned and sent across or delivered by mail when we felt that the internet might be too open a space on which to exchange information about sensitive topics. I spoke not only to childhood friends and family members who remembered the Bhutto children at their youngest and most uncomplicated, spread out across continents, but also to police officers, members of my grandfather Zulfikar Ali Bhutto's cabinet, founding members and foot soldiers of the original Pakistan People's Party, judges, lawyers, and South Asia experts and professors. There were many who asked that I protect their identity; it is not an easy task to speak out against the status quo, to criticize the legacies of serving parliamentarians and presidents, but they spoke to me still and interviews were conducted in crowded meeting places to circumvent our voices being picked up by the recording devices that logged conversations at home. Other times, when it might have been too dangerous to be seen speaking to me, interviews were done in confined private spaces, without notebooks or pens, memory serving as my only transcriber until I was safely at home and able to put pen to paper and record what I had learned. 70 Clifton, our family home, is an archive in itself. It is a living testament to the Bhuttos. There are still wardrobes filled with my great-grandfather's suits and shelves that hold my grandfather's cologne, Shalimar, his glasses and his cufflinks. Bookcases rise towards the ceiling cluttered with velvet-lined state albums and official government memoranda in musty green leather folders bearing the insignia of the Prime Minister's office. Documents, both written by hand and officially typed, served to build a political as well as a personal chronology.

It has been difficult to surround myself with the lives and scandals of the dead, to immerse myself among their personal effects and to speak to them through interlocutors acting as mediums. I have struggled to imagine people I have loved and known as human beings independent of my recollections. My detective work has been shocking and painful at times, but it was, for me, an uncomfortable and necessary pursuit. Milan Kundera once said that the struggle of people against power is the struggle of memory against forgetting; this is my journey of remembering.

{ I }

I9 September 1996. It was close to three in the morning and we were sitting in the drawing room downstairs, a room typical of the house's abstract art deco style, boxed in with no windows, with maroon velvet walls and decorated with modern Pakistani art. We had just come back from dinner at the Avari Hotel. Papa's birthday had been the night before and some friends had invited us for a belated celebration. He was forty-two.

The Avari is one of Karachi's grander hotels, founded by an old Parsi family patriarch, Dinshaw Avari, who eventually passed it, as is the custom in Pakistan, to his son, Byram. It's rather a plain hotel, painted blue and white on the outside, not too ostentatious, unlike the spate of foreign chain hotels that are the Avari's neighbours. In the days before skyscrapers captured the imagination of the city's architects, the Avari was advertised as the country's tallest building. Now banks compete with each other over whose building is the highest as they struggle upwards to escape from the smog and poverty of the city. In the mid-nineties, the Avari Hotel was known for being home to Karachi's only Japanese restaurant, Fujiyama. We had eaten there that night.

That Friday evening Papa was wearing a navy blue suit, one of the few he had that still fitted him. Like his father, my grandfather Zulfikar Ali, Papa was a dandy when it came to clothes and grooming. He was an elegant man, nearly six foot three with salt and pepper hair and a neatly trimmed moustache. Papa had put on weight over the past two years, the busy and tense months that marked our return to Pakistan and the start of a newly public life, and we teased him about it. He took it good-naturedly, insisting that he was going on a diet soon, while my younger brother Zulfi and I patted his belly.

Papa signed the Avari guestbook that night. The staff at the restaurant presented the book to him with a great flourish and opened it, ironically, on the very page where General Zia ul Haq had signed an effusive note. It was the absolute worst page they could have turned to. General Zia presided over the military coup that deposed my grandfather's government. Two years later, after arresting and torturing him, General Zia put my grandfather to death. They say he was hanged, but my family never saw the body. The army had buried my grandfather's body quietly, not even notifying our family, before they released the news of his execution to the public. Papa looked at the General's handwriting. He calmly read the General's thoughts on Fujiyama's fine cuisine before making a face at me, sticking his tongue out and frowning comically, one of the few light moments we had that night at dinner, and then turned several pages on and began to write.

At dinner Papa was quiet. He sat across the table from me with his arms crossed in front of him, his chin resting in the bridge made of his intertwined fingers. It made me nervous to see Papa, usually animated and boisterous, so subdued.

Two days earlier, Papa had returned to Karachi from a trip to Peshawar feeling calm and rested. He had arrived late and was eating dinner and telling Mummy and me about his trip when, shortly after midnight, the intercom phone in the drawing room rang. It could only be someone in the kitchen or in the office next door at 71 Clifton: no one else was awake. The kitchen was close by and Asghar, our bearer, could have walked over if he needed to tell us anything. It had to be the office. Papa picked up the phone on the first ring. '*Gi?*' he said, yes? He listened quietly for a few minutes. '*Gari tayar karo, jaldi*,' he said, get the car ready, quickly. His relaxed mood was gone. Papa put down the phone, stood up and walked towards the door that connected to my parents' bedroom. 'What's happened?' I asked. 'They've taken Ali Sonara,' Papa replied. 'They just raided his house and took him.' 'Where are you going?' I asked slowly as Mummy's hands went softly to steady my back, patting me and reminding me

14

that she was still there, that things were going to be OK. 'I'm going to find him,' Papa said and walked out of the drawing room.

Ali Sonara was from Lyari, one of the most densely populated, politically radical and poorest neighbourhoods of Karachi. He belonged to a Katchi Memon family, a small Sunni community whose roots in the region can be traced back to the Ran of Kutch and Sindh desert regions. He had been a loyal supporter of the Bhutto family since his early schooldays. After Zulfikar Ali Bhutto had been overthrown and arrested by General Zia's military coup in 1977, Sonara abandoned his studies and became one of Lyari's most prominent activists.

He joined the Save Bhutto Committee in his community and worked tirelessly to oppose General Zia's abrogation of the 1973 constitution. After Zulfikar Ali Bhutto was killed by the military government in 1979, Sonara joined the Movement for the Restoration of Democracy (MRD) and worked closely with my aunt, Benazir Bhutto, for the next ten years. He was a member of the movement's Karachi Committee and spent his time distributing pamphlets against martial law and the illegality of Bhutto's execution, holding covert meetings to enlist local support and organizing protests and demonstrations.

In 1984, during the height of Zia's dictatorial repression, a bomb was planted in central Karachi's popular Bori Bazaar. Bori Bazaar is a busy market named after the religious sect of Bohri Muslims who wear distinctive long petticoats and blouses with hijab-like hoods. When the bomb exploded, scores of women and children who frequent the bazaar to shop for fabric, beads and colourful homeware were among the injured. Upon hearing the news Ali Sonara ran to the bazaar from his home nearby in Lyari.

He was certain that the bomb had been planted by the military but if Bhutto activists raised protests, the neighbourhood would be swept and men would be swiftly carted off to jail or, worse, to stadiums for public lashings. Resistance was dealt with severely by General Zia, and Sonara, who had spent several stints in Karachi jails for his leadership role within the Sindhi community, knew that the harder you fought, the more vicious was the punishment.

When Sonara arrived at Bori Bazaar he ran back and forth between ambulances helping to shift bodies onto stretchers. He coordinated blood donations and was dealing with the panicked families of the dead and injured as best he could when Zia's Chief Minister, Ghous Ali Shah, turned up surrounded by film crews to survey the wreckage.

Ali Shah claimed that the blast had been the work of the anti-military activists, terrorists they called them then, and that the state would soon find these terror mongers and punish them without mercy. As soon as Sonara saw Ali Shah, he raced over to him and punched him squarely in the face. It was the desperate act of a desperate man. The Chief Minister promptly arrested Sonara for planting the bomb in Bori Bazaar.

He was later released without charge.

When, in May 1986, Benazir returned to Karachi from self-imposed exile in London, it was Sonara, with the help of several other prominent activists, notably Ali Hingoro, who arranged for her reception in the city. At the time, General Zia's supporters in Sindh, the Muhajir Quami Movement (MQM) party, had been set up in Karachi to present an alternative to the People's Party, whose power base was in the province. The MQM were created to present an alternative, and, failing that, simply to frighten people into switching their allegiance. Lyari had been one of the neighbourhoods first seized upon by the MQM and it was a dangerous time to show your party colours, but Sonara took the risk. He organized a *jalsa* or rally for Benazir at Kakri Ground, an enormous sports stadium in Lyari. Benazir thanked him and the others at the rally, calling Sonara out from behind her where he was acting as her chief bodyguard. 'This is my brother,' she said. '*Yeh mera bhai hai.*'

Benazir, new to organized party politics and intent on building a career that would see her reach the pinnacle of power, came to depend on Sonara. He was one of the *naujawans*, or youth leaders, who organized public meetings for her throughout the city and travelled with her as part of her security detail as she visited cities across Sindh. As a member of the Karachi Committee Sonara was a key player in the Pakistan People's Party grassroots politics and provided the backbone for Benazir's election victory.

But Sonara soon fell out of favour. His loyalty to my father Murtaza, Benazir's younger brother in exile, was proving difficult for Benazir to handle. By 1988 as Benazir began to appoint her first cabinet and bestow ministries upon those brought into the party fold by her new husband, Asif Zardari, Sonara's fondness for plain speaking had become wholly inconvenient. At a party meeting at 71 Clifton, the dispute between Sonara and Benazir came to a head. He was objecting to the apparent favours that were being distributed to members of Pakistan's business and feudal community when Benazir, who famously had very little tolerance for dissent or criticism, reacted. 'Sit down, Ali!' she commanded. 'Behave properly. I'm the chairperson of this party and you have no right to speak in front of me this way. '*Mohtarma*,' Sonara began, using the title that Benazir now insisted on being addressed by, 'it is absolutely my right. I am a political worker and it is my right to tell you what I see going wrong.'

After Benazir's government fell in 1990, Sonara went underground. He had made too many enemies, powerful men who pushed him out of the party that he had helped build as a bulwark against military dictatorship. He resurfaced in 1993 when national elections were called. When my father filed his nomination papers, Sonara joined his campaign. It was what Benazir had feared.

———◆••◆———

That night Ali Sonara had been visiting Seema and Inayat Hussain, two old PPP stalwarts. Seema Hussain is a former labour leader who joined the party under Zulfikar Ali Bhutto. She worked briefly with Benazir, but also found herself falling out of favour as the party began to veer blindly towards the pursuit of power and money. Seema, too, joined my father and worked as a leader within the women's wing of the Pakistan People's Party (Shaheed Bhutto or 'Martyr Bhutto', the party my father founded as a reform movement in 1995).

Things had become edgy around Lyari, especially for those who dared to openly criticise the government. Fearing the police might be looking for him, Sonara had moved with his wife Sakina and their two young children over to the Hussains'. But the police had tracked him down. Shortly after midnight they raided the house. The police produced no arrest warrant; they entered, picked up their target, and left. Sakina called our office at 71 Clifton minutes later. Sonara had made some phone calls from the Hussains' house and it seemed the police, waiting for some sign that he was nearby, traced the calls and swooped. 'Where are they taking him?' sobbed Sakina on the phone. 'What has he done?'

I remember Mummy being calm that night as Papa hurried out the door. It was close to one in the morning and I was scared. I tried to stop him. I followed Papa out of the drawing room and walked with him to the door, begging him not to leave. It was so late, couldn't he wait till the morning? I reasoned, pulling on my father's arm as he walked, trying to halt his movement. Why did he have to rush off like this? When I grabbed Papa's arm again, he removed my hand. 'Fati,' he said, 'I have to go and be with my people.' I felt my eyes sting. 'Let me go now,' he said, softening his voice, 'please.' I stepped back and nestled myself into my mother's arms, both of us silent as Papa got into the car and drove away into the Karachi night.

<hr />

Karachi is often described as one of the most dangerous cities in the world. Home to somewhere between 16 and 18 million people, our city is overcrowded, underdeveloped and poor. Its police force, perpetually violent and corrupt, lends itself easily to crime and has a sinister reputation among citizens irrespective of their neighborhoods. In the 1990s, under Benazir's second government, extra-judicial killings were rife. Assassination squads within the police force were known by special theatrically coded nicknames, and so-called 'encounters' or police target killings disguised as shoot-outs were commonplace. This was the city that my father was to cross that night in his search for Sonara.

Papa's first stop was the Central Investigation Agency Centre[1] in the Garden area of Karachi, near the busy Lee Market on the threshold between Lyari and Karachi's old colonially constructed commercial hub of Saddar. My father entered the *thana* or station and approached the officer on duty.

Through what information had been gleaned at the time, it seemed that Sonara's arrest had been ordered under the CIA Garden's jurisdiction. If it was a legal arrest there should have been paperwork attesting to the time, place and charges levied against him, but, despite my father's official request, no evidence of Sonara's imprisonment was produced that night. Papa and his guards, who always travelled with him in Karachi, left CIA Garden and drove towards SSP South, the police station near the Sindh Governor's residence – quite a distance from Lee Market and a rung or two up the hierarchy of powerful police *thanas*. SSP South was commanded by a notorious senior superintendent of the police named Wajid Durrani.

As the minutes ticked by and the clock neared two in the morning, the chances of finding information about Ali Sonara's arrest and whereabouts grew slim. The police in Karachi are famous mercenaries, known for not playing by the rules. No warrant meant no official culpability when a dead body surfaced on the side of a highway or in a jute bag on one of the city's many garbage heaps. My father entered the SSP South station and found it, like CIA Garden, empty except for one Pathan assistant superintendent seated behind a large wooden desk. Papa moved towards the desk. As an elected member of parliament he had the right to enter any government office, whether it was a hospital, school or ministry. 'Where are the records of Ali Sonara's arrest?' he asked again. The assistant superintendent shrugged his shoulders, 'I don't know.' My father repeated his question.

As Papa told me later, the assistant superintendent slowly put his hand on the handle of a drawer underneath his desk and steadied himself, extending his arm and pulling the drawer closer to him. As he slowly opened the drawer, there was no rustle of papers, no clicking of pens as they rolled against each other. The drawer was empty save for a gun. Papa reacted as his guards feared he might. '*Utt Jaho!*' he yelled, 'Stand up!', pulling the police officer towards him by his collar. 'Tell them all – the Deputy Inspector-General, the Inspector-General, the SSP – everyone: if you produce proof of Sonara's arrest, I'll go home. If not, if he's in danger, then none of you are safe.' They drove to one more station, the CIA Centre on Napier Road, after which they returned home without incident, two hours after they had first left the house.

A trap had been laid. My father, impetuous and fiery, had reacted just how they thought he would. By the next afternoon we noticed the first tank parked outside our house.

———◆••◆——

18 September, a Thursday, was Papa's forty-second birthday. I woke up in the morning and ran down the stairs to find him. I could hardly sleep the night before, restless with worry over Sonara's arrest and what Papa's midnight search might mean. Typically, the front pages of all the papers carried the sensational news of my father storming several police stations. No mention was made of Sonara's illegal arrest or of the complicity of the police force in his kidnapping.

We passed the day waiting: Papa for news of Ali Sonara and us for the evening celebrations that would mark Papa's forty-second year. That afternoon as Papa was in his room getting ready for the evening I went in to speak to him. He was polishing his shoes – he was fastidious about a multitude of seemingly innocuous things that had to be done in a specific way – the order of his books, the arrangement of his pens, the manner in which cups should be placed in a cupboard, the evening polishing of his shoes. 'Papa, can I ask you a question?' I said, leaning against the bedroom door. He looked up at me and smiled. 'Anything, Fatushki,' Papa said, using my Soviet nickname.

'Is Mummy my legal guardian?' I asked nervously. Papa was still smiling at me, moving back and forth between his bedside and his shoeshine station by the closet. 'Yes, of course. Why are you asking?' I didn't know why I was asking; it had never occurred to me to check my guardianship before. I just knew that if anything happened to my father I wanted to be safe. 'Papa, are you sure? Are you a hundred per cent positive that Mummy's my legal guardian after you?' I pressed. Papa put his things down and came over to me. He put his hands on my chin and lifted my face towards his. 'Of course I am, don't you worry,' he said and kissed me on my forehead.

We both knew why I was asking. I had a biological mother somewhere in America, a woman my father divorced when I was three years old. Fowzia. I hadn't seen her for years. As a child it had been my father who had brought me up: making my food, cutting my hair and taking me to school. I never felt I had a mother till he met Ghinwa sometime after my fourth birthday.

'Papa, are you sure you're right?' I asked. He nodded to me. 'Yes.' 'Well, can I have the papers that prove it?' Papa let go of my head and laughed out loud. Wherever did I learn to become so paranoid? he asked. Yes, yes there were papers – did I need them that instant? 'No,' I said, 'I just want to make sure you have them.'

The evening celebrations came and went. Friends joined us and brought sweets and bouquets of flowers and funny cards and I sat next to my father in our velvety drawing room throughout the evening. We ate dinner in the dining room, the table set by Mummy and laid with silver from my great-grandfather, Sir Shahnawaz's time. We ate Middle Eastern *mezze* and *taboule* and barbecued meats. It felt as if we were home in Damascus, far away from all the danger and violence of Karachi. But we weren't. We were in the thick of the danger, though we didn't realize it at the time. Papa kept excusing himself to go to the phone and check whether Ali Sonara had been found, but he did so discreetly not wanting to scare or upset us. We hadn't heard anything all day. More disturbingly, it looked as if the state was building a case against Papa. There had been some small blasts around the city, small *pathakas* or firecrackers put in the dustbins outside trade centres and government offices in Saddar. No one was hurt, but the tension was palpable. Late editions of city newspapers quoted the authorities as laying the blame on the workers of PPP (SB) and on my father.

By the evening, we spotted another tank, this one behind the first. The next morning there was a third, on the right-hand side of the house, hugging the corner of the office at 71 Clifton. By 20 September, two days later, there were four armoured vehicles, one on each side of 70 Clifton. We were surrounded.

'Do you regret your life?' I asked Papa after we returned home from his sombre birthday dinner at the Avari Hotel. He was sitting on his green chair, his legs crossed and his elbows resting on the arms of the chair. He paused for a moment, stroking the crown of his head as he often did when he was lost in thought. 'No.' Papa leaned forward towards me. 'I fought the government that killed my father and brother and I'm proud of that. What we failed in, we failed in, but we didn't take the coup lying down. We resisted. I'd do it all again,' he said and leaned back into his chair. We had, my parents and I, been having a light-hearted conversation – escaping briefly from the day's madness into our own private world of late-night jokes and memories. Papa was teasing Mummy and she was giggling back at Papa; they had been flirting absent-mindedly until my question brought us back to the dangerous present.

'You should write a book,' I said. Papa laughed loudly and threw his hands up in the air. 'I can't write a book while I'm alive. They'd never let me come out into the open with the things I know.' 'What do you mean? You have to do it – write a book about your life, Papa, it would be *so* interesting.' But he just laughed again, this time more quietly. 'No, I can't. You'll do it for me. You can write the book on my life.'

He smiled at me. Papa had the most beautiful spirit of any grown-up I had ever encountered. No matter that his life was often fraught with uncertainty and danger, he never let anything cloud his smile. I picked up a pen and a scrap of paper from the table, ready to take preliminary notes. 'Not now,' Papa said. 'You can write it after I'm dead.' 'Why when you die?' I felt my mood dropping and the anxiety of the past few days returning to the pit of my stomach. 'It's too dangerous before then,' he said, looking at me. Papa's eyes were sad. I don't know if he felt it too, the uncertainty of what was ahead, the growing nervousness that had rumbled inside me for days. I think he did.

20 September was a Saturday.

By the evening my father would be dead.

In the morning there was a flurry of activity in our house – bearers were rushing to prepare the meals and Mummy was planning a belated party for my brother Zulfikar's sixth birthday the following day. We had planned to hold his birthday party at a children's amusement park, Sinbad. It was ten minutes away from our house and had been built in the 1970s as a casino but was now an Islamically acceptable games centre. With its kitsch, windowless architecture Sinbad lorded it over Sea View, staring out at the grey sand on Clifton Beach and the Arabian Sea beyond.

My room was being redecorated, being made my own after two years of living in the bedroom my two aunts had shared as angsty teenagers in the 1970s, so Papa came upstairs to the TV room, used as a makeshift bomb shelter during the 1965 war and where I now slept, to wake me up. After I'd got dressed we walked over to take a look at the renovations. My parents had waged a mini-war over who was going to decorate my new bedroom. The problem was that Papa had no taste at all when it came to décor. He tried to woo me with the promise of a disco ball in the centre of the room. It almost worked. Otherwise, his plans were wholly embarrassing. While Mummy knew that I wanted light green walls and a girly flowery look, Papa hadn't a clue. He still thought of me as an eight-year-old tomboy. 'We can put in Western-style swinging saloon doors like the ones in the old movies.' No, Papa, we can't. 'OK, well how about rounded windows like in a submarine?' No. The glittering disco ball was his finest moment.

We walked into my freshly painted room. It was all white – only the base coat had been applied – and empty except for the wrought iron bed, which was pushed to one side of the room along with two side tables that hugged each other at another corner. The room looked clinical, like a hospital. 'Nice,' smirked Papa. 'I bet you're really happy you went with Mummy's design.' He laughed. *Khe khe khe.* Papa sounded like a naughty schoolboy when he laughed like that, his eyes wrinkling at the corners and his cheeks widening with each *khe.* Papa had brought back some panes of traditional stained glass from the interior of Sindh a while earlier. They were orange, blue and green. They were, in truth, repellent, but Mummy had vetoed putting them anywhere else in the house so I sided with Papa and insisted they were gorgeous. My reward was a set of my own Sindhi glass windows. They had already been installed and with the sun so bright that day and the room so white, their colours bounced across the room. 'Good windows though,' Papa murmured as we walked out of the room and down the stairs.

At two that afternoon my father held a press conference. Journalists from various local papers and television crews were assembled in the press hall in 71 Clifton, an open room with windows facing towards the garden. Papa entered the room and sat at a long wooden table facing the press. Next to him sat Ashiq Jatoi, the president of the Sindh chapter of the party, and Malik Sarwar Bagh, an elderly gentleman who was PPP (SB)'s Karachi division president. Papa was wearing a midnight-blue *shalwar kameez* that day, so dark it seemed almost black, and at his neck he wore the two-pointed sword of Hazrat Ali, the courageous disciple of the Prophet who became the first Imam of Shia Islam. Papa was not a religious man but he revered the warrior who fought for the struggling Muslims in the days when they were outnumbered and under threat. The sword, small and golden, had the words *la illah ill allah*, there is no god but Allah, with small criss-crossed etchings finely imprinted around its curved shape. It hung on a black thread around Papa's neck. He almost never wore jewellery, only a watch given to him by his father on his left wrist.

Before coming in to speak to the press, Papa called Yar Mohammad and Sajjad over to speak to him privately. The young men were his two bodyguards. They were political workers too, but once my father was released from jail they rarely ever left his side. They protected him as if he was their own father, never moving too far from him. He had information from the police, Papa explained. He asked Yar

Mohammad and Sajjad to leave Karachi. 'Go where you want, it doesn't matter where, but I don't want you or your families nearby. We don't know what they've done to Sonara and I want you safe until we find out.' Yar Mohammad and Sajjad were not to accompany Papa to his public meeting in Surjani Town after the press conference; he made it clear that he would not risk their lives. The men protested, without effect. Things were just too dangerous to take a chance. They didn't ask where the information about their lives came from or what it meant. But Papa was insistent. They were to leave him today and get out of the city, end of discussion.

When Papa started the press conference, there was a weighty silence in the room. The papers had been full of stories, some falsely titillating, some accurate, about Papa's midnight visits to the police centres two nights earlier. On 18 September, General Naserullah Babar, Benazir's powerful Interior Minister who would proudly herald the Taliban in next-door Afghanistan as 'my boys', had taken to the floor of the National Assembly in Islamabad. General Babar announced that there were going to be, according to his top-level information, two bomb blasts in Karachi as a protest against the arrest of the terrorist Ali Sonara. He informed the assembly members and the press that the perpetrators of the violence were going to be from the MQM party or the Shaheed Bhutto party. Sure enough, there were 'blasts', and the government was quick to blame my father's party. The journalists at the press conference on 20 September were eager to hear what Murtaza Bhutto had to say about all this. General Babar's clairvoyance was making for serious copy in all the papers.

Papa began his statement. 'There is a plot against me, formulated by the most criminal elements within the police force, such as Wajid Durrani and Shahbaig Suddle.' Papa named two notorious police officers. Rumour had it that they had achieved high rank owing to their close personal friendship with Benazir's husband, Zardari, and also to their well-documented penchant for violence. Suddle was the District Inspector-General of Karachi and Wajid Durrani was the Senior Superintendent of the Police, heading one of the police stations my father visited on the night of the 17th. But Papa mispronounced one of their names; it wasn't Shahbaig Suddle, it was Shoaib Suddle. We wouldn't forget Shoaib Suddle's name again, not ever.

'These men,' my father continued, 'under the supervision of Abdullah Shah, the Chief Minister of Sindh, want to kill me. My life is in danger today. I'm giving this press conference to tell the government that my bags are ready. Bring a warrant for whatever it is you are accusing me and my party workers of and I'll come myself and sit in your car.' In fact, Papa's packed briefcase had been sitting by the side of his bed since the night of the 17th.

'I want to answer the allegations the government has made about my visits to several police stations. Regarding this, let me remind you that I am an elected official, an MPA, and it is my right to enter government offices.' At this Papa held up a picture of Ali Sonara. It is a photograph of one of Benazir's *jalsas*, her political rallies; she is standing up with her head and shoulders poking out of the sunroof of a jeep, and waving at a crowd swarming around her. Several men stand behind her, eyes fierce, shielding her from every side; they are her bodyguards. Sonara is circled in the picture. 'This is the man taken by the government,' Papa said and pointed to Sonara. 'Naseerullah Babar, the Minister of the Interior, said on the floor of the National Assembly that there would be blasts after Sonara's "arrest" and that the MQM or SB would be behind it. If he had this information what did he do to avert any danger of the blasts actually going off? Nothing. There was nothing to do. This is a crackdown on the Pakistan People's Party (Shaheed Bhutto). The Interior Minister knew about these supposed blasts because it is his office that planted them. I want to tell the government that we are a political party and we will resist these illegal, warrantless arrests and extra-judicial killings politically ... We will not go into hiding. We are ready. It is not my style – in times of trouble – to hide behind my workers for protection. I stand on the frontline, they are behind me.'

We ate lunch at home in 70 Clifton while Papa was giving the press conference next door, and left afterwards for Sea View, to continue the preparations for Zulfi's party. As Mummy and I returned home, we ran into Papa, who came striding across the lobby. He was on his way out. The press conference was over. Ashiq Jatoi was waiting for him in the car outside on our driveway. I ran over to talk to my father but he was in a hurry and looked tense. 'I'm late. I have to go,' he said, stroking my back, as he moved towards the heavy wooden door. 'Papa, wait,' I said. 'Let me change, I'll come with you.' I had only climbed one or two stairs, bounding towards my bombshelter bedroom, when Papa gently caught my elbow, stopping me in my tracks. 'No, Fati, you can't come,' he said. 'Things aren't safe right now. Stay here, I'll be back soon.' I stood on the stairs and watched him walk out of the door, pulling it shut on his way out.

As Papa walked towards the car he spotted Yar Mohammad and Sajjad. He walked over to them, visibly upset. 'I told you both not to come with us today.' The threats against the two men were serious. They were very close to my father and he depended on them greatly. 'How can we leave you now?' Yar Mohammad asked. 'If things are as dangerous as you believe them to be,' continued Sajjad, 'then our place is not at home, but by your side.' They would not be dissuaded. Papa called the other guards forward, there were seven men that day. 'If the police try to arrest us on the way to the *jalsa*, surrender peacefully. Don't try to protect me, I'll be fine. Let them produce the warrants and we'll go with them.' The men nodded, they understood.

Four cars set off from 70 Clifton that Friday. Papa sat in the passenger seat of a blue Land Cruiser belonging to Ashiq Jatoi, who was driving the car. Yar Mohammad sat in the back, behind Papa, along with Asif Jatoi, Ashiq's family driver, and Asghar, a bearer from our house who often joined my father on his trips. Ahead of them was a red double-cabin pick-up truck carrying six people. Mahmood, Qaisar, Sattar Rajpar, Rahim Brohi – my father's guards – and two others. A small white Alto car, matchbox shaped and compact, drove alongside Papa's. It was carrying three people, two men who came along that day for the *jalsa*, and Sajjad. It was at Sajjad's request that the Alto drove next to my father's car, so it could act as a buffer in case anything happened. The last car was a white Pajero jeep belonging to a gentleman who had also decided to tag along to the public meeting; he was not a political worker but a well-wisher of sorts.

Wajahat Jokio, the last of my father's seven guards, sat with the Pajero owner and another passenger.

The drive to Surjani Town, a suburb outside Karachi, is a long one, more than an hour in Karachi's traffic. But it's an opportunity to pass through most of our hectic city, caught unawares on a weekend afternoon. Papa's small convoy drove towards Surjani Town on the road that leads towards Las Bela in Balochistan. Passing Clifton, they travelled north past the monument of the three swords, or *teen talwar*, emblazoned with the motto 'Unity, Faith, Discipline' on each of the large white marble swords pointing skywards. They would have driven through Saddar and its various markets – Zainab market where women's clothing and children's romper suits hang on wires outside storefronts, towards Gentila Men's Tailors near the cooperative market and close to Karachi's central post office, past the electronics market full of buzzing mobile phones and gadgets sold at half price. My father's last journey was almost a beautiful one. He drove by Quaid-e-Azam Jinnah's *mazaar*, or tomb, past the young hawkers preying on children and tourists with their cages containing small orange-beaked birds for sale. Further north, their convoy, having now grown to around thirty-five cars, sailed past Guru Mandar, an area named for an old Hindu temple but now known for its cluttered bus terminals, ferrying passengers in and out of the city.

It must have been nearly 6 p.m. by the time my father's car passed the gaudy marriage halls that mark the beginning of Surjani Town, whose boundary begins at a small police *chowki* or kiosk at a dusty roundabout. Circling inwards towards the small suburb, one leaves behind the big city's flyovers and huge concrete bridges. There are no more fast food outlets or large cars parked outside fruit stalls and shopping malls. No, there's none of that in Surjani Town.

It's a town marked only by weedy shrubs growing on the sides of the road, festooned with plastic bags that get punctured and caught as they float by. Papa was travelling to Youseff Goth, a small *Katchi Abadi* or slum within Surjani Town limits. He would be speaking to the poorest inhabitants of the area. Many party workers tried to dissuade Papa from even going to Surjani Town. 'He'd had a very large meeting in Lyari in August,'[2] Malik Sarwar Bagh remembers, speaking with such resignation that it is almost difficult to make out the words. 'Everyone told Mir Sahib, don't do the Surjani Town *jalsa* – you had such a reception in Lyari! Just like your father's! Why bother with a small place like Surjani?' But Papa refused to cancel. He had given his word to Maqbool Channa, a dedicated supporter from Youseff Goth. Bashir Daood, another party worker who had come from nearby Goli Mar, remembers my father insisting that the plan to visit Surjani Town and open a party office for religious minorities in the community was set in stone. He would not cancel.

A huge crowd of about 2,000 people had gathered on a large stretch of land bordered on two sides by arbitrary manmade ditches full of sewage and rubbish. Papa got out of the car and saw that the police had come out in force too. They had parked their battered cars on the outskirts of the neighbourhood. The police, Qaisar and Mahmood remember, had close to thirty mobile units along with several large trucks commonly used to transport prisoners. There were close to a thousand officers in Surjani Town that September evening and they were visible everywhere. They stood behind the makeshift stage erected for the *jalsa* on the edges of the crowd, with their arms folded and their walkie-talkies beeping with static. But they did nothing. The police just stood by and watched, trying to intimidate the thousands who had come out to see my father.

Papa first walked with a Christian party worker, Yousef Gill, to the new PPP (SB) office for minorities that Gill had opened in the slum. Papa and Gill talked as they walked, followed by enthusiastic supporters chanting slogans. '*Aiya, Aiya, Bhutto Aiya,*' they shouted. 'He's come, he's come. Bhutto has come.' '*Mazdoor ka leader*, Murtaza!' 'The leader of the workers, Murtaza!' '*Hari ka leader*, Murtaza! *Gharib ka leader*, Murtaza!' 'The leader of the peasants, of the poor, Murtaza!' After opening the office by cutting a ribbon and taking a brief tour of the one-roomed office, Papa hoisted a party flag on a grey metal post outside before moving on. As Papa walked over to the stage, which faced east and was made of wood, he stopped. The *azan* was sounding, it was time for the evening prayers and the sun was beginning to set. It wasn't the call of the *muezzin* that stopped Papa though, it was the light of dusk. He called Siddiqe, a jolly fellow who worked as the party photographer, and asked him to take a picture of the horizon. It was beautiful and he wanted to remember it, Papa said, as he moved towards the crowds of people waiting for him.

He climbed slowly onto the stage, waving at the people gathered before him. As he moved towards the sofa that had been placed at the centre of the stage, a group of women approached him with rose and jasmine garlands. Papa bowed his head and received the ladies, two at a time, as the garlands were placed on his neck. Behind him Ashiq Jatoi, who had only recently been elected as the Sindh president of the party, was shaking hands with several workers who came to offer him their congratulations.

Papa was still standing, meeting a new group of women who had come forward to introduce themselves and their children. One of them carried a young girl dressed in shiny blue-and-silver fabric with two pointy pigtails tied tightly on the top of her head, and after being lifted up to place a garland around my father's neck she presented him with a bouquet of roses. The bouquet was sheathed in plastic and folded into a diamond shape. It was trimmed with red ribbons and had small staples holding it together. When my father and Ashiq Jatoi sat down, guarded by Yar Mohammad, who was dressed in black and standing behind them, the bouquet rested on the sofa between Papa and Ashiq.

Malik Sarwar Bagh, the president of the Karachi division, spoke first. He called for a protest vigil at the Karachi Press Club the following day, Sunday, 21 September. Ashiq Jatoi rose next. He too was wearing a dark black *shalwar kameez* with garlands resting on his neck and shoulders. He introduced himself and said a prayer of thanks: '*Bismillah arahman uraheem.*' 'We thank God, the kind and the merciful.' It was the third time that he had come to Youseff Goth to speak to its people and he thanked them for their reception. He too raised Ali Sonara's illegal arrest. 'He has been taken and we still do not know in whose hands his life rests,' Ashiq said, speaking forcefully. He continued, speaking in a strong, steady voice, 'Not Nawaz nor Benazir will rule the people of Pakistan,' he said, gesturing at the crowd. Ashiq had also worked with Benazir during the MRD era of the 1980s and was eventually jailed by General Zia ul Haq. By the time her first government came to power, Ashiq no longer believed in Benazir's promises of true people's power and left the party. 'The people will rule, they must rule themselves, once and for all.' He was a gentle man. *Ashiq*, his name, means the one who loves, a lover. His normal demeanour was temperate and kind. He had a light and powerful spirit that didn't need to resort to volume and theatricality. But as he spoke, Ashiq changed into something larger than himself. He clenched his hand into a fist and raised it above his head. 'Our symbol is the *mokka*, the fist, and we will show those two that the strength of this *mokka* comes from the people – from Balochistan, Punjab, the Frontier, and Sindh. You are our strength and together we will return Pakistan to its rightful leaders – the people.'

The last speaker of the evening would be my father. As he walked the short distance to the podium, the crowd swelled and began to raise their *naras* or slogans. '*Zinda hai Bhutto!*' they cried. 'Bhutto is alive.' '*Jab tak suraj chand rahaiga, Bhutto tera waris rahaiga*' and the more romantically emotional, 'As long as the shadow of the moon exists, Bhutto, your heir remains.' They threw rose petals at the stage and clapped their hands loudly in welcome. Papa walked towards the podium, which was draped in an *ajrak*, traditional Sindhi fabric, printed in natural dyes of maroon, white and black. As he walked Papa ran his fingers through his hair freeing the stray deep pink rose petals that had been caught there. He removed the necklace of garlands from around his neck and placed it on one side of the podium, only to be instantly garlanded in four more threads of jasmine. Papa adjusted the two old metal microphones to his height. They didn't extend as far as they should and so he leaned into them.

He began with a thanks. 'In spite of the pressure of this administration, the gathering of all of you in Youseff Goth is a referendum of our dissent. It is a referendum in support of Ali Sonara and his fellow workers and against the violence of this regime. The people of Youseff Goth are not afraid. Today you are with us, and we are not

31

scared, despite the government's actions.' At this the crowd roared and my father's voice was drowned out for a minute. He patted the air with both his hands. *'Baat sonao'*, 'Listen,' he said.

'In history, whoever fights the corruption of the state, whoever raises his voice against forced unemployment and abuses of power, whoever fights *awam ki huqooq ki jang*, the war to defend the peoples rights, they call them terrorists. But today in Pakistan, it is the state that is drinking the blood of its citizens. The government People's Party is not your party. It is *kamzor*, weak, *begharat*, without decency or dignity. This is your party, we are the party of *quaid-e-awam*, the leader of the people, Shaheed Zulfikar Ali Bhutto's party, so don't try to frighten us.' Papa shook his hand forcefully in the air.

His voice now growing hoarse, Papa turned to Wajid Durrani and Shoaib Suddle, addressing them directly in his speech. 'We aren't afraid of your CIA centres and we aren't afraid of your police. We aren't afraid of your Chief Minister, Abdullah Shah.' At this Papa grew angry. 'Abdullah Shah, *sonao*, listen. It is not possible for dogs to fight with lions. Your corrupt and criminal police force has been filling the papers for the last week with political statements, statements that are not their right, as protectors of the people with a neutral mandate, to make. They have put armoured vehicles around my house for the last several days and they have been threatening to arrest me. "We're waiting permission to arrest Mir Murtaza Bhutto," they say arrogantly. "We're only waiting because he is an MPA and the approval has to come from *high above.*" *Auw!* Come! *Begharatoon*, you indecent men, I'm not afraid of your corrupt police.'

Once more Sonara's arrest was raised. It was perhaps the most pressing issue at the *jalsa*, more so than the current atmosphere of danger imminently focused on my father. 'Remember,' Papa continued, shaking with the force of his words, 'we are a political party. This injustice, this political violence against our workers, will not stand. We will go to the people, we will fight politically, and we will not be silent – *Dham damadam Must Qalandar*,' he repeated, quoting Sufi poetry.

The *naras* picked up again as Papa, his brow furrowed throughout his speech, smiled as he walked off the rickety stage. Maqbool Channa, the organizer of the *jalsa* in Surjani Town, had invited Papa for a cup of tea in his home. Malik Sarwar Bagh begged leave, he had to go and prepare for the Press Club the next day. 'I wish I had known,' Malik Sarwar Bagh tells me twelve years later. 'I wish I had known what was coming, I wouldn't have left your father then.'

--- ◆••◆ ---

Back home at 70 Clifton the day had passed painfully.

It was evening. Mummy was in the kitchen cooking and I went into my parents' bedroom and sat with Zulfi as he watched TV on the bed. He was a little child then and was always so easy to take care of with his easy-going and affectionate nature. We were lazily watching *Lost in Space*, a show made in the 1960s about missing astronauts; there was nothing else on. Zulfi was lying down on his stomach, his head in his hands, and I sat on Papa's side of the king-size bed, reclining and resting my head against the headboard. It was close to eight when the intercom phone rang. It was Nurya, a girl from my ninth-grade class at the Karachi American School. She was calling to arrange for us to meet over the weekend to discuss a school history project. I slumped down, leaning against the bed but sitting on the floor with my knees bent talking to Nurya. We were speaking when I heard the gunfire. It was a single shot and it sounded very close. I moved the phone from my ear and waited to see if Zulfi had heard it.

The sound was still ringing in my ears when several seconds later, the echo of the first shot was interrupted by a barrage of bullets. They were coming from right outside the window; I could hear the shooting as if the guns were firing over our heads. 'Nurya, I'll call you back!' I screamed into the phone. I leapt across the bed and pulled Zulfi into my chest. He was so close to the window and though I had no idea what was happening, I knew that was the one dangerous position to be in in the event of gunfire. I carried him, skinny six-year-old Zulfi, into the dressing room, a small windowless corridor. I slammed the door shut and went over to the bathroom door. The bathroom had windows and connected to the dressing room. I closed the door tightly before sitting down with my back against the wall. Zulfi was small and gentle. His shiny black hair was parted neatly across his head. His bird-like features betrayed his sudden fear and confusion. While the shooting lasted, five minutes at the very least, and with no pause in the crack of the bullets, Zulfi huddled against me. I hugged him and pushed his face into my arms and chest, as if I could protect him from the sound. 'Where's Mummy?' I didn't know. I hoped she was still in the kitchen, it faced the other side of the house and the gunfire wouldn't have been as close to her as it was to us.

We waited for a few seconds. It had stopped. I told Zulfi to wait for me; I was going to check where our mother was. As I stood up, Mummy burst into the bedroom screaming. 'We're here!' I yelled and she threw open the door to the dressing room instantly pulling me into her arms and pulling Zulfi up off the floor. 'Let's go to the drawing room,' Mummy said, breathing quickly. It too had no windows and was not as confined as the yellow dressing room we had been hiding in.

We sat in the drawing room for close to half an hour, waiting. The shooting had stopped and we asked our *chowkidar*, our gatekeeper, to check outside and tell us what had happened. The area was thronged with police, he said. They wouldn't let him out of the house. 'There's been a robbery, there are *dacoits* outside,' the police told the *chowkidar*. 'Stay inside until it's safe.' Mummy sat on the sofa in the drawing room with her hands to her face. I paced up and down the room. There were no mobile phones in Pakistan then. They had been banned by the democratic government (who managed to keep a few for themselves before closing down the market for the rest of the country). We had no way of reaching Papa and no choice but to wait for him, patiently.

It was past eight in the evening and he should have been back home, but we tried not to worry. I grew more agitated with every minute. Not for one instant did I imagine Papa had been hurt. Maybe he had been arrested and the firing was the police signalling their victory. I worried out loud – there had been a lot of gunfire, more than the typical burst of bullets one heard in Karachi in those days. 'Don't worry, Fati,' said Zulfi as he swung playfully behind Papa's green armchair, 'it's only fireworks.' It must have been close to nine, forty-five minutes later, when I'd had enough. I couldn't wait any longer. I told Mummy I was calling my aunt, the Prime Minister. By that point I was convinced that Benazir had had Papa arrested and I wasn't going to sit by while my father was taken to jail. I picked up the red intercom phone and asked whoever answered in the office to connect me to the Prime Minister's residence in Islamabad. 'Don't take no for an answer,' I said fiercely. 'I have to speak with Wadi.'

The phone rang minutes later, much sooner than I thought it would. It was usually a considerable hassle getting through to the Prime Minister, even – or especially – if she was your *wadi bua*, or father's elder sister in Sindhi. I picked it up and was placed on the line with the Prime Minister's aide-de-camp. I sat down in Papa's armchair to take the call. 'Hello, *bibi*, is everything all right?' The ADC sounded shaky, scared even. I didn't know whom I was speaking to – we certainly didn't have a relationship this ADC and I. 'Yes, everything's fine. Can I speak to my aunt please?' I was curt, but he kept speaking. 'Is your family OK? Is everyone fine?' Yes, yes, I responded. Satisfied with my grunts and promises that everything was fine, the ADC put me on hold.

The music on the other end of the line was soon interrupted by a click and a silence. 'Hello? Wadi?' I said, calling my aunt the name only I used for her. 'No, she can't come to the phone right now,' came the reply. It was Zardari. It was no secret that none of us in the family liked Asif Zardari, my aunt's oleaginous husband. On the few social occasions where I saw him, we shared nothing other than a cursory hello. 'I need to speak to my aunt,' I said tersely, not wanting to speak to Zardari. 'You can't,' he replied, equally brusque. 'It's very import-ant, I need to speak with her now.' 'She can't come to the phone right now,' Zardari replied. 'It's very important and I don't want to talk to you, I need to talk to her,' I insisted, my voice quickening. I had wasted enough time on this phone call already. 'She can't speak, she's hysterical,' Zardari replied. As if on cue, there was a loud wailing sound in the background. It had been quiet before, with no indication that anyone was in the room with Zardari, and all of a sudden there was an almost desperate crying shattering the silence. 'What? No, I have to speak with her, please put her on the phone,' I continued, growing confused at what seemed like a theatrical attempt to keep me from talking to the one person who was in charge. 'Oh, don't you know?' Zardari responded. 'Your father's been shot.'

{ 2 }

The Bhutto family, it is said, originated in the deserts of Rajasthan and was swept over time onto the banks of the River Indus in Sindh. Mitho Jo Mikam, a small village in between Mirpur and Garhi Khuda Bux, is where the Bhuttos first settled in Sindh. The village was named after its original settler, a fierce Rajput warrior. Rajputs, from the Sanskrit *Rajputra* or son of a king, hailed from Northern India and were known for belonging to the Kshatriya or warrior castes. They trace their lineage as far back as the sixth century and had historical dalliances with the Mughals and with the British through the Indian army. Mitho Jo Mikam fled Rajasthan, they say, due to a family feud. It is ironic that the Bhuttos of Pakistan managed to mould themselves out of a feud in the family, but fitting nonetheless.

As they settled across the province of Sindh, some Bhuttos scattering as far south as Thatta and others further north in the Punjab, Mitho Jo Mikam made a name for himself and his tribe settling land disputes. Whenever a problem occurred between two land tillers, one would invariably reach out to Mikam, who easily out-bullied the larger of the two bullies and settled the dispute, usually in exchange for land or a gift of produce.

Though they were only a minor tribe, it was water that serendipitously brought the Bhuttos into local prominence. Some time after the Mughal era, when the British were running India as they once ran the East India Company, the Raj found that it needed help managing large tracts of unirrigated land. In Begari, Jacobabad, on the border between Balochistan and upper Sindh, there was a large watercourse, a *vah* in Sindhi, that had not yet been made into a canal. The water was open and abundant. At the time, however, there were no large *zamindar* in Sindh to exploit the water and till the land around it. The government wasn't terribly fussed over who the land should belong to, but was certain that it didn't want to take on the trouble of cultivating the open land alongside the large *vah*, so it offered up a challenge: anyone with enough manpower and guts to try was welcome to the land.

In stepped Doda Khan. Doda Khan believed himself a Rajput if ever there was one. He had four able sons and the warrior blood of their ancestors had not yet been diluted by their exile. Doda Khan called his sons forward and together they rounded up Bhuttos from across the province – if you can cultivate it, it's yours. That was the promise. And so the Bhuttos came. Many men were wounded in battles over the control of the *vah* and the land, but they fought on. The nearby Baloch, themselves inflated with a proud warrior tradition, would not let the land go easily. And so they fought.

The Bhuttos fought and suffered casualties; wounded men who were returned to the villages were replaced on the battlefront by Bhuttos from other areas. They battled, led by Doda Khan, the brains behind the operation and not an easy man to confront, until the Bhuttos had secured themselves land that stretched fifty to eighty miles from Naudero, near Larkana, to the Sindhi–Baloch border in Garhi Khairo in Jacobabad. In those days the Bhuttos believed it was taboo to sell the land they had fought so hard to possess and so their holdings grew and grew. Ashiq Bhutto, a debonair man who was once a model with striking good looks until a devastating car accident robbed him of his career, and a cousin of Zulfikar Ali Bhutto, told me the legend of Doda Khan. 'You're now known as the Bhuttos of Larkana, but make no mistake – the Bhuttos were all over the place in those days and most of the land was in Jacobabad, well, until Zulfi's land reforms changed that.'[1] Finally, the tribe settled into three areas, led by three distinct branches. In Garhi Khuda Bux, you have the Bhuttos of Larkana. In Garhi Bhutto there is the line that traces down from Ilahi Bux, down to Ashiq's family and his brother, Mumtaz, the *sardar* or chieftain of the Bhutto tribe currently. In the third town of Naudero, Amed Khan, the only son of the very wealthy Rasool Bux, carried the local Bhutto line. The three towns are within sprinting distance of each other, a worrying fact since Bhuttos are not known to share easily (or at all).

In a corridor in Ashiq's house in Clifton there are photographs of all the Bhutto ancestors. The walls on both sides of the corridor are covered with photographs of the Garhi Bhuttos: Ilahi Bux, his son Pir Bux, his grandson, Wahid Bux who later became the Sardar, down to his son and Ashiq's father, Nabi Bux. There are photographs of Zulfikar Ali Bhutto as a young man, with his cousins, a photograph of my father Murtaza wearing a leather jacket, and pictures of Ashiq's three beautiful daughters.

At the very end of the corridor, far away from prying eyes, is a little piece of Doda Khan. Ashiq shows it to me one sweltering Karachi summer morning. It is a certificate on paper so old, it has greyed. In sunburnt brown ink that must have once been red, it reads: 'By command of his Excellency the Viceroy and Governor General, this certificate is presented in the name of her Most Gracious Majesty Victoria, Empress of India, to Doda Khan Bhootta in recognition of his loyalty and good service as a landholder.' It is signed by the Viceroy and dated 1 January 1877. Uncle Ashiq turns to me and says, 'I don't like the bit about "loyalty" to the British, so I keep it here out of the way.' And behind a rather large and leafy plant.

And so the Bhuttos multiplied, aided by the powerful empire of their time. The myriad of Bhuttos from the three branches continued to receive accolades from the Queen and presents of titles and land from the Raj. Rasool Bux, of the Naudero Bhuttos, had a ferocious reputation. He was a stout man with short white hair and a stubbly white beard. In a photograph on Uncle Ashiq's wall, Rasool Bux is captured sitting on a simple chair in trousers, boots and what seems to be a long-sleeved undershirt. He is holding a conspicuously large hunting rifle in one hand and a dead deer, its throat bleeding, lies in front of his feet. In family lore there is a story about Rasool Bux, who bore only one son – the very rich Amed Khan. He had a particularly nasty habit of swearing; he cursed everyone in sight and everything that crossed his path. One day, his *munshi* or land manager, a poor man who had crept into his good graces through years of servitude, approached him. '*Sain*', 'Sir', he asked, 'please don't get angry at me, but could I ask a favour?' Rasool Bux grunted. The *munshi* continued, 'Could you possibly go an afternoon without cursing? I'll offer prayers to Allah and all the saints in your honour if you would.' Rasool Bux held his tongue. 'And if I swear?' 'Then you will have to give me five months' pay, but if you don't, *sain,* then you can dock five months off my salary.' Rasool Bux, the story goes, was endeared into the deal by his affection towards the loyal *munshi* and agreed. He finished his morning tea and headed off to take a bath. Five minutes later, as he lathered his face and began to shave Rasool Bux burst out into a barrage of swearwords: '*Haram zada!* You bastard! How dare you try to fleece money off me? Take your money you swine but the next time you try to play funny with me I'll kill you!'

Then there was Ghulam Mir Murtaza Bhutto, my father's great-grandfather and the man after whom he was named, the forebear of the Garhi Khuda Bux Bhuttos. They say he was a handsome man, dashing and charismatic. They also say he was having an affair with the white wife of a British emissary. Some debate remains over whether the woman was indeed a hundred per cent white or Anglo-Indian ('they acted even whiter than the whites,' Uncle Ashiq insists), but regardless it was a torrid affair. It was said in our family that the woman's husband found out about the illicit dalliance and one after-noon invited Ghulam Murtaza to his house, where he offered him some refreshments. Ghulam Murtaza, not one to refuse the hospi-tality of a host, even a host whose wife he was planning to run away with, accepted graciously. He died shortly after the meeting; poisoned to death, legend has it.

Bhuttos very rarely, even then, died natural deaths. Many of them died violently and before reaching middle age. My father used to tell me the story of one Bhutto, a powerful local landlord. He felt that he had begun to lose favour with the locals he lorded over, but wasn't sure whose continued loyalty he could count on and whose he could not. So he faked his own death. His family was forced into announcing his funeral and made to stand around his very undead body wailing and grieving. He lay there, on a small *charpai* or cot, shrouded in white, and kept very still. He peeked when he could but assigned a servant to make a note of who came to pay their respects and who didn't. Everyone who failed to show up for the funeral was summarily punished. It was typical Bhutto shock and awe. When this Bhutto finally died, there was no seating space at his funeral to be found. The entire village turned out to pay their respects, just in case.

◆◦◦◦◆

In 1935 the India Act created councils within the various provinces in the Raj and elections were held in October 1937. In those days there were no political parties in Sindh, so it was an election that was open to very few – the powerful – and no one else. Sir Shahnawaz Bhutto, son of the poisoned Ghulam Murtaza and controversially knighted by the British occupiers, stood for election from Larkana, his home town. He was a large landowner, a respected man and a local of great influence. But he lost. A complete unknown, Sheikh Abdul Majeed Sindhi, defeated Sir Shahnawaz at the polls. Sindhi was not a resident of the district; he was an outsider with no reputation to fall back on. It was rumoured at the time that Sindhi was brought in and backed by a section of the Bhuttos themselves who were desperate to relieve Sir Shahnawaz of his local power.

'Politics is like building a temple, a house,' Zulfikar remembered his father telling him, 'or else he said it was like writing music, or poetry and he mentioned Brahms, Michelangelo.'[2] Sir Shahnawaz was an old-fashioned man. He felt betrayed by the loss of what should have been an automatic win, but did not push the issue further. He simply packed up his family and left Sindh.

By 1938, the Bhuttos were in Bombay, including Zulfikar who was preparing for his foray into college. Sir Shahnawaz had three sons, Imdad, Sikandar and the youngest, Zulfikar Ali. He had three daughters, Benazir, who died as a young girl, Manna and Mumtaz. Zulfikar's brothers were many years older than him and were noted Lotharios. Imdad was the most handsome. He wore three-piece suits and always carried himself with an air of purpose and grace. His younger brother, Sikandar, idolized him and copied his style of dress and mannerisms. Sikandar was once reprimanded by their father, who admonished him for being directionless in life. 'Why don't you comb your hair properly and get your act together?' his father said. Sikandar wore the same three-piece suits as his brother did but let his hair go wild, never slicking it back. He told his father, quite bravely, that he was an artist. He wrote poetry and wore his hair in the manner befitting a poet. Most *zamindar*'s sons in pre-Partition India were not artists. They were landowners or military men or politicians. Even business was out of the question, it was a low-caste job, kept for Hindu money-lenders and traders. Both the elder sons did as they fancied. Elegantly dressed and big drinkers, they were popular with all the young society women. They were playboys and they lived their lives freely, always followed by a gaggle of admirers. Both men, Imdad and Sikandar, died young. Their health gave out, owing to the demands of their lifestyle. They were in their early thirties and left behind young families. Imdad and Sikandar went out of the world as easily as they came in.

In Bombay, Sir Shahnawaz took up the post of the Chairman of the Sindh Public Service Commission. He was offered the chairmanship by Sindh's first Chief Minister, Allahbux Soomro, and found that a life of simple bureaucracy suited him, especially after the fickleness of local politics had cost him his home seat. Some years later, the Nawab of Gunaghar, a friend of Sir Shahnawaz, fell ill and was about to set sail to Europe for treatment. Things in India had become politically precarious for the princes, with all the rumblings of Independence and sovereignty, and the Nawab wanted to leave the running of his state in the hands of a trusted well-wisher. He asked his friend, Shahnawaz, to come and administer the Chief Ministership of Gunaghar in his absence. And so, with Partition on the horizon, Sir Shanawaz moved his family to Gunaghar. He remained there until India split, when with the Nawab and his family and the prince's twenty pet dogs (people who were obviously not dog lovers said the dogs were either Dalmatians or Great Danes), the Bhuttos moved back into what was now Pakistan.

Zulfikar spent his adolescence between two Sindhs: Larkana, in what was later to be Pakistan, and Bombay, the capital of Sindh in India. He was an athletic young boy, spending his time playing cricket and going on *shikars* or hunts with his elder brothers. When he was thirteen years old, the issue of land and his feudal stature first affected the young Bhutto. Amed Khan, of the Naudero Bhuttos, was by far the largest landowner in the Bhutto tribe. He was the only son of Rasool Bux Bhutto and cursedly bore three young daughters and no male heirs.

Sir Shahnawaz and Amed Khan came together one afternoon to arrange a mutually beneficial arrangement between their two families. Amed Khan had three daughters to marry off but wanted to keep his share of fertile agricultural land in the family. His eldest daughter, who had been abducted by a neighbouring tribe in a land dispute, was married to a Bhutto who was a local teacher. His second daughter married Imdad, Zulfikar's elder and dashing brother, who bore more than a passing resemblance to Errol Flynn.

Amed Khan's third daughter, Ameer, or Shireen as she was known among the young cousins, was a petite young woman of twenty-three when she was finally married. Zulfikar was ten years younger than his bride when their wedding was arranged. He was a thirteen-year-old boy – though some stories make Zulfikar as old as sixteen when he was bribed into the feudal marriage. If he went through with it, his family told him, they would buy him a new cricket bat. Zulfikar, barely a teenager, had been offered a deal he could not refuse. So he married Ameer. He was too young to understand what was expected of him and it would be years before he visited Ameer Begum as a man visits a wife. His cousin, Ashiq, remembers Zulfikar laughing about the story of the cricket bat years later, amused by his own innocence. Some say the marriage was never consummated; certainly no heirs were ever produced. The only thing gained by the union was a sizable amount of land in Naudero, land the family still owns to this day. It was land that made the Bhuttos' fortune and it was, for many years, a vast and intimidating fortune. At their feudal height, the Bhuttos were among Sindh's largest landowners, making them one of the wealthiest families in the developing province.

By the time the Bhuttos moved to Bombay, Zulfikar complained to friends that he had fallen in love with a girl named Soraya Karimbhoy and he had proposed to her family, only to be shot down by Soraya and her parents when they learned their daughter would be Zulfikar's second wife. Sir Shahnawaz paid little attention to his youngest son's heartache. Zulfikar was going abroad to study, a cachet few young men could boast of in those days, so his father urged him to concentrate on his future and waste no more time moping over his lost lady friend.

India was still one country when Zulfikar left to begin his undergraduate studies at the University of California at Berkeley. There was no talk of Pakistan or of Partition. The country Zulfikar left would be broken by the time of his return, and some of his detractors would later insist that he was still legally an Indian citizen. But Zulfikar's identity was constantly shaped by the shifting boundaries that surrounded him. It was in Bombay, on the eve of his departure to California, that he first read Marx. His privileged existence faced its first challenge. He was a feudal master, a large *zamindar*, but he never imagined himself as the perpetrator of capitalist aggression. He later said that it was his reading of Marx that stirred a shift in his thinking and in his attitudes towards the feudalism that those of his generation – and many still – took for granted. Decades later, when speaking of his government's land reforms, in which Zulfikar surrendered his own land (mainly the land in Jacobabad, fought for and won by Doda Khan), he said, 'I'll lose still more, my children will lose still more . . . I've felt no fear of giving up what I own ever since the day I read Marx.'[3]

At Berkeley he studied Bertrand Russell and Carl Jung and was haunted by the words of his mother, Khurshid, who was born into great poverty. Her poor origins led to the rumours that she was a Hindu and therefore from a lower social stratum than her husband, an aristocratic landowner she married out of love. Khurshid always reminded her favourite son that 'the paradise of politics lies under the feet of the people'.[4] He would be nothing without this truth at the forefront of his mind, she insisted. His potential was enormous – even as a child he was considered brilliant – but never forget, she reminded him, you come from a poor land.

Events in the US further radicalized Zulfikar. It was in San Diego during his Berkeley days that he was refused a hotel room because of his olive skin and because the employee at reception told him he 'looked like a Mexican'.[5] Zulfikar wasn't a *zamindar* any more, nor the son of Sindh's most notable bureaucrat. He was a nobody in California and the isolation and alienation he felt there followed him throughout his political career. It was after the humiliation in San Diego that Zulfikar would leave the old-boy confines of Berkeley and go down to Maxwell Street to get away. He would sit for hours with the African-Americans who lived in the rundown neighbourhood, because they 'felt real'[6] to him.

He was a contradiction in so many ways and often used to say of himself after his sojourn in California, and later Oxford and Lincoln's Inn in England, that his mind was Western but his soul Eastern. He later told his children, only half jokingly, that they were not to apply to university in California because its beautiful weather would distract them from their studies, but perhaps it was because he feared they would not weather the brutal jolt to their sense of self as successfully as he had. Zulfikar's children would attend Harvard, where self-realization would be fleeting and inconvenient among students from the world's elite.

In a letter he wrote to his son Murtaza, when he was about to graduate from Harvard, Zulfikar, by then Prime Minister, wrote:

You are halfway through your academic career. I am sure that the other half will be equally exciting and inspiring. And that you will remember the obligation of the people of your country. America is a great country. It has attained formidable power on the strength of its learning and technology. The American is full of vitality. His curiosity remains with him up to the end of his life. He is always on the move – learning, observing, and building. He is the great builder. Look at what he has done to his country. The average American does not have a penetrating mind, he does not possess the sophistication of the genuine Eastern intellectual whose brain cells go back centuries and whose contours are shaped by the old civilization.'[7]

He continued the letter with some personal advice, a haunting reminder of the courtesies he had been refused in the West while a student himself:

I am sure you will make good friends at Oxford. On my part, I consciously broke most of the links I developed with the friends I made in England and America, of course there are exceptions, but generally speaking, I thought my re-integration in the setting of our country would be speedier if I broke those links because I never wanted to feel nostalgic about America and England when I returned to the village of Naudero.[8]

Zulfikar's childhood friend, Ilahi Bux Soomro, whose father had offered Sir Shahnawaz his bureaucratic posting in Bombay, remembers Zulfikar coming to visit him in New York, where he was studying at Columbia University. Soomro is a sprightly eighty-year-old whose political roots go back as far as the Bhuttos. He called Zulfikar 'Zulfi' as many of his friends did and Zulfi in turn called him 'Iloo'. 'We would be sitting in the International House on Riverside Drive, near Harlem, and would be engaged in discussions on foreign affairs with these students from across the world, but Zulfi always came out the best. He was brilliant.'[9] It was with Iloo that Zulfikar stayed in New York on his way to embark on graduate studies in England.

When he returned to Pakistan, a new nation, Zulfikar came as a barrister. He had few friends in the new country, some cousins – including Mumtaz and Ashiq, who remembers Zulfikar calling his house on the telephone and putting on a shrill girl's voice to ask for

'Ash-tec' in order to irk his mother – and Iloo. He began work at Dingomal Ramchandani's law firm. His office was on Bandar Road, in old Karachi, near the current Sessions Court and quite close to the Palace Hotel, where the Bhuttos were staying until their house in Clifton was built.

As his reputation as a barrister grew, Zulfikar shifted to the offices of A. K. Brohi, another respected Sindhi lawyer. One day, Iloo remembers, Zulfi mentioned that Brohi had given him a legal draft to vet. As they drove around the city in Iloo's car, Zulfikar mentioned that it was a big step in his career and he'd have to spend proper time going through the document. The next day, as he often did, Iloo picked his friend up from his law office, which was near Mohammad Ali Jinnah or Quaid-e-Azam's tomb. 'How did it go with the draft?' Iloo asked, since Zulfikar hadn't mentioned it. Zulfikar smiled. 'I changed every line of it. I thought Brohi would go mad, but he accepted it.' Iloo knew his friend only too well. 'Zulfi,' he cautioned, 'you shouldn't do these things deliberately.' Zulfi continued smiling at his friend. 'I wanted him to know I know more than he does,' he replied and laughed, not joking in the least.

While his career was creating ripples in legal circles and his adjustment to life in a new country was going well, socially things in Karachi were slightly dry. After so many years abroad, in California and London, Zulfikar didn't know too many people in Karachi. He loved to go out to restaurants and nightclubs, but hadn't managed to find a suitable partner to accompany him. Sindhi families are notoriously conservative; men didn't take their wives out to social functions, let alone their daughters. It was by chance that one evening, at a wedding, Zulfikar came across a beautiful Iranian who had moved with her family to Karachi from Bombay after Partition. Nusrat was tall and slender with chiselled cheekbones and dark auburn hair. She was new to the city too and had only learned English a short while before. She had a gaggle of sisters, but none of them was of any importance when she was in the room. They all faded into the background like shadows when Nusrat was present.

Nusrat and Zulfi made an attractive couple. They were both elegant and lively, both rebellious and charming. Soon Zulfikar had fallen in love. He approached his parents to ask if he could have their permission to send a proposal to Nusrat's family, but they were not amused by their son's suggestion. Khurshid Begum put up the strongest opposition to the notion of Zulfikar marrying an outsider. Nusrat was not Sindhi; she was entirely foreign. She came from a religious Shiite family and the Bhuttos were Sunni. She wasn't even a *zamindar*'s daughter. Her father was a soap maker who had owned a factory in Bombay – even their name bore the mark of their profession, *Saboonchi*, the one who makes soap. He was a businessman, the lowest of professions in the feudal Bhuttos' eyes. Khurshid Begaum put her foot down; her son was not going to marry Nusrat. Besides, she reasoned, he was already married.

But Zulfikar was as headstrong as his mother. Early one afternoon in 1951, Zulfikar drove to his friend Iloo's house, near Quaid-e-Azam's dome-shaped marble *mazaar* and honked his car as a signal for Iloo to come outside. He was sitting calmly in the car when Iloo walked out of his door. 'Do you have any money on you?' Iloo nodded. 'Get in the car, we have to go now.' 'Go where?' asked Iloo, still confused over the surprise visit. 'I'm going to get married. To Nusrat. Today.' Iloo reminded him that under Islam he would need two witnesses, and he was just one person. He suggested they pick up a friend of his, Karimdad Junejo, a young fellow from another one of Sindh's prominent families. They sped towards Karimdad's house and yanked him into the car. 'Hurry,' Iloo told him, 'Zulfi's going to get married.' 'To whom?' Karimdad asked, astonished that he had been picked up to help Zulfi elope. 'Nusrat,' Iloo replied. 'Nusrat? That *lambhi*?' That tall girl? Karimdad laughed clucking his tongue, 'She's too tall!'

The three men drove over to Clifton to pick Nusrat up from her house, a stone's throw away from where 70 Clifton was being built for the Bhuttos. The only male in her house was her old father, who was nearly blind and not disposed to be of any help with an elopement. Nusrat's sisters met the groom's procession with the opposition that their father would have mustered if he had been of sound body.

'Have you brought the *maulvi*?' asked one of her sisters, referring to the mullah who was to conduct the marriage. The three friends had no idea they were supposed to provide the clergy.

'The closest mosque at that time was just behind the Sindh Club, ten minutes away,' remembers Iloo, leaning in conspiratorially as we speak about the famous elopement more than fifty years later – it is the first time I've heard the story directly and I lean in too, feeling momentarily involved in the hatching and planning of my grandparents' secret marriage. 'I picked a fellow up and raced back to Clifton so he could conduct the ceremony, but as we entered the house Nusrat's sisters said, "He's Sunni. We want a Shiite *maulvi*. Send him back", so I dropped the fellow all the way back to his mosque and asked him if he could direct me to where I might find a Shiite mullah. He opened the car door, got out, and abused me heartily.' Iloo has always been a religious man, and as he drove around in circles scouting out other possible mosques, he stopped to say his *asr* or mid-afternoon prayers at a mosque near Bori Bazaar in the middle of the city.

As he walked out of the mosque having completed his prostrations he stopped a *maulvi* and asked if he was Sunni or Shiite. For the second time in the day, Iloo had a hail of curses flung at him by a member of the clergy. 'As I was walking out sheepishly after having been yelled at, a gentleman approached me. He had overheard my conversation and said, "*Beta*, son, you won't find a Shiite *maulvi* at a mosque." So I asked him where I could find one and he told me that I should go to the Imam Bargha, or Shiite mosque. I had no idea where the Imam Bargha was. In those days we didn't think of ourselves, Sunnis and Shiites, as so separate – what did we know? The gentleman told me it was nearby in Bolton market.' After crossing Bolton market, Iloo caught sight of a friend on the road and stopped him to ask for help. His friend laughed at him. 'You're never going to get a Shiite *maulvi*, you need to book them days in advance.' Iloo explained his predicament to his friend, who ended up saving the day. 'Go to Sindh Madrassah – there are two schools, one preaching the Sunni teachings of Islam and one for the Shiites, you might find someone willing to perform the *nikkah* there.'

By now it was dusk, nearing the time for *maghreb* prayers, and Iloo pulled up at the madrassah just as a *maulvi* was walking out. 'I stopped him and asked him to please come with me to Clifton to read a *nikkah* for your grandfather. The *maulvi* was reluctant to come with me. "How much will it cost for you to perform the ceremony?" I asked him and he shrugged his shoulders and grumbled that it would cost fifty rupees. I pulled out the hundred-rupee note from my pocket and handed it to him. "There," I told him, "that's your advance" and pulled him into the car.'

After the ceremony was read and the marriage contract signed, Iloo packed the newlyweds into the car and drove them to the Palace Hotel. They were married, finally.

Two days later Sir Shahnawaz hosted a reception for his son and his new wife, but he was not the least bit pleased about it. Khurshid Begum was even frostier to her new daughter-in-law. A week later, Zulfikar and Nusrat took off to Turkey for their honeymoon. They would stay with his sister Mumtaz, who had married an army man posted by the Bosphorous. In the black-and-white photographs from their honeymoon, the only ones taken marking their union as man and wife, Zulfikar has his coat collar pulled up to his chin and Nusrat is wearing a sari under her overcoat. They looked beautiful, my grandparents, like old-time movie stars.

＊•••＊•＊

In the 1950s, Pakistan, like most other nations, was caught up in the quagmire of the Cold War. Neutrality or non-alignment was not considered an option by the military coterie that even then pulled the strings of Pakistani politics. Impartiality was deemed impractical on the basis that the emergence of an equally powerful third force was unforeseeable in the near future. Pakistan rejected the possibility of bipartisanship and joined forces with the United States in its urgent quest to rid the world of communism.

Even as a young student, this angered Zulfikar who felt that 'the central motif of the so called bipartisan policy of the United States was to tie up all the nations outside the Iron Curtain into an intricate net of interlocking alliances which would embroil them all in any attempt by the communist states to spark off a conflagration.'[10] It was under this guise that Pakistan was to become a part of SEATO, the supposed South-East Asian counterpart of Europe's NATO, in 1954. Zulfikar felt it ridiculous for Pakistan to ally itself with this monstrous power, claiming to have common interests, when, 'while blood flowed in Kashmir, Jeffersonian America kept aloof with remarkable nonchalance, whereas the first shot out of a trigger-happy communist in any theatre of the world can cause such a reaction throughout the non-communist bloc.'[11]

The world was being ripped apart by dissension and attempts to disrupt the balance of power. This disarray in world politics meant that 'in one breath, the leaders of the world preach peace and in the next threaten to obliterate civilization with atom bombs . . . our position', wrote Zulfikar, speaking of Pakistan, 'is pathetically unstable'.[12] Fifty-odd years years later, Zulfikar's assessment rings frighteningly true: Pakistan remains in a desperately unsound state.

The frustration the young Zulfikar felt towards the state of world affairs was matched by his feelings of solidarity towards the Third World. While still studying at Berkeley he insisted that it was necessary for us to 'halt this moribund pattern of our politics and rearrange our world in a revolutionary way'.[13] He felt himself most strongly attached to the fate of fellow Muslim nations. When looking at the state of world affairs at the time, Zulfikar reflected, 'I am not a devout Muslim, I do not say my prayers regularly; I do not keep all the fasts . . . my interest is soaked in the political, economical, and cultural heritage of Islam.'[14] Sindhis, especially, born into a culture rich with Sufi Saints, Hindu lore and tribal ancestry, aren't known for their observance to orthodox Islam. The Bhuttos were never devoutly religious, unusual for Pakistan's political elite, but Zulfikar must have been only twenty-one years old when he committed himself to the renewal of his Muslim brethren, saying, 'I genuinely consider any accomplishments of the Islamic people as a personal feat, just as I consider any failure of the Muslim world as a personal failure.'[15] It was a romantic notion, the idea that in order to break the chains of the status quo and to ease the plight of future generations of Asians and Muslims alike, it would be necessary for the people of such diverse blood and myriad heritages to come together as a unified whole, putting aside their cultural, political and linguistic differences. He truly believed that a unity of this kind would 'give to the world a blueprint of the brotherhood of mankind'.[16] Considering the lay of the land in today's world, Zulfikar's political desire to see the dispossessed come together to defeat centuries of ruthless exploitation sounds fanciful, but Zulfikar carried this dream with him for many years to come. When he later became Prime Minister of Pakistan, Zulfikar would write long letters to his eldest son, Murtaza, then away at Harvard, detailing in an almost lecture-like way all that was happening in Pakistan and around the globe. In one letter, after discussing the Vietnam War and the tragedy of its people, Zulfikar reminded his son, 'I am telling you this because you are an Asian. You belong to this part of the world. You have to live here and work for the people of your country. You can never think of leaving your homeland.'[17]

———◆———

The Pakistan Zulfikar returned to after his time abroad was entirely new to him. It was, after all, only a few years old. He had finished Berkeley, carried on at Oxford and then passed the bar at Lincoln's Inn, where Jinnah himself was schooled in the field of law. Education, Zulfikar always told his children, is the one thing no man can rob you of. 'There is no last phase in education, it continues from birth to death, from the time one begins to see and observe and understand till the time one ceases to see, observe and understand.'[18]

In 1953, the Bhutto house at 70 Clifton was in its final stages of completion. The gate had two plates: one in a dull gold with the name of Sir Shahnawaz Bhutto and another, directly underneath it in a muted bronze colour, that announced the name and title of the first professional Bhutto: Zulfikar Ali Bhutto: Bar at law. At this time, Zulfikar, married to Nusrat, became a father. Their first child, a daughter, Benazir, born in June 1953, was named for her father's sister, who died as a young girl. Her mother delivered her in one of Karachi's Christian hospitals. Begum Mazari, the sister of the renowned Baloch fighter Akbar Bugti and the wife of the *Sardar* of the Baloch Mazari tribe, remembers visiting Nusrat in the hospital after her first delivery.

'It was hard for her, she had tears in her eyes,'[19] Begum Mazari says of the friend she remembers as a lively young woman. All the family had expected a son, and the delivery of a girl was one more reason to resent the woman who the Bhutto family had fought so hard to ostracise. 'Nusrat said that hardly anyone had called on her to congratulate her on the birth,' Begum Mazari says, even though Zulfikar doted on his daughter, treating her tenderly and spoiling her rotten. 'You know,' she continues, 'he was a very progressive man. He broke many taboos. In Sindh you only saw males, only the men would be out in public, but Zulfi took Nusrat everywhere with him, even on state trips.'

Begum Mazari visited Nusrat in the same Christian hospital a year later, in 1954, when Mir Murtaza was born, and noticed a world of difference in the atmosphere in the maternity ward. 'When Mir was born, her mother-in-law cooked her food and brought it to her in the hospital. She gave her gifts of jewellery and looked after Nusrat in a way she had never done before.' Not that this is unusual, especially in Pakistan. Even today the birth of a girl means dowry, wedding arrangements, and sadly little else. 'I remember I asked her, Nusrat what are you doing? I keep coming to the hospital to see you! And she laughed, she was much happier this time, and said what can I do? Zulfi likes children.' In quick succession, two more children were born. Sanam, a girl, and Shahnawaz, named for his grandfather. Zulfikar and Nusrat's small family was complete.

In Pakistan, separating rumours from fact is often a laborious job, especially when it comes to politics. It was at this time, shortly after the birth of his children, that Zulfikar left his practice in law to join active politics. It is said that it was Nusrat, his foreign-born wife, to whom Zulfikar owed his political career. An Iranian friend of Nusrat's had married Iskandar Mirza, the President of Pakistan. As the government was facing a steady stream of unsettling upheavals, Nusrat mentioned to her friend Naheed Mirza that she might ask her husband to invite Zulfikar to join politics; he was from a good family and had a brilliant young mind lauded in his professional sphere. Mirza, it was known in certain circles, was looking for someone fresh to represent Sindh.

On 7 October 1958, General Ayub Khan, a dapper blue-eyed military man, took power from President Iskandar Mirza in a quiet and largely uneventful coup d'état. The illegal seizure of power came at a time of immense chaos and political uncertainty within the country and most people seemed indifferent to the General's takeover; some may have even been relieved. In order to understand the realm of the ridiculous that domestic politics had entered, it may be worth noting that in the decade of the 1950s, Pakistan had had seven different Prime Ministers, each intending to carry out a five-year term by law. What seemed aberrant in the late 1950s has now become a sad trademark of Pakistan's feckless political landscape.

As a result of the coup, President Mirza was forced to abrogate the admittedly flimsy constitution and dissolve all assemblies and ministries. President Mirza, who assured the nation that martial law would be lifted within three months (they all do that, it must be force of habit) and that a referendum was soon to take place, justified his actions by blaming political parties for the poor state of affairs. 'The mentality of political parties has sunk so low,' he reasoned, 'that I am unable any longer to believe that elections will improve the present chaotic internal situation.'[20] Military dictators and those who passionately enable them are nothing if not trite. In the late 1950s this may have been somewhat of an original rationale, but by Pakistan's sixtieth anniversary of independence and three dictators later, the 'elections don't help anything' reasoning has become a remarkably familiar refrain. Mirza, none the wiser, was ousted from power by the army twenty days after martial law was instituted.

It was at this time that Zulfikar was approached and asked to join the new government. Like many Pakistanis undergoing their first coup,

Zulfikar's reservations about the military government were eased by the promise that martial law would soon be lifted. Pakistan was a country still in its political infancy; maybe the military would work to restore order, maybe they would pave the way for an earnest era of democracy. And so it was at the age of thirty that Zulfikar joined the government, serving as the Minister of Fuel, Power and Natural Resources.

As Zulfikar had entered politics with a clean slate, his presence within the new government was looked upon positively; he was young, spirited and intellectually determined. It was often said that in a government 'dominated by the strong, central figure of Ayub, Bhutto was reputed to be the one man who stood up for his views, was listened to with respect, and assigned the most delicate tasks despite his young years'.[21] In 1960 Zulfikar was given the sensitive task of negotiating an oil agreement with the Soviet Union. Throughout his short time in office, Zulfikar was openly frustrated with the compromising position Pakistan was constantly put in vis-à-vis the major powers and had consistently argued for a turnaround in foreign policy. Pakistan's relationship with the Soviet Union was difficult at this time, mainly because of Pakistan's stubborn insistence on standing by the United States, thus allying itself on the other side of the Cold War's equilibrium. The Soviet Union, in turn, had a thriving relationship with Nehru's socialist India, supplying it with massive amounts of military aid and economic assistance. Zulfikar's visit, however, was a success. He returned home with the Soviet promise to fund further oil exploration within Pakistan, credit of 120 million roubles and a deal to supply experienced experts and equipment for the programme. What further endeared Zulfikar to the Soviets was his insistence on travelling around the Soviet Union. He spent a day in Samarkand and spoke to his hosts of the 'grandeur of Islamic architecture and culture so richly visible it made one feel proud to be a part of its history, race and religion'.[22]

Even though Zulfikar's government duties busied him with commerce, industry and finance, it was Pakistan's image and position abroad that most concerned him. 'Our salvation lies in one world . . . in which we shall not only eliminate wars but also offer the promise of a new social and economic order,'[23] Zulfikar wrote, fired up against all the injustice he had witnessed, but thus far had not yet suffered. 'We must have fearless minds, our spirit should never be daunted . . . we can only improve with the improvements of humanity, for we are an inextricable part of it. Let our achievements be for all.'[24]

But Pakistan's achievements, under the directive of General Ayub, were not to be for all. Military dictators in Pakistan tend to cuddle up to any power that promises to protect them and it is no small surprise that the power which most frequently enables militarism in Pakistan is the United States. Under the pretext of modernizing its military, already impressively modern, Pakistan signed a Mutual Defence Agreement with the United States in May 1954. As part of the agreement, Pakistan was 'encouraged' to join SEATO, the South-East Asian Treaty Organization, in September 1954 and later CENTO, the Central Treaty Organization, in 1955. The growing power of communist China was the catalyst for the creation of SEATO. Countries like Thailand and the Philippines were eager to band together under SEATO, fearing a Korean War-inspired outbreak in their own countries, but Pakistan, miles away from communist Korea, was hardly at risk. India, Burma and Indonesia refused point blank to be part of SEATO and Ceylon eventually wriggled out of negotiations too. The great alliance was to be made up of three countries: Pakistan, Thailand and the Philippines. CENTO was later introduced as a corollary to protect US interests in the Middle East and again, Pakistan parlayed its strategic importance into access to the American-drafted CENTO pact. CENTO caused a great deal of disruption within the Arab world as it was seen as a ploy to destroy Arab unity. Pakistan, by virtue of being a signatory, became suspect – and not for the last time – in the eyes of Arab states. Pakistan did nothing to improve its PR when it played a subversive role during the Suez crisis and came out on the side of the aggressors on all the aspects of the conflict: the nationalization of the canal itself, Anglo-French collusion with Israel and aggression against Egypt. As a result, Pakistan's image in the Middle East was pitiful. A Syrian newspaper, *Al Badra*, wrote that Pakistan, like Israel, was solely a creation of British imperialism.[25] No implication could have stung more, especially for Zulfikar, who yearned for Third World unity and was about to join the stage as Pakistan's Foreign Minister in 1963. Furious at the perception of Pakistan as an unthinking US stooge, he maintained that 'CENTO is not and was not meant to be an expression of Iranian–Turkish–Pakistani–British–Iraqi community . . . its ineffectiveness has been manifest.'[26] There is no doubt that CENTO was extremely detrimental to Pakistan's relationship with Arab and Middle Eastern Nations, but it was SEATO that cemented the notion that Pakistan acted wholly as an American tool.

As Foreign Minister, Zulfikar made no secret of his disgust at many of the decisions of the government and isolated himself from the machinations of the state when he spoke out in the National Assembly, pointing out that:

> It was said that the foreign policy of Pakistan was bankrupt; that we must walk out of the alliances of CENTO and SEATO, but the next day on getting into office, there were dazzling somersaults and it was solemnly said that without CENTO and SEATO Pakistan would not survive. These are some of the people who have played havoc not only with our internal life, but have made us feel ashamed in the world outside in our external dealings.[27]

Such dissent was not welcomed by the government, especially not by General Ayub, who may have been charmed by Zulfikar when he was Minister of Fuel but rarely saw eye to eye with him as Foreign Minister.

Zulfikar felt that under Ayub's governance, Pakistan was 'in danger of becoming a mere satellite, without any policy of its own'.[28] Pakistan's continual political and diplomatic immaturity would have distressed Zulfikar, had he lived to see his country's current place in the world. Foreign policy was an extraordinarily weak point of Ayub's, who couldn't have cared less about diplomacy so long as American money kept flooding in through military pipelines, but for Zulfikar it was paramount. A year into his post as Foreign Minister he wrote that 'the foreign policy of a nation is a manifestation of its sovereignty. If a people enjoy all power, except the right to conduct foreign relations, it cannot be regarded as independent.'[29]

Pakistan was increasingly putting all its energy into relations with powers like the United States and the Soviet Union and wilfully neglecting Asian and non-aligned states. Zulfikar saw the danger of Pakistan placing all its eggs in the Cold War basket and as Foreign Minister declared, much to General Ayub's displeasure, that:

> we are in the vortex of grave historic events, in which the difference between a right and a false move might well mean the difference between survival and disaster . . . Instead of generating hope and providing for an easing of international tensions, the Titans, through their animosity, are leading the world to the brink of total annihilation.[30]

Zulfikar refused to jump either way, in the words of the historian Hugh Trevor-Roper, and it was this characteristic that most grievously annoyed General Ayub.

While bilateral relations were the centrepiece of Zulfikar's foreign policy, there was no easy way to avoid the fact that relations between Pakistan and China had seriously deteriorated under General Ayub. The General was constantly pushing China out in order to make room for the United States, blind to the glaring fact that Pakistan was no longer America's favourite client. Relations with China, and conversely with the United States, took a sharp turn in 1963 when Zulfikar, seen as the architect of Pakistan's bilateral foreign policy, took up the position of Foreign Minister. In anticipation of Pakistan's possible rapprochement with China in December 1962 and the young Foreign Minister's socialist leanings, the United States transferred 300 million rupees in counterpart funds, meant to initiate credit expansion, from the State Bank of Pakistan to US commercial banks operating within Pakistan.[31] It was a clear warning to Pakistan.

But Zulfikar did not respond well to threats. An emissary of the United States – rumours point to Henry Kissinger – told Zulfikar once that if he were one of their senators, they would have dealt with him before he got out of hand. I wouldn't be a senator, Zulfikar cockily replied, I'd be your president.

Three months later Pakistan and China signed a historic border agreement. Engineered by the Foreign Minister and his Chinese counterpart, Chen Yi, the agreement formally demarcated the boundary between China's Sinkiang region and the contiguous areas whose defence fell under Pakistani control. It was heralded as a great achievement, one that would 'not only give full expression to the desire of the peoples of China and Pakistan for the development of good-neighbourly and friendly relations, but also help safeguard Asian and world peace.'[32] The United States was considerably miffed. It pronounced that the border agreement was 'an unfortunate break in free world solidarity' and promptly withdrew an offer of funds it had promised towards the construction of an airport in Dhaka.[33]

Undeterred, Zulfikar only continued to improve Pakistan's relations with China. The two countries resumed official trade relations, with Pakistan exporting its jute, cotton and textiles among other goods, while importing Chinese chemical dyes, machinery and paraffin wax.[34] In 1964 China gave Pakistan an interest-free loan of $60 million to replace the American money that had dried up since Zulfikar took over as Foreign Minister. The bond between the two countries strengthened and Foreign Minister Bhutto spoke of the upswing in diplomatic relations, ominously foreshadowing the coming war with India, when he warned that 'an attack by India on Pakistan would also involve the security and territorial integrity of the largest state in Asia now'.[35] While Ayub may not have been comfortable with China as a new ally, the people of Pakistan responded warmly to the change in best friends. *Pak-Chini bhai bhai* or Pakistanis and Chinese, brothers, became the slogan of the day; we were no longer feeling like pariahs. Pakistan had opened up new frontiers and the removal of the previous insecurity of only having one bossy international ally was met with great enthusiasm; when Chen Yi visited Pakistan in 1965, he was welcomed by scores of Pakistanis, to the point where even the rigid establishment English newspaper *Dawn* had to admit that Yi received a reception 'never before accorded to the Foreign Minister of any country'.[36]

Withholding economic aid to Pakistan was not enough, so under President Kennedy the United States increased its allocated amount of funds to India. In 1964 Senator Hubert Humphrey called for an Indian-led coalition to counterbalance China's communist threat. The sibling countries were once again pitted against each other by imperial powers, playing ping-pong with the countries' security and edgy foreign relations.

In 1965 General Ayub was uninvited to Washington after Zulfikar refused to support US policy in Vietnam. Zulfikar's time as Foreign Minister was electrifying, possibly his finest time in government. He was a giant among men and his dissent regarding the war in Vietnam makes my heart pound with pride every time I consider the Uncle Tom obsequiousness of Pakistan's politicians since Zulfikar.

I wrote my undergraduate senior thesis on Zulfikar's bilateral foreign policy. I had grown up on my father's stories of the time and saw the period as the greatest accomplishment of my grandfather's political career. One of my thesis advisors, understandably from an academic point of view, warned me that I was verging on the hagiographic when writing about Zulfikar's time as Foreign Minister. It was too emotional for me to explain to my advisor how I felt sitting in New York in the midst of the United States invasion and occupation of Iraq and Afghanistan, two countries my ancestry ties me to – Nusrat had Kurdish blood in her family – and watching my country shamelessly collaborating in the unjust wars. I tried to step back, to take enough space to remove the emotional, but I couldn't. Zulfikar deserves the hagiography there. As a young Pakistani who came of age in the era of dictatorships, civilian and military, I had never felt proud of my country. It was an alien feeling; I knew it existed but I had never felt it until I studied my grandfather's foreign policy.

The breaking point between Zulfikar and General Ayub came as a result of the 1965 war with India. The catalyst for the war was the passing of the Integration Bill by the Indian parliament, which converted the state of Jammu and Kashmir into a province of the

Indian Union. Kashmiris, those Muslims who identified themselves with Pakistan and not India, crossed the ceasefire line into the Indian-ruled area of Kashmir and began to engage in acts of sabotage. There are no just wars, no wars where one side is vindicated by their violence; between Pakistan and India, fresh from the scars of Partition, no war could be seen as any one side's fault. But this is the story of the 1965 war as seen from Pakistan, an infant nation, still mourning the loss of Kashmir, the valley promised to them by their ancestors, while at the same time trying to build a home of their own.

The Indian army began to send troops into Kargil and occupied strategic posts in Pakistani-held Kashmir, ensuring that an all-out war was on the horizon. Both countries saw the war as inevitable, both countries saw the war as their neighbour's fault. Nehru believed that Pakistan was ruining the Kashmiri landscape with its continued aggression, while India was motivated only by thoughts of peace. The major difference between the two countries' policies, he said, stemmed from Pakistan's 'deliberate propaganda of hatred and disunity'.[37] Zulfikar, on the other hand, saw India's occupation of Kashmir as typical of a country with colonial designs. 'There is no difference whatsoever between India's hold over Kashmir and Portugal's hold over Mozambique and Angola,'[38] he wrote.

So for two months in the autumn of 1965, Pakistan and India engaged in an undeclared war. Pakistan was in an incredibly precarious position; while India produced approximately 80 per cent of its military requirements at home,[39] Pakistan embarrassingly had zero self-sufficiency, having been brought up to rely on the handouts of the often moody United States. The United States was Pakistan's only donor of military aid. India, however, played the non-aligned card and received military assistance not only from the United States but also from the Soviet Union and other socialist countries.

India's twenty-two military divisions, equipped with American weaponry, greatly outnumbered Pakistan's six and a half. It was obvious that, without the help of its allies, Pakistan would be easily crushed by India's superior military strength. To make a bleak scenario even bleaker, the United States failed to come out in support of Pakistan.

It was a tremendous betrayal for the United States' principal ally in the region, counterbalanced only by China's loyalty to Pakistan in its time of need.

At the outbreak of the war, the United States' first action was to cut off military aid to both sides, demoralizing Pakistan, which was under the impression that their 'special relationship' and having joined SEATO and CENTO, against its regional interests, meant that the United States was committed to keeping Pakistan safe from harm. General Ayub, already persona non grata with his patrons, called on President Johnson to intervene on Pakistan's behalf. The Johnson administration responded by saying that it would withdraw its support from any country seen as being friendly towards China. President Johnson also made it abundantly clear that economic aid was not to be restored.

While India enjoyed the support of the Soviet Union during the 1965 war, Pakistan had been dumped by its own Cold War giant. By the end of 1965, the break-up was fiscally clear. The United States had given India $246.6 million in loans and grants and another $38.2 million in import/export bank loans, while Pakistan received considerably less – $182.3 million in loans and grants and nothing in import/export bank loans.[40] The *Daily Telegraph* had even gone so far as to suggest that the United States had encouraged India to attack Pakistan to unseat the politically unstable General Ayub, writing that a 'coup d'état to dethrone him was imminent' and that the 'Indian decision to reoccupy posts across the ceasefire line in Kashmir was "cleared" with the United States Embassy in New Delhi'.[41]

China's reaction, however, was swift and sharp in support of Pakistan. As Indian forces crossed the international frontier to attack Lahore, China came out and branded the Indians as aggressors, rejecting India's claims that it was acting defensively. China also accused the United States of showing partiality towards India. The Prime Minister, Chou En-lai, insisted that India 'could not have engaged in such serious military adventure without the consent and support of the United States'.[42] Chou En-lai did not stop at a condemnation of the

United States, but also blamed the Soviet Union for playing 'a most unseemly role'.[43]

As the danger of an Indian attack on East Pakistan was mounting, China took its support for Pakistan a tactical step further. On 16 September 1965, China issued an ultimatum to India, calling on it to dismantle all its military installations on or over the China–Sikkim border within three days or face 'grave consequences'.[44] Faced with the mortifying threat of war with China, India backed off and eased the pressure on their Western Pakistani front.

Pakistan's Foreign Minister spoke out in China's favour in the National Assembly, repeating what he had foreshadowed in an early speech, by saying that 'there were three considerations which prevented India from attacking East Pakistan – God, monsoon and the ultimatum from China.'[45] He was being generous; China was the only reason India did not attack East Pakistan.

The ill-fated war ended only when both countries accepted the United Nations Security Council resolution to cease all hostilities, but by then the damage had already been done. There was land to be redistributed, again, and prisoners of war to be repatriated, so at the Soviet Union's invitation General Ayub was called to Tashkent to meet Indian leaders. As Foreign Minister, Zulfikar was adamant that Ayub should not kowtow to the Soviets, whom he felt had played a dirty role during the war. It was China, not the Soviets, who had defended Pakistan and once again China was being edged out. General Ayub disregarded his Foreign Minister's advice not to go to Tashkent, and ignored the protests from the Pakistani people, who believed they had been double-crossed by the Soviets. Dictators tend to do as they please – it is one of their less endearing traits – so General Ayub flew to Tashkent in January 1966.

Signed by General Ayub and his Indian counterpart, Lal Bahadur Shashtri, the Tashkent Declaration detailed the withdrawal of troops from Kashmir, the restoration of the ceasefire line, the repatriation of POWs, and the promise to adhere to good relations based on a principle of non-interference in each other's internal affairs. General Ayub had no sense of irony when he arrived at Tashkent and thanked his hosts by saying that India and Pakistan had both 'suffered under long and dark periods of foreign domination' and that it was now that both countries had finally regained their freedom, oblivious to the fact that he had once again placed Pakistan's fate in the hands of two great world powers.[46]

The official line was that the war had ended in a stalemate; Pakistan had not liberated Kashmir, but had also resisted subjugation by the Indian army. A movement of opposition swiftly grew within the country among those who felt that Pakistan had won the war, but failed in the critical objective of freeing Kashmir. Zulfikar felt betrayed by General Ayub's willingness to sign away Pakistan's fate at Tashkent. For him, withdrawing the troops without an outline for a solution to the Kashmir issue was a glaring sign of the General's weak governance. He had advised Ayub against making such a monumental mistake, but to no avail.

Kashmir holds an almost mythic importance for Pakistanis and Zulfikar felt that General Ayub's handling of the situation was a total collapse of power and judgement. Zulfikar himself felt that 'Kashmir must be liberated if Pakistan is to have its full meaning'[47] and could not abide by the dictator's wavering any longer. The United States, meanwhile, was pleased that Pakistan had forgone China at Tashkent and announced its decision to resume military and economic aid to both Pakistan and India. Two days after the announcement, Zulfikar Bhutto resigned as Foreign Minister and left General Ayub Khan's government.

'It was a special period in history,'[48] Miraj Mohammad Khan, now eighty years old and fighting heart disease tells me. 'You had Nasser nationalizing the Suez Canal, Sukarno in Indonesia, Patrice Lumumba in the Congo, and the Vietnam War was energizing the youth the world over. Politics was so radical and so romanticized. I had gone to speak to Mr Bhutto during Ayub's time but the Intelligence wouldn't allow anyone, especially not us students, anywhere near 70 Clifton. They used fear and intimidation to keep us away from Mr Bhutto, but us lot, we weren't afraid.' Miraj was president of the National Student Federation, the most radical element in political activism at the time. He was and still is, even in old age, a political firebrand.

'They were restricting Mr Bhutto so much in those days, they knew he was going to leave the government and they wanted to isolate him as much as possible. The newspapers wouldn't even print so much as a square inch of his news. We at the NSF had daggers drawn against the regime. We belonged to completely different backgrounds, but that's why he respected us, respected me.' Miraj speaks to me in Urdu, stopping only to cough into a roll of toilet paper he keeps at his side. He pauses every once in a while to make sure I'm keeping up with him as I'm taking notes in English. 'In 1946 during a sailors' revolt against the British, I threw a big pot on a British truck from the fourth floor of a building during a curfew. They beat me badly after that so I don't like to talk in English. I have an allergy against it even today,' he explains.

Miraj is an old Marxist, a radical student leader who spent much of his life fighting against imperialism and elite domination of the poor of Pakistan. 'When we heard of Mr Bhutto resigning from Ayub's government, we collected NSF students and went to meet him at Cantt Station when he returned from Rawalpindi to Karachi. We were there in our thousands to receive him, we took him back to 70 Clifton in a huge *jalsa*. Before we left him, we gave him a paper on our foreign policy ideas. He told me to come back in the evening to speak to him. He had read the paper by then, very quickly, and had appreciated it.

'We spoke quite often in those early days, we used to talk about the *haris*, the peasants, about the middle class, about the labour unions. He used to say, "I'm with the poor, with the barefooted, with the rootless." People loved him for this.' Zulfikar had not left General Ayub's government to sulk; he had left in protest and people were waiting eagerly to see what he would do next. Miraj, a young activist, was perhaps an unlikely ally to the feudal family of the Bhuttos, but he joined Zulfikar because he saw something different in him, something that most *zamindar* didn't possess. 'Let me tell you, I loved him very much,' Miraj says, speaking to me decades later and generously ignoring their bitter falling out, a consequence of Zulfikar's governance when in power. 'Yes, he was my leader, but I would argue with him at any time and he would tolerate it. I wanted to save him because I believed very firmly that he had to abolish feudalism. I used to tell him that. Please, Mr Bhutto, abolish feudalism. We are not free people, he used to tell me. Freedom is what we have to fight for after years of economic exploitation and rule by dictators. Freedom is our goal and that has to be clear.'

The Punjab is the seat of power in Pakistan. Most of the armed forces and bureaucrats come from the Punjab province. If you win in the Punjab, they say, you take all of Pakistan. 'It was the status quo we were fighting,' recalls Dr Ghulam Hussain, an elderly comrade of Zulfikar's. 'We wanted class consciousness, we wanted real change.'

But this was not going to be easy, not with the military still in power. They pulled the strings in Pakistani politics – they still pull our strings – and nothing that they can defeat ever slips past them. It never happened before. It's never happened since.

General Ayub's regime, meanwhile, was not coping well with the expansion of Zulfikar's popularity since he had resigned. Those who were coming out to support him were ordinary people, activists, students and labourers – not bureaucrats or military lackeys, the kind of crowds they could control. The state consoled itself with the belief that the strength of the army and the state was far greater than any support that the people could muster; the establishment in Pakistan pays little heed to the voters (who rarely get a chance to vote, and almost never get a chance to vote freely). At that point, elections, free and fair general elections, had never been held in the twenty-year-old country. What did bother the state, however, was the support Zulfikar received internationally.

The state in Pakistan is empowered by outside forces, by the hegemony of large countries and international agencies; these outsiders constitute a power base the establishment never ceases to cultivate. For their part, the Chinese were disturbed by Zulfikar Bhutto's exit from government, suspecting that the split was the work of 'US imperialists and Soviet revisionists'.[49] China's Prime Minister, Chou En-lai, made a hurried stop in Karachi on his way home from state visits to Albania and Romania, to hold talks with General Ayub to establish whether the pro-China Bhutto's departure from government would affect China adversely. It would. With Zulfikar gone, General Ayub had no one to stand in the way of the 'go slow' strategy he had adopted regarding China.

Abdul Waheed Katpar, a lawyer from Larkana, Zulfikar's home town, recounts a story Zulfikar told him. 'After his resignation from the government, Ayub called Mr Bhutto to come and see him. When Mr Bhutto went to see him, he was threatened by the President. Ayub spoke to him while pulling his socks up, fiddling with his dress as though the meeting was an afterthought. He told him, "Look we are Pathans, we don't leave our enemies in peace, even when they're in their graves."'[50] The message was clear.

Pakistanis regarded the declaration at Tashkent as confirmation that Kashmir had been lost, that something had been wrongfully taken away from them once again. It was Bhutto who spoke out against Tashkent; other politicians and pundits allied with the government were characteristically silent. As Zulfikar continued to speak out against his former boss, he was harrassed more and more.

In those days, the Sindh government had ruled that rice sellers could only deal with the state. Some ten wagonloads of rice were automatically handed to the state, who offered typically inadequate compensation, and permitted the sellers to sell only one wagonload freely to the buyer of their choice. Taking advantage of the fact that Zulfikar belonged to a feudal family, the government launched a case against several workers at the Bhutto rice mill on the grounds that they were caught trying to sell three wagonloads of rice in Peshawar.

Abdul Waheed Katpar, the young lawyer from Larkana, was in Quetta with his family on vacation when he heard the news of the smuggling charges brought against Zulfikar. His family advised him to go to Larkana and assist in the defence. He had never met Zulfikar Ali Bhutto at that time, he knew him only by name. 'Why should I go?' he asked his family. 'Doesn't Bhutto have many young lawyers around him, friends of his, that should be handling the case?' In Katpar's eyes, the case was obviously political; it could be thrown out of court easily. No, he was told, none of those men were around Bhutto any more. Since he left government and had fallen out of official favour, they had all abandoned him.

'So I got into my small Russian car and drove through the night to reach Larkana', Katpar remembers. 'I filed bail applications for the arrested workers, some of them women, and got interim bail handed down from the local sessions court. It turned out the workers had a permit to sell the rice they had been caught with. A legal permit. It was a case built on misconceptions and on deceiving the public. I confronted the Peshawar police who had made the arrest and produced two witnesses who could back up the facts, and that was it. The case was dropped.'

Zulfikar was away in Paris during the whole rice debacle and returned to Larkana to find that a stranger from his city had fought the case and had it dismissed, freeing the workers from the family mill. He rang Katpar up and invited him to Al Murtaza House, Zulfikar's home in Larkana. 'That's where we started,' says Katpar. 'He thanked me for my help, and asked how much he owed me for my services. I told him to forget about the fees, I was just doing my job. Mr Bhutto then took out a notice from his pocket – it was a letter from the District Commissioner of Larkana telling him to surrender all the arms in the house.' (I interrupt Katpar with my laughter and he smiles at me wondering what's so funny about this very unfunny story. I tell him that that was how the police continually harassed my father, Murtaza – arms. The family owns several antique weapons and had been *shikar* hunters all their lives. They all had legal permits, but it was the easiest way for the authorities to create some bother for us. Katpar leans forward and tells me it's always been their favourite trick against their enemies, his eyes twinkling at our common story.) 'I took his note,' Katpar continues, 'and went to file a petition in the courts. That's how I became close to Mr Bhutto.'

While the government continued with its petty persecution, Zulfikar was at work drafting a political manifesto. He had spent time travelling the country and speaking with young activists and local leaders within the four provinces and East Pakistan. He had decided to found his own party. At that point, Katpar was spending a lot of time at Al Murtaza with Zulfikar. They ate many meals together and sat late in the evening listening to Sindhi folk music. 'He never listened to Urdu songs, only Sindhi ones. It was Sufi music,' Katpar tells me proudly. At that time a young engineer from Lahore, Dr Mubashir Hasan, and J. A. Rahim, also from Lahore, were in Larkana with Zulfikar. Together they were the authors of the manifesto that would launch the Pakistan People's Party. They were from middle-class not feudal backgrounds, degree-educated and intellectual. As the autumn changed into winter and the launch date of the party neared, Zulfikar approached his friend and lawyer Katpar. 'Would you like to come to Lahore with us?' he asked. Katpar shyly refused. 'I'm not a politician,' he protested. He was in fact president of the Larkana Bar Association, which was, and remains, a highly political post. 'You'll come with us,' Zulfikar insisted and together he and Katpar travelled to Lahore.

The city of Lahore is unlike other cities in Pakistan. It is large and winding with canals to guide one through the urban sprawl that has grown all around this historic fort city. In the summer the roads are full of people riding their bicycles and tongas to work across large avenues lined with shady trees. The canals are dotted with young children and men splashing about in the water to escape the sweltering heat. In the autumn, however, the climate is cool – unlike in the rest of the country – and slowly, as the winter months draw near, a mist descends over Lahore.

In contrast to the craziness that one finds in other metropolitan areas in Pakistan, Lahore always has a sense of calm about it. The neighbourhoods are spacious, the restaurants teeming with lazy eaters out to sample some of Punjab's finest dishes, and the schools and universities carry on educating their students in some of the finest institutions the country has to offer. Lahore lacks that sense of urgency, of needing to prove itself, as if it has already arrived. Lahore is quietly aware of its envied place in Pakistani history.

It is the city that the Mughals built as their capital this side of the border and holds not only the tomb of Jahangir, the *Shish Mahal* or palace of mirrors, but also the Shalimar Gardens, designed by the architect of the Taj Mahal for the emperor Shahjahan. Lahore is also the home of the sandstone Badshai Mosque and Kim's gun, made famous by Rudyard Kipling, and is heralded as the birthplace of Pakistan – it was in Lahore that the original Muslim League, led by Jinnah, passed the Pakistan Resolution at its annual session on 23 March 1940. Lahore is where the dream of Pakistan was born. Lahore added another notch to its historic record, as the birthplace of the Pakistan People's Party, when in 1967 Sindh's famous son came to the Punjab to make his own history.

When news had spread that Zulfikar, free of General Ayub's regime, was about to launch his own political platform, the General's government took steps to ensure that this would not go smoothly. Assembly in public spaces in Lahore city and its neighbouring districts was banned under Section 144 of the criminal code to prevent Zulfikar from holding a massive public gathering that would potentially embarrass the government. Section 144 is an establishment favourite. It has been put into effect on numerous occasions – it was used during the 1971 civil war, employed to halt union and trade demonstrations, and more recently put forward by General Pervez Musharaff to thwart people from rallying around radical Islamic parties in the aftermath of the US-led invasion of Afghanistan.

Regardless of the fact that Section 144 was reserved for situations of grave national emergency, the law was pushed through, forcing the nascent PPP to meet privately. The party had been originally scheduled to announce its creation and present its manifesto to the people in one of the city's large parks, but because of the looming threat of violence from the state, the announcement of the party's establishment was shifted to the home of one of its founding members, Dr Mubashir Hasan, in 4-K Gulberg. Dr Mubashir offered his home because no assembly hall was willing to take the risk of upsetting the General by welcoming Zulfikar Bhutto. Section 144 had effectively scared the owners of any private spaces from opening their doors.

On 30 November 1967, delegates from all across the country, the rich and the poor, the secular and the religious, both men and women, met under a large *shamiana*, or tent, in Dr Mubashir's small garden to usher in the birth of the Pakistan People's Party. Though delegates from East Pakistan were stopped from entering Lahore and those travelling from Sindh and Balochistan were continually harassed by their local authorities because of their association with Zulfikar Ali Bhutto, hundreds of people came. Abdul Waheed Katpar stood outside Dr Mubashir's residence and issued permits to the five hundred or so delegates streaming into the house. The permits were issued by the party to ensure that there was a modicum of safety and order.

Over the next two days the Pakistan People's Party was founded by unanimous decision of all delegates present. On the morning of 30 November, once all the delegates had registered their names, the first session began with a recitation from the Koran. Next, two poets, Aslam Gurdaspuri and Dr Halim Raza, recited poems in Urdu that they had penned especially for the occasion. Following the poetry, the principal delegates were introduced to the convention by name, and included the likes of Dr Mubashir, Katpar, Miraj Mohammad Khan, and Begum Abad Ahmad Khan.

After being introduced by Malik Aslam Hayat, Zulfikar Ali Bhutto rose to address the convention and was greeted by a standing ovation that ended only as he began to speak. He spoke eloquently and emotionally, calling the occasion 'the hardest of all and the most challenging I have had to meet as our country, Asia, nay the whole world, all are passing through a dangerous period of transition'.[51] Zulfikar condemned Pakistan's 'monstrous economic system of loot and plunder'[52] that guaranteed that the rich few (twenty-one families at the time of Partition, twenty-seven families by the millennium) got richer while the poor of Pakistan sunk into desperate poverty.

He explained that, in contrast, the new party's economic programme would be aimed towards social justice and led by the principle that the means of production should never be allowed to become the means of exploitation. He outlined the need for the nationalization of certain industries such as banking, transport and fuel resources and their inclusion in the public sector. Zulfikar maintained that the root cause of Pakistan's economic and political problems lay in the fact that 'fundamental national problems had not been referred to the people at any time. The people alone could finally settle the issues and the final nature of their state and government.'[53]

As well as economics, Zulfikar also spoke about the importance of Kashmir, without which, Pakistan was as 'incomplete as a body without a head.'[54] He also called for an end to the bombing of North Vietnam, adding that as Pakistanis 'we pay homage to the indomitable people of Vietnam'[55] and warned that the present atmosphere in Pakistan of police violence, cultural degradation and lawlessness would eventually lead the country into destruction.

Zulfikar concluded his introductory remarks by reaffirming the fact that it was these very economic and political conditions that brought the need for a new party to a head. He ended his speech with a promise. 'We respect tradition, but will oppose the bad in the old. We respect only those traditions that are beneficial to the people of Pakistan, not those that are dragging the country backwards . . . We will give our country a new outlook, we will give Pakistan a new revolutionary form.'[56]

Dr Mubashir described it to me later as 'the day of your life' and gave an example of the excitement and energy that was felt that day. 'Take the case of Khursheed Hasan Meer, a very politically active lawyer from Rawalpindi, a former president of their District Bar Association. Z.A.B had invited him. He came and told me in private that he had not come to join the new party, but only to observe. As the convention proceeded, he asked for the floor, made a very fiery speech and announced his decision – from the podium! – to join the party.' Even Katpar, another lawyer who had always been suspicious of politics, gave a speech, speaking publicly for the first time in his young life.

The second session began later that afternoon at 3.30 and lasted about three hours, during which four committees were formed: the steering committee, the constitutional committee, the resolution committee, and the draft declaration committee. Zulfikar was elected chairman of each of these committees. The inclusion of elections was one of the greatest precedents set by the party, but it was a system

74

that was to be swiftly abandoned after Zulfikar Ali Bhutto's death. Following a general discussion about the responsibilities of the various committees, the day's activities came to end.

The third session met the following day, 1 December, and after the initial poetry readings and recitations, the party passed twenty-five resolutions and the draft declaration committee put forward a working paper outlining the manifesto of the party.

Kashmir was the subject of the third resolution passed by the convention, and it declared that 'no solution to the question of Jammu and Kashmir is possible except on the basis of self-determination as accepted by Pakistan and India as well as the United Nations'.[57] No compromise, such as the one at Tashkent, would be accepted on the matter. Zulfikar felt there was no duty more incumbent on Pakistan than 'redeeming the pledge given to the people of Kashmir'[58] and later spoke of the political mess that General Ayub had created when he suggested that if nations could not resolve their disputes, they should put them aside and move on with life. The consequence of such inane statements, commented Zulfikar, was that when Britain's Foreign Secretary last visited Pakistan, he brusquely repudiated the UN's commitment to hold a plebiscite in Kashmir.

The issue of military alliances, the fifth resolution, held an important place within the party's framework and for Zulfikar personally. It was SEATO and CENTO that had mired Pakistan in a network of subservience and slavish allegiance to the world's superpowers. The convention called upon the government to leave the two alliances since they had 'in no way contributed to the security of Pakistan when their assistance was needed'.[59] The resolution also called for the Mutual Defence agreements between Pakistan and the United States to be declared null and void since the US had failed to come to Pakistan's assistance during the 1965 war with India. It was a spectacularly one-sided deal, Zulfikar explained. There was nothing mutual about it when, during the war, Pakistan, 'the country of three military alliances had to run from pillar to post in search of armaments and spare parts'[60] rather than receive them from the United States. The resolution ended by calling for Pakistan to ask the Americans to return all its military bases in Pakistan.

Two resolutions were passed respectively about Vietnam and the Middle East. Zulfikar wrote that 'As Muslims, we entertain no hostility against any human community; when we say this, we do not exclude the Jewish people.'[61] However, the occupation of Palestine was seen as an illegal and systematic victimization of a people, and that, like the carpet bombing of the Vietnamese, was an injustice that the party recognized. In calling for the unity of the oppressed, Zulfikar was very clear about the impetus for doing so. 'Our unity is not directed against any creed, religious or secular. It is not nourished by hate or rancour. Its drive and force is a passion for justice.'[62]

It is this sentiment that leads to one of the most important resolutions, the eighteenth, which calls for the solidarity of the Third World. This was an issue integral to Zulfikar's political philosophy. He saw the world as broken down into 'the hewers of wood and drawers of water on one side, and those who wield mastery over the planets' resources on the other'.[63] There was no economic justice in the Third World, where the large industrialized states still enforced their dominance over a colonial economy. This was possible, in Zulfikar's eyes, because 'our terms of trade, our markets, and our resource flows are overwhelmingly dependent upon the economic and political policies in the richer countries'.[64] Since the peoples of the Third World had always been united by their common suffering and struggles against exploitation, it was they who had the mandate to rid themselves of such unfavourable conditions.

The solution Zulfikar envisioned was not a class war or some sort of global battle for power, but simply the redistribution of economic wealth and the creation of a Third World summit that would open up the space for those underdeveloped nations to speak. This was progressive Zulfikar at his best. Those critics that expend all their energy attempting to denigrate the man's politics (by either their antipathy or their supposed allegience to the PPP and Zulfikar's legacy) wilfully ignore the visionary quality of Zulfikar's political philosophy. The Third World, Zulfikar maintained, did not want charity; it only wanted its fair share. 'We are trying to create an environment of opportunity, an ethos of dignity and hope for the underprivileged majority of our peoples. We cheerfully undertake the toil and sweat for a better life for our masses; we accept the denial of immediate comforts.'[65] If the Third World did not act immediately and purposefully there was the inevitable danger that 'our collective capacities will then remain immobilized and we will have failed to translate the abstract into the concrete, poetry into politics and romance into reality'.[66]

The fourth and last session of the founding convention of the party opened at three in the afternoon on 1 December and dealt with the basics of the party. The convention adopted a document on the necessity for such a new political forum and then moved to decide upon a name for the as yet untitled party. Names such as the Socialist Party of Pakistan and the People's Progressive Party were bandied about and sampled until rejected as the convention collectively voted to call itself the Pakistan People's Party.

The convention unanimously passed the interim constitution of the party and moved to elect a chairman. The delegates all shouted out Zulfikar's name and refused to propose any other candidates. Zulfikar Ali Bhutto was unanimously elected, after which he addressed the delegates in Urdu and promised to serve the party, the peasants, the working class and the nation of Pakistan with all of his being.

{ 3 }

Mir Murtaza Ghulam Bhutto was born on 18 September 1954. The first son welcomed by Zulfikar and Nusrat, he was born a year after his sister Benazir and arrived just as 70 Clifton, the family's house, had been completed. The family, four in all now, moved into an upstairs section of the house that they shared with Sir Shahnawaz and his wife, Begum Khurshid. Murtaza, named after his great-grandfather, was a sunny child with a warm disposition. Photographs show him playing in the garden as a young child, dragging a bicycle by its handlebars and sticking his small feet into the garden pond.

As a boy, Murtaza, who was soon joined by a younger sister, Sanam, and a baby brother, Shahnawaz, four years his junior, enjoyed all that his world offered him. He would yearn to go hunting with his father and his uncles in Larkana, shooting wild boar and deer. His foray into the world of *shikars* was brief, however, as Zulfikar, then a young minister in Ayub's cabinet, was shifted to Rawalpindi, where the children were raised outside the parameters of a laissez-faire landed elite. A Swiss governess, Noreen, was hired to look after Zulfikar and Nusrat's boisterous children as they began to travel, both inside Pakistan and abroad, more often. The children delighted in torturing their prim nanny and years later Papa still chuckled, his *khe khe khe* laugh spreading light across his face, when he recounted poor Noreen's attempts at discipline. For one, she would insist the young Bhutto children finish their spinach, their daily hated vegetable, before they were excused from the dining table. Soon the children found an ingenious way of disposing of four large servings of the leafy vegetable – they would take turns chucking their spinach to the pet dog, who obediently waited for each dish under the table (he eventually got sick). Murtaza, Sanam and Shah – nicknamed Gugail, or Gogi for short, by the family – mischievously tormented Noreen on as regular a basis as they could muster. Benazir was less naughty, often siding with the nanny and abiding by her strict codes, soon becoming her favourite in the house. Her siblings, meanwhile, were less inclined to 'apple polish' as the boys would say, and invented new ways to circumvent Noreen at every turn – spitting out their daily vitamins as soon as she'd turned her back was one such small act of resistance – in the hope that she would volunteer her resignation.

'We were in Pindi by force of circumstance because my father was a minister,' explained Murtaza in an interview with a Karachi magazine a few months before he was killed, 'so our exposure to the feudal set-up was kind of limited. And even when we did visit the village, there were strict checks on us to see that we didn't get up to any mischief. And because we were expected to concentrate on studying, we didn't have time to run off for *shikar* and things like that – which is generally what kids in feudal families grow up with.'[1]

'We were never brought up as the children of a typical feudal family,' continued Murtaza.

> My father always said to us that everything can be taken from you, but your mind and thoughts cannot . . . He placed a lot of emphasis on education as did his father before him. I remember that as kids when we used to go to the village, we already knew that when somebody bows down to touch your feet, you should stop him before he gets there. So, no, we were not raised as the kids of a feudal family.[2]

Murtaza began riding classes. His mother Nusrat framed a photograph of him standing perfectly upright in riding jodhpurs and a grey leather jacket. Murtaza's hair is gelled impeccably, parted on the right, and he is smiling broadly, holding a riding crop in his gloved hands.

Later on he remarked that while he enjoyed hunting and riding, 'these were not the things I did night and day. It wasn't a lifestyle.'[3]

When it came time for Murtaza to begin his schooling, he went first to Aitchison College in Lahore, a colonial institution built to educate the country's young sons in a conservative and archaic environment and atmosphere. Murtaza lasted only a few months at Aitchison – which has since become internationally infamous for educating Omar Sheikh, the alleged murderer of the American journalist Daniel Pearl – before begging his parents to free him and bring him back home to Karachi. The college, a boys' school, 'encouraged what I would for lack of a better term describe as feudal traits', remembered Murtaza. 'The *pagris* (turbans), the riding, the personal servants – all these things are the surface indications of a feudal lifestyle.'[4] Students at Aitchison were required to attend Friday prayers at the school's mosque every week. Cricket was the school's crowning glory, cricket, cricket and more cricket. 'They promote this image of a rigorous public school kind of atmosphere,' continued Murtaza in the interview, 'you know, the cold showers and all that, and yet there is this odd paradox because you are made to feel like you're some sort of *chota sahib* (little master).'[5]

After leaving Aitchison, Murtaza attended Karachi Grammar School, the city's elite Jesuit school set up by monks and Freemasons during the colonial days of the Raj. 'It was a more liberal kind of place,' he recalled. 'There was a much better mix of people there. True, everyone was largely well-to-do, but their backgrounds were varied: there were kids of land-owning families but there were also children of writers and professionals.'[6] He made friends with many such children but it was Gudu, who hailed from an intellectual and media-oriented Lahori family and was several years older than Mir, who was his best friend. Murtaza excelled in school, but managed to fail spectacularly in mathematics, something of a family trait. When my turn came to bomb at maths, no matter what grade I was in or how adept my teachers were, Papa was both reassuring – 'Don't worry, it's genetic' (it is) – and supportive – 'You'll never have to use it later on in life' (I did). His blue Grammar School maths notebooks are covered with his doodles and practised signatures. 'Maths is a boaring subject,' Murtaza scribbled confidently on his geometry notebook.

Murtaza's Grammar School report cards were bound together in a black leather book, a sign of the school's status. Murtaza's report for his eighth year is written in carefully marked spaces in blue fountain pen. Under the subject religious knowledge his teacher has written, 'Must show more interest'. That remark is echoed in the report book every term, until somewhere around tenth grade, where the remarks change, begrudgingly almost, to 'has improved'. The general remarks, which noted that Murtaza was absent only once that term, sound especially Victorian. 'Young Bhutto has taken to his studies very seriously and I do hope he perseveres during the next scholastic year . . . Mir is a well-behaved lad, obedient and exemplary.' The report is signed by Nusrat, though previous terms show the name P. Bhutto under the signature of a parent or guardian. Pinky, his sister Benazir.

While Benazir tended to treat Murtaza with the distance elder children precociously reserve for their subordinates, Murtaza adored his oldest sister. He teased her for her aloofness while protectively fussing over her and making sure she was treated as seriously as she wished to be – when they were young children, at least. An old family friend of Zulfikar's, who often spent time at 70 Clifton with the Bhuttos and later with Mir and his siblings when they were adults, spoke to me about his obversations of the rivalry among the children. 'Benazir always kept a keen eye on Mir. If he had a new tricycle, she wanted one too. It didn't matter that her parents told her that boys had separate toys from girls or that her own play area was well stocked with dolls and the like. It must have been hard on her, because her brothers were so instantly likeable and charming and she was shy and introverted, so that she felt like an outsider when forced to compete with her male siblings.' After double-checking that I would shield his identity the family friend said that he had been an official guest of Benazir's prisons during her second term and did not fancy his chances of remaining a free man in the current environment. 'Whenever Zulfi and Nusrat came home from state trips or official visits, there would often be a separate suitcase with gifts for the children, books that

Zulfi – an avid reader – had bought on his travels and various memen-toes given by their hosts. One time, I had been to the airport to welcome Zulfi and Nusrat and was at the house in 70 Clifton when their luggage arrived. All the children were giddy with excitement, they were all looking forward to seeing what treats their parents had brought for them, but Benazir parked herself on top of the suitcase in question and demanded that she receive her presents first, since she was the eldest child and in her eyes the most important one.' I laughed at the story. People would tell me the strangest things when I told them I was writing a book, bizarre anecdotes and tales that I had never heard before. I thought it appropriate to break the ice with a joke. How old was Wadi, I asked, fifteen? The family friend thought quietly for a minute, ignoring my attempt at humour, and then turned his head to the side, as if mystified by the answer. 'Yes,' he replied with no sign that he was joking.

The dynamic between the four children had been established early on in their lives. Sanam, who was spoilt rotten by her brothers and allowed to roughhouse with them and hang out with their friends because she was considered cool enough to be one of the boys, divided her time between her brothers and her sister, who engaged in no such roughhousing and recoiled at the thought of hanging out with the boys and their friends. Sanam was the sister they could count on to join in their bawdy jokes and naughty pranks; she was always up for a good time. Benazir was more formal, more distant, except with regard to her sister whom she treated like a lady-in-waiting. The two sisters shared a room, arranged to have the walls painted black and the curtains finished with striped white and black cloth that looked like fabric prison bars, and smoked secretly in their dressing room, wearing leather gloves on their hands and wet towels on their heads so the smell of smoke would not stain their nails or get stuck in their poker-straight hair. They sounded so rebellious and impossibly cool to me when I heard the stories as a child; I was always desperate to hear more stories of my aunts' renegade teenage years, imagining that one day I too would learn to smoke cigarettes in dressing rooms with such laid-back nonchalance, though since punks were big when I was young, I imagined myself forgoing the towel for a pink Mohican. Papa would make angry faces at me when I expressed delight at hearing of my naughty aunts' antics and I would collapse in laughter and tell him, no, no I was only kidding, I didn't want to smoke cigarettes with leather gloves on! How silly that must look . . .

Murtaza and Shahnawaz shared a room across from their sisters, until they moved into the annexe outside the main 70 Clifton house that had been built for their two uncles, Imdad and Sikandar. The boys painted their room 'communist red' and covered their walls with posters of Kiss and the Beatles, fabric wall hangings of Lenin that their father brought back from the Soviet Union for his sons and a large red and blue painting of Che Guevara. As Murtaza and Shah got older, and lazier when it came to the rigours of school and alarm bells, they would stay up late at night talking and bouncing around their room, dress for school sometime around 2 a.m. and then hop into bed and try to sleep in perfectly still positions so their school uniforms wouldn't crease too much. Murtaza, ever obsessive-compulsive when it came to his appearance, would still wake up with enough time to brush his hair and shave what few stray bristles there were around what he hoped would be a fine moustache. Shah, meanwhile, would shuffle out of bed with minutes to spare, brush his teeth, fill the sink to the brim with cold water and dunk his head in before racing down the stairs to get into the waiting car. Later, both boys would develop a demanding sartorial regimen they would call 'suiting and booting'.

In eleventh grade, under the remarks for Chemistry, a teacher with a pink pen has written: 'It would be a prudent move to drop Chemistry altogether.' By his junior year in high school, Murtaza's standing academically had improved significantly. Religious knowledge education had been completed, he dropped Chemistry and managed an almost miraculous 'excellent effort' in Algebra. A different class master, as Grammar School insisted on calling its teachers, wrote: 'Murtaza's improvement in most subjects and his dropping of science has made a great difference – this is splendid.' He graduated second in his entire class.

Murtaza managed good grades in his A levels, the British equivalent of twelfth grade, but didn't put as much effort into those exams – he had applied to college on the strength of his O-level results – tenth and eleventh grades – and spent his time towards the end of her school career in pursuit of other knowledge. Murtaza was part of the tae kwon do association of Karachi, becoming a black belt. He got himself certified in first aid through the St John's Ambulance Association of Pakistan for two years in a row, and received several Duke of Edinburgh awards.

Together with his brother Shah, Murtaza enjoyed an idyllic childhood amidst the uncertainty of Pakistan's fragile new nationhood. As the 1965 war raged on, bringing the sounds of air-raid sirens and emergency warnings to Karachi, Murtaza dreamt of becoming a fighter pilot. He confessed, 'I was fascinated with fighter jets . . . I guess it was because at that time the war had broken out and I used to watch the planes take off and land – it was a fairly impressionable age.'[7]

It was during these early childhood years that Murtaza and Shah developed the bond that would carry them through adulthood. Naturally close and protective of each other, both boys, but especially Murtaza as he was the first-born son, were treated strictly by their father, who kept them on a tight leash. Murtaza and Shahnawaz received an allowance of fifty rupees a month, meaning that the brothers had to pool their funds if they ever wanted to live it up or splurge on something special. 'Two governments before,' Murtaza's best friend in adulthood, Suhail Sethi, explains politely, wriggling around Zulfikar's apparent stinginess, 'Ayub Khan's sons ran wild with the bounty their father's excesses in government provided them with. ZAB was very determined to avoid the same thing happening to his family and was determined to keep his children on the straight and narrow.'[8] Suhail and I sit quietly for a minute. Urm, I venture, all his children? 'You know, he directed it at his sons who in those days were the representations of your family' Suhail says. 'In his first speech on television, after he assumed the presidency, ZAB said very clearly: this government will be different, there will be no nepotism under my regime.' I've seen the speech Suhail is referring to. It's Zulfikar at his best, at his most upfront. He wears his thick black-framed glasses and speaks from notes, which he shows the cameras at some point, telling them these are only notes, he's speaking from the heart. Zulfikar speaks in English, apologetically telling his audience that it pains him to do so – that he often speaks in Urdu, though small children laugh at his mistakes in the language – but that the world's eyes are watching Pakistan after the break-up of its eastern province, so he speaks in a language that everyone can understand. He says there will be no nepotism, no corruption from within his family, he swears it. 'I have a talented cousin,' Zulfikar says as an aside, referring to Mumtaz Bhutto who was a founding member of the PPP and later Chief Minister of Sindh, and says that he would like his assistance in government. But that's it, he promises. That's the extent of it. Zulfikar saw it as his duty to groom his sons from an early age, toughen them up and turn them into men, even though they were only young boys. Zulfikar was neither as lenient nor as relaxed with his sons as he was with his daughters; he demanded nothing short of perfection from his sons and wasted no time mollycoddling them or playing around with them. On a trip to Larkana, the two boys went hunting with their cousin Bhao – who, having lived the feudal life Zulfikar allowed his sons only sparingly, was prone to reckless *chota sahib* behaviour. As the boys sat at the dining table in the family room waiting for their lunch, Bhao picked up his hunting rifle and jumped on his chair, aiming at his male cousins as if they were hunting marks. He stomped his feet on his chair, making Bollywood-style *dshoom dshoom* shooting noises, all the while thoughtlessly keeping his finger on the trigger. At some point in Bhao's stupid game, a shot was fired, hitting Murtaza in the back, above his shoulder blade. Murtaza slumped forward onto the table and Bhao and the girls giggled, thinking Mir was pulling one of his famous pranks. Then Shah, who watched over his brother with a concern unique among the siblings, noticed that there was blood seeping through Murtaza's *shalwar kameez*. Shah shoved Bhao off his chair and didn't leave his brother's side until he had been taken to the hospital and the bullet had been safely removed.

For his part, Murtaza doted on Shah. He indulged him, never

pushing away his younger brother when he had friends around, and guarded him vigilantly. Any schoolyard tussle that Shah – proud and combative towards anyone who tried to goad him or was unchivalrous about his family – found himself in always saw Murtaza standing alongside his brother. He defended Shah to their father too, pleading with him not to send Shah off to boarding school – or cadet college in the heart of Sindh when he had been especially egregious – whenever he broke some cardinal rule of Zulfikar's. Sanam and Shah were both sent off to boarding school at one point or another and both children would manage to escape: Shah by having his brother plead for his parole on the grounds of good behaviour and Sanam by jumping the school wall and hitching a ride with a truck driver down to whichever official residence Zulfikar was living in at the time.

⬥••⬥

It wasn't until Murtaza was twelve years old that he became aware of the political dynamics surrounding his family.

> We didn't really understand what this minister stuff was all about initially. Of course, we had policemen around all the time and the normal privileges that come with the territory, but it didn't really seem that inspiring. I mean, we knew my father was important because we heard his name on the radio all the time, but it was only in 1966, when he came out of jail, that we realized this was serious business.[9]

Zulfikar was on the cusp of founding the Pakistan People's Party and he went, overnight it seemed, from being a minister to being a political icon.

> We saw all the crowds, the hysteria and the passions that were being evoked in front of our eyes, especially at the Lahore railway station (where Zulfikar had gone to launch the PPP), and it had a very powerful impact on us children. I was about twelve at the

time and after that I wouldn't miss any opportunity to go along with my father. But I was largely drawn to politics as a spectator at that time, I wasn't thinking of myself as an actor at any stage.[10]

Murtaza began keeping newspaper clippings, charting the politics of Pakistan and every rise and fall of his father's party. He hoarded newspapers as they came in, combing them hungrily, marking in pen the articles he felt worth removing first and then carefully – he was a fastidious Virgo; clean lines meant the world to him – clipping them out of the broadsheets to archive. He bought simple notebooks, some with seventies psychedelic flowers on their covers, others plain and looking like they'd belong to a chartered accountant, businesslike and austere; one of the notebooks, made by the Hamdam Book Binding Works in Karachi, has a watercolour painting of the Shalimar Gardens. There is a white box, hanging over the Shalimar pond, with the words 'name/subject/class/sec' written in navy blue with long lines attached to them, waiting for answers. It is empty. The answers are inside.

The clippings are from Urdu and English newspapers, kept in place with Scotch tape. Some are of photographs of Zulfikar addressing large crowds of people across the country, in Murree, in Korangi, in Kahuta. Some are pictures of riots, mainly religious Jammaat Islami gatherings pitched against Zulfikar and his new party. There are also statements, strong confident statements: 'Mr Zulfikar Ali Bhutto said here yesterday that his party does not believe in political alliances.' 'Our alliance is with the people,' reads a clipping from the *Daily News*, Monday, 27 July 1970. Another article from a Lahore newspaper, dated 2 October, blares the headline 'Bhutto says: NOBODY CAN DARE . . .' followed by the words: 'Chairman of the People's Party Z. A. Bhutto declared here yesterday that even if all the political parties of Pakistan joined together they could not beat the People's Party . . . He added we will wipe out bribery, corruption and nepotism from this country.'

Murtaza kept everything. No story was too small or too large; this was a habit that stayed with Murtaza throughout his life. Later, when I was a child and we were living in exile in Damascus, my father and

I would sit together in the evenings clipping newspapers. We each had our own notebooks. I cut out cartoon strips, 'Garfield' mainly, while Papa clipped news stories from Pakistan.

It was around this time, his early teenage years, that Murtaza discovered the world of politics and it did something to him – something strange. It consumed him and electrified how he thought of himself and the world. He began to read, to study. Che Guevara's diaries and Mao's dialectics were the cornerstones of his ideological material at the time. Gudu, who befriended a young Murtaza at the age of fourteen, remembers his friend as 'quiet, pensive' but 'very ideological towards Pak-China friendship. He was reading a lot of Mao at the time and we'd go to the embassy and watch movies there when they had screenings.'[11]

Gudu and Murtaza organized Che marches to commemorate the most famous moments of their hero's career and martydom. They wore black berets, carried Che posters and once managed to convince a bunch of Russian soldiers on leave, who were wandering around the market in Saddar, to join their procession. Otherwise, young Murtaza and Gudu followed a fairly spartan schedule. Most days they would go to swim at Clifton Beach, timing their visits to coincide with the Karachi police cavalry, who would bring their horses to the sandy beach for their afternoon plunge in the salty waters. The two friends would go to visit the Sufi shrine of Mango Pir in outer Karachi, where Mango Pir's *Sheedi* disciples fed and tended to a pack of crocodiles they believed to be avatars of their saint. Murtaza would yearn to touch the crocodiles, Gudu remembers, but never did. When time was a factor, Gudu and Murtaza would bike to the shrine of Abdullah Shah Gazi, Karachi's patron saint, or the Hindu temple near 70 Clifton. They would sit with the Muslim or Hindu devotees and eat delicious oily food before excusing themselves. When they were feeling especially maudlin or unsure of their place in the world, Murtaza and Gudu would sit in the empty black ceramic bathtub in Murtaza's bathroom and stay up talking, knees bent and cramped, late into the night.

One day, Gudu and Murtaza took a tent and a flashlight and camped out in the garden of 70 Clifton. 'I think he was rebelling or something,' remembers Gudu. 'We'd go inside for food but we were trying to live out in nature.' As the night progressed and their conversation about Che Guevara and worldwide socialism heightened, 'We realized we wanted to do something', says Gudu. 'It was a very political time – Zulfikar Ali Bhutto had just left Ayub's government – and we wanted to do something. Let's start a magazine, I said.' And so they did.

They had come across printers as they travelled with Zulfikar on his campaigns across the country and Gudu and Murtaza managed to wangle a deal whereby the pages of the magazine were printed at nearly no cost, so long as they paid for the colour on the cover. They gathered friends and schoolmates who knew enough about the world to appreciate their obsession with progressive socialism and convinced them to write for the magazine. Together, Gudu and Murtaza selected the articles that would be printed in each issue. They had a vision and they worked hard to make sure the magazine reflected the idealism of their youth 'We worked in the slums in Lyari during the elections,' remembers Gudu. 'We all felt for the poor people, they influenced us a lot, it was the late 1960s – a very radical time.'

Shah, too young at the time to write for the magazine, joined up as a supporter and hawker of the magazine. However young he was though, he never missed out on accompanying Murtaza on the campaign trail or on trips with their father across the country. Zulfikar encouraged his youngest child to accompany his older brother, pleased that the brothers displayed the stamina and interest to keep up with the gruelling day-to-day intricacies of local campaigning and political tours. One of their main jobs during the build up to the 1970 election, as they travelled around the country campaigning for local PPP candidates, was to help print pamphlets and posters. Murtaza found printers who were sympathetic towards the party and hostile enough to Ayub's dictatorship for them to be willing to print party material for free. The PPP barely had any funds at the time; it was not the mega conglomerate it is today, but a young party with the poor running as its candidates – with professors and trade union activists at its helm, not feudals landowners and businessmen, not yet.

Murtaza, hardly eighteen, went to Larkana, his father's constituency, and met with villagers in *panchayats*. 'Young people wanted to follow him around,' remembers Gudu, who accompanied him to many of these gatherings. 'They wanted to touch him, to be around him. He listened to everyone,' says Gudu. 'Mir spoke to the people and discussed their problems with them. His father also spoke to him a lot, it was private, between the two of them, but they had a connection when it came to the political work and Mir always listened to him.' In time Murtaza began to receive legal petitions from workers who had no access to the law. One heading reads: 'Lawlessness of police in Garhi Yasin in taking of my daughter illegally.' The petitioner is a citizen of Naudero, where the Bhutto agricultural lands are based, and he submits: 'Seeing no other source, I request your honour to kindly help me get back my daughter, Roshan Khatoon, whose suit has not been decided by the civil court of Larkana. For this I will remain ever grateful, thank you in inticipation [sic] Ali Sher.' Murtaza spoke to all petitioners who wrote to him and did what he could. 'It was his purpose', explains Gudu, unfazed that such things could be asked of a young man like him. 'His heart was in it. Mir met the people with great dignity and they trusted him, even at that young age.' Years later, I found those petitions, sent to Papa at college in the United States in some cases, in a small cardboard box. He never threw them away.

It was with the elections in the foreground of their minds that Murtaza and Gudu decided to call the magazine *Venceremos*, Spanish for 'we will overcome' and a battle cry long associated with Castro and Che Guevara and the Cuban Revolution. The first issue of *Venceremos* has Alberto Korda's iconic portrait of Che, printed in block red, on the cover. It opens with a message from the two editors:

With harmonic emotions perhaps to be shattered, we publish the first edition of VENCEREMOS. It is our hope, it is our aim and determination, that VENCEREMOS will kindle into the flame . . . that a fire will start in the mind of men. VENCEREMOS we hope will make the people realize, especially the proletariat, because for them we have a message, the evils of this society, the absurdness of their lives, their useless sense of values . . . That they should break away, tear down this social structure, and thus cleansed build a new society, a new nation based on the fundamental laws of human nature: for the love of humanity. We want to put a stop to this exploitation of man by man.

The introduction's rapid-fire internationale ended with a poem: 'VENCEREMOS, Arise ye prisoners of starvation, Arise ye wretched of the earth, for justice thunders condemnation, a better world's in birth.' For all its excitement and lack of grammar, the introduction set the mood of the magazine, but it didn't colour the content of the magazine, which was surprisingly serious. 'Indonesia: The Downfall of a Nation', 'The Disastrous Policy of the Americans in Vietnam' and 'State of the Pakistani Economy'. Murtaza wrote articles for the magazine such as 'God's Forgotten Land', which begins: 'The Valleys of Kashmir, the most beautiful in the world, have for decades been stained by the blood of their own people . . . The people of Jammu and Kashmir must be aware that "a revolution is not a dinner party" nor is it a protest march, a revolution is more or less a war between the exploiters and the exploited.'

When I finally tracked Gudu down after months of searching and exhausting the kindness of strangers by leaving emotional voicemails for him on their answering machines, I found my father's old teenage confidant, who now lives in Washington DC, working as a short-order cook, as well as practising as a licensed naturopath, to fund his ambitious travels across the world to study with shamans and healers. He speaks in a light, almost frail voice, about the lift-off of the magazine. 'At the time, there were student revolts going on against Ayub, so we went and distributed *Venceremos* to Karachi University students and had some copies sent to Lahore to be passed around Punjab University. Mir wanted to keep the magazine ideologically geared towards the youth.' Gudu and I spent a spring day together, sitting on the porch of the shared house he was living in – where he still kept decade-old copies of *Venceremos* with him – and in Meridian Hill park, also known as Malcolm X park in the racially diverse Columbia Heights neighbourhood. The park, alternatively described on DC tourism websites as a hippie, drumbeating haven or a notorious vice den of the city's more seedy elements, was beautiful on the sunny April day we visited. Lugging my camera bag and inadvisably wearing a sweater, I was exhausted by the time Gudu and I sat down by the park's thirteen basin cascading fountains. I showed him pictures of my brother Zulfi. He smoked and I cried. Alternatively, every twenty minutes or so I would open my notebook to jot something down and Gudu would cry. When we parted company, I promised to send him a copy of the book I was writing. 'I don't know where I'll be,' he said in his whisper. I promised to track him down again when the book was ready; I had already found him once, after all.

Future editions of *Venceremos* with Ho Chi Minh on the cover and angry articles lambasting the Shah of Iran, an ally of Zulfikar's (whom he found obnoxious and insufferable, but an ally nonetheless) inside, were taken to Saddar and distributed on the roads to workers and passers-by. The thought of the son of such a political powerhouse standing on the road, trying to foist Lenin upon whoever went by made Gudu laugh as he remembered it. 'It was a beautiful youth,' he said.

In the autumn of 1972, Murtaza won an academic scholarship to Harvard University. 'Dear Mr Bhutto,' the letter, dated 9 June 1972 read, 'The Committee on Admissions and Scholarships' decision to admit you is clear evidence of its belief that you are well qualified intellectually and personally for Harvard.' Chase N. Peterson, the chairman of the committee, signed the letter with a rounded C and an elongated P. Murtaza set off from Pakistan as an independent young man for the first time.

◆•••◆

By the late 1960s Ayub Khan's government was beginning to lose its hold over the country. The United States cut off military aid to Pakistan in 1967.[12] Ayub's unilateral foreign policy was entirely ineffectual;

Pakistan had been cut off financially and diplomatically isolated and further had lost face as the United States became closer to India, its traditional enemy. Pakistan had lost so much standing with the Americans that they did not bother to renew their base at Badebar, near Peshawar, in 1968.[13]

Domestically, Ayub had become the 'symbol of inequality, of all that had gone wrong',[14] and he had begun to lose ground politically. But Zulfikar Ali Bhutto's PPP was not the only party that threatened Ayub's stability. In East Pakistan, it was the Awami League, founded in 1949, that had become a force to reckon with.

Since Partition the ethnic Bengalis who populated most of the new country felt alienated as East Pakistanis, and the time to act, to demand more, was finally upon them. East Pakistan made up more than 50 per cent of the nation's entire population, yet it was physically separated from West Pakistan by more than a thousand miles of Indian territory. But it was not only the distance from the central government that so estranged East Pakistanis; economically there was a tremendous disparity in the funds allocated to the various provinces, with Bengal or East Pakistan getting the short end of the stick. Culturally, East Pakistanis felt slighted by the fact that Bengali was never adopted as an official language, as Urdu – spoken by the ethnic Muhajirs who crossed over from India during Partition – and English were.

It was under the direction of Sheikh Mujibur Rehman, a former student leader active in the cause of building Pakistan and head of the Awami League, and so committed to the new country that he reportedly bicycled across the new borders to reach the promised homeland, that East Pakistan announced its political grievances with the Six Point programme of 1966. The Six Points voiced the party's demands for a parliamentary form of government with a central parliament directly elected by the people; for the powers of the federal government to be restricted to defence and foreign policy, leaving all other affairs to constituent units; for separate fiscal policies or currencies to be introduced to stop the flow of capital from East Pakistan; limited powers of taxation for the federal government; provincial rights to enter into trade agreements with foreign countries and full control over its earned foreign exchange; and finally for the provinces to have their own militaries and paramilitaries if necessary.[15] Essentially, politely, the Awami League was asking for more than provincial autonomy; it was asking for its own country.

None of the six points were accepted by Ayub's government. The dictator only felt threatened by what he saw as the Awami League's separatist leanings. In 1968 he had Mujib arrested for the treasonous act of plotting seccession from Pakistan. Zulfikar was also arrested, his new party hadn't been asking for much less than a complete turn-around of the political system and the end to Ayub's disastrous reign, so he too was thrown into jail in late 1968 – and was shifted from jail to jail for the next three months until his release in January 1969. On the issue of the Awami League's six points, the PPP, as Dr Mubashir Hasan puts it, 'accepted five and a half', rejecting mainly the notion of separate assemblies and a new Bengali currency.

Ayub's weakness and political insecurity against the two rising threats paved the way for martial law. On 26 March 1969 General Agha Mohammad Yahya Khan, the army's Commander-in-Chief, proclaimed martial law and installed himself as its chief administrator. Four days later, the 1962 constitution – a document hardly worth the paper it was printed on – was abrogated and Yahya Khan assumed the presidency of Pakistan. Ayub, beleaguered by poor health, left quietly and elections were called for the following year. Zulfikar, who had a wicked sense of humour, kept one reminder of his former boss – a large portrait of the General in uniform. He hung the portrait, painted at his commission, in his drawing room in Larkana. To this day, members of the General's family have asked for the portrait but family rules – handed down from Zulfikar himself – forbid it. Ayub hangs in our drawing room still.

The return to constitutional government was initially set for October 1970, but was postponed until December, after which Pakistan would be presented with a brand new constitution. The election campaign was fierce. The Awami League stood resolutely by its Six Point platform, not conceding an inch on its agenda. Zulfikar embarked on an intense campaign and toured extensively around West Pakistan at the helm of the PPP's strong leftist and national platform. 'He was a man of great energy,'[16] remembered Miraj Mohammad Khan, one of the party's founding members. 'He would stand in the rain to talk to ten people as if they were a thousand.'

The PPP's 1970 election manifesto took a strong stand against Ayub's unilateral policies, maintaining that Pakistan had been 'made use of as a pawn in the international game by the neo-colonialist allies'[17] and that the only way to create an independent Pakistan would be to leave its existing international alliances. Foreign policy and Pakistan's sovereignty made up the introduction to the manifesto and while there were similarities between the document and the PPP's earlier tract, *Foundation and Policy*, which set out to define the scope of the new party, such as the strong sense of solidarity with Muslim peoples the world over and with fellow Third World nations, there were some key additions.

Zulfikar, while writing the manifesto with his colleagues, translated his vision of bilateralism more clearly than he had previously. He was the lone voice in Pakistan calling for the nation to leave the British Commonwealth which, in his estimation, had 'lost any meaning it might have had at one time' by serving colonial interests and taking the side of the United States in its war against Vietnam.[18] Zulfikar did not see Pakistan's relationship with the Commonwealth as beneficial to Pakistan and enunciated this in his party's manifesto, stating that Pakistan would only engage in relations based on reciprocity and mutuality of interests. (Under Zulfikar Ali Bhutto's presidency, Pakistan voluntarily withdrew from the Commonwealth in 1972. Pakistan voluntarily rejoined the Commonwealth in 1989, under the premiership of Zulfikar's daughter, Benazir.)

The first ever general election held in Pakistan, on the principle of one man, one vote, took place on 3 December 1970. Twenty-three political parties contested 291 seats in the National Assembly, putting up a total of 1,237 candidates. Three hundred and ninety-one candidates ran as independents.[19] The results were predictably divided; the Awami League took East Pakistan and the PPP won the majority of seats in the West, sweeping Punjab and Sindh. East Pakistan, however, made up 56 per cent of Pakistan's population and so the balance hung in the Awami League's favour. However, any constitutional settlement hinged on the two parties reaching an agreement to share power, which would leave Mujib with East Pakistan and Zulfikar with the West and General Yahya Khan in charge of the military.

Mujib wanted the constitution to be framed by his party, allowing him to form the government, while Zulfikar was not comfortable with the army's assurances that the PPP would be given as equal a hand as the Awami League in the proceedings. Effectively, promising power and position to both parties, the army played the two men against each other and ensured that no harmonious settlement was reached. After decades of Western hegemony over the country, the army – based in Western Punjab – had no interest in handing over power to its compatriots in the East. However, it was equally reluctant to allow the socialist Zulfikar to translate his party's victory into government. On 1 March 1971, the National Assembly proceedings were postponed and General Yahya Khan dissolved his civilian cabinet. The army vetoed the proposed coalition government and the Awami League's opportunity to form a national government was over. Riots broke out across East Pakistan. The bloodletting began.

In East Pakistan a campaign of civil disobedience was undertaken by Bengalis refusing to pay taxes and wilfully ignoring the radio and press censorship enforced by the military.[20] On the other side of the world, Murtaza, now at Harvard, discovered that he was being watched by the US State Department. His father, not yet the head of the country, did not have enough power to merit having his son followed at college. There were death threats made against young Murtaza, from Bengali quarters, and the State Department began to take them seriously. Eventually, Zulfikar was notified that his son's life was in danger and security was arranged, aided by the Iranians, who sent over some young-looking agents to watch over the former Foreign Minister's son. Two of Murtaza's Harvard roommates, Peter Santin and Bill White, remember finding out about Mir's precarious situation much later. He had downplayed it in order not to worry them.

When I asked both former roommates about the incident years later, they pursed their lips and said little. It was a sensitive topic. An Iranian agent followed Murtaza around college, eating Chinese food with the students and playing cards with them in their dorm for a time. They couldn't escape Mir's Iranian shadow then, and were reluctant to discuss him with me. It was too uncomfortable a topic.

The military, unsurprisingly, reacted with brute force to the rumblings in East Pakistan, most notably by sending General Tikka Khan, a soldier known for his eager use of force, to act as the military's chief authority in the province. General Tikka Khan, a graduate of the Dehra Dun school and a Second World War officer who fought on the Burmese and Italian fronts under the banner of the Raj, enjoyed an infamous reputation. He was nicknamed the 'butcher of Balochistan' for his role in quelling the province's secessionist unrest in the early 1960s. He would soon add 'butcher of Bengal' to his CV.

By 25 March 1971 talks between Bhutto, Yahya and Mujib had stalled and the military put into effect an emergency plan: within the next twenty-four hours Mujib was arrested, the Awami League banned and a cessation of all political activities throughout Pakistan enforced.[21] At midnight, General Tikka Khan led the assault on Dhaka University and various other points in the city's old quarters. Thousands were killed. Pakistan was plunged into a bloody civil war as the East Pakistan Rifles, a paramilitary group, mutinied and joined the rebels fighting to take East Pakistan. The army countered the insurgency by mounting a fierce offensive against the Bengalis. Within six months, on top of thousands dead and wounded, a refugee population of approximately 10 million had been created, with thousands fleeing across the border into India.

The violence of the conflict was staggering. Reports from East Pakistan placed the number of civilian casualties in the millions, citing figures of around 3 million killed. Pakistani officials, via the ludicrous Hamood-ur-Rehman commission – whose pages were edited by the army and whose full copy no one has yet seen – insisted the number was closer to some 30,000, a mere by-product of the war. International figures, treading lightly, estimated around 200,000 dead on the Eastern front.

While the numbers differ, there is no dispute regarding the sheer force used by the Pakistani Army against civilians, most notably women.

In her moving and disturbing work, *Against Our Will: Men, Women and Rape* Susan Brownmiller claims that some 400,000 women were raped by the Pakistani Army as a tactic of war. The women were singled out in an effort to destabilize and stigmatize the Bengali people. Brownmiller recounts the story of a thirteen-year-old girl, Khadiga, from Dhaka with shocking effect.

> Khadiga . . . was walking to school with four other girls when they were kidnapped by a gang of Pakistani soldiers. All five were put in a military brothel in Mohammedpur and held captive for six months until the end of the war. Khadiga was regularly abused by two men a day; others, she said, had to service ten men daily . . . At first, Khadiga said, the soldiers tied a gag around her mouth to keep her from screaming. As months wore on and the captive's spirit was broken, the soldiers devised a simple quid pro quo. They withheld the daily ration of food until the girls had submitted to the full quota.

In addition to reports of sanctioned violence towards women, there were charges levelled against the Pakistani Army for its use of violence towards intellectuals, academics and minorities, Hindus specifically. Word had spread to Karachi that the Pakistani Army, having killed 200 intellectuals in Dhaka, was planning to carry out the same kind of massacre in Sindh to quell inconvenient questions of their brutality in the civil war. Abdul Waheed Katpar, the Sindhi lawyer who worked with Zulfikar early on his career, was present when the news reached the ears of the People's Party chairman. I asked Katpar if he meant to say that Zulfikar believed the rumour that the army was planning to massacre Sindhi intellectuals. 'Yes!' replied Katpar ardently. 'They don't believe in anything, these *Khakis*'. [22] Zulfikar picked up the phone and called General Gul Hasan, the corp commander of Sindh. 'He was furious,' remembers Katpar. 'He told him, "I'm hearing you're killing intellectuals in the East. If you bring this vicious tactic to Sindh, I'll be your second Mujib and rise up against you!"'

The Hamood-ur-Rehman commission, headed by the Chief Justice of Pakistan, denied any wrongdoing on the part of the Pakistani armed forces and deflected blame for the war away from the army. Similarly, Sarmila Bose, an Indian Harvard-educated professor and granddaughter of the nationalist leader Sarat Chandra Bose, made ripples in 2005 when she claimed that Bangladeshi allegations of mass rape and religious targeting committed by the Pakistani Army were greatly exaggerated for the new country's political purposes.

While the Pakistani Army has always denied that rape was used as a means of fighting the East Pakistanis, the occurrence of rape during the war was so commonplace that Mujib ultimately coined a term for victims, *Birangona* or heroines, and attempted to honour the rape survivors after the war had ended, a miscalculated initiative that only further shamed and alienated the women survivors among their communities and families.

As the civil war spread across the borders of Pakistan, India began to play a dangerously flirtatious role with East Pakistan. By the end of March, the Indian parliament had passed several resolutions in support of the 'people of Bengal', a term no one had used internationally at that point, still referring to East Pakistanis as Pakistani citizens. As Bengali nationalists and secessionists engaged in their own acts of violence against Pakistan, Pakistan closed its high commission in Calcutta and India shut its own consulate in Dhaka.

By the summer of 1971, the Mukti Bahini, a Bengali liberation army, began to receive training and equipment from India.[23] As India continued funding and instructing the East Pakistani secessionists, reports began to surface of increased border shelling between the two countries. On 29 November 1971 the provisional government of Bangladesh was announced, just one week after General Yahya instituted a state of emergency and told his countrymen to prepare for an all-out war. As the year drew to a close, it was not only inevitable that Pakistan would be broken into two, but also that war with India was once again on the horizon.

On 3 December, the Pakistani Air Force struck Northern Indian military targets. The escalation in border shelling had reached its peak and this time India reacted with its full military might. By 4 December, India had launched an air, ground and naval attack into East Pakistan, converging on Dhaka. Two days after their spectacular invasion, the Indians had all but taken over East Pakistan, tightened their grip around the soon to be capital city of Dhaka and recognized the provisional government. The Indian government violated a tenuous peace between the two countries and continued to violate Pakistan's sovereignty by securing its hold on Dhaka.

It was in the early weeks of December that Zulfikar was sent by General Yahya Khan to plead Pakistan's case at the United Nations Security Council. It was on the 15th of the month, after the UN had ruled in Bangladesh's favour by supporting its claim to independence, that Zulfikar angrily declared, 'So what if Dhaka falls? So what if the whole of East Pakistan falls? So what if the whole of West Pakistan falls? We will build a new Pakistan. We will build a better Pakistan . . . We will fight for a hundred years.' Zulfikar had felt from the start, leaving aside his respect for Mujib as a compatriot, that the Awami League's Six Point programme would divide the new and fragile country. Now, disgusted with the proceedings at the Security Council, Zulfikar ripped up his papers and walked out, angry and frustrated. 'My country hearkens for me, why should I waste my time here in the Security Council?'

$\{4\}$

On 16 December, Pakistani forces surrendered and the following day a ceasefire was put into effect. Yahya Khan resigned his position four days later and Zulfikar, having just left New York, flew to Islamabad to assume the presidency.

In 1972, Zulfikar and the People's Party took direct control of the government and worked to bring the party's vision of socialism and Third World solidarity to the national stage. Having played a mediatory role in Nixon's détente with China, Zulfikar visited Beijing shortly after the famous trip in February 1972. He was received graciously by China; in order to ease Pakistan's transition back to life after its harrowing civil war, the Chinese government agreed to write off some of its earlier loans to Pakistan, totalling $110 million.[1] Several months later, in the spring of that year, China sent Pakistan sixty Mi-G fighter jets and one hundred T-54 and T-59 tanks as part of the new $300 million economic and military assistance package negotiated during the President's earlier visit.[2]

Diplomatically buoyed by Zulfikar's new socialist leadership, China supported Pakistan wholeheartedly. It used its United Nations veto to keep Bangladesh out of the international body, refusing to recognize the new state as a legitimate sovereign nation. In fact, China did not recognize Bangladesh until October 1975, long after Pakistan had extended its recognition, which it did in February 1974. China also refused to exchange ambassadors with India until it had fully restored diplomatic relations with Pakistan in the summer of 1976.

It was also reported that China, a nuclear state since 1964, had exported nuclear aid to Pakistan, whose nuclear programme was started by Zulfikar in 1972. A 1977 report by the United States Arms Control Disarmament Agency concluded that 'China had assisted Pakistan in developing nuclear explosives' and had also provided Pakistan with highly enriched uranium (HEU) as part of its nuclear assistance programme.[3]

For his part, Zulfikar committed his Foreign Office to aiding China within Asia whenever it could, most notably by helping to bring about an upswing in relations between China, the Middle Eastern nations and Iran, with whom Pakistan enjoyed close relations. Pakistan also turned its back on the Soviet Union, shunning its 'Asian Security' scheme because of its aggressively anti-Chinese tone.[4]

Pakistan under Zulfikar's leadership enjoyed its strongest period of Pak-Chinese friendship, but the young President also opened his country's foreign policy up to numerous other Muslim and Asian states. For once, for the first time in Pakistan's history, Pakistan was not simply an American or Soviet lackey, but an independent nation exercising its sovereign powers through decidedly bilateral relations. Pakistan was part of Asia, no longer a satellite of the great powers. 'Pakistan has sought to take the right position based on justice,' Zulfikar wrote to his son Murtaza while he was studying at Harvard. 'As long as I am in charge of the affairs of Pakistan, this shall always be the case whether it is the Middle East or any other theatre of the world.'[5]

Meanwhile, the issue of Bangladesh and the fallout of the war loomed. In late June, the summer Zulfikar assumed the presidency, he travelled to the Indian hill station of Simla to meet with Indira Gandhi, his Indian counterpart, to discuss the subcontinent's new borders and the prisoners of war who remained captive in Indian and Bangladeshi jails. Zulfikar travelled to India from Lahore with a large delegation, apprehensive that the meeting would require Pakistan to recognize the new state broken from its borders and agree to a no-war pact with India.

The first session of the Simla talks was opened by welcoming words from Mrs Gandhi, who acknowledged the difficulties of the two parties in meeting to negotiate. Zulfikar reciprocated. 'I want to say, believe me, we are interested in peace. That is our objective and we will strive for it. We want to turn the corner. We want to make a new beginning.'[6]

The warmth of the first meeting, however, did not last. The second day of talks produced no concrete results. Both delegations met and discussed the roadblocks, including the Indian insistence on a refigured Line of Control in Kashmir – a matter of importance in the 1971 war that remained an eternally perplexing one for the two countries – and the Pakistani insistence on a plebiscite in Kashmir. On 1 July, near the end of the official summit, newspapers were reporting that the talks had stalled. Nothing firm had been agreed upon and both parties were reluctant to sign a treaty that belittled their respective countries. The following day, even Zulfikar was said to have admitted to the press that there was 'some kind of deadlock'.[7] Both sides continued to hold their breath and wait.

That evening as Indira Gandhi walked alone in the gardens of the hill station where the negotiations were taking place, Zulfikar, himself frustrated by the failure of their talks thus far, went out to join her. The two leaders walked alone, without delegates and advisors, for some time. They spoke freely and without the usual tension that seemed to dog their relationship on every other occasion. Both of them had come to Simla for peace, a peace that did not leave their countries beholden or indebted to the other but that guaranteed them both a measure of political equality. As they walked in the evening cool of Simla's summer, Zulfikar and Indira came to an agreement.

The signing of the eleventh-hour Simla treaty was a diplomatic miracle. Neither Pakistan nor India lost ground and neither vanquished the other. No vital concessions were made, a feat between two aggressive and territorially proud countries; calm between India and Pakistan was once again a promised possibility. A new ceasefire line in Kashmir was agreed upon, trade, communications and flights were resumed between Pakistan and India and cultural exchanges were no longer blocked. The prisoners of war were not yet to be released, but it was the success at Simla that ensured they would be – 90,000 Pakistani soldiers would soon return home. People say that the agreement between the two leaders was so sudden and unexpected that Zulfikar didn't even have a pen on him when the treaty was passed to him to sign.

Upon returning home, Zulfikar told the crowd that met him at Rawalpindi airport that the success at Simla belonged to the Indian and Pakistani people who had struggled through three wars to reach this momentous peace. Twelve days later, the National Assembly approved the Simla agreement. A large oil portrait of the signing of the Simla peace hangs in what was Zulfikar's office in 71 Clifton; he must have hung it himself. For so long as I can remember, it has always been the centrepiece of my grandfather's book-laden office.

Zulfikar's foreign policy triumphs continued as his time in office progressed. In February 1974, Pakistan played host to the Organization of Islamic Countries' second ever summit. The city of Lahore was spruced up and its roads cleaned – citizens were told that they were to welcome their guests, the heads of thirty-eight Islamic states, even offering them their homes. Hotels and government guest houses were not sufficient to handle the number of dignitaries and functionaries coming so Zulfikar called upon the people of Lahore to open their houses and they did so with the knowledge that they were for once included in the solidarity movement of people across the Islamic *umma*. Sadat of Egypt, Boumedienne of Algeria, Gadaffi – who had a stadium named for him in the Mughal city – of Libya, Hafez al Assad of Syria, King Faisal of Saudi Arabia, whose country helped with the preparations, and Yasser Arafat, head of the PLO, all attended. While the Shah of Iran did not deign to make an appearance, Idi Amin did – uninvited and with a substantial familial entourage.

Zulfikar roused his guests and heralded the success of the OIC summit by declaring that 'We, the people of Pakistan, shall give our blood for the cause of Islam . . . Whenever the occasion arises the Islamic world will never find us wanting in any future conflict.'[8] The architect of Pakistan's solidarity movement with the Muslim world would have had a coronary had he lived to see the day when Pakistan entered a war on two Muslim neighbours, Afghanistan and Iraq, at the behest of the United States, no less, and meekly opened the frontiers of its borders and skies so that a foreign army's planes could bomb undisturbed. He would have been all the more disgusted to know that the party he founded sits at the helm of such spineless collaboration.

Zulfikar had made good on his pre-election promises to strive towards closer bonds with Third World nations and fight for Pakistan's sovereignty; since becoming head of state Zulfikar had withdrawn his country from the British Commonwealth and removed Pakistan from SEATO, the South East Asia Treaty Organization sponsored by the United States. He fostered close ties with Middle Eastern and African countries, the culmination of which was seen at the OIC summit where Colonel Gadaffi called Pakistan 'the citadel of Islam in Asia' and promised his country's resources to Pakistan whenever it required Libya's friendship and aid.[9]

I found myself in a bizarre scene, thirty-five years later, when, travelling across Europe researching this book, I found myself at the dinner table of one of Colonel Gadaffi's son's. I knew who he was, but I don't think he had figured out who I was, genetically speaking. I leaned across the table and introduced myself, received a polite nod as we exchanged pleasantries in Arabic and then proceeded, in rapid fire, to tell him about the OIC summit (I had just finished my notes on what would be this chapter), concluding with the stadium, a place that has a unique history in many Pakistani imaginations. Poor Mr Gadaffi listened politely and when I ran out of breath, we moved on. Discussing Pakistan's current President Zardari and a new bill he has signed punishing with imprisonment anyone found guilty of 'character assassinating' his person or his past, Mr Gadaffi asked about Pakistan's tenuous future. I tried to reassure him that things would change one day, they always do. He smiled broadly and recalled some of his father's and elder brother's visits to the once glorious country.

The OIC summit itself was a success and concluded by forming the Islamic Solidarity Fund and setting the foundations for the Islamic Commission on Economic, Cultural and Social Affairs. Pakistan also used the summit as an occasion to announce formally its recognition of Bangladesh and in return Bangladesh withdrew criminal charges against some 200 Pakistani soldiers in its custody.

The OIC summit brought Zulfikar closer to those leaders in Asia who were natural allies: Muslim states coming out of recent liberation movements since the fall of colonialism in the post-war world. He spoke frequently to several of the heads of states, Saudi Arabia's King Faisal and Sheikh Zayed of the United Arab Emirates among them, with regard to future summits and a proposed Treaty of Non-Aggression among Muslim countries.[10] Besides détente with India, Zulfikar had moved Pakistan closer to China, continued the country's relationship with America, now on more equal terms, and fostered stronger ties with neighbouring countries like Iran and Afghanistan.

Besides a radically altered foreign policy, for which Zulfikar will always be recognized in Pakistan, he made brave moves towards change in two other significant spheres – the formation of the country's new and first democratically proposed constitution and in the field of feudal land reform.

The 1973 constitution came into law in August and built upon the foundations of the country's previous constitutional charters with several important and far-reaching additions and amendments. First, the constitution put the structures in place for a bicameral legislature, giving the senate equal representation in the provinces by calling for its members to be indirectly elected by the provincial assemblies and having the national assembly given power by direct vote.[11] The problem of provincial autonomy was remedied, at least in part, by these directives, which decentralized what had always been an enormously centralized state. A Council of Common Interests was set up to regulate policies covering the fields of oil and gas, industries, water and power, which also contributed to the more balanced governing of Pakistan's most valuable resources.

Under the new constitution, Zulfikar assumed the post of Prime Minister, changing the mode of government to prime ministerial as opposed to presidential.[12] As for the army, the constitution had previously contained – and would again later contain – the necessary strings to allow for acts of emergency to be called for under the dubious 'doctrine of necessity'. If the army deemed it necessary to take over, the constitution of Pakistan always granted it the excuse to do so. Under the new constitution, however, the federal government was empowered with 'control and command' over the armed forces.[13] The soldiers in service were required to 'uphold the constitution' and avoid 'any political activity whatsoever'.[14] The new constitution chafed the army, which was not amused at being singled out for a reduction in its power. Eventually the Prime Minister would feel the same way too and he would seek to amend the constitution to lessen the restrictions on his power. Though it was, at the time of its drafting, a far-sighted document – the constitution, by virtue of a clause that obstructed the passing of any laws contrary to Islam, negated the notion of ever bringing Sharia law into a federal position at any time in the future – it was lacking largely in its treatment of the Ahmedi sect of Muslims, keeping this community's second-class-citizen status and refusing to acknowledge them as Muslims.

At least initially, though, the army were not the only ones who suffered at the hands of the new people's government. As part of his political campaigning Zulfikar had promised that his government would seek to amend the injustices of feudalism. It's worth noting that Zulfikar's family was one of the foremost feudal families in the country. There's a story, popularly recounted, of a census taken during the Raj when a British officer instructed a subordinate to tally up the various holdings of Sindh's elite. 'Call me when you've finished detailing the Bhutto land,' the officer was said to have instructed. Several days later, he had not heard from his colleague and returned to ask why he had not reported back. 'I'm still working on the Bhutto lands,' was the subordinate's reply.

At its inception the PPP was made up largely of writers, intellectuals, union leaders and other progressive elements of Pakistani society. Feudalism was an ill that was universally recognized within the party apparatus and a vow was made to amend the inequities of Pakistan's landed elite. Zulfikar held true to the promise of land reforms. The government instituted a ceiling of 250 acres of irrigated land and 300 acres of unirrigated land, making the reforms the most radical in

Pakistan at the time. Zulfikar lost much of his family's land in the reforms, slicing away his children's inheritance.

But there were still problems that plagued the reforms, mainly that land was transferred in name only: large landowners managed to hold the bulk of their titles through changing the names on the deeds to those of powerless peasants and contractors while still raking in the cash themselves. Many landowners also attempted to sidestep the reforms by donating their time and services generously to the PPP, hoping closeness to the chairman would exempt them from having to surrender their land. Zulfikar acknowledged that the reforms had further to go and formulated stricter ceilings, 100 acres for irrigated land and 200 for unirrigated land, to be put into place during the second stage of land reforms, but they were too late. He would not have the time to implement them.

It was not only the landed gentry who saw their fortunes placed in jeopardy; the country's industrialists felt the brunt of Zulfikar's socialist policies early on in his government, when the regime introduced nationalization. Initially, only thirty substantial firms were nationalized – with more to follow – as the government saw the programme as vital in tackling Pakistan's economic inequality and endemic poverty. Though nationalization seems to antagonize most serious capitalists the world over, those affected in Pakistan never ceased to blame Zulfikar for their economic castration. When my brother Zulfi, named for his grandfather, was in third grade – starting at a new private school in Karachi – he had a fight with another child in the playground. The child explained himself to Zulfi: 'We can't be friends,' he insisted. 'Your grandfather took away my grandfather's bank.' It wasn't only the bankers' relatives either. We heard similar tales of woe from the grandchildren of shipping magnates, insurance company founders, steel mill owners and various other beleagured captains of industry. Nationalization wasn't personal – it was a matter of national policy. Unfortunately, in Pakistan, politics is nothing if not personal – it seems to be the country's one constant. But rather than engage in the pros or cons of nationalization, it suffices to say that in a country where twenty-one men controlled the nation's economy, nationalization was the only available means to redistribute wealth. The move might not have been permanent, but only a short-term remedy on the way to a mixed economy. But, again, Zulfikar was not to have the time to test out his economic theories.

While it is fair to say that Zulfikar's time in office remains memorable owing to his advances in social programmes and foreign policy, it is important to recognize that it was hindered by many setbacks and mistakes made by the Prime Minister himself. He was a polarizing figure; you either loved Zulfikar or hated him. Without looking at the problems of his regime, there is no way to understand the manner in which violence and power attached themselves to the Bhutto family. And there is no larger problem than the role Zulfikar played in Balochistan.

Balochistan is a province blighted by Pakistan. The origins of the Baloch people, tribal in their formation and groupings, are said to be Semitic or Iranian, depending largely on whom you ask. Those who identify linguistically with the Aryans across the border claim a Persian heritage, those others who speak Balochi or one of the other regional languages claim that they abandoned their lives as shepherds in Syria sometime during the first millennium and travelled nomadically across the landscape of Central Asia before settling in the Baloch province.

By the time of the Raj, Balochistan had been part of the Mughal, Persian and Afghan kingdoms and had added culturally, linguistically and ethnically to its population. By the nineteenth century, the province was divided into four princely states, the majority of which were brought under the suzerainty of the British Raj. Wars and imperial struggles further unified the larger area that is now Balochistan, a province rich in mineral resources, namely gas, but whose population is poor.

As the subcontinent began to break apart, two states were asked where they wanted to go: Balochistan and Nepal. As the Baloch remember it, the people of the province voted to be independent – like Nepal, they didn't choose to belong to either Pakistan or India. The centres of Baloch authority unanimously rejected the idea of joining Pakistan and declared their independence. However, they were ruled by princes, who were easily bribed. The Pakistani Army was sent in and forced Prince Mir Ahmed Yar Khan of Kalat to change his tune; the Khan of Kalat signed an agreement revoking Baloch claims to independence and brought his people into Pakistan. His brother, on the other hand, refused to bow to Pakistani pressure and was later killed in his quest for Baloch national sovereignty.

The mode of operations had been set. The second conflict between the province and the state of Pakistan took place a mere ten years later in response to General Ayub's One Unit centralization policy. Balochistan was not going to go quietly into Pakistan's fold. The third struggle – they were averaging one per decade – happened in the early 1960s as the Pakistani Army began to build garrisons for its troops in Balochistan. Militants, insurgents belonging to various tribes, took up arms and attacked the state's army. General Yahya quelled the violence by erasing the One Unit structure and signed a ceasefire with the various warring factions. But the Baloch, formally and forcefully brought into Pakistan, were not held peacefully for long.

'Pakistan is a colony,'[15] Khair Bux Marri, the head of the Marri tribe, insisted to me when I went to speak with him at his Karachi home. I was met at the gate by burly men with large *shalwars* and Kalashnikovs hanging from their shoulders. The Bhuttos are not particular favourites of *Sardar* Marri, but the elder tribesman met my request for an interview graciously, received me courteously and offered me orange juice as we spoke.

'Very few countries are independent,' he continued, 'but Pakistan has been an imperial colony from the British to the Americans now. How can a colony have an independent attitude? Pakistan accepts the dominant position of imperialism. They chose to call this country Pakistan, land of the pure, because they believed the Koran is here, as if all other nations are pagan. To call it Pakistan is a grave mistake. It is *na-pakistan*, land of the impure.' I asked Marri how it was that the Baloch found themselves perpetually pitted against the state. 'There's a saying in Balochi,' he explained, speaking so quietly I had to keep edging closer towards him, this tribal chieftan who famously loathed my family, so that I might hear him. 'A man comes into a railway compartment and he sits in a corner as if he is there out of other people's generosity. You can tell him to move back in the carriage until he has nowhere else to go. But when pushed to the wall, he will draw his dagger. At that point, he'll either kill you or he'll die.'

In 1972, the Baloch found themselves pushed against the wall once more. They had voted alongside the Awami League and were further isolated when East Pakistan broke away from the union. Members from a range of political parties in the province grouped together to form the National Awami or People's Party, NAP, and pitted themselves as a bloc against Zulfikar Ali Bhutto's government. Various Baloch leaders demanded more representation in the federal government and began to formulate a secessionist plan of their own. The following year a large consignment of arms was found at the Iraqi embassy in Islamabad. The weapons, police alleged, were en route to the Marris of Balochistan. Zulfikar reacted quickly; he called the actions of the Marri insurgents treasonous and dismissed the provincial Baloch government.

The issue behind closed doors was admittedly larger; there was pressure from the Shah of Iran, who believed that the ethnic Baloch on his side of the border were arming themselves against Pahlavi rule. Worried at the prospect of an armed revolt, the Shah asked Pakistan to intervene. The army was sent into Balochistan once more. Zulfikar was not the first premier to take excessive measures against the Baloch, but he shouldn't have acted in conformity with his predecessors, all insecurely prone to excessive violence against the Baloch people. Khair Bux Marri, the same man who served me orange juice, put together the Baloch People's Liberation Front, BPLF, and began a guerrilla war against Zulfikar's government and his troops. Estimates, shrouded as they are, put Pakistani losses at around 3,000 with close to 10,000 Baloch separatists killed.

I asked *Sardar* Marri about the operation carried out in the 1970s. He demurred. 'You are his granddaughter, it wouldn't be proper,' he said politely. I was surprised by Marri's formality with me. I assured him that I was there to listen to him, to hear whatever he had to say. 'I have within me great fire against the PPP,' he cautioned. I insisted that I would not take anything he had to say personally. I am not my grandfather's keeper, I said with a laugh, please speak freely. He shrugged. I had asked for it. 'Bhutto was no different from Hitler,' *Sardar* Marri began. 'Before the operation he initiated, death only touched certain areas of the province. Then it affected all of Balochistan. The violence was expanded. Before our resistance had been traditional, tribal. Then it became more nationalistic.'

Marri was jailed on Zulfikar's orders. Many tribesmen were. Their dissent was silenced forcefully and they have never forgiven him for it. Yousef Masti Khan, another Baloch politician my father's age, also agreed to speak to me about the role Zulfikar played in Balochistan and was less old-fashioned and reticent about his views. He too had been arrested in 1974. Masti Khan was kept in barracks across from the passport offices in Saddar, Karachi, for fifteen days before he was moved by the army to a jail in Quetta. He was a young activist, a small player in provincial politics, and his father, Akbar Masti Khan, was an old friend of Zulfikar's. They used to argue about his policies. After the younger Khan was released, his father was called by his old friend, the Prime Minister, and offered a contract to build a highway across the province.

'I told my father, if you do it, I will leave here and take up arms in the mountains,'[16] Yousef Masti Khan told me, speaking animatedly. 'My father said, I can't just refuse Zulfikar, he's very vindictive.' Eventually, according to Yousef, his father went to see Zulfikar. He knew he couldn't take the deal and had to find a way out. He reached the official residence of the Prime Minister in Rawalpindi and found Zulfikar sitting on the staircase in his pyjamas, smoking a cigar. They talked for a while about old times, shooting the breeze as if things were normal, until finally Zulfikar asked him how things were in the province. 'Do you want to hear the answer for a Prime Minister or for a friend?' Akbar Masti Khan asked him. Zulfikar told his friend to speak openly. 'Why are you killing people in Balochistan?' he asked him. Zulfikar spoke about the violence, about the attacks on the state by the insurgents, about the sabotage. I don't want violence, he said, but what can I do? 'Withdraw the army,' insisted his friend. With that Zulfikar hung his head. 'I can't,' he replied.

It was a familiar refrain. He had, like all those before him, no power against the army when he was engaged in a war against his own people. The moment that Zulfikar began to fight Pakistanis, treasonous ones or not, he began to distance himself from his power base, from the source of his ultimate strength, and then the army, finally back in business, began to turn against him. Akbar Masti Khan was also arrested. And the army remained in Balochistan till the end of the decade.

'The Balochistan operation gave the army a lot of strength,' [17] agreed Miraj Mohammad Khan. 'They saw that the government needed them. Zulfikar was fighting his natural allies – the NAP were socialist, progressive, he missed these crucial alliances and that's what broke him.' Miraj left the PPP in 1974, in protest against the government's violent attack on Balochistan, and because of the about-turn Zulfikar had taken against the unions.

'The feudalists betrayed him. They infiltrated the party and then used its apparatuses against the people and because he had become insecure by that point, because these feudalists distanced him from the people, Zulfikar let them,' Miraj explained to me in Urdu. 'I walked out of a meeting in 1972 when we were discussing the union protest in Landhi, Karachi. The workers were striking and causing disruptions and Zulfikar said to us, "I assure you the strength of the street will be crushed by the strength of the state." So I walked out. He called me later and said I'd broken protocol. I told him why I left, why I broke party protocol. "It's the situation, Miraj!" Zulfikar replied, justifying what he had said. But the police, under the orders of the Chief Minister, had fired on the workers. The workers, the people, before this shooting believed that everything had changed with Zulfikar Ali Bhutto, they believed they had come to power and this terrified the industrialists. So, Zulfikar Ali Bhutto placated them.'

For Miraj, a lifelong Marxist so committed to the idea of a new Pakistan he still refuses to speak in English, this U-turn was unacceptable. Though he was one of Zulfikar's closest associates, Miraj left the party. 'I told him, you're being taken over by Intelligence. They're alienating you from your strength. J. A. Rahim was pushed out, Dr Mubashir Hasan was pushed out, so was I – all the founding members, all of us the most radical elements. Intelligence would send him reports saying we were plotting to kill him and as he got weaker, he became more paranoid.' The year after he left, Miraj was arrested. J. A. Rahim, one of the writers of the party manifesto, was brutally punished for his dissension. Dr Mubashir Hasan, the Finance Minister at whose house the PPP was founded, resigned from his ministry post, but stayed – one of the few – with Zulfikar.

{ 5 }

A ll of the men who gave their youth and their commitment to the party with Zulfikar that afternoon in Lahore were, one by one, sent to jail. 'He was not a prophet,' Miraj, now frail and ill, told me. 'He was a great man and a great leader, but in our culture we have a tendency to make prophets out of men.' The conclusion of Zulfikar's power was near, and in his weakness he didn't even see it coming.

Towards the end of his political reign, Zulfikar floundered. Despite the United States' hostility towards Pakistan's burgeoning nuclear programme, the building of the 'Muslim bomb' was pushing ahead, though it was winning the Prime Minister no friends in the process. Henry Kissinger, who publicly rated Zulfikar an able and intelligent politician, was said to have warned him that the Americans would 'make a horrible example' out of him if he were to proceed with Pakistan's nuclear ambitions.

Losing his solid footing, Zulfikar became nervous and started to appease the opposition at home, hoping the turnaround would placate his traditional enemies. He amended the 1973 constitution several times, enhancing his own powers by allowing the federal government to ban political parties and curbing the power of the courts so that, under the third amendment, 'no order could be made prohibiting detention or granting bail to a person so detained'.[1] Imagining his position secure, Zulfikar curried favour with the religious parties, small in number but powerful in terms of their fear factor, by amending the constitution to define the parameters of who was a Muslim. The Ahmedis, a small sect of Muslims who believe a prophet after

Muhammad, called Ahmed, will one day walk the earth, were officially defined as non-Muslims. Zulfikar went further: he banned alcohol, drove the country's gambling and entertainment industries underground and declared Friday, the day of prayers, a public holiday.

But he could not stave off the decline that had already begun. The feudalists, who had infiltrated the PPP in a bid to secure their own positions, began fighting among themselves. Abdul Waheed Katpar, one of the founding members of the PPP, remembers this period as one of intense paranoia for Zulfikar. 'He thought the army would kill him. He called them the *Khakis*. When the big *zamindar* in the party began to destabilize the party's image with their public feuding, Zulfikar told them, "Your fighting won't destroy me, the army will not spare me now – don't think they will spare you either." '[2]

In 1976, when the butcher of Bengal, General Tikka Khan, retired from the army, Zulfikar replaced him with General Zia ul Haq 'over the heads of five senior generals',[3] promoting him to Chief of Army Staff purely because Zulfikar believed him to be a meek, subservient man. Zia swore his undying loyalty to the Prime Minister on a Koran and bowed feverishly whenever Zulfikar walked into a room. Zia was a 'cunning man', remembered Katpar, 'always acting over-courteous with Bhutto. He was very ambitious and that made him very cruel.'[4] A stout man, with pomaded hair parted severely in the middle, and a moustache dyed black and carefully combed, Zia came from humble origins. He was not known for his political aspirations, but for his obedience to orders and religiously inspired simple-mindedness.

A story often repeated in my family, and used to defend if not explain Zulfikar's decision to promote the army general who later had him killed, went like this: Zulfikar had called his army chief to the Prime Minister's office for a word. Zia arrived on time, early even, and was taken into the office, where he sat down nervously, shaking his feet and twitching his legs. He had begun to smoke, a habit he indulged in to calm his nerves, when the Prime Minister walked in. Zia, various family members would exclaim, jumped up deferentially and shoved the lit cigarette into his pocket. It began to burn through the fabric of his jacker. Smoke came billowing out of Zia's uniformed military jacket, but he was so anxious around Zulfikar that he was too embarrassed to admit he had been smoking – hardly a crime – and too polite to put out the fire.

But the quiet and unassuming general would not have to wait long. His designs on the presidency were already in motion, even as his pocket linings burned. 'I know the bloodhounds are after my blood,'⁵ Zulfikar raged publicly, in one of his last sessions before parliament. He could feel it coming.

⋯⋯

Despite the political turmoil of these years, Zulfikar still found time to stay in close touch with Murtaza. When Murtaza first arrived at Harvard, Zulfikar wrote him a letter, the first to his son at college, on official stationery.

> In the beginning you will be homesick and anxiously expect to hear from your parents, your brother and sister . . . but the more you settle down you will not get as excited in the future as you will get now in getting news from home. This does not mean that you will lose interest in what is happening in your country but that intense eagerness will lose its flavour. Most probably, I am writing to you all the things I wrote to Pinky in my first letter. Now this is natural because I am the same person, writing with the same sentiments and values to my son instead of my daughter under exactly the same circumstances. The thoughts and the feelings will be approximately the same. I could have well written: 'Hullo, Mir, how are you? Please read the first letter I wrote to Pinky when she went to Radcliffe. If she has not cared to preserve it, I will send you a photostat copy. Goodbye son, I am very busy, I have some important work to attend to. Do well and look after yourself.' But I am not made of that kind of wood. I have great love and affection for you although I rarely gave over demonstration of my affection for you. There are many reasons for this reticence. I tried to explain them to you when

you were here, ever since you were young. In the first place, you are my eldest son and it is essential for me to see that you are not spoilt. I must make sure you grow up in this cruel world as a hard and a brave man. By hard I do not mean cruel, because all of us have a great deal of art in us. By hard I mean tough enough to face the bad side of life as a man. As my eldest son, more than the other children of mine, you personify me and the family. That is why it is necessary to deal with you differently. I would like you to grow up to be an immaculate individual, sharp in intelligence and smart in appearance. You have the making of such a man. With hard work and diligence I am certain you will do well, very well I hope. A person can be jealous of others but he can never be jealous of his own children. This is what my father told me again and again. And this is what I tell you. I will be the happiest man in the world if you come back with a first-class education and with all the right ideas to do better than I have done. I have succeeded in some respects but I have also failed in a way. I do not want you to fail in any way. There is no substitute for hard work. A hardworking mediocre is less of a curse than a lazy genius. Hard work does not kill anybody. Time passes and the temptations of life pass faster. They go by with the flash of the moment. God has created the world and given it unparalleled beauty. In the whole of this beauty there is nothing more beautiful than the human body and nothing more creative than the human mind. What we make of this body and mind is for us to determine. It will be for you to finally determine what you want to make of your life. You will have to take the decision. You will have to decide if you want to leave behind a good name or a bad name.

Zulfikar wrote his children letters that he must have known would have a place in history. He spent hours crafting them, taking the time to write them on aeroplanes, in base camps, in various state offices around the country, until they were ready to be typed up by his aide-de-camp. The letters are sometimes funny, sometimes casual with a joke here or there, but mainly they are tutorials: instructional and conscientious. Papa kept all his father's letters in their original envelopes, stamps untouched, seals unbroken. He would delicately remove each letter as if performing open-heart surgery, careful not to destroy any part of the envelope. After Papa read them, he placed all the letters in a blue plastic folder. He had left them, a great big pile of envelopes, in Karachi but he spoke about them often. After we returned to Karachi and Papa came home, one of the first things we did together at 70 Clifton was look for the folder of letters. It was the one thing that had not been touched or aged by time, the one artefact, more precious than any others, that no one had removed and claimed as their own; the folder was where Papa had left it, on a shelf in his father's library.

As if Zulfikar was certain that the time he had with his children was not going to be nearly enough to tutor them in the lessons of his world, he wrote:

You do not get excited easily and this is a good thing. You have received all the political education necessary to do well in the subjects you have decided to take. You have travelled a great deal, you have been to the Soviet Union and the People's Republic of China, you have seen politics and diplomacy from close range and in reality. You have learnt your politics not from thick books but from being close to me. I took you with me to the Soviet Union and to China with a marked purpose. I sent you again to China with the same purpose. [Murtaza spent a summer travelling around China, his father sent him to see more of the country and to learn about the history of socialism on the footpaths of Chinese cities and villages.] In the study of your field you have advantages which others would envy. Make full use of your previous experiences.

This letter, in particular, is the most tender Zulfikar wrote. His lesson-giving is brief. Here he adopts a helpful tone, explaining issues his young son cannot possibly know, but should.

Americans tend to be argumentative. They like to quote from books. They get so involved in details that they fail to fathom the main points. They do so much shadow boxing that they do not grasp the central issue. They have so many prejudices, they postulate so many theories and notions that they lose the essential factors. Ironically, the essential factors are quite straightforward and simple. The Americans like to make problems complicated. Their egos get involved. They place far too much reliance on the machine, the gadgets they have made. They have become the creature of their own creation. Partly for this reason they get bogged down in detail. They do not visualize the broad horizon. They do not go over the rainbow. To show their wisdom they will ask you to read a number of books. They will ask you to write many papers. They will use impressive expressions without fully comprehending the thinking behind them. They find it difficult to go straight to the heart of the problem and it is the heart, my son, that you must touch and hold.

Zulfikar reminds his son, once more, to study hard. He warns him against the futility of memory as an educational tool, arguing that a refined mind is infinitely more valuable than a photographic one. He tells him he has both capabilities and reminds Murtaza that he is his father's son. That is why this letter is so important for him to write.

Mir, my son, take things in their normal course, in their stride. Do not get depressed by a setback and do not get exalted by success. Have your feet always on the ground. Never lose heart. Always learn a lesson from a setback, always be humble in success. Speak with confidence, maintain your point of view courageously but not obstinately. Keep an open and objective mind, always be anxious to learn from others to acquire knowledge. Maintain a sense of balance. Above all, at no time should you be ashamed of your background or your culture. In upholding your rich heritage you do not have to be offensive. Be natural and normal. Do not lose the strength of your conviction either by prejudice or by complex. Do not get provoked. Good or bad, your roots are here in a history coming from a thousand years. I think they are good roots. A manifestation of national pride does not mean the demonstration of chauvinism or arrogance. You do not have to prove that Pakistan is good by proving that America is bad . . . Never be ashamed of your culture, never be ashamed of your background, never apologize for the conditions in Asia. Never be afraid of upholding honourable principles. Europe brought about the miserable conditions of Asia and we are trying to remove them. Remember that despite all the advances of science and technology, Islam is the last message of God. Try to keep in touch with your religion as much as possible . . .

Like any father, Zulfikar digresses into a 'just say no' discussion. He talks to his son about the myriad of human failings, of vice and of other 'soul-destroying habits'. He asks him not to smoke cigarettes, but says it is better that he does that than drink. Then anxiously points out that cigarettes cause cancer and he should probably not do that either. Zulfikar warns Murtaza that many students in America take drugs. He does not realize that many students in Pakistan take them too. But he nervously, you can tell, tells his son that those students out there will tell you, 'Why don't you take a puff?' It's innocent-sounding enough, but BAM. Your life will be over, you will have lost your soul to drugs. Destroying your life destroys mine, he pleads. Don't do it, son, don't, he beseeches.

Before concluding, let me again assure you that my thoughts are always with you. I would request you to overlook the day I slapped you in the Clifton House on Sunny's [Sanam, his younger sister] false complaint in 1962. We look forward to your visit to your home in the coming summer. The winter winds will pass and you will be happy to be back with us for your holidays. Till then look after yourself, be careful of the cold, study hard and remember us. God bless you!

The letter is signed in blue ink, 'Your loving Papa, Zulfikar'.

———◆•◆•◆———

Murtaza walked into his dorm room at Winthrop House in the autumn of 1972. His roommate was a young man with a rich baritone voice from the frontier of Texas. His name was Bill White and he had requested a roommate from Asia, someone preferably with an interest in politics. Bill recognized the name Bhutto on their door, he knew the name was from Pakistan, he was a keen student of all things political, but he didn't realize that his Bhutto roommate would be the son of the premier who made the name sound familiar. Both Bill and Murtaza were from warm countries, both had scarcely experienced snow. They were both fuelled by their fascination with politics. Bill didn't care much for the bust of Lenin that Murtaza kept in the room or the requisite posters of Che Guevara and Chou En-lai, but Murtaza wasn't crazy about Bill's country music either. They became fast friends.

I had already graduated from college in New York and was midway through studying for my master's in London when I felt brave enough to begin the search through my father's past. The first step, I reasoned, would have to be the college years. I was in the throes of finding my own independence and remembered how Papa had spoken of his time at university as uncomplicated and beautiful and so decided, in a preemptively nostalgic strike of my own, to visit the Harvard Alumni Association online. I wrote to the 1976 class officers cautiously explaining my situation and trying not to frighten them with the details of my father's life since college or with my intention to move backwards through time so that I could be with my father again. My request, tame as it was, was ignored by three of the four Class of '76 representatives, but then, a reply. Nancy emailed me and threw herself into my search and would become a formidable ally in my time-travelling. She sent emails, SOSs for information on my father, updates to the newsletter; Nancy regularly posted my plea for help and worked as though she felt phantom pains, as if she understood how important it was to me and my journey to start at the one place that seemed the hardest to manoeuvre in.

One by one the emails started rolling in. It was as if the universe and the Harvard Class of 1976 Alumni conspired together, as if they had been waiting for me to come so that they could relieve themselves of information they had been holding on to, keeping it only for me. I got bites of information from strangers, people who never knew Papa in college but remembered him being friends with this person or the other. I received emails, heartfelt letters from people who took classes with Papa, others who lived on his floor, and soon I had the names of his friends and roommates, phone numbers and addresses of the people who loved my father when he was a lanky teenager freshly thrown into American college life.

There was, to be honest, only one exception. Only one person received the news of my quest and my request for help with trepidation and misgivings. Oddly enough, the person in question was a professor who taught at my undergraduate college. He declined to meet and speak with me. It was 2005, I was twenty-three years old and perhaps a little naïve. I tried to persuade the professor to see me; I offered to fly to his city whenever he might have time to spare. The tenth anniversary of my father's death was the following year, I was desperate. I needed to fill in the blanks, to have something to give to my brother, who was turning sixteen and needed now more than ever to know the father he lost when he was only six years old. The professor did not budge. He was a friend of Benazir's. 'I was a classmate and acquaintance of Benazir at Harvard,' he wrote to me, 'and she and I renewed our acquaintance and became closer friends at Oxford (partly through Mir). I have remained friends with Benazir over the years, seeing her occasionally in Boston, New York, and Oxford.' I read his email and felt my stomach hurt. I knew where he was going but thought it unimaginably cruel. 'I trust you have talked with Benazir about getting her contribution to your project?' he asked. Though I knew he was a dead end, it hurt me more than I was prepared for at the time to find that even friendships are political and that there, in a totally separate and seemingly safe place, was a familiar roadblock. It made me worry about the reach of power, but I wrote the professor one last email.

> It saddens me that my aunts cannot be helpful resources to me at this time, but I must make clear that my aim here is not to launch a vitriolic attack on anyone but simply to honour my father's life through a meaningful remembrance. If you feel that you would rather not participate, I will of course respect your wishes. However, if you would feel comfortable talking about Mir and the time you knew him, I would be most grateful for your help.

He never replied.

The professor was a glitch in the machine. Everyone else I found connected me to webs of other people who welcomed me into their homes and lives when I made plans to travel back to the US and start my interviews. My father's friends were a family, that was my biggest surprise. He never lost their love and affection and, when I found them, they easily and warmly transferred that love to me.

'Your father and I were best friends some of the most critical years of our lives,' Bill wrote to me after he received my letter. 'Fatima, if you ever want a home away from home or a visit to a part of the United States which you may have not visited, please feel free to come to Houston. I can tell you more about your father that would make you proud.' I flew to Texas to stay with Bill and his family. When Bill and I finally met, I was sitting at his kitchen counter eating a cookie. We spent several days together, time-travelling.

In their freshman year, Bill bought the television and Murtaza the stereo. A typical day in their dorm room saw the two roommates waking up around nine in the morning – they both liked to rise early, regardless of their penchant for late nights – and heading towards their classes. They studied together in the library or in their room till eight in the evening. Then they'd have friends over, play liar's dice, socialize and listen to reggae – *The Harder They Come* was their favourite album – late into the night.

At the end of each semester, as the time to return home approached, Murtaza and Bill had a standing agreement. They would bring each other newspapers from their cities and when meeting again in the autumn or spring they would spend hours sitting together poring over daily news items from Texas and Pakistan with curiosity.

They roomed together for the rest of their time in college. They added other roommates from time to time, essentially to get better housing, but they remained especially close to each other. 'Murtaza was a politically sophisticated eighteen-year-old,' Bill, then the Mayor of Houston – America's fourth-largest city – and a prominent member of the Democratic Party, told me when I met him, exactly thirty years after he and my father graduated from Harvard. 'He had a natural dignity to him, a certain gravitas. Both of us were idealistic and populistic about what we thought of the world . . . we both had a yearning to get into politics. He had no desire towards making money – we talked about it especially as a public servant where it's a weakness. There had been attempts on his father's life, so he knew it was risky, but it's just what he wanted to do. He had a genuine interest in history, ideology, policy.'[6]

But he was also just a kid, away from his family for the first time in his life. Another friend of Murtaza's at Harvard in his freshman year remembered him as gregarious and outgoing. Milbry recognized instantly that Murtaza was someone who knew he was going somewhere in life, somewhere big, but he never showed it. She saw it, this strange glimmer of his, through time; Mir was easy-going and relaxed, not a crazed Harvard connector like so many others in their class. He was young, carefree. Two or three weeks after their first meeting, at a Woody Allen movie they both walked out of, Murtaza called Milbry up to complain that all his clothes were dirty. 'I told him to wash them,' Milbry recalled, laughing, 'and he had never done his own laundry before, so I walked him through getting quarters and putting in the detergent. Two hours later Mir called me back screaming, "What did you tell me to do? All my suits have shrunk! My shoes!" he had dumped everything into the machine, expecting it to come out neatly pressed and clean!'[7]

Together with Milbry, Murtaza tried out for a Harvard letter. They joined the rifle team. Milbry had learned to shoot in Texas and Murtaza out in Larkana on occasional hunts with his father. When they turned up at the team's practice grounds, however, they were strapped into a tiny space where whether you got a bullseye or not depended on a fraction of a centimetre. It was very professional, very little was left to chance. Milbry remembers they went back a couple of times until Mir whispered during one session, 'This isn't really a sport, you know', and they decided to quit. His extracurricular activities at Harvard were thus limited. Murtaza and his friends, who all knew him as Mir, watched movies at the student centre on campus, especially the Bond films, and went out to Elsie's for sandwiches, to Tommy's, the local twenty-four-hour diner, for midnight snacks, and to a Chinese restaur-ant called the Hong Kong, which was known locally for its especially bad food.

Benazir and Murtaza overlapped at Harvard, Benazir was at Radcliffe and a year ahead of her younger brother, but what distance didn't exist naturally was quietly created. The siblings had different friends and interests and though they knew each other's groups and spent time together, Murtaza was content to leave Benazir in her own world. He was closer to their younger sister Sanam, who joined her siblings at Harvard two years after Murtaza. As in childhood, Sanam flitted between her brother and sister, adapting to each but promising no exclusive loyalty to either. Sanam, easy-going and not fussed about politics, was malleable and fun, whereas Benazir was prouder and more remote, even to her contemporaries. She also famously despised all her brother's girlfriends. In one of our letters, I once asked my father to tell me about his old flames, desperate to have some dirt on my near perfect Papa. 'Ask Wadi,' he wrote back. 'She hated all of them.'

'If I hadn't known that his father was Prime Minister at the time, I would never have suspected it,' Peter, one of Murtaza's three room-mates from his second year onwards, told me, still surprised at the thought all these years later. 'He was very down to earth, even-keeled, he never got angry but I think he carried it with him, as a burden maybe. I think he felt a certain responsibility, he was part of something larger.'[8] Peter remembers Murtaza fasting during the month of Ramadan. Peter was from a blue-collar background in Buffalo, New York. He hadn't come across many Muslims before. 'But how can you not drink water all day?' he would ask his roommate incredulously, and remembers Mir saying, in a Pakistani accent – which he imitated for me when we met at his Phoenix office – 'You just have to do it, man.' Peter also remembers Bill's frustration that he just couldn't get Murtaza to fully embrace the joys of country music.

'Mir was completely comfortable anywhere,' remembered Magda, a comparative literature major who was a part of Murtaza's circle of friends, all formed during his first year at college. Magda looks like a brunette Kathleen Turner, she has a husky voice and she wears a string of pearls that bounces on her chest with every beat of her laughter. Magda is part Cuban, part Basque, and she dated one of Mir's later roommates. They would go dancing. 'It's in my blood, I'm Cuban, I can move,' Magda told me. 'But your father . . .' She stood up and imitated him, a notoriously enthusiastic but bad dancer, standing perfectly upright with his hands at breast level flaying this way and that with a robotic kind of rhythm, all the while bobbing his head to the beat of the song. 'We called it the Mir dance,' Magda explained. Magda cried several times as we spoke. 'Your father was one of the kindest people I ever knew,' she told me. 'He had an enormous heart.'[9]

All of Papa's college friends had been rocked by his assassination and they all reacted to meeting me by examining me for signs of my father – you look like him, you're shorter than he was (how did that happen?), your hands are the same – and then, when comfortable, by peppering me with questions, trying to understand how the Mir they knew had been killed. Before each interview, each visit, I coached myself not to get too emotional and break down in front of the people I was so nervous about meeting. But I didn't cry, not really, I was too amazed and taken aback by this world I had discovered to allow my sadness to take over. My universe expanded exponentially, as did my knowledge of my father, all in a matter of weeks. I was elated that I had discovered an important part of my father's past. But I also felt upset, angry that these people, Papa's alternate American family, had been kept from me and my family when it became clear that everyone I interviewed knew my aunts, both Benazir and Sanam. Or rather, my aunts knew them. They had kept in touch with Murtaza's friends, especially the important ones, over the years, had their phone numbers and email addresses, exchanged condolences and Christmas cards, details of their children and their spouses. And here I was, playing amateur private investigator, running from pillar to post with only shadows to chase and footprints highlighted by kind strangers to follow. I tried not to dwell on the unfairness, on being kept in the dark; I had found everyone I needed to, no matter how. Milbry, whose warm laugh and hugs saw me through my first day of the journey back in time, gives me feedback on my articles and career advice now; I'm on Bill's email list of supporters as he campaigns to be governor of Texas; and Magda – who my journey ended with – emails me comforting thoughts when the news in my country is depressing and we speak of meeting again soon so she can show my mother the Mir dance.

───◆•••◆───

At Harvard Murtaza studied government – he was a major in the politics department – but branched out and took classes on sociology, environmental science – a class called 'future of the earth' was his favourite – and history, mainly focusing on Russian and Soviet politics. Robert Paarlberg was a teaching fellow who had returned to Harvard to work on a doctorate after his service in the Navy, when he took over a class on International Relations and Security Policy in the spring of 1975. 'I didn't know what to expect when I saw Murtaza's name on the list of students assigned to me,' Professor Paarlberg confessed in his office at Harvard, where he still teaches. 'He was the son of a Prime Minister. I wasn't at Harvard when his sister was there, but she had a reputation for being outspoken, conspicuous and drawing on her connections. But the first time I met Murtaza it was pretty clear that he was there to take advantage of the undergraduate classroom experience. He was serious about his studies ... he was unassuming, affable. I thought, OK, this is interesting, he's just another good student.'[10]

Murtaza had a specific interest in foreign policy. Across the oceans, Bangladesh was being formed, broken off from Pakistan. In the United States Vietnam was tearing apart a generation of young Americans and the Cold War was expanding its client list and moving across the lines drawn at the end of the Second World War. Paarlberg had served in the Navy as a Naval Intelligence officer. Murtaza found his record fascinating and they spent time talking together in and outside class. 'He struck me as someone who would be a very effective politician,' his professor remembers. 'Mir connected with people so easily and paid attention to them. He had a light touch and a sense of humour but he wasn't getting ahead of himself, trying to be a politician while he was a student at Harvard. He seemed to live in the moment.'

Professor William Graham, now the Dean of the Divinity School at Harvard, taught Murtaza an Islamic Civilizations course. 'I think he was curious about me, a white Anglo-Saxon teaching Islam,' Graham recalls with a laugh, 'but in the course he was very interested in expanding his knowledge of Islam outside of Pakistan – we covered the African world, for example, and that greatly interested him.'[11]

In one of his blue Harvard exam books, marked with a slightly deformed-looking B grade on the cover, Murtaza threw himself into Professor Graham's material. 'The Islamic system is a society, a state, a thought and art,' begins his answer, quoting Bernard Lewis (not yet known as the academic-cum-state-department advisor who pushed America to war after 9/11 or even, I suspect, as academia's premier Orientalist). Murtaza reaches further, connecting his interest in government with the subject of Islamic order. 'The prophet was a religious head as well as the legislature, the executive and the judiciary. He was a man with absolute and religious powers.' He scribbled maps beneath his answers, maps of dry farming zones in the north of the Sahara desert and south of the Turkish mountains, explaining the nomadic nature of early Islamic communities. The comments at the end of his answers, written in pencil, read, 'Good essay moving from general points to practical illustrations.'

'I had no sense in class or in our interactions that Murtaza wanted everyone to know who he was,' said Professor Graham, who also knew the two Bhutto sisters during their respective times at Harvard. 'He was just Mir as Mir. It was very attractive about him. He didn't have an *idée fixe* about position or power. He wasn't pushy, he didn't come across to me as someone gearing up to be a politician. He didn't push himself on you, but when he opened up and you began talking to him he was very warm and sociable, easy to talk to.'

In class, Murtaza's political connections and family gene pool rarely, if ever, came up. He had grown up the son of a politician in Pakistan; that relationship formed the basis of how people saw him back home and he was determined not to let it follow him to college. The times when it slipped were more humorous than anything else. Professor Paarlberg remembers a day in the spring of 1975 when Murtaza, his eager student, missed class. He came over the next time the class gathered for its recitations and discussions and apologized to the professor, saying he had been out of town. Where were you? asked Professor Paarlberg. Washington, Murtaza answered. What were you doing there? his professor pressed on, 'Well, I had to go to a state dinner,' Murtaza replied, 'I thought it might be interesting'. His father had been in town on a state visit to the United States, meeting President Gerald Ford, whose predecessor, Richard Nixon, had been very friendly to Zulfikar and Pakistan. Professor Paarlberg had opened up a can of worms; one of the other students jumped in and asked whether Ford's daughter, known for her looks, had been a good dancer. 'Murtaza said she wasn't as good as he was,' Paarlberg remembered, laughing, 'but it took a lot of prodding to get that out.'

On a previous state visit to the Nixon White House, the President was informed that it was his visiting Prime Minister's son's birthday. So Nixon sat at the piano and sung 'Happy Birthday' to Murtaza. It must have been Murtaza's twentieth birthday, and he spent it like no other twenty-year-old – listening to wooden Dick Nixon serenade him. That story, however, Murtaza kept to himself.

———— ◆•••◆ ————

Towards the end of his junior year at university, Murtaza started to prepare himself for his dissertation. It would be the culmination of all his hard work at Harvard. He discussed the matter with Professor Paarlberg. He wanted to write, he decided, about Pakistan and the nuclear issue. 'It was the only time his father ever came up in our discussions,' says Professor Paarlberg. 'I was concerned about how he would get all the information needed to write a thesis in the face of secrecy and governmental blocks, but Murtaza laughed it off and said he was going home that summer and that he was confident he'd get the required information.'

At the start of his senior year, Murtaza was accepted as an under-graduate associate at Harvard's Center for International Affairs. His acceptance letter, which is postmarked 19 November 1975, sets the guide-lines of his association with the Center, a prestigious honour for 'seniors engaged in research and writing their theses' and reminds the lucky few that while they have access to the Center's activities and special semi-nars they 'do not normally have access to Center supplies and Xeroxing'.

He was assigned an advisor in the government department to guide him through the process of writing his undergraduate thesis – the only problem, Murtaza wrote in his letters home, was that his advisor, a big name in the department, was also infamously known at the time as the 'butcher of Vietnam'. His name was Samuel Huntington. Samuel 'clash of civilizations' Huntington was then known for his advisory role in Vietnam. Huntington advocated the herding of villagers into clusters away from the Vietcong, not appreciating that it made it much easier for the US army to bomb civilians in their separated enclaves. When I travelled to Cambridge in the spring of 2006, I found Huntington a frail old man. He wore a woolly navy sweater in April and drank Coca-Cola from a Starbucks espresso cup. He shrunk into his brown leather armchair as we spoke and seemed to be so much smaller than his frightening legend suggests. Huntington told me he remembered Murtaza as a student but 'not terribly well'.

When I told him that they had worked together on his senior thesis, for which Murtaza was awarded honours, Huntington nodded and mumbled, 'That's good', sounding impressed at his involvement in this particular process. He told me that he and Murtaza met several times a month to discuss his progress on the thesis and that Murtaza 'wanted very much to write on nuclear proliferation and that we discussed it and I encouraged him'. Of course you did, I thought. You're Samuel Huntington. Nuclear proliferation must produce a Pavlovian response in a fellow like Huntington; I imagined it excited him terribly. He recalled that he and Murtaza had 'lively discussions' (unlikely), that they talked about Vietnam though 'I can't remember what he said or I said' (thankfully), and that he knew the young student's 'background was extraordinary but that it didn't affect him as a student'. He was impressed he didn't flog his family connections as he struggled to research and write the thesis. I asked Huntington if he remembered my father's work. 'As I remember, it was a very good thesis,' he replied, but struggled to give me more than that. He was a tough person to interview, most of our eleven minutes together were spent with Huntington sifting through notes printed out for him – most were, I noticed eerily, about me – and shrugging his shoulders admitting that he just didn't remember. 'I have to tell you,' he said to me at one point, 'I have a lousy memory.'[12]

Murtaza barrelled away at his thesis and threw himself fully into writing and researching it. 'He was an oddity at Harvard because his senior thesis was on Pakistan having the bomb,' remembered Bobby Kennedy Jr, another one of Murtaza's Harvard roommates and friends, when we met at his New York home before an imminent *Rolling Stone* deadline. We had a spot of lunch – I did a lot of eating on my American research tour – and discussed old times. 'Everyone, including his friends, was aghast at the idea – but he was unafraid to argue it. He had the capacity to defend his beliefs.'[13]

The final product, 'A Modicum of Harmony', was a neatly bound dissertation arguing Pakistan's right to obtain nuclear power in order to safeguard its position in the region. Pakistan's nuclear proliferation, Murtaza argued, would guarantee military moderation between it and its neighbouring nemesis, India, and would further stabilize the new country's position in the region. Murtaza argued that India's explosion of the bomb demanded that Pakistan follow suit, and if it did so, the proliferation of nuclear weapons in the subcontinent would not have an overly destabilizing effect on the international system; rather, it would balance it out.

In a letter to her son around the time he had been drafting his thesis, sending his father sections to read, Nusrat writes:

> Papa remarked how well you write now and how very mature you are and I suddenly felt you are a grown-up person and not my little baby. I suppose subconsciously I looked on you as a little son of mine, now you are my grown-up son and a man; oof I don't know what I am writing I have become sentimental – can't help myself, I love you too much. May you have a happily successful life and may you live to be a hundred years old.

Where Zulfikar was strict and orderly with his sons, Nusrat was effusive and affectionate with all her children. She was a devoted mother who sparkled when she was around her babies, ignoring all norms of discipline and protocol that Zulfikar would strictly insist upon. While Murtaza was at college it was his mother who carried on his habit of cutting out newspaper articles, diligently posting him a packet every two months or so.

'A Modicum of Harmony' was read and marked by three college readers. The first called it 'perversely refreshing' and found the author's insights 'quite elegant'. The examinor continued to applaud the thesis's integration of political philosophy, mainly that of Hobbes, Rousseau and Machiavelli, 'a linkage of technical policy analysis and the larger problems of politics which is unfortunately all too rare in writing on nuclear weapons'. The thesis was deemed 'provocative and well argued'. The second reader, however, was less impressed. Michael Ng Quinn found that the author failed to 'answer one central question: despite his recommendation that Pakistan should also go nuclear, why hasn't she done so?' The third reader was caught somewhere in the middle. While he found the thesis was 'argued persuasively' and felt that the author was 'able to argue, against what one might first think, that nuclear proliferation may have positive effects on world order and, in particular, may raise the Indo-Pak dispute to a higher level of responsibility', he had objections with the author's analysis of the regional dispute in 'abstract' and theoretical terms.

But critical though the readers were, the thesis was awarded a distinction and Murtaza Bhutto was awarded honours. His father, Zulfikar, sent a telegram through Western Union on behalf of the family when he received news of Murtaza's success. The telegram, dated 16 June, is excited and rushed; almost none of the words are spelled correctly. 'Mumjy, Gugail and I actullay everone of us here join in congratulating you on graduating with honou rzgfrom Harvard (.) It is the outcome of your vhard and devoted labou (.) may you score greater su ccesses in the ffuture. Your loving Papa'. Murtaza graduated from Harvard in 1976 in the top 15 per cent of his class, cum laude.

{ 6 }

In the autumn of 1976, Murtaza was en route to England.

He had applied to his father's alma mater, Oxford, and had been given a place at Christ Church to read politics, philosophy and economics. The letter offering him a place was dated 28 November 1975, and cautioned that he might have to do some preparatory work in economics – further proof that one does need maths now and again – before starting his degree, but that, nevertheless, 'it will give everyone here great pleasure that the family tradition is being continued'.

At Oxford, Murtaza would once more be around his elder sister Benazir. They had overlapped at Harvard, along with Sanam, their younger sister, but though they lived close enough to each other their circles were poles apart and they led conspicuously different lives. They communicated, it would seem, mainly by letter. Benazir sent her brother postcards from her travels. One card from 1974 reads: 'A fortune teller told me I'd marry at 27 live abroad at a farm and look after sheep and cows' and is signed BB. Another, from when she started at Oxford, a year before her brother, began: 'My dear creep' and goes on to complain that Benazir 'had to pick up Michael Foot, the minister of unemployment, in my little MG sports car'. That letter is signed Pinky, her childhood nickname. From New Zealand, on a state visit with their parents, she writes, 'New Zealand was terrific and I met lots and lots of charming people – charming being all those who fell in love with me.' From Sri Lanka, on another state trip with their father, on a postcard of male Kandyan dancers, 'Last night three Sinahlese minister's [sic] helped to cover me so I could smoke a cigarette after the banquette without Papa seeing.' But the best was sent from Paris: 'Had to walk for one hour through the Louvre for Mummy's sake. I loved Versailles. Will you get it for my birthday? Love Pinky.'

As Murtaza's October arrival at Oxford neared, the Dean of Christ Church wrote to the senior censor regarding the young man's arrangements. Murtaza had been housed at No. 2, Brewer Street, and it was decided that his address would not be printed in the list of lodgings and residences. The Dean instructed the porters not to give out Murtaza's address or confirm that he was a student at the college. The note ended presciently. 'If at any time during his residence here, tension builds up about the politics of Pakistan, special measures may have to be taken, e.g. advising him never to take the same route at the same time of the day if it can be avoided.'

It was summer when the army finally struck. Elections were getting close and the embattled Zulfikar had been doing his best to appease his opponents. As an understanding between the PPP and a newly formed alliance of opposition parties was reaching its culmination, General Zia declared martial law. He closed down the country on the night of 4 July 1977 and appointed himself chief martial law administrator. Elections would be held in ninety days, he promised on television, adding that the Prime Minister, Zulfikar Ali Bhutto, was under 'protective custody'.

Zulfikar was released several weeks later. He immediately set off on a political campaign across the country, rallying crowds and attacking the military's attempt to discredit him and seize power. As millions of people came out to hear him, whatever political credit Zulfikar had lost during his time in power had been regained. He was unstoppable. General Zia realized that Zulfikar would not lose the election, no matter when it was held. 'It's either him or me,' the General is said to have prophesized. 'Two men, one coffin.'[1]

It was summer in Karachi, hot and stifling, and Murtaza was home from his first year at Oxford. As soon as his father was arrested, a message was sent to his eldest son: 'Go to Larkana, begin the campaign.' Murtaza went straight to the family constituency, accompanied by his younger brother, Shahnawaz. He was twenty-three years old and singlehandedly, as Zulfikar and his lawyers began a process of legal protection, began to work for his father. He met with peasants, with local notables, with those he had first worked alongside as a young boy campaigning for his father's first election.

After several arrests and releases the military government placed a 'conspiracy to murder' charge against Zulfikar, accusing him of attempting to murder a political opponent, Ahmed Raza Kasuri. Three years earlier, gunmen had fired at Kasuri's car, killing his father. At the time Kasuri – a former member of the PPP – blamed the government. A tribunal was called to investigate the matter and rejected the allegations, after which Kasuri rejoined the People's Party – the party he claimed had attacked him and killed his father. The claims, sensational and provocative, were factually weak. But a man, even a Prime Minister, could be hanged for murder. Kasuri cooperated with the military and charges were filed against Zulfikar. They finally had him in their sights.

It was in Larkana that Murtaza saw his father a free man for the last time. Zulfikar had come to the city from Lahore. He hadn't slept in two days. Gudu was working in the ruins of Moenjodaro, thirty minutes from the Bhutto home, at a job Nusrat had recommended him for, and was living with Murtaza at the time. It was late at night, past midnight, when Gudu, who was in the bathroom, opened a window because a noise outside had startled him. There was a commotion of sorts, but not the familiar noise of crowds outside Al Murtaza that one grew used to hearing, the chants of slogans and exuberant chaos. There was something more orderly and alarming about the racket. Upon opening the window Gudu saw that the walls of the house were being scaled by men in uniform. 'I panicked' he recalled. 'I ran to Mir and told him what I had seen. He was as calm as ever. He told me to calm down and then we went to tell his father.'

By the time they reached Zulfikar, an army officer was standing in front of him. Gudu remembers the soldier apologizing to the Prime Minister. 'Sorry, *sahib*', he said before escorting him to the car waiting outside.

Mir, Shah and I were alone in the house then. We stayed up all night, I packed my clothes and planned to quit my archaeological gig at Moenjodaro in the morning. Mir was worried, of course, but he held himself together. Zulfikar told him something before he was taken away. It was private. The next morning he got on a plane to Rawalpindi to join his mother, Nusrat.

In Rawalpindi, the sons met with their mother. She had been cloistered in the compound since the arrest and was sick with worry. Since Zulfikar's first arrest in July, Nusrat had been unable to sleep at night. The sound of boots climbing the steps to her bedroom to arrest her husband, frightening her children, haunted her. She wore earplugs from then on. I remember her always putting them in when she retired to her room for the night, to block off the sound of boots in her sleep. It simply wasn't safe for Murtaza and Shahnawaz to be in Pakistan. The regime was building its case against Zulfikar personally, not just politically, and the danger to those around him grew. Zulfikar sent word to his sons to leave the country. He asked one of his friends to arrange to send Murtaza and Shahnawaz out of Pakistan. Do it legally if you can, he asked, but if not then find other channels. If there was a vendetta against Zulfikar being played out at the highest levels of the state's military, his sons would be the next natural targets. Murtaza tried to argue, but Zulfikar's reply was final.

Murtaza returned to Oxford and Shahnawaz to his college in Switzerland, but not for long. The brothers immediately mounted an international campaign to save their father's life, the Save Bhutto Committee, and its base of operations was to be in London. Sometimes with their mother, who remained in Pakistan with her daughters, but most often travelling with other political workers belonging to the PPP or alone, the brothers set off on diplomatic missions. They met Colonel Gadaffi, a close friend of their father's, in Tripoli. He offered his support to Murtaza and Shahnawaz, going so far as to extend asylum to them should they ever need it. After the General's military junta was firmly in place in Pakistan, the government several times asked Gadaffi to extend an invitation to General Zia for a state visit. Gaddafi always refused, out of his affection for Zulfikar and his memory, even though a number of Pakistani servicemen were stationed in Libya for long-term training.

Murtaza and Shahnawaz flew to Beirut to meet the Chairman of the Palestine Liberation Organization, Yasser Arafat. A Palestinian friend from college arranged the meeting for Murtaza and his brother, and for his part Arafat confidently told the Bhutto brothers that their father's life would be spared. He recounted a story of running into General Zia at Mecca while both men were performing the Hajj. Arafat told the brothers that he asked General Zia in front of the Kaaba to spare Bhutto's life and that the General had promised clemency. They met Giscard D'Estaing of France, who sent a strong letter of support for Bhutto to General Zia, called on Kurt Waldheim, the Secretary-General of the United Nations, and received support from the Pope and the friendship and assistance of Hafez al Assad of Syria among many others.

Murtaza and Shahnawaz, twenty-three and nineteen years old respectively, were carrying out a gruelling schedule. Together they met with dignitaries, spoke at press conferences, picketed Pakistani embassies and lobbied journalists and Pakistani communities to raise their voices against the abrogation of the 1973 constitution, all the while carrying on with their studies and sending in their work by post or speaking to their tutors by phone. But they were still young men, raising their eyebrows at each other over Arafat's effete and handsome young assistants. They often found small moments of levity to amuse each other in the face of such daunting odds.

Travelling in the States alone, without his brother, but accompanied by Bhutto's one-time Chief Minister of Punjab, Mustafa Khar, Murtaza became exhausted by the older man's finicky ways. Khar, a man whose chequered domestic history prompted his wife Tehmina Durrani to write *My Feudal Lord*, a wildly successful tell-all about their marriage, could not start the day without half an hour of yoga in the morning, which he insisted on practising in the nude. Murtaza would have to wait outside the room until Khar had found his morning zen. He quickly grew tired of the monotonous morning schedule. One day, to liven things up, Murtaza decided not to place the 'Do not disturb sign' outside their hotel door as Khar had asked him to do. Instead he hung the 'Please make my room' sign. Murtaza waited in the corridor for the housekeeper to arrive and collapsed laughing when the startled housekeeper ran out of the room screaming after she had walked in on Khar in a naked downward dog pose.

Shahnawaz would return to Switzerland in the spring of 1978 to concentrate on his studies. He had planned on leaving school to campaign full-time for his father's life alongside his brother, but Zulfikar, a very stern father, would not hear of it and instructed Shah in no uncertain terms to return to his university. Education was non-negotiable. Murtaza remained in London organizing marches to Trafalgar Square and meetings with Pakistani Britons while he worked on his master's thesis. It was in the summer of 1978, when the activities of the Save Bhutto Committee were at their peak, that my father fell in love.

The Save Bhutto Committee was running its operations from London but there were chapters of the organization across the United Kingdom. Murtaza travelled to Manchester and Birmingham to speak to chapter members and supporters and to enlist allies to rally around the cause of saving Chairman Bhutto's life. The Save Bhutto Committee held rallies in parks and public halls where Murtaza spoke openly and passionately against the dictatorship that had taken hold of Pakistan.

The People's Party newspaper, *Musawat*, had recently been banned under the Zia regime in Pakistan and Murtaza took charge of resurrecting the paper and began to publish it from London. He gathered several journalists and former political activists to edit and write articles for it, but took charge of the paper's editorial line, submission guidelines and the logistics of having *Musawat International*, as it was now called, printed and distributed.

Suhail Sethi, Murtaza's childhood friend who would follow him into exile, frequently travelled to London with messages for Murtaza from Nusrat in Pakistan. Suhail came from a privileged Peshawari family, and he had only recently got married. Because of his loyalty to Murtaza and the Bhuttos, the army routinely harassed his family, raiding

urshid and
ahnawaz Bhutto
th their children.
ilfikar is wearing
uit and standing
xt to his father

Nusrat as a young
woman in Bombay

Foreign Minister
Zulfikar Ali
Bhutto with John
F. Kennedy in the
White House

Zulfikar with his Indian counterpart,
Indira Gandhi

The Bhutto children, Murtaza,
Benazir, Sanam and Shahnawaz,
in China with Chou en-Lai

Shahnawaz, Benazir, Murtaza, Sanam, Nusrat and Zulfikar in Northern Pakistan
in one of the last family photographs taken of the Bhuttos all together

Prime Minister Zulfikar Ali Bhutto with Chief of Army Staff General Zia standing behind him, watching an army parade in Islamabad

General Zia ul Haq

A portrait taken of Murtaza around the time he embarked on his undergraduate studies at Harvard

Murtaza clowning around in Karachi during his college days

Benazir, Shahnawaz, Murtaza and Sanam Bhutto in Shanghai, China

Murtaza and Bill White at their Harvard graduation

Police arresting a student
in Lahore during General
Zia ul Haq's martial law

Workers of Pakistan People's Party
chanting slogans 'Bhutto Ko Raha Karo'
'Free Bhutto' in Thatta, Sindh

Nusrat after being attacked at Gaddafi
stadium in Lahore during a protest
against General Zia's dictatorship

Murtaza campaigning for his father in Larkana
during the 1977 elections

Shahnawaz in Kabul

Murtaza leading a rally of the
Toronto chapter of the Save
Bhutto Committee
(Photograph courtesy
Milbry Polk)

his house and his wife's parents' home, and he was regularly warned to stay away from politics. But he didn't. He was, and remains, my father's most trustworthy friend. 'It was difficult, we were working in secret most of the time. At one point, *Begum Sahiba* – Nusrat – was in Lahore and we knew she would be travelling to Peshawar for the death anniversary of one of the founding members of the PPP, especially to show party solidarity against Zia. She was a strong woman; I knew she'd make it, no matter how hard the authorities tried to stop her, but I didn't know how. I went to the airport one evening, knowing that a Fokker flight was coming in from Lahore and I stood there in the arrivals hall waiting to see *Begum Sahiba* but couldn't spot her. And then I noticed a rather tall woman walking towards me in a burqa, which no one wore in those days, especially Mrs Bhutto, and it was her – she came in disguise!

'Other times the problems came from within the family. Pinky—' Suhail stops, it's instinctive to call Benazir by her childhood nickname rather than the various formal titles she acquired in later years '– intercepted a message for me once. Mir needed me to come to London to assist with the *Musawat* relaunch and asked her to relay the message but she didn't think it was necessary to pass it on. She didn't understand the importance of what Murtaza was doing in London publishing *Musawat*. He ran that newspaper from the end of 1977 till 1982, he was in charge of it. And not just that. People only talk about Murtaza and Shahnawaz with guns and guards, but they have no idea what they were doing at that time.' Suhail takes a deep breath and smiles. 'One time Benazir sent Mir a confidential letter through one of her gaggle of girlfriends. This friend of hers had a boyfriend who was travelling to London and Pinky allowed her friend to pass on the letter to this fellow. Mir only knew a letter was coming, he didn't know who was bringing it but assumed it was someone dependable since his sister had stressed it was an important letter.' At this Suhail starts to tap his cigarette packet, his fingers drum quicker as the story crescendoes. 'The boyfriend reaches London and lo and behold goes straight to the Pakistani embassy and gives them the letter. We didn't know what had happened, we were still waiting for the letter to reach us until we read excerpts of it in *Nawa-i-waqt*, a Pakistani newspaper.'[2]

Indeed, it was the failure of those diplomatic and political efforts that changed Murtaza and his brother's life. But they did not know what was in store, and if they did, they showed no signs of wavering as they fought on. They worked day and night to spread the news of the injustices being done to the state of Pakistan under the military junta. The military made countless accusations against Zulfikar Ali Bhutto through their courts in Lahore in the form of White Papers. Zulfikar, who spent hours in his cell in Rawalpindi jail writing legal rejoinders to the Supreme Court, penned a response to the accusations against him. Naturally, the junta banned Zulfikar's response from being carried in the media – the newspapers were not allowed to print even extracts of Zulfikar's rejoinder.

A copy was smuggled out of the country to Murtaza in London and he arranged for it to be printed as a book, titling it *If I am Assassinated*. 'Murtaza should have written a foreword to it,' remembers Suhail. 'In those days he was so desperate that the truth got out he didn't even ask the publishers for the royalties.' It was published first by Biswin Sadi publications in Delhi. 'Mir didn't ask for a single penny,' Suhail says exasperatedly. 'His mission was that it should reach the people and in one year they printed nine or ten editions of the book.' Later it would also be printed and distributed by the international offices of *Musawat* from a small office on Brushfield Street in London.

The Indian edition of *If I am Assassinated* has a photograph of Zulfikar on the back along with quotes from the text.

If I am assassinated through the gallows . . . there will be turmoil and turbulence, conflict and conflagration . . . The events of the last twenty years have made me arrive at the unambiguous conclusion that, at present, the greatest threat to the unity and progress of the Third World is from coup-gemoney . . . More than my life is at stake. Make no mistake about it. The future of Pakistan is at stake.

At the bottom of the printed quotes is Zulfikar Ali Bhutto's slanted signature. The book is more than just a compendium of the legal flaws in the case against Zulfikar presented by the junta's White Paper; in the chapter called 'The Prejudice', Zulfikar dealt with the various propaganda attacks against his government and presents a rare insight into the conditions he was being held under.

'Since 18th March 1978, I have spent twenty-two to twenty-three hours out of the twenty-four in a congested and suffocating death cell,' Zulfikar writes.

I have been hemmed in by its sordidness and stink throughout the heat and the rain of the long hot summer. The light is poor. My eyesight has worsened. My health has been shattered. I have been in solitary confinement for almost a year, but my morale is high because I am not made of the wood which burns easily. Through sheer willpower in conditions that are adverse in the extreme, I have written this rejoinder. Let all the White Papers come. I do not have to defend myself at the bar of public opinion. My services to the cause of the people are a mirror in front of them. My name is synonymous with the return of prisoners of war, with Kashmir, with the Islamic summit, with the Security Council, with the proletarian causes.

Ordinarily, I would not have bothered to reply to the tissue of lies contained in this disgusting document [which included charges of Bhutto being a 'bad Muslim' as well as the Kasuri murder charge], but the circumstances are not ordinary. A principle is involved: the principle of the right of reply, the principle of the right to face the lie with the truth . . . As I said at the trial in Lahore forget the fact that I have been the President and Prime Minister of Pakistan. Forget the fact that I am the leader of the premier party of this country. Forget all those things. But I am a citizen of this country and I am facing a murder trial. Even the ordinary citizen – and I consider myself one – is not denied justice.[3]

If I am Assassinated was not simply a tract on innocence and justice; it was like his letters – detailed, thorough, and resounding in its eloquence and force. Zulfikar weaves in an analysis of the political coalition that rose against him, the non-aligned movement, and General Zia ul Haq's Afghanistan connections.

Papa kept one of the first copies of the book on his bookshelf when I was growing up. One winter, when I was around nine years old, I took the book off Papa's shelf and sneaked it into my bedroom. I never really understood Pakistani political lingo – White Paper, red tape, all kinds of official acronyms and officials – but I wanted to and commenced with highlighting the yellowed pages of *If I am Assassinated* with a pink Bic pen. If Papa was annoyed when he saw that I'd graffitied the pages of his one copy in Damascus, he managed to hide his feelings well. 'I'm going to write a book on grandpapa,' I apologized sheepishly. Papa knew the book by heart, he could quote from it citing page numbers. I never asked why and in all those years Papa never mentioned his role in its publication.

◄•••►

It was an ordinary London night in May 1978 when Murtaza and Shahnawaz took some time off to have dinner with friends at the Hilton Hotel on Park Lane. That night, in the Trader Vic's restaurant, my father's attention was caught by a different kind of political lobbyist.

Della Roufogalis was born in Veria, Greece, the birthplace of Alexander the Great. Her father, Anastasios Pasvantidis, was a small merchant who had once fought in the underground resistance against the Germans when stationed in a small Albanian town during the Second World War. Della, eight years older than Murtaza, was in London to attend a conference of the United Nations and to lobby for the release of a loved one jailed in Greece. She was eating with the Somalian Ambassador to the United Kingdom when she noticed a handsome man staring at her. She could hear him and his friends speaking English, but they had accents; she noticed that the man who

154

was staring at her was half a head taller than the others at his table, even though he was sitting down. She smiled at him and he smiled back. She remembers that when he returned her smile, a light spread across his face. The Ambassador noticed Della's distraction and pointed towards the man she was glancing at and asked if she knew who he was. 'He's the son of the ex-socialist Prime Minister of Pakistan,' he told her. 'His government was removed by a military junta and he's now in jail.' Then the Ambassador added piquantly, 'Just the opposite situation from yours,' and continued to eat his dinner.

Like the Bhutto brothers, Della's young life had also been wildly tempestuous. As a young girl in Greece she wrote poetry and composed lyrics, writing to find an outlet for her thoughts and fantasies. There is evidence that Veria existed as a city as far back as 1000 BC and it grew in glory long before Alexander fled its soil to build his empire, notably in the texts of Thucydides and through the preaching of Paul the Apostle. As a teenager Della was restless; she was tall and beautiful and was waiting to burst out of the small world she felt stuck in. She married young, at sixteen, and moved with her husband, a mechanical engineering student, to South Africa. Their mutual wanderlust took them to Johannesburg at the peak of apartheid. Trapped in a marriage that was violent and abusive, Della became a model. She was a local sensation; delicately tall, blonde and olive-skinned, Della soon won an international contract with Wilhelmina models in New York. She eventually left her husband and returned to Greece, where at a dinner party she met and fell in love with Michael Roufogalis, General Roufogalis to the men who feared him.

Twenty-five years her senior, the General – head of the State Information Department, the most dreaded office in military-led Greece – proposed to Della and married her a mere three months before his government was overthrown, with the junta dictator President Papadopolous serving as Roufogalis's best man at the Greek Orthodox ceremony. In their wedding pictures, Papadopolous is waving a finger at Della, looking beautiful with her hair temporarily dyed red, as if warning her of something (the dangers of marrying into the junta? Probably not). She returns the dictator's bizarre remonstration by smiling gracefully.

The police came to take General Roufogalis to jail early one morning in 1974. Under the new government's courts, the General was found guilty of treason and given a life sentence. Della, the General's new bride, immediately took to lobbying for her husband's release both in Greece and abroad.

She spoke to Aristotle Onassis months before he died, and travelled to the United States to meet CIA representatives sympathetic to the jailed Greek junta. There was no real hope that she could get her husband's life sentence lifted, he had already been spared the initial death sentence meted out to his colleagues, including the former Prime Minister, Papadopoulos, but Della wasn't used to sitting back and letting the blows fall without offering some serious resistance. After his trial, General Roufogalis told his young wife to carry on living instead of fighting. 'This will last for a long time,' he told her. 'How long, I don't know . . . you're young, you're beautiful and you need companionship. Try to find someone of your calibre.'[4] So she did, but not as he had requested; she honoured her commitment to her husband through her work. Carrying sensitive messages and organizing support from right-leaning governments and leaders around the world, Della believed she had a mission: she was the voice of the jailed Greek junta leaders, and she sought reversals of their sentences on the grounds that they were indicted under retrospective laws.

It was this charge that brought Della to London and seated her at a table in Trader Vic's basement restaurant with the Somalian Ambassador. Trader Vic's was always packed with an international clientele; it was the hottest place in town. The Pacific island feel of the restaurant, complete with rattan furniture and décor, meant Trader Vic's served the meanest ribs in London and packed equally exotic cocktails into flower-laden goblets and punchbowls. The Ambassador asked Della if she wished to be introduced to Murtaza Bhutto, the young man she'd been exchanging glances with all night, but she replied that it wasn't necessary; they didn't have to cut their discussion short to make introductions. A little later Della excused herself to go to the ladies, and when she came out, Murtaza was waiting for her. They swapped phone numbers and returned to their respective tables. As they were both leaving, the Ambassador approached Murtaza, enquired about his father and formally presented Della Roufogalis.

Murtaza called Della the next day at eleven in the morning and they arranged to meet for lunch back at Trader Vic's. They spent the afternoon exchanging their life histories: Murtaza sharing stories from his own fight against his father's imprisonment and Della speaking of her mission to free her husband. She knew they were treading on delicate ground; if anything, their experiences should have made them adversaries, each fighting against the other's allies, but it didn't. Della noticed that Murtaza listened when she spoke fondly about her imprisoned husband, not criticizing or judging. And for her part, she felt a tenderness for him as he talked about his father and the junta in his country. The next day they went dancing at Annabel's and on the third day after a fast and frenzied courtship, Della had to return to Athens.

Murtaza and Shahnawaz took her to the airport but it was clear that the couple were not ready to say goodbye. Della walked through to the departure lounge feeling sad about leaving Mir behind. It was an unfamiliar feeling for her, this affection, after the last four years of frustration and isolation. By the time she made it to her flight she was distracted and annoyed to find a man sitting in her seat reading a newspaper. She cleared her throat to tell him that the seat was hers when he lowered the paper. It was Murtaza. 'How did you do this?' she asked him, incredulous. But he would have done anything to be with her.

Della was an unexpected relief for Murtaza, who had missed living his own life since General Zia ul Haq's coup. She understood his work and how draining it was on the spirit and together they created a small shelter from the fear they had grown used to living under. Murtaza would surprise Della many more times. He would call her in Athens and tell her that Shah was passing through town on his way somewhere and that he would call on her to drop a letter or a book off for her. After sitting home patiently waiting for Shah to call, the doorbell would ring and Della would answer it to find Mir, suit-case in hand.

During his first trip to Athens, Mir stayed at the Caravel Hotel and he and Della would spend the afternoon at Colonaki Tops in Kolonaki Square reading the *Herald Tribune* and chatting to other tourists and Greek friends of Della's who happened to be passing by. Two days into his stay, Murtaza took Della to see a friend's father – Milbry Polk's father, who worked at the US embassy. William Polk's brother George was killed in mysterious circumstances in Greece and the Polk family still maintains a journalism scholarship in his name. On the ride to the embassy, Murtaza gave Della a ring with green and blue enamel as a birthday gift. They had known each other for less than a week.

On 5 June Murtaza returned to London. He and Shahnawaz were trying to get a documentary made about their father's trial – a work that would take many years to finally complete – and they had to meet various producers and directors back in London. He wrote to Della the following day, 'My dearest Della, I have been involved with a lot of work here since I arrived, but that has not stopped me from thinking of you. I miss you dearly. I intend to be with you in Greece by the 15th of this month. Your embassy people better give me a visa.'[5] (They did.)

When he was travelling, Murtaza often wrote to Della. He sent her postcards and love letters, scribbling on the back of air mail envelopes 'with all my love, all my sleep, all my drinks, all my white hair, all my thoughts . . .' I'd never known that my father wrote love letters. After Papa was killed, I turned to the boxes of correspon-dence he kept in his room, among his books and magazines, poring over every letter and envelope. I would scour the pages hoping to find something romantic and passionate, but I never did. I don't think he knew how to write them then. I don't think he knew until he met Della. From the New York Hilton he wrote to her on hotel stationery: 'Maybe our relationship is tragic. It is, in a way, very sad. We love each other and are very happy together, but what obstacles we have. In the end, after all is over, a very sad love story can be written about us.'[6]

On his second trip, there was more than just lunch at Colonaki Tops to organize. Staying with Della at her flat at Pakgrati Square, Murtaza called Minister Lamprias, the secretary to the Prime Minister, Karamanlis. He enlisted Della's help in speaking to those who didn't understand English and got an appointment with the Prime Minister, a friend of his father's. Karamanlis, a one-time right-wing politician turned moderate, had only recently returned to Greece after some time in exile. He was friendly to Murtaza and received him warmly. Murtaza asked for his support in the fight for Bhutto's life; he asked the Prime Minister to put pressure on Zia not to kill Pakistan's first elected Prime Minister.

Della did not accompany Murtaza on this visit; she was, officially, the enemy. She worried that the government would know about her and the young Pakistani and wondered whether it would affect the government's handling of her husband and the other jailed junta leaders. But Della was nothing if not brave. In the end she figured it might even make her position in Greece slightly safer, making her look like less of a junta firebrand.

In 1978, Murtaza visited Greece around ten times, stopping over after trips to Turkey, Syria and within Europe. He came to Greece to meet and speak with politicians in the new government and travelled around the country with Della. They went to the island of Aegina, where General Roufogalis was jailed, and while Della visited her husband in prison, Murtaza read the newspaper at a local coffee shop. They went to Veria and Murtaza met Della's mother and two sisters, Nana and Vou, and together they went sightseeing around Alexander the Great's hometown. Nana took Della and Murtaza to Mount Parnassos, near Delphi, when the first snow of winter came. She was a good skier, Della not so much and Murtaza not at all. Typically Pakistani, Murtaza scarcely ever wore winter clothes, and he very rarely hit the slopes. As Della was struggling down a small hill she saw a figure with a shawl on his head waving at her from the bottom of the peak – it was Mir, he had written her name in large letters with twigs and leaves in the fresh snow.

Della often came to London and it was there that Murtaza gave her a copy of *If I am Assassinated* and signed it 'with best wishes to Della'. Shah, more effusive, signed below 'with lots of love'. In London the brothers changed apartments regularly, Della didn't know if it was to do with security but Murtaza always wrote the different numbers and addresses in her diary himself. She used a small deep purple Asprey diary and Murtaza's slanted cursive handwriting fills several boxes – 42 Lowndes Square is one address, oddly close to the Pakistani embassy, and 72 Stanhope Mews was the last address he wrote. On his birthday, his twenty-fourth, Della joined him in London and they went back to Trader Vic's to celebrate. He wore Azzaro cologne that year, Della remembers, switching to Gray Flannel the next – he would wear the Geoffrey Beene cologne for the rest of his life – and wore, Della insists, only Turnbull & Asser shirts and silk suits. She wore long gypsy dresses, in fashion at the time, and embroidered peasant blouses. Murtaza often smoked Romeo y Julieta cigars, Che's favourite brand, and slipped the red cigar bands onto Della's fingers. Together, they visited Oxford and met Murtaza's tutors – he still had a master's thesis that occupied him – and Della accompanied Murtaza to Parliament, where he gave a briefing on Pakistan to a gathering of MPs. Murtaza was shy, Della remembered; she thought it would take a few months before he became comfortable with this sort of thing. But it wasn't the MPs, it was Della; Murtaza had grown up with crowds and had campaigned vigorously for his father, giving speeches and doing door-to-door from an early age. He was shy of her. He had never felt like this before. Neither had Della.

It was still early in General Zia ul Haq's dictatorial rule. He promised to hold elections after ninety days in July 1977 but swiftly reneged on his promise on the grounds that he felt it more prudent to start an 'accountability' process in regard to politicians first, a vetting process that led to the filing of the White Papers against Bhutto. The veneer of Zia's power seemed thin. Murtaza believed that General Zia would not kill his father. Most people thought of the religious army general with the slicked-down hair as an aberration – his reputation as a sycophant preceded him and most Pakistanis didn't think Zia would dare kill Zulfikar in the face of the international uproar created by

Murtaza and Shahnawaz's determined lobbying. The family's lands were still safe; it wouldn't have gone over well in traditional Sindh for the General to confiscate them, and it was the revenue from its combined land holdings that kept the family afloat during the frantic Save Bhutto years.

In October, just a month after his twenty-fourth birthday, Murtaza travelled alone to America and Canada to meet American statesmen for the first time. His old college roommate, Bobby Kennedy Jr, was at law school in Virginia and had been working hard to arrange for Murtaza to see top-level officials. He had written and published a number of editorials in the *Washington Post*, with information gleaned from Murtaza, about the state of martial law in Pakistan and the injustices of Bhutto's case. Together, Bobby and Murtaza went to Washington to meet senators, including Bobby's uncle, Ted Kennedy. 'Mir's diplomatic work was effective,' recalls Bobby. 'He worked hard and people wanted to help him.'[7]

They travelled to Plains, Georgia, to see Lillian Carter, President Jimmy Carter's mother, who had been in the Peace Corps in South Asia. She had an interest in India and Pakistan and, as Bobby remembers it, 'Mrs Carter was delighted to meet Mir. She was very cordial but was worried that she wouldn't be able to influence anything, though she genuinely tried to help us in every way she could.'[8]

Bobby spent a considerable amount of time with Murtaza helping him raise awareness of his father's case. They travelled around the South together, going riding and raccoon hunting at night to unwind. 'We went to a bootlegger named George Kelly, a large black man with one eye, in Lowns County, Alabama – a dry county. He had a small shack where he would play music on a jukebox and sell beer to the mainly black residents of the county, so we went down there with some raccoon we had caught because George Kelly was known for his barbecues too. We went there one night and ate and danced and spoke to people there.'[9]

In between flying over to New York to speak to members of the UN General Assembly or to Pakistani communities around the States, Murtaza tried to be with his college friends as much as possible.

It was too difficult a time to be alone. 'I loved Mir,' Bobby tells me when we are talking about that trip, and meeting for the first time, eighteen years later. 'He was one of my closest friends because he had all these qualities we call virtues. He was honest, he was a loyal friend. He wanted to commit himself to people who did not have the advantages he had. He really was a populist, you know. He cared not just about wide swathes of people, he cared about individuals – he was curious and would question them. In Alabama he would talk to black people, very poor people who had never been out of Lowns County, he would talk to them about their lives.'[10]

Next Murtaza travelled to Canada to address a gathering of the Toronto chapter of the Save Bhutto Committee and to speak to the Canadian press and various politicians. Milbry, his Harvard friend, travelled with him around America and to Toronto and saw Murtaza in an entirely new light. 'It was a very difficult time and he carried himself very maturely. He had a heavy burden but Mir always loved life. He was always engaged in what he was doing.'[11]

In Toronto, Murtaza continued his efforts to garner interest in the possibility of making a documentary on the judicial trial of his father. 'It just didn't happen,' remembers Milbry, apologetically shrugging off the disappointment years later. 'We met with commentators and TV stations and we got close a number of times but we were awfully young – the whole campaign in the United States was very frustrating. Americans don't often look beyond their own borders and Pakistan was a border very far away. But Mir had to keep going, trying to free his father consumed his life; if he expected his father was going to be killed he would have lost heart.'[12]

Della and I met thirty years after she and my father fell in love. It felt like a reunion, although we had never met before. She contacted me – I had tried to find her for years – asking all my father's old friends whether they knew her, the Greek love of my late father's young life. I didn't know Della's last name. It wouldn't have mattered; she had changed it. Two years after I had been in the United States, a man I had only spoken to on the phone, an old boyfriend of one of my aunts, met Della at a dinner in Palm Beach. She introduced herself and something must have clicked. Or maybe they spoke about Pakistan and how they had both dated Pakistanis, before the names came up and struck a chord. Somehow my father's name came up and the man told Della that Mir, whom she loved, had a daughter and that she was looking for her. That was all it took – once Della knew that we wanted to know her, she and a friend Googled me and quickly found my email address.

In the summer of 2008, I flew to Greece to meet Della. She was in her early sixties but still very beautiful. She reminded me of Nusrat, my grandmother. She had fine cheekbones and she carried herself well, just like my *Joonam, my life*, as I called my grandmother in her native Farsi. I landed in Athens and we flew to her home in Mykonos, where she showed me my father's letters and photographs. It was hot and breezy in Mykonos and the smell of basil plants, natural Greek mosquito repellents, permeated the evening air with their sweet scent. Della told me that she and Papa had listened and danced to Ma Baker and Mammy Blue (both mother songs, I thought to myself). Della picked up on my funny expression and said that Papa had often told her that she reminded him very much of Nusrat and that he used to tease her by calling her Ma Baker, making her squeal and squirm with laughter at his naughty sense of humour. She reminded me of the smoke rings Papa blew as he smoked and somehow Della managed to bring him back to life in a new manifestation. I met his friends, friends I never knew he had, all over Greece. On our first night in Mykonos we went out for dinner; Della's sister Nana was with us, and Della told me about a trip she had taken with my father to Monte Carlo, along with a friend of hers, Kryssa. They had spent a weekend there at the beginning of their love affair and when it was time for Kryssa and Della to leave, they couldn't find a taxi. They were running out of time, their flight was scheduled to leave early in the afternoon. So my father chartered a helicopter to fly them to the airport. I couldn't imagine him doing something so wild, so reckless. He was in love, I suppose, and love makes us do remarkably unhinged things. First I laughed at the story, then cried over my main course, because I had never known that Mir.

After dinner, Della led us down the narrow white alleys of Mykonos to a restaurant. I didn't know where we were going, but I knew it wasn't the way we came. At the restaurant she went up to the owner and hugged her, chatting away quickly in Greek. It was Kryssa; her name means 'golden' in Greek. She was shorter than Della, with a raspy smoker's voice and a lit cigarette in her hand. It was around midnight. Della brought Kryssa to me – I didn't know she was Kryssa from the helicopter story – but I introduced myself only as Fatima and held out my hand. As she shook it, she stared at me. 'Don't tell me,' Kryssa said to Della in Greek. 'Is she the daughter of the Pakistani?' Della nodded and she and Kryssa began to cry. Wiping away her tears, Kryssa grabbed me, hugging me and squeezing my arms. She kissed my hair and told me in her accented English, 'It's the eyes. I can see from your eyes that you're Mir's daughter.' I cried for the second time that night. Kryssa asked me if I had any pictures of my father. I had one, a photograph of us together when I was a baby. It's a beautiful picture of my father; he's smiling and holding me close to his face. 'He looks so sad,' Kryssa said, shaking her head.

'Can you believe what happened to our Mir?' Della asked her, smoothing her face clean of tears. Kryssa shook her head. 'If I think about it, I go crazy.'

{7}

The start of 1979 was marked by a frenzied effort to increase the international pressure on Pakistan's military regime to save Zulfikar's life. His death sentence had been passed; from Benazir in Karachi, Suhail delivered the news that the junta was going to execute Zulfikar to Nusrat in Lahore. Both women were among the first to know and were devastated, unsure of what they could do to save him. As Zia ul Haq's government busied itself with asserting its control over the country, Zulfikar's health was rapidly deteriorating.

Word from Pakistan was bleak. Zulfikar, who had never expected a fair trial from the military, was sure that he would be killed, but Murtaza continued to be convinced that the Save Bhutto Committee could exert enough pressure on the Pakistani government from foreign quarters to keep his father alive. In a file of clippings he kept from the time, Murtaza highlighted a grainy black-and-white photograph of an austere-looking man with a caption that read:

Stan Newens, MP, put down a motion in the House of Commons on the matter and obtained 100 signatories: 'I stand on the left of the Labour Party . . . but I can say that from the left of the Labour Party to the right wing of the Conservative Party, right across the spectrum, there was a deep sense of revulsion at this trial, at the verdicts they called and, now, at the so-called sentence being carried out. I myself take the view that what we have here is an assassination which has been cloaked in a political or judicial form.'

Murtaza, working as the head of the Save Bhutto Committee in London, organized a two-day conference to discuss the legal inconsistencies of the junta's case against his father. The Convention of International Jurists on the Trial of Mr Zulfikar Ali Bhutto was convened to discuss the judicial process against the former premier and participants came from around the world in an extraordinary show of legal solidarity. From England there was the (later disgraced) MP Jonathan Aitken, the editor-in-chief of the *Observer*, law and politics professors from Oxford and the London School of Economics. Amnesty International sent two participants. The Chairman of the Executive Committee of the International Commission of Jurists flew in from Geneva along with trial lawyers from the United States. The heaviest legal hitter on the panel was undoubtedly Ramsey Clark, the former Attorney General under the US President Lyndon B. Johnson. Murtaza's friend, Suhail, remembers Clark's presence as powerful. 'He not only attended the law conference but he gave a statement saying that Bhutto's case was not a trial of murder, rather it was the overt murder of a trial – it was very promising to have him come out so forcefully for the Chairman.'[1]

After reviewing the case files and documents pertaining to Bhutto's trial at the hands of the military regime the jurists issued a statement that would be released to the international press. They agreed that Bhutto's trial clearly failed to meet several necessary standards of justice in 'at least' the six following ways: maintaining a distinct bias in regard to the trial judges and lawyers, the failure of the junta to hold an open trial, the failure of the courts to maintain an accurate record of Bhutto's trial, the failure to institute a proper trial structure, and the court's decision in moving ahead with clear evidentiary improprieties and insufficiencies. Lastly, the jurists noted that Bhutto's physical maltreatment at the hands of the state was ominous and a cause for international concern.

Spring began with a letter from Zulfikar to his eldest son. A messenger came to London with the news that Zulfikar's health had worsened. He had lost a lot of weight and had asked to see a dentist; his teeth were rotting. I remember my father telling me that Zulfikar used to find shards of glass in his prison food and that his gums would be cut as he ate, mixing his blood with the prison gruel. The messenger also delivered a letter, the last one Murtaza would receive from his father.

Della was with Murtaza when he read the letter. 'Go to Afghanistan,' directed Zulfikar, 'be close to your country.' Afghanistan was still a socialist country, not yet invaded by the Russians or the bearded fundamentalists that would follow. Zulfikar's letter took a more serious tone, one of vengeance. 'In the letter, which I saw and read many times with my own eyes,' insists Della, 'Zulfikar told Murtaza, and through him Shah, "If you do not avenge my murder, you are not my sons."'[2]

'Mir began to prepare immediately,' remembers Della. 'I would tell him that I felt the military government wouldn't kill his father, but he would answer me back seriously, "Yes they will. You don't know Pakistan."'[3]

In the span of a year, Murtaza's hope that his father would be spared from the gallows dimmed. Tariq Ali, the prominent Pakistani writer, historian and activist, was based in Britain at the time. Though he had a somewhat rocky history with Zulfikar – he had refused to join the PPP on the grounds that it was not radical enough and had been open in his criticism of the feudal landlords who had continued to prosper in the party – Ali became very involved in the Save Bhutto campaign. 'Once the death sentence had been passed, it became obvious that we had to save his life,' Ali told me. 'The whole thing was corrupt to the core. The army wanted to kill the country's first elected Prime Minister – it was unacceptable. Whatever disagreements Bhutto and I had became irrelevant. Murtaza knew that I had differences with his father, but it wasn't a problem for him. He was pleased, rather, that we were participating in the campaign. Many a time he would give me a hug and say "Thank you for what you're doing."'[4]

The campaign had grown exponentially. The Save Bhutto Committee was holding large rallies across the United Kingdom and galvanizing Pakistani communities in cities across the world – in Sweden, in France, in the Gulf states, and in Canada and the United States.

Stories of the international protests against Zia's junta were carried across to Pakistan on the BBC overseas service, bringing news to a country whose own press had been brutally silenced. 'Deep inside, despite everything,' recalls Tariq Ali, 'there was a feeling that they couldn't do it – they couldn't kill Zulfikar Ali Bhutto – that something would stop it from happening. I think, initially, Murtaza and Shahnawaz felt that too. He was the most popular leader, there'd be mass uprisings, people would storm the prisons . . . but what we didn't take into account was how badly Zia had brutalized the population.'[5]

Public floggings, stonings and humiliating displays of torture were being carried out in Pakistan. There had never been such an overt display of the state's capacity to commit violence towards its own people before. There couldn't be a mass uprising to save the country's first Prime Minister, people were too frightened.

Murtaza and Shahnawaz addressed the question of the Pakistani people's resistance, or lack of it, at a press conference in London before Zulfikar's death sentence had been handed down. A journalist with a faint Australian accent asked Murtaza to comment on the lack of public support for his father, to which Murtaza replied, 'There is little unrest. First of all, thousands of his supporters have been arrested. There have been large-scale arrests. Troops have been called in from the border regions, border patrol units have been called – the security measures are truly overwhelming, truly oppressive.'[6] Shahnawaz was seated next to Murtaza at the press conference. He was wearing a dark brown suit but had not yet grown a moustache like his brother. Shah's voice was deep and resounding and he spoke slowly, measuring his words. 'I hope General Zia does bow down to the international pressure . . . but if he does not then I fear very grave consequences for Pakistan.'[7] Neither of the brothers mentioned the idea of armed resistance, not yet.

But it was percolating through their minds, given urgency no doubt from Zulfikar's letter. 'It was at one of the campaign gatherings that Murtaza first brought up the idea of guerrilla war with me,' remembers Tariq Ali. 'He asked me what I thought of the notion and I said to him, "Murtaza, I'm not sure this is the correct tactic, but even if it is you cannot do these things in public – everything is being watched – you can't operate like that." I didn't think it would have worked and Murtaza said to me, "What else is left to save my father?" I told him, "It's not going to do that. It won't work. He's surrounded."[8]

—————•◆•——————

Rawalpindi, situated in the Potwar Plateau, is a short distance from Pakistan's capital, Islamabad. It is, and always has been, a garrison city. Home to the Raj's British forces and since independence the Pakistani Army, Rawalpindi sits higher up than the land surrounding it, instantly cooler and breezier, but it has a sinister reputation, at least among politicians. It was once the home of the exiled nineteenth-century Afghan king Shuja Shah. It is where the man Mohammad Ali Jinnah had appointed as Pakistani's first Prime Minister, Liaqat Ali Khan, was assassinated, and it is where the army had taken Zulfikar Ali Bhutto to die. Almost thirty years after his murder, his eldest child, Benazir, would also lose her life in Rawalpindi. I've never liked the place. It's a desolate, eerie town.

Rawalpindi jail has long been destroyed; Zia razed it to the ground in the 1980s, wary of its potential to become a Bhutto-ist symbol. Only one of the prison's original walls remains now, old red bricks covered with deep green ivy. The rest of Rawalpindi jail has been turned into a banal shopping mall. Situated in between the old Prime Minister's residence and various military offices, the jail has now been renamed Jinnah Park and it is home to a McDonald's, a Cinepax cinema and a Pappasalis pizza joint franchised from Islamabad. At the entrance of what was once Rawalpindi jail is a two-storey yellow building. The top storey is covered by a sign that reads 'Blacks' next to a large photo-graph of a women's eyes, maybe it is a beauty parlour, I don't know. The bottom half of the building just reads 'Tequila City', and it's anyone's guess what goes on there in alcohol-free Pakistan.

It is here that the army killed Zulfikar Ali Bhutto and then erased all traces of his blood.

Della remembers the night before 4 April 1979 as a busy one. The Stanhope Mews house that Murtaza and Shahnawaz were living in in central London had been packed with people. The flats the Bhutto brothers lived in were always full of Pakistanis – men visiting from home and carrying letters and news, associates and supporters of the SB Committee, journalists and political activists from Manchester, Birmingham and Leeds. That night there were people sleeping in the living room and the corridors, and home-cooked Pakistani food had been communally eaten with everyone gathered to share a meal sitting on the floor. It was between six and seven in the morning when the phone rang.

'Is this the Bhutto household?' asked the voice on the other end of the telephone. Della, careful not to wake Murtaza, answered that it was. The man on the line identified himself as a BBC reporter and asked Della if she was aware that Zulfikar Ali Bhutto had been killed at two in the morning, Pakistani time. She was careful not to repeat what the reporter was saying; no, she answered quietly, she wasn't aware. The BBC reporter asked to speak to Murtaza, the official family spokesperson. Della didn't answer; she was in shock. She nudged Murtaza awake and handed him the telephone. 'Mir, it's for you,' Della told him, and then to soften the blow of what he was about to hear, 'It's the BBC.'

Murtaza sat up, his legs bent over the bed. He took the phone and Della moved to sit opposite him. Immediately, his hands and face started to shake. His teeth chattered. Murtaza was overcome with emotion and instantly swore revenge. 'They have killed a hero,' he said. 'They will pay for this.' Murtaza put the phone down. Della remembers that he looked like a bird about to break. She held Murtaza and tried to comfort him, rocking him in her arms and telling him to be calm, to be careful.

They had been expecting this. Murtaza had begun to prepare himself since receiving his father's last letter in March.

He rose and went into the bathroom to shower and change into a white *shalwar kameez*, the Muslim colour of mourning in South Asia, sent especially from Pakistan for this day. By the time Murtaza went to the next room to speak to his brother, he was back in control.

He went into the room alone, woke Shah and told him that their father had been killed. Murtaza handed his younger brother another white *shalwar kameez* and told him to wash. There were already mourners outside and the media were beginning to gather.

Murtaza, normally so at ease in front of the press, didn't want to go outside. 'What am I supposed to say?' he asked Della, his head in his hands. 'Not what you said on the phone,' she advised him softly. 'You have to be careful, your mother is still in Pakistan.'[9] Followed by Shahnawaz, Murtaza went out to face the press. The cameras were already rolling as Murtaza opened the door. The brothers looked tired and defeated. Murtaza cleared his throat and began to speak. 'I don't want to say much. I came just to tell you that of course it's a personal tragedy. They tried to break our father, they tortured him for two years, they couldn't do that. They tried to ruin his political name and now they have killed him. We have nothing to be ashamed of. They have buried a martyr today.'[10]

The military buried Zulfikar before announcing the news of his execution. His family never saw his body. There is no proof, medical or otherwise, that he was hanged as the military junta claimed he was. The family have long believed that he was tortured and killed. Bobby Kennedy Jr remembers what a shock the assassination was for Murtaza. 'It was devastating, it really challenged his faith in government, his country – in all the things he believed in.'[11]

In Pakistan the news of Bhutto's killing was met with an outpouring of grief, despite the strict measures the army had put in place to prevent a public show of mourning. Men set themselves on fire in Zulfikar's constituency of Larkana and the roads across the provinces were full of cars, driving in a spontaneous procession to the Bhutto ancestral home of Garhi Khuda Bux to pay their respects at the Prime Minister's freshly dug grave.

There were, however, people who celebrated. Nisar Khuro, a member of the Khuro feudal family from Larkana had been agitating for Zulfikar's imprisonment and murder; Abdul Waheed Katpar, one of the PPP's founding members and another Larkana native, recalls Khuro chanting, 'First hang Bhutto then try him!'[12] at gatherings around the city. 'And when they killed Bhutto *sahib*, Khuro distributed sweets, *mithai*, around the city – it is well known,'[13] Katpar says, clenching his teeth. The story is painful for him to recall. Nisar Khuro was brought into the People's Party after Zulfikar's death by his daughter Benazir, and was made head of the Sindh branch of the party. Khuro remains an integral part of the PPP till this day, currently serving Benazir's and her husband's PPP as the speaker of the Sindh Assembly.

Later that morning, the mews house was once again filled with people, this time crowding in to offer their condolences. Margaret Thatcher, not yet Prime Minister but well on her way, came to see Murtaza and Shahnawaz, and gave them a letter to pass on to Nusrat. Various MPs and supporters of the Save Bhutto Committee made up an endless stream of mourners. The anger, partnered with people's grief and shock, was palpable. 'If the United States had said, let's be blunt, if they had come out and said this is wrong and we don't want you to execute Bhutto, the junta wouldn't have done it,'[14] Tariq Ali says, summing up the feeling among the Pakistani community. Henry Kissinger had made good on his promise: a horrible example was made of Zulfikar Ali Bhutto.

'Murtaza was clearly in a traumatic state,' remembers Tariq. 'On Murtaza's face emotions showed very clearly. When his father was finally executed, the grief was visible.'[15] Shahnawaz was furious. The youngest child of the family, he had become incandescent with rage. Della remembers the police knocking on the door of the mews house a few days after Zulfikar's execution. There had been a bomb threat phoned into the Pakistani embassy and the police had traced the call to the house. In those days, there wasn't really the technology to figure these things out, but the police had the means. Shahnawaz answered the door. He had made the call. There was no actual bomb threat, no means to carry out any such attack, but he was young and he was angry and he wanted the embassy to feel afraid, to feel that their actions in Pakistan had consequences. The police took Shah to the station; Murtaza insisted on going with him, and he was eventually let go. The police understood that he made the call under immense stress; his father had just been killed.

The Save Bhutto Committee organized a *namaz-e-janaza*, a Muslim prayer for the dead, in Hyde Park. Thousands of people came, wearing white, to offer the Islamic rites for the dead. 'There were lots of us who were incredibly upset,' recalled Tariq Ali. 'I remember speaking with Murtaza and Shah and Murtaza saying to me, "Well, that's it now." His grief had given way to anger. "We have to fight them till the end. There's no other way left. It's the only language these people understand." He was so enraged; there was a real anger that his father had been executed, that the world had watched it happen and that he couldn't do anything to stop it.'[16]

Della postponed her trip back to Athens to remain with Mir. He was destroyed by his father's execution. For forty days, the traditional Muslim mourning period, Murtaza slept on the floor of the flat, with no blankets or pillows. 'I want to remember,' he would tell Della when she asked why he insisted on sleeping so uncomfortably when what he needed to do was rest properly and gather his strength. Her sisters, Nana and Vou, fussed over Murtaza and Shahnawaz too, trying to make sure they were eating and getting through the day. Nana also asked Murtaza why he insisted on sleeping on the cold floor. 'I want to feel the same as he did,' he told her. When he and Shahnawaz went to see President Hafez al Assad in Syria one month later, Murtaza was still sleeping on the hard floor.

———◆◆◆———

After two years of fighting to save their father's life through diplomatic and media channels and losing the battle to an armed and violent state, Murtaza and Shahnawaz began a different kind of campaigning. Spurred on by their father's letter and the increased brutality being waged against the democratic process in Pakistan, the two brothers, who as young men had both idolized Che Guevara and the resistance movements of Latin America and Africa, began to organize a more dangerous defiance of the Zia regime. Suhail, who would leave behind his family and his life in Pakistan to join Murtaza and Shahnawaz, sums up the feeling that drove them to the idea of armed struggle: 'When a constitution is abrogated, when the legal and political agreement to live together is cut, and you're running a country through the barrel of a gun, it becomes every citizen's duty to fight against this.'[17] Tariq Ali, who watched the campaign closely, concurs. 'The failure to win diplomatic support from governments around the world played a big part in convincing Murtaza that the only option was armed struggle.'[18] He had tried everything – printing newspapers, speaking to journalists, holding press conferences, protesting outside embassies, speaking to foreign ministers and legal advisors the world over, and none of it had worked. None of it had managed to save Zulfikar Ali Bhutto's life.

In May 1979, Murtaza flew to Damascus, accompanied by Shahnawaz, to seek President's Hafez al Assad's support. The President had long been a close friend of their father's and had offered the brothers asylum in his country. Murtaza didn't tell Della why he was travelling to Damascus, but she sensed that something was different. 'He changed after his father's execution,' she remembers. 'He became very serious. Before he was a student, the son of the Prime Minister – he went to nightclubs, to beaches, he liked the best of things, clothes, food, and then he just stops. He goes to places like Syria, Libya, Afghanistan. He stopped smiling, laughing, Mir was putting himself in training. He was torturing himself.'[19]

By telephone Murtaza asked Della to come and meet him in Kabul, where he would be heading after Syria. By the summer of 1979, Murtaza and Della were no longer two lobbyists, commiserating with each other and trading war stories; they were seriously in love and committed to each other. Murtaza had given Della a simple ring from a jeweller on Sloane Street and asked her to marry him. She couldn't. She was already married. With her husband, General Roufogalis, still in prison in Greece, Della told Murtaza that she couldn't think about it then. Maybe later. Maybe.

Della flew out to Kabul on 12 June. Murtaza was waiting for her at the airport. The government had given him a small villa and he was beginning to get his new life in order. The villa, near Chicken

Street, so called on account of the butcher's shops nearby, was simply furnished, and propped up against the walls of the bedrooms Della found newly unpacked automatic weapons. She tried to contain her shock and Murtaza, who had previously stacked the floors of his bedroom with books, laughed it off. 'They're just toys,' he said. 'Nice toys,' Della replied. 'I don't think he realized at the start how dangerous the task was,' Della tells me thirty-one years later. 'How large it was. It was very obvious what he gave up to do this. Even with my husband and his situation, I couldn't have done it. It shocked me, but I admired him for it. How is he going to live like this every day? He was driven by the will of his father, that's indisputable.'[20]

After a dinner of Kabuli *naan* and lamb, Della raised the subject of the weapons again and why Murtaza was in this strange country alone. She told him plainly that she thought the way he and Shah had chosen to avenge their father's death was wrong. Murtaza bristled. 'You can't understand, they hanged my father. You do not know how that hurts.' He told her that he had flown from the Middle East with the weapons, the lone passenger on a plane full of arms. She couldn't reconcile this image of Murtaza with the one she had known only two months earlier. They tried to spend a few pleasant days in Kabul – Murtaza took her to buy *shalwar kameezes*, which Della wore indecently by tucking the long tunics into the trousers, thinking them more fashionable that way, but exposing the one part of the suit meant to be hidden – the crotch. She told me that she spoke to Murtaza's dog, an Alsatian called Wolf, in Greek and walked around in her untucked baggy *shalwar kameez*, stumbling over guns.

A week later, Della left for Athens, stopping in Karachi to deliver letters Murtaza had given her for Nusrat and his sister Benazir. It was the first time that Della had visited Pakistan; upon arriving at 70 Clifton she was taken straight to see Nusrat. They embraced, looking closely at each other. This was the first and only time that they would meet. Nusrat is a slightly shorter, brunette version of Della – their resemblance is striking. Both women have regal and defined cheekbones, long elegant noses and perfect ballerina-like posture. Nusrat nervously asked about her son and Della handed over Murtaza's envelope, trying to answer all her questions. At one point in their hushed conversation, Nusrat held Della's hand as she was speaking and moved her across the room, out of the light of the chandelier they had been standing under. 'The house has ears,' Nusrat said, pointing overhead. Della was sweaty and dirty from the trip and was desperate for a shower and a change of clothes, but Nusrat insisted she meet Benazir first to give her the letter her brother had sent for her. But Benazir was not there to receive Della. After some time, Della got tired of waiting and asked to be taken to Benazir.

She was taken through to 71 Clifton, the adjoining house and office, and entered a room to find Benazir sitting at a table, typing. She didn't look up; she didn't even acknowledge the blonde stranger in front of her. 'I wait so long that it begins to bother me. What is she trying to prove?' Della writes in her memoirs.[21] 'I've come all this way from Afghanistan with news from her brothers, whom she hasn't seen for over two years, and she doesn't seem to be in any hurry to hear it.' Della was eventually given an audience with Benazir, seven years her junior. It was long enough only to exchange names and for Della to hand over Murtaza's letter. She acted like a political heir, Della recalls, remembering Murtaza telling her that Benazir had always wanted to lead the political charge after their father and explaining that he loved his sister enough to step aside for her. It was a tense visit; Nusrat would only speak to Della in whispers, certain that the entire house was bugged – while Benazir wouldn't speak to her at all. Della left the next morning for Athens.

While Della was in Greece and Murtaza in Kabul, they corresponded by letter. Murtaza and Shahnawaz had abandoned the idea of a diplomatic solution to Pakistan's junta – their two years out in the world convinced them that there was no peaceful way of dealing with the military regime. Zia's violence was too powerful, the military's grip on the country too strong. The only way to fight the junta was with force. The brothers formed the People's Liberation Army, modelled on the guerrilla outfits they had idolized as young men, but quickly found that their romantic ideal of a people's armed resistance against a gargantuan military apparatus was not an easy one to operate.

Writing to Della about the PLA's organizational developments since she left Kabul in June, Murtaza jokes:

> We, the PLA, are unique in many respects: 1) Our official spokesman is a dog (Wolf) 2) we have more commanders than fighters 3) We are the first organization in Pakistan's history that believes in fighting 4) We consider secrecy nothing to be secret about 5) the PLA's chief can make enemies much quicker than friends – and he thinks that's interesting 7) No one yet knows exactly who the chief is 8) the official spoksman has ticks and likes to chew on bones – also, the official spokesman shits on carpets.[22]

He continues:

> The people of Pakistan, whom the PLA seems to be fighting for, are an even stranger breed of people. Their 'war' for 'independence' was 'won' by them one year before they had wanted it. Independence was forced on them; they were begged to become independent and free . . . The Pakistani Army effectively reflects the valour and determination of the people it lives off. 1) When a soldier fell on his backside he suffered brain damage. 2) It believes in equality: it constitutes 00.06 per cent of the population but consumes between 70 and 80 per cent of its wealth . . . The official spokesman of the PLA, Wolf, feels he can take on the Pakistani Army any time in an intellectual confrontation. We have advised him to refrain from challenging them as it will only provoke the heroic Pakistani Army into committing mass suicide. This is a very predictable reflex in the character of our brave army. They are also world-famous for surrendering heroically. A very shrewd British statesman once remarked, 'War is too serious a business to be left to the soldiers.' How true. And then when given the government to run . . . Soon the rule of the Generals will come to an end for ever. The rule of the lash and the barracks will be buried. First they broke half the country. And now it's

turn [sic] for the rest. Thus will end the short and sad history of Pakistan, a nation that killed its protector, that bit the hand that fed it; an artificial nation made to be broken on an ugly murderous scaffold. Pakistan will pass into history, shameful and forgotten.

Murtaza ends the letter with love and signs it 'Salahudin'. It was his *nom de guerre,* a salute to the Arab liberator of Jerusalem.

By the end of July Murtaza and Shahnawaz left Kabul to travel to Libya for a meeting with Colonel Gadaffi. From there they went back to Damascus. Della joined the brothers in Syria, and when she accompanied Murtaza on a visit to meet President Assad, Murtaza introduced her as his fiancée. At one of their meetings with Syrian officials, a general asked Della how her husband, General Roufogalis, was faring. She was taken aback. What an impossible position to be in. Della stammered that General Roufogalis was fine, trying to keep nonchalant, but she was shaken. Murtaza took Della to Maa'lula, the southern Syrian city where Aramaic is still spoken, and they visited a monastery on a short break from Murtaza's official meetings. A woman offered to read their cards. She told Della that she would never have children but that the man she was with would. How had it come to this? Della wondered. She was the wife of a right-wing jailed junta leader and the fiancée of a left-wing would-be revolutionary.

In their search for support for their newly formed People's Liberation Army, Murtaza and Shahnawaz went to all the countries that had close relations with Zulfikar's socialist government, and while thanking them for all their efforts in lobbying General Zia to spare their father's life, the brothers explained to presidents and diplomats alike that they had decided to take another course. They were going to wage an armed struggle against the junta in Pakistan. Yasser Arafat, fond of Zulfikar, congratulated them on their commitment and spoke of his own battles, hoping to inspire them with tales of the Palestinian experience, but that was it. Many legends swarmed around that meeting – people whisper that Arafat sent PLO operatives to Kabul to train the men gathered by Murtaza and Shahnawaz.

They claim that he diverted arms from the PLO to the PLA, that he personally advised the Bhutto brothers on guerrilla warfare. It isn't so. The brothers took to wearing *keffiyehs*, chequered Palestinian scarves; Murtaza wore the red *keffiyeh*, as he was the senior commander, and Shahnawaz the black. But that's it. Knowing my father, I'm sure he would have loved the rumours, flattered by the myths that people dreamt up around the organization.

In September, Murtaza and Della met again in Geneva. He was there to meet Sheikh Zayed, the leader of the United Arab Emirates, another friend of Zulfikar's. Murtaza went into the meeting on 13 September imagining that Zayed would agree to bankroll the PLA. He left disappointed. Murtaza returned to the hotel visibly angry and told Della that Zayed disagreed with the road the brothers had taken. 'He told Mir that he should return to London and start a family. Zayed told him that "Time will pay off and things will change. Be patient." Mir was furious.'[23] The sheikh had refused to fund the PLA, giving Murtaza a token sum of $10,000. 'What am I supposed to do with this?' Murtaza said, flicking his hand at the envelope. Della tried to calm him down; she agreed with the sheikh — she wanted Murtaza to have nothing more to do with an armed liberation army, no matter what the cause. 'Get up, let's go for a walk,' Murtaza told Della, rushing her out of the hotel. He took Della to the Rolex store and bought her a watch. 'This is from the Sheikh of Abu Dhabi,' he told her. Murtaza didn't want the man's money; his mission didn't need it.

'He felt he had no choice about relocating to Kabul,' Murtaza's college friend Milbry Polk, who now runs Wings World Quest, an NGO that supports women explorers, tells me. 'He had to put a lot of his own personal dreams on hold . . . he had to make a cut in his life — in his lifestyle, with his friends, his mobility. It was an extreme choice, but he probably couldn't have lived with himself had he not done it. He was a good son, a good Pakistani, and the leadership burden was on him.'[24] Before returning to Kabul, where the foundations of the PLA were almost ready, Murtaza made one last stop in London. He saw two of his close friends from college. He knew he would not to be able to travel to the United Kingdom for some time. There were rumours that General Zia had directed Pakistan's International Airline pilots to divert their planes to Pakistan if either of the Bhutto brothers were on board. There was an element of danger everywhere.

In London, Murtaza met his college roommate, Bill White, who was disturbed by the marked change in his friend. 'The last time, we met, Mir said, "I don't know if we'll see each other for a long, long time," ' Bill tells me, speaking slowly in his deep baritone voice. 'And I told him, "What are you talking about?" Mir replied that he didn't know if I'd want to see him. "I may do things you don't approve of," he said. "What I'm going to do is fairly dangerous, plus I might not live that long." I told him that was ridiculous. I told him we'd keep in touch. I'd always had the sense that in twenty or thirty years' time we'd be in touch, see each other's families and keep notes on each other's lives. As I was leaving, Mir said, "Really? You think we'll be able to keep in touch?" '[25] Another friend, Magdalena, had a similarly ominous farewell. 'I saw him last in London in 1979 and it was before we knew that he was going to be in Kabul and he said to me, "Don't think I'm not a good friend if I can't be in touch often." '[26] Magda stops mid-sentence and begins to cry. She never saw Murtaza again; neither did Bill.

'Mir took Zia's actions very personally,' Bill tells me, trying to find a way to explain his friend's sudden new life plans. Kabul is a bit of a tricky subject these days. How do you tell your best friend's daughter, whom you've never met, why her father changed everything – changed his life, his sense of peace, his family's security – to lead an armed guerrilla movement? 'He believed Zia crossed a line when he took Zulfikar Ali Bhutto's life and he believed he had to pay for that. Mir was a risk taker. For someone who grew up in a privileged environment, he was pretty tough.'[27]

On 17 September 1979, one day before his twenty-fifth birthday, Murtaza flew back to Kabul. It would be his home for the next three years.

{ 8 }

In Pakistan, Nusrat and Benazir were being shuttled between jail and house arrest in Karachi and Larkana. Whenever a moment of political uncertainty approached, the junta locked them up, setting them free only when the tension had passed. One afternoon while in Al Murtaza house in Larkana, I decided to clear out some space for my books and started rummaging around in the old closets in my room, where I came across a stack of old registers. I dusted them off and opened them gingerly to find that they were Benazir's diaries and notebooks from this period. The diaries were only sporadically dated and were written between the autumn of 1979 and sometime in 1981.

Like the Benazir I knew in life, the entries in the notebooks are conflicting and divergent. They often read as though they have been written by two entirely different people. A letter from 18 November to the jail superintendent at Larkana who oversaw Benazir's house arrest is fierce and bold.

For several days I have not been feeling well. When my health worsened yesterday, I asked for a doctor. Twenty-four hours have passed but no doctor has come. Is it part of your policy to ensure that political detenus [sic] should be so maltreated? You better look into your Jail Manual for Allah and the people of Pakistan will judge you according to your duties . . . Your attention is also drawn to the fact that a) reading material has been illegally stopped from reaching me; b) eatables are being stopped by the Frontier Force from reaching me; c) writing material has been stopped from reaching me; d) my sister informed me that my lawyer has not been allowed to visit me.

But another note written in her register displays a different sort of prisoner. 'There are so many mosquitos around. Waking at noon. Massage for an hour. Lunch. Massage for another hour. Wash up. Dress. Make up. Read a book. Tea at four. Feed the deer. Walk. Wash the windows or walls. Play Scrabble. Read a bit. Dinner at 8:00. Read/Scrabble. What a waste.'[1]

There is the Benazir who suffered the horrific death of her father and saw herself as a political apprentice, hungrily pulling together shreds of local knowledge and political notes, names and dates. 'A couple of evenings ago, we decided to draw up a tentative cabinet,'[2] Benazir writes in her tight cursive script. Another day she draws up a list of local bodies' leaders, noting names and by how many votes each man had secured his position. At other times, she writes of her father and Zia: 'With the end of term of the corps commanders in March, it seems that Zia won't be able to "settle things" in his narrow personal way until at least then. That bloody murderer, the *Yazid* of the twentieth century.'[3]

Then there is the Benazir who is generally easy-going, sounding more like someone on a life enhancement course rather than under house arrest. 'It took ages to mate the good quality roses,' she writes on 14 November, days before her letter to the jail superintendent. 'Made buddings of the blue rose and have called it Machiavelli the Blue Prince, the yellow rose is the Blonde Borgia, the maroon red velvet Enchantress' and so on and so forth. Three days later she notes, 'Today they stopped candy floss, food from *Bua's* (aunt) and any other cooked food from coming to us.'

And then at other times, she is a bit of both. Complicated, infinitely so, and manipulative. 'Sugar,' Benazir starts, writing on a Friday, 'came meowing at the window demanding to be let in. She had caught a mouse which she wished to show us. Sugar behaves like a human so often. It's almost as if she can communicate. Sunny' – Sanam, her younger sister – 'came on the 23rd. Was rude and upset me. Her selfishness knows no bounds. She does not think what it is like for us to be cooped up. What would it have cost her to be polite?'[4] Or else, she is ominous. On an undated page, Benazir summarizes a book she has recently read. 'The man who reached the top reaches it by climbing . . . The qualities of a leader: he observes. He reads. He listens. He thinks' (he does a lot of stuff). 'Advertising when you advertise, write as you talk. A well-written advertisement, with a striking illustration and a good headline, placed in the right publication, has the best impact.'

The choice of Kabul was made for Murtaza. His father directed him to Afghanistan in his last letter, knowing that to be there was to be as close as possible to Pakistan. 'There is a historical tradition of exile in Pakistan,' explains Suhail, who joined Murtaza in Kabul that September. 'During the Khilafat movement in the subcontinent around the Second World War there was a fighter named Obaid Ullah Sindhi – he too was Sindhi – who based his resistance against the British Empire from Kabul.'[5]

There is also a family tradition of exile in the northern borders of Afghanistan. Murtaza's great-grandfather, Ghulam Murtaza Bhutto, after whom he was named, had been carrying on with the wife of a British commissioner during the Raj. When their dalliance was discovered, Ghulam Murtaza fled to Kabul and was received as a guest of the city's Emir. He was eventually offered a peace by the British (and his lover's husband) and returned to Larkana, where he was promptly killed.

As well as the Bhutto connection, Afghanistan was full of Baloch and Pushtun nationalists banished by the federal government. It was a country that shared a cultural and religious affinity with Pakistan, even some ethnic heritage, and it was considered a far more manageable option for Pakistani exiles than India or Bangladesh.

Shahnawaz did not move to Afghanistan with his brother immediately. He was still in London, dealing with some personal business. He had been engaged to a young Turkish girl, Nurseli, whom he had met in college in Switzerland. They had dated for several years before Shahnawaz proposed. Nurseli was from a wealthy Turkish family, a plain and plump girl, but Shahnawaz loved her and was faced with an ultimatum. When he informed her that he and his brother had planned to wage an armed struggle against the junta in Pakistan, Nurseli's family baulked. Give up your 'activities' they warned Shah or we break the union. There wasn't much he could do. So he settled his affairs in London, broke his engagement, and packed his bags for Kabul.

The brothers moved into the Chicken Street bungalow on Wazir Akbar Khan Road in the autumn of 1979. The house was called Palace Number 2 and was opposite the German embassy, to the left of the Libyan embassy and a half a kilometre from the residences of the Pakistani embassy. It was a simple one-storey house with three bedrooms – one for Murtaza, one for Shah, and one for Suhail – a study, a kitchen, and a large drawing room/lounge. The walls were painted off-white and the sitting areas panelled in wood. Outside, there was a large lawn and the three young men put up a net where they would play badminton. They carted a grill outside and would often have barbecues in the evenings.

In Kabul, Murtaza went by the alias of Sulaiman Khan. One couldn't be too careful, especially with Pakistani officials living down the road. He didn't know much Dari, only a few words – formalities and pleasantries that could get him by – and no Pushto, unlike Suhail, whose family hailed from Peshawar. Shah spoke the most Dari out of the three, not because of their Iranian mother, but more because he had a large number of Persian-speaking friends in college. Together, they were almost fluent.

Wolf, the dog Della spoke Greek to, had been brought to Kabul from London by Murtaza. He always loved dogs and claimed it would be useful to have a guard dog. But Wolf was more of a pet than a guard dog. There were a bunch of Russians – no one knew why then – who lived in the adjoining portion of Palace Number 2. They had their own entrance and their own lawn, but they often stopped outside the gate to play with Wolf. When they left, Wolf mysteriously disappeared with them and Murtaza was certain the Russians had stolen him. He brought another German Shepherd home after Wolf's departure and promptly named him Wolf 2. When Murtaza left Kabul three years later, Wolf 2 went with him.

The President of Afghanistan, who came to power after a communist revolution in 1978, welcomed the Bhutto brothers to his country and allowed them free rein to organize their liberation army in Kabul. They were given a permanent driver, Abdur Rehman, whom Murtaza grew very fond of. Abdur Rehman was in his mid-forties and used to drive them all over town as well as delivering the meals that the presidency insisted on sending over twice a day. 'They had a strange system in Afghanistan,' Suhail remembers. 'In every office from the President's to the peon's, government employees were given subsidized rates for food. They'd get rice, two pieces of double *roti* (white bread), some curry and potatoes. Dr Najibullah, the head of Intelligence and a member of the politburo, used to get the same meal – only with a bowl of yoghurt on the side. Afghans don't grow rice, but they're mad about it – they ate the same thing every lunch! When the Russians invaded, because of the curfew, we used to get our dinner at around six in the evening, so we used to wait till late at night and then 'pakify' the food, adding onions and tomatoes and *masala* to it, then we'd heat it standing over the stove and eat it all up.'[6]

Dr Najibullah, who was later to become President of Afghanistan, had two people working directly under him, *muawans* or helpers as they called them in Dari, and his *muawan* number one, a Mr Nooristani, was assigned to deal with the newly arrived Pakistani exiles. Nooristani was a shortish, clean-shaven man, his greying hair balding at the top, who always met the Bhutto brothers dressed sharply in a suit. 'We became friendly with him,' recalls Suhail. 'He would come by and see us two or three times a week and update us on the situation in the country and what they were hearing about Pakistan. He came from a well-known political family – his brother was in charge of Kabul airport and his brother-in-law was the head of the Supreme Court.'[7] Suhail and Murtaza had a chance meeting with Nooristani in Peshawar, where he had fled, their roles reversed, after they returned to Pakistan in the mid-1990s. I asked Suhail if he knew where Nooristani was now, was he still in Peshawar? 'I don't know,' he says, shaking his head. 'We heard that his brother-in-law, the head of the Supreme Court, was killed by the mujahideen. I don't know what happened to him or his brother, Sultan, who ran the airport.'[8]

Kabul was lonely for the three young men. When the Russians invaded, two months after they moved to Kabul, a 9 p.m. curfew was imposed. 'We used to make long-distance calls to our families and loved ones in the evenings when we were stuck inside', laughs Suhail, 'and the lines were so bad that we'd give up and just stay on the phone chatting to the operators. Time would pass so slowly. We'd be so bored some evenings, we used to forget whether we'd already had dinner, only remembering when we entered the kitchen and saw the sink full of dirty utensils.' Once the curfew was imposed, there was no more mobility, no more operators willing to stay on the line and shoot the breeze, and the boredom intensified. 'There was only one channel on TV, the state channel, and at the weekends they would broadcast a half-hour programme called *Ranga Rang* or "The Colourful",' Suhail tells me, smiling. 'It was a music programme that would feature six songs, including one Urdu song and one English song. It was our favourite programme. Otherwise it was propaganda all day! We'd wait for it all week, sitting in front of the television at the ready with our paki-fied food and snacks.'[9]

While the Russians had been moving troops into Afghanistan from the autumn of 1978, they launched a full-scale deployment in December 1979. For those living in Kabul, the Russian invasion was not a surprise: there were plenty of them around already – even living next door. But the news of the invasion was carried with typical sensationalism on the international airwaves. Della was watching television in Athens when she heard of the Russian move into Afghanistan and was shocked by the news that President Taraki had been executed. He had been in charge during Della's last visit and the violence with which events seemed to be unfolding unsettled her. She has notes in her purple Asprey diary, taken from Murtaza as he tried his best to explain the complex dynamics of Afghan politics. He wrote down names for her to read up on, Babrak Kamal, Hafizullah Amin, Noor Mohammad and so on. Her own notes are written in small handwriting, squeezed in between dates and appointments, and when she goes back to the diary to seek some answers explaining the sudden about-turn in Afghanistan, she's less comforted than she hoped she might be. 'Kyber, one of Kamal's men, said too much in a speech, is killed,' reads one entry. 'Amin killed in Taraki's house,' reads another.

Panicking, Della tried to reach Murtaza by telephone, but the lines were dead. She called his friends in London and was told they hadn't heard from him either. Everyone was worried, but Della acted. She went to a friend, a lawyer, who through his stock holdings at the *Acropolis* newspaper got her a press pass, slung a Nikon camera around her neck and headed off for the airport. Della departed on Alitalia flight 788 from Athens to New Delhi, hoping to catch a connecting flight to Kabul from India. She reached Delhi in the middle of the night only to find the Ariana Airlines desk empty. She spent what was left of the night sleeping on her black suitcase in the dank surroundings of the Indian airport.

The following afternoon Ariana Airlines announced that the next flight to Kabul had been cancelled. Della mingled with the disappointed passengers and found an Italian diplomat with a briefcase chained to his wrist and an American dressed in jeans and cowboy boots. The American introduced himself as a traveller en route to Kabul to buy carpets. It wasn't a terribly subtle cover, and Della tells me later that he reeked of the CIA. At least she had a camera to help her disguise. Where were the cowboy's carpet accoutrements?

The strange trio left the airport and booked three rooms at the nearby Taj Mahal Hotel. They spent the evening at the hotel's rooftop restaurant and got to sleep early, hoping to find a way out of the country in the morning. However, the next day's flight to Kabul was cancelled too. Della left Delhi airport with her odd companions and, finding no rooms at the Taj Mahal, headed towards the Asoka Hotel, an older and infinitely cheaper establishment. The Italian diplomat, who only ever removed the chain that connected him to his briefcase at mealtimes, decided to give up and go to his embassy, so Della and the American carpet buyer were forced to count their pennies and share a room with two beds at the thriftier Asoka Hotel.

It was with great relief that on the fourth day of waiting they finally found a flight to Kabul and began the journey to a new Afghanistan. Their flight landed safely and Della found Russians everywhere; she distanced herself from the American, who was having a hard time explaining why a connoisseur of Afghan carpets would travel with a trunkload of camera film. When she phoned Murtaza from the airport he was shocked that she had spent four days trying to get to Kabul. Why hadn't she called? 'Stay there,' he told her. 'I'll send someone to come and get you.'[10]

Suhail was dispatched to pick Della up from the airport and drive her back to Palace Number 2. It was the peak of Kabul's winter and the roads, mostly empty, were paved with mud and snow. Della, warming to her new role as a journalist, noticed a Russian tank on the street outside the house. A Russian soldier was leaning against the tank, watching everything. Della leapt out of the car to take a photograph. Immediately the soldier lifted his rifle and marched towards her. Suhail grabbed Della and pushed her into the house's garage, speaking quickly in pidgin Russian to the soldier. This wasn't the Kabul Della remembered. Something ugly had happened to it.

Murtaza comforted Della and tried to make her feel at ease in a city that seemed on the brink of violence. A dinner guest announced himself in the evening, a lean man who went by the name of Azmuddin and, Murtaza warned Della, was part of the new government. Still in journalistic mode, Della asked Azmuddin about the situation. He spoke fluently, going back over a hundred years of Afghan history and stopping at Taraki's murder. Azmuddin was casual about recent developments, telling Della that the word on the street was that the former Prime Minister had been suffocated in his sleep and rudely refused to die, taking a whole ten minutes for his life to be snuffed out. Della pressed him further, asking why the pro-Russian Taraki should be killed in such a manner. 'He was dangerous. So we eliminated him,' Azmuddin replied, staring straight at Della.[11] Murtaza touched her, urging her not to continue. Azmuddin was with the Afghan secret service and the new fellows were not as congenial as the ones he and Shah had dealt with before.

One evening Della, Murtaza, Suhail and Shah went to the Intercontinental Hotel. Della noticed that when speaking of Pakistan and Zia's military regime, Murtaza had become more resolute, more hard. Like Kabul, he'd changed. At the hotel there was a board with the day's wire stories tacked on to it. Above the board were the words 'Bulletin Board'. As they left, Della grabbed a pen from her bag and drew lines in between the letters so the sign now read, 'Bullet/in/Board'.

At home with Murtaza, Della began to realize how much she loved him – how crazy she must be to have flown all this way just to see that he was OK. Murtaza explained that while he was happy to see her, things in Kabul weren't safe. Because of her husband the Russians might assume she was with the Americans, working for the CIA even. People had been warning him of this since they first fell in love, but now it was serious – for Della's own safety she had to leave Kabul as soon as possible.

They spent the next morning, a Sunday, trying to find a way out of the city for Della. Finally, her press pass proved to be the golden ticket and a Canadian TV crew that was flying out to Peshawar on a private plane agreed to take one more on board. They parted with a promise to see each other soon – Murtaza had to be in Turkey in February. Della didn't ask why – she had stopped asking questions – and he promised to come to Athens to see her.

After the Russians invaded, television programming became a little more bearable. To tease the Islamist mujahideen, Egyptian belly dancers were often broadcast wriggling and writhing on screen: *Raqse Arabi* the show was called – 'Arabic Dance'.

During the day the brothers worked at drafting a manifesto for their movement, whose name they changed to Al Zulfikar, the name of the two-pronged sword carried by the Shiite Imam Ali, who was known to be a fearless warrior and a brave leader, and of course there was the connection with their father, who took his name from the Imam's sword: Zulfikar Ali, the sword of Ali. They spoke to activists in Pakistan, student leaders, university students, engineers, young men who had been fighting the military junta at home and who would form the bulk of Al Zulfikar's recruits. Oddly enough, Murtaza still had his Oxford thesis on his hands. He snatched as much time as he could to work on editing and typing his dissertation, carrying on an anachronistic side life as a student in between the demands of setting up an armed movement against Pakistan's military dictatorship. As the new recruits trickled into Kabul, Shahnawaz and Murtaza spent days and weeks settling the men into the organization and holding meetings to discuss how best to fight the dictatorship. 'Those young men were so grateful for that support and solidarity,' Suhail tells me. 'Once, after the Russians invaded, in the early days when there was fighting across Afghanistan, the mujahideen sent out a warning that they were going to attack Kabul, and Mir didn't want all these men, who had come to join us – to fight our cause with us – to feel that they were alone, so he took his things and went over to their lodgings and spent the night with them.'[12]

After her trip to Afghanistan, Della went back on the road lobbying for her husband. She flew to America and found herself meeting with Ahmed, the former Somalian Ambassador, who had since been posted to the United Nations. Everywhere she went, it seemed, she was speaking either for her husband or for Murtaza. Ahmed asked about Murtaza and how things had been since Zulfikar's execution, but there was little Della could offer – there was no longer much she could do on Murtaza's behalf.

In February, in between a trip to Turkey and Libya, Murtaza stopped over in Athens to see Della. He was back to his old self, scribbling notes in her diary when she wasn't around. 'Club', Della had written in a date marked for March. '*Which club?*' wrote Mir, underlining it for emphasis. He flipped forward to September, his birthday, and wrote under the date 18/9 'A historic date'. As soon as it seemed that the old Murtaza had resurfaced, he was gone again.

In Pakistan, ever since Zulfikar's imprisonment there had been a concerted smear campaign against the Bhutto family. The junta printed stories of Zulfikar's 'un-Islamic' nature, calling him a communist and an atheist. They ran photographs of Nusrat and her daughters – their heads superimposed on bodies of women cavorting in swimsuits or knocking back drinks at raucous parties. But they saved the fiercest attack for Murtaza and Shahnawaz.

Since their move to Kabul and their declaration that they were going to fight the military regime until the democratic constitution of 1973 was restored, the regime began to portray them as terrorists. Al Zulfikar had – thus far – done nothing except release statements, invite support, and speak out about the government's use of torture and violence against the Pakistani people. But there was large covert support for the organization among students and activists in Pakistan. They were part of a larger framework of resistance and that wasn't received kindly. But Murtaza always kept his sense of humour, no matter how dour the situation. He wrote funny letters, teasing Della about her country in one. 'Greece is internationally famous for three reasons. First it has more islands than people. Second, it used to be a part of Turkey. Third, its national hero, Alexander the Great, was a Yugoslavian.'[13] In Libya, he sent Della a postcard of a camel and told her he was wearing a ring she had given him, though he never wore jewellery, except for a watch his father had given him. 'I think of you all the time,' Murtaza wrote and asked Della to come to India with him in the summer.

Della could not make the trip; her health had been bad and she was exhausted. She was paying more attention, finally, to herself after neglecting the health problems she had been suffering from for years, so instead Murtaza flew to Athens on his way to Delhi. In another of Zulfikar's prison letters, one I have heard about from my mother, Ghinwa, but never seen, Murtaza's father praises his sons for their hard work through the Save Bhutto Committee. He makes notes and sugges-tions here and there, ending the letter with another directive – he forbids his sons to go to India. It is not a request and a reason is not given; it must have been obvious to the sons, though they were not to listen.

In Delhi, Murtaza met with Indira Gandhi, who had a famously rocky relationship with Zulfikar, and her son Rajiv. I remember the day Rajiv Gandhi was assassinated. My father and I were in a supermarket in Lebanon and we passed by a television set near the electronics section just as the news of his death was coming on.

Papa stopped and watched it, shaking his head. I never even knew that they had met.

Murtaza flew to Athens twice more: on his way back from India and for four days to celebrate his birthday en route to Damascus in September. Della didn't ask where he was going; she didn't want to know any more. In October, Murtaza went to see her for the last time. They weren't to know that they'd never see each other again, but still the visit was bittersweet. Murtaza was pensive – Della watched him smoothing down the hair at the crown of his head, something he only did when he was anxious. She noticed that he smoked too many cigarettes and was less talkative than usual. Della was still not well and Murtaza asked her to stop neglecting herself.

On 18 October, before leaving for the airport, Murtaza wrote a tender letter to Della that he left for her to read after he had gone. She drove him to the airport in Athens and they embraced and kissed as Murtaza was about to board his flight. They would see each other soon, they promised.

{9}

At the other end of the world, Pakistan was beginning to burn. The movement against General Zia, initially held back by the sheer force of the regime, was growing. After executing Zulfikar Ali Bhutto and ordering a strict curfew to halt movement across the country, General Zia banned all political parties and political activity of any kind, forbade public meetings and instituted complete and total press censorship.[1]. Zia's total disregard for civil rights, human rights, sexual liberties and basic democratic freedoms inspired the most concerted resistance Pakistan has ever seen. The General's regime, for its part, came down strongly against the movements his brutality generated. Zia's state was not only excessively brutal – ordering public floggings and hangings – but also well versed in the art of humiliation. During the Islamic month of fasting, Ramadan, Zia ordered water lines in Karachi to be cut, ensuring that no running water was available for un-Islamic drinking from sunrise to sunset, forcing the fast on those who were less than willing (that sewage lines were also closed demonstrates in what esteem the regime held secularists). For the rest of the year, General Zia made the five-time-a-day prayers mandatory in all offices, businesses and schools.

The resistance movement in Pakistan was represented by four large groups: the press, lawyers, women and union workers, and the agitation was led by political groups and activists, of which Murtaza was a part.

As soon as General Zia reneged on his promise to hold elections in October 1979, the junta instituted blanket press censorship. Six daily newspapers were permanently shut down – *Musawat*, which Murtaza carried on printing and distributing from London, *Tameer*, *Hawat*, *Aafaaq*, *Sahafat* and *Sadaqat*. The weekly *Mustaqbul* and monthly *Dhanak* were also closed.[2] Martial Law Regulation No. 19 was enacted and gave the government the right to censor matters deemed 'prejudicial to Islamic ideology', Pakistan's security, and 'morality and maintenance of public order'.[3]

Local and international media outlets, including the BBC, were subject to twice-daily checks by the junta censor, who alone had the power to decide what would and would not be reported. What was considered offensive to 'Islamic ideology', a pet cause of the funda-mentalist General, was often absurd and arbitrary – one over-eager TV producer went as far as censoring Popeye's girlfriend Olive Oyl out of the cartoon because she wore a skirt.[4] Women anchors on Pakistan state television, PTV, were required to wear a *hijab* before being allowed on air. Mehtab Rashdi, a newscaster, was the first woman to quit in response to the mandatory *hijab* edict.

The reporting of any item that made the military regime look bad was considered 'anti-state'. Hussain Naqi, the Lahore bureau chief of the Pakistan Press Institute, lost his job in 1984 when he reported that the US President had stated during a press conference that Pakistan wasn't a democracy.[5] Such a close watch was kept on the press that news of hunger strikes, student protests and political rallies were made known to reporters and editors only to prevent them from covering such events.[6]

While previous governments in Pakistan – in fact, one could be generous and say all governments – had imposed restrictions on the press at some point or other, no other government was as ruthless in meting out punishment for press disobedience as Zia's. In 1978, the editors of the Urdu dailies the *Urdu Digest*, the *Sun* and the PPP's *Musawat* were arrested and sentenced to one year of rigorous impris-onment and ten public lashes for 'publishing derogatory remarks against Zia'.[7] They were later pardoned and released but the message was clear. Disobedience to the state was unacceptable. Siddiqueh Hidayatullah, a teacher who was at the start of her career at Kinnaird College in Lahore, witnessed the frenzy around the city's first public flogging and described the spectacle for me. 'The lashing was being held on a large *chowrangi* or roundabout on Jail Road, right there in the open, in the middle of a busy street. People came in what looked like the thousands to watch, some were called from the nearby bazaars and others must have just turned up to have a look. Some men even climbed trees to have a decent view. It was sick. There was such a *tamasha*, or commotion, created around the floggings so that all of us would know how ferocious the regime was.'[8] The same year, the editor of the Karachi daily *Sadaqat* – which would eventually be permanently shut down – was arrested for the crime of criticizing the government's central budget.[9]

Local playwrights, poets and writers were also subject to Zia's lack of tolerance for creativity and were punished or silenced, and forced to leave the country when their writing made the junta unhappy. Notable writers from this time who fled Pakistan include the poet Faiz Ahmed Faiz, who took refuge in Beirut, Rehmatullah Majothi, Naseer Mirza and Tariq Ali.

While reporters and editors continued to resist government censorship and were punished for their defiance with prison sentences or fines, the turning point came in May 1978 when four newsmen were publicly flogged for their dissidence.[10] Never before in the history of Pakistan had journalists been so brutalized. But the punishment failed to have the desired effect among the populace – instead of scaring the press into submission, the public floggings pushed members of the press towards actively resisting the government and they did this in two ways.

First, journalists began to invite arrest by staging highly visible sit-ins, hunger strikes and rallies and by printing material critical of the government. In the two months after the floggings took place, 150 journalists were arrested.[11] Zia justified his regime's unforgiving treatment of the press by declaring, 'I have no respect for these newspapers and journalists who blindly use the stick of the pen to harm national interests.'[12]

His comments only further enraged the press corps. As well as courting arrest, newsmen began an indefinite hunger strike at the offices of *Musawat* in 1979 as a protest against the paper's closure. They agitated until they were carried away and arrested by the police.[13] Nine Urdu dailies in Muzzafarabad were shut down by a local magistrate's decree in 1979 as they refused to cease printing material critical of the government.[14] Ten journalists in Lahore lost their jobs in 1983 for taking part in a civil disobedience campaign protesting the extensive government repression, and as further punishment were banned from working in the media for the duration of Zia's rule.

Second, the press, which has never been braver since, fought against martial law through covert resistance, or as the government called it 'deviant behaviour'. Newspapers, under the orders of the board of censors, had to submit each and every article ahead of publication. Often, the board crossed out entire stories and news items it considered unfit to be edited, let alone published. Instead of filling their papers with large swathes of meaningless items, the newspapers began to leave the spaces blank. When the largest English daily newspaper, *Dawn* – an establishment mouthpiece – printed almost an entire newspaper of empty columns, the government threatened it with permanent closure[15].

Many other newspapers followed suit, changing their tactics only once the government censors caught on. When blank columns in newspapers were forbidden, journalists like Mazhar Abbas, who wrote for the *Daily Star*, began resisting the censor's pen more caustically. 'In the blank spaces we would print a picture of a donkey or a dog and print news of Zia speaking or his ministers speaking underneath the pictures. So, they realized then that something fishy was going on, Then they said you had to inform the censorship board specifically of what news you would use to fill the blank spaces!'[16]

When the censors tightened their reins further, cutting items in the evening that they had approved in the day's check, the papers began circumventing them altogether. News items that the Karachi censors had cut would be printed in the newspaper's Lahore edition, which had entirely separate printers and censors[17]. The efforts of the press, acting more or less as a unified front against Zia, successfully resisted the attempts to make the fourth estate into an agent of martial law.

During Zia's time, half my family was in exile and the other half in jail. When I began my research into the period, I turned to journalists – who, as luck would have it, had taken Zia's repression personally enough to share their detailed memories with me when my textbooks and newspaper clippings became too dry.

I was twenty-two and in England studying for my master's, and flirting with the idea of a journey through my father and family's past, I decided to write my own master's thesis on resistance to General Zia's dictatorship. It was a timely topic; Zia's successor, General Musharraf, was in the sixth year of his rule and a new Afghan war was on Pakistan's horizon. But it was more than just intellectual curiosity that shaped my dissertation. I wanted to understand my father. I wanted to break the taboo of talking about what happened in Afghanistan. I grew up idolizing my father's decision to take up arms against Pakistan's military junta, but as I got older and had to grow up without my father I began to stuggle past my childhood reverence. Why had he gone to Kabul? It was a decision that altered all our lives. It wasn't enough just to know he had gone. It wasn't enough just to love him, regardless of his choices. I had to dig deeper and understand what happened through retrospective lenses. My reverence for my father did not change, but my method of questioning did. I buried myself in libraries, consuming resistance theory and history during what should have been an unencumbered and self-congratulatory time of study. My choice not only gave me the tools to understand a period that had been mythical for me growing up, but also gave me the added benefit of distance when working to understand a history that had deeply personal consequences.

Along with journalists and other members of the press, lawyers were also vocal critics of Zia's regime. Since the earliest days of the junta, Pakistani lawyers 'intermittently held conventions, organized protest marches, boycotted the courts and offered themselves for arrest'[18] to press for the demand that martial law be withdrawn, the judiciary freed, and civil and political rights restored. The lawyers' movement that rose against Pervez Musharraf's regime in 2007 was by no means the first of its kind; it had its roots in the lawyers' movement against Zia ul Haq.

In the first few months of 1981 alone, 460 lawyers were arrested for demonstrating against martial law.[19] The lawyers' resistance was a clear reaction against the junta's co-opting of the judiciary and its interference in the state's legal affairs. The infamous Doctrine of Necessity, which claims that 'that which otherwise is not lawful, necessity makes lawful', had been used retroactively by Pakistan's courts to justify every period of martial law imposed by the army, and was also used to condone Zia's seizure of power.[20]

Once the way had been cleared by the doctrine for Zia's regime to remain in power, the General began to cultivate a judiciary favourable to the junta. By 1979 those judges who had demonstrated their lack of enthusiasm for the military in government had been swiftly sacked and replaced.[21] The power of the civil courts had been clipped and Sharia courts and military tribunals were created to do the bidding of the regime.

The federal Sharia benches were comprised of clerics, often lacking any background in civil legal affairs. It was their job to examine whether laws were 'repugnant to the provisions of Islam' and on that basis declare the offensive laws immediately null and void.[22] Meanwhile, the military tribunals were given a greatly expanded jurisdiction and were able to operate without civilian review. According to Ordinance 77, the tribunals were afforded the authority to hear all cases involving 'political offences, violations against martial law regulations and all other offences under the Pakistan penal code'.[23]

The military tribunals wasted no time in discarding basic civil and legal liberties; under the new draconian court system prisoners did not have the right to be charged, could be held for indefinite periods without charge, the court was under no compunction to keep records of the charges or the ensuing legal proceedings, the number of cases tried under such courts were not made public, and legal counsel for the accused could only observe, not participate in, the proceedings against their clients.[24]

Several cases came to light in 1984 that encapsulated the illegality of the regime and spurred the legal community to further resistance. Two cases, both involving gross legal violations, especially galvanized it. The first was the Rawalpindi Jail Case in which eighteen defendants were arrested for 'anti-state' activities, though it would be a year before specific charges were lodged against them. Eventually their trial was held *in camera* in prison and they were convicted of conspiring to overthrow the government with the aid of an unnamed foreign power. The defendants were denied a fair trial and refused access to their families, the press and often to their legal counsel.[25]

The second case, the Kot Lakhpat Jail Case, was an escalation of the previous one: fifty-four defendants were held on similar charges. However, in this case their lawyers were required to take a 'secrecy oath' by which they swore not to reveal any details of the trial, which was also held *in camera* in prison. Fifty of the defendants in the Kot Lakhpat Jail Case boycotted the trial and went on hunger strike to protest being held in subhuman conditions and denied the right of a fair trial.[26]

While these two particular trials garnered tremendous media attention and legal outrage, bringing more lawyers to the streets in protest, it was only the beginning. The regime had begun putting people to death for 'anti-state' activities at an alarming rate. It's estimated that between 1979 and 1985, the peak of the junta's brutality, anywhere from 100 to 1,000 people were put to death by the state. While mercy pleas were allowed, by the mid-1980s General Zia had not once commuted a death sentence.[27]

Zia had a penchant for the theatrical; along with sweeping midnight arrests and raids, it was possible to go to a neighbourhood stadium or cricket ground – it is worth noting that the national cricket team never protested and seemed more than happy to be used by the regime whenever necessary, such as in Zia's foreign policy triumph of 'cricket diplomacy' with India, which was as one-dimensional as it sounds – and watch public floggings, public executions and, in time, public stonings of women. According to Foucault, public torture and executions do not re-establish justice, but rather 'reactivate power'.[28] They are highly political rituals wherein the injured ruler is restored to grandeur and sovereignty by manifesting his power at 'its most spectacular'.[29]

————◆•••◆————

While women were active in the political resistance and were members of the press and legal community, the Hudood Ordinances of 1979 opened up a new front for opposition led largely by women. The

Ordinances, which still remain in place today, are a compilation of laws dealing mainly with women's bodies and the notion of *zina*, which in Arabic denotes sexual intercourse between an unmarried man and woman. *Zina bil jabr* is a variant taken to mean rape; however, under the junta's new definition, consent was not the issue, but intercourse. A woman could be convicted by law after being raped because, willingly or not, she had had intercourse out of wedlock. Under the Hudood laws, rape victims were prosecuted alongside their rapists for engaging in *zina bil jabr*. The Ordinances also dealt with adultery, basic sexual relations and prostitution.[30]

The Hudood laws carried clauses prohibiting alcohol and narcotics, untoward activities carried out by minorities (whatever those may be), theft and other petty crimes. They were unusual not only in their puritanical reordering of private life but also in the punishments they prescribed for these 'crimes'; most commonly public flogging and imprisonment, but also public stoning to death, amputations and fines.[31]

Prior to the implementation of the Hudood Ordinances, Pakistan's penal code did not label fornication a crime, but rather had provisions for dealing with the crime of marital rape and viewed rape itself as a crime where the rapist, not the victim, was the sole party to be indicted under law.[32] Moreover, *zina* laws under the Hudood Ordinances stipulated that an individual could be 'found guilty with or without the consent of the other party',[33] which meant that women, as a result of medical evidence, were more likely to be convicted under the Ordinances than men. A simple examination could prove that a woman had recently had sex, or that she was no longer a virgin, but men's innocence rested simply on their word.

The Hudood Ordinances define Zia's medieval and barbaric rule, but he did more than just brutalize the nation's laws; he fundamentally changed its people and society. In 1983, Lal Mai from Liaqatabad became the first woman to be publicly flogged on adultery charges under the Ordinances. Reports indicated that 8,000 men witnessed Mai receive her fifteen lashes.[34] It's unclear whether the spectators at Mai's punishment were brought to the scene by the police and made to watch her public torture, as happened in Afghanistan under the Taliban, or whether they were there out of morbid curiosity. But they were there, in their thousands.

Women all over Pakistan took to the streets calling for the removal of the Hudood Ordinances and were viciously beaten and arrested by the police for their protests.[35] In addition, women lawyers organized under the Pakistan Women Lawyers Assocation (PWLA) and called conferences, under the threat of severe government harassment, in 1982, 1983 and finally 1985 to bring attention to the brutality of the Ordinances.[36] Besides the PWLA, other women's groups that exist in Pakistan today trace their origins back to the movement of resistance against Zia's archaic laws. Several groups sprang up to organize women and campaign for increased rights, notably the All Pakistan Women's Association (APWA) and the Women's Action Forum (WAF).[37]

No section of society was safe from the army's interference in the early 1980s. Besides insinuating itself politically and legally into all corners of daily life, the army began to meddle in the running of Pakistan's economy. If the army could not set the price of goods in the economic market, those goods would simply disappear. If the army could not take a cut out of black market profits, those vendors would be arrested and often flogged.[38]

Marx's 'dull compulsion of economic relations' did not produce a compliant labour force, but exactly the opposite, at least until 1985, when politics destroyed the resistance movement against the junta. Merchants and small street vendors were politically powerful in terms of numbers and engaged in visible grass-roots resistance. Traditionally, the group had not 'actively supported any government except Zulfikar Ali Bhutto's'[39] and thus made up a lively section of the resistance movement against the military junta. The short-term economic restrictions of making a living did not hinder merchants, traders or labourers from hitting back against the junta. Zia squeezed the group by attacking their rights and working conditions. They resisted by staging strikes, boycotts, demonstrations and marches in the streets throughout Zia's tenure.[40]

Labour unions were broken by the regime and Zia actively oversaw the weakening of unionization and the labour rights movements. In 1981, the General banned all union activity in Pakistan International Airlines. PIA's union offices were sealed and union office bearers and workers were arrested when they resisted the government's decision.[41] When workers of the newly commissioned Karachi Steel Mills demonstrated for more labour freedom in late 1981, they were beaten by the police and the president of the workers' union was carted off to jail.[42] The Pakistan Labour Conference, set to be held in Lahore that same year, was closed down by the government as their forces worked overtime blocking the entry of labour leaders into the Punjab province.[43]

The more union members resisted Zia's anti-labour laws, the more ruthlessly they were punished. A trade union leader was notoriously held in both Camp and Kot Lakhpat jails and after being stripped on arrival in both prisons was stretched out on a *tiktiki* – an A-frame to which his hands, feet and midriff were tied – and whipped.[44] Factory workers all over the country were routinely arrested, beaten and tortured by prison authorities for opposing the government's anti-labour dictates and rallying for better working conditions.[45]

Urban professionals and intellectuals also played a substantial role in resisting martial law. The medical profession, otherwise neutral, took a unique and unprecedented stand against the junta. The Hudood Ordinances ordered that thieves be punished by amputation of the hands, and as the sole group qualified to mete out the punishment doctors refused to comply.[46] Ghulam Ali from Okara was convicted of stealing a clock from his local mosque and sentenced to have his right hand removed; yet not a single doctor in all of Pakistan could be found to carry out the amputation, whereas we know that in countries where similar punishments are prescribed against theft, such as Afghanistan and Saudi Arabia, amputations were and are still carried out with the aid of the local medical communities. The courts had no choice but to convert Ghulam Ali's sentence to six years of rigorous imprisonment instead.[47]

The initial wave of political resistance, however, came uniquely from members of Bhutto's own PPP. It is estimated that immediately after Zulfikar's murder, some 3,000 party workers and activists were jailed in order to quell an uprising against Zia's decision to execute the country's first democratically elected Prime Minister. Former prisoners that I have spoken to described extreme measures being used against them in jail as a matter of principle. Male prisoners were often moved nightly to different cells, or in extreme cases to different jails, to disorient them; although political prisoners, they were made to share small cells with hardened criminals (who were luckily politically liberal and mostly anti-Zia); their food was searched in front of them before they were allowed to eat. And two prisoners I spoke to had their fingernails removed when they dared to shout pro-Bhutto slogans. Activists and individuals loyal to Zulfikar, in the Sindh province especially, continued to stage daring acts of resistance, setting themselves on fire and chanting slogans such as 'Zia *hatao*' – 'remove Zia' – in public squares. In one extreme case, party workers threw rocks at Zia's army helicopter as it attempted to land in Dadu, in the interior of Sindh.[48]

Zulfikar's widow, Nusrat, was famously attacked in Lahore as she attended a cricket game at Gaddafi stadium. She knew her presence would excite the large crowd gathered; furthermore, PPP activists had planned to unfurl a banner calling for Zia's removal during the game and Nusrat offered herself as protection. Instead, when the police noticed that Nusrat Bhutto, the dictatorship's public enemy number one, was in the audience and that her strong and stoic appearance was creating palapable ripples in the stadium, they came and demanded she leave. No, Nusrat replied, I'm here to watch the game. At that, the police clubbed Nusrat on the head with their batons. She suffered gashes on her forehead and head that required stitches and was photographed being carried out of the stadium, semi-conscious, her hair matted and her face stained with blood.

Not all PPP members, it is worth noting, sacrificed themselves in the fight against the junta. The party's current Prime Minister, Yousef Raza Gilani – who bears more than a passing resemblance to Saddam Hussain – spent his time not in jail but serving on the dictator's *majlis e shoora* or religious parliamentary council, rubbing shoulders with General Zia's protégé Nawaz Sharif. Gilani's junta background did not prohibit his entry into Benazir's PPP; instead it earned him the second-highest post in the land under the Zardari-led party.

-------◆••◆•------

As a response to Zia's absolutist politics, the Movement for the Restoration of Democracy or MRD was formed in 1981 and included a hodgepodge of alliances. Spearheaded by the PPP, and eventually taken over by Benazir, the movement was comprised of the National Democratic Party, the Pakistan Democratic Party, the Islamic Jamaat ul Islami, the peasant-based Mazdoor Kisan Party, the Pashtoon National Alliance Party and several other organizations.[49]

The MRD's programme, which called for the end of martial law through the holding of free and fair elections and the restoration of a democratic government through said elections, simultaneously inspired popular support and the concern of the military junta. Ultimately though, the MRD proved to be ineffectual, partly for reasons of its own creation and partly owing to government interference and infiltration.

At its inception, the MRD announced plans for country-wide agitation in February 1981. Fifteen thousand people were immediately arrested for breaking the junta's ban on public rallies and political gatherings as they came out to support the movement's first call to action.[50] The regime acted quickly to suppress the nascent power of the MRD, and the hijacking of a PIA aeroplane the following month gave a perfect pretext. The junta's jails had become too full. Human rights organizations the world over were calling attention to the overcrowding of Pakistan's prisons and something needed to be done to rectify the situation. Through the hijacking, the junta found a way to do both – many of Pakistan's most prominent political prisoners were released and the MRD was contained as its political leaders were placed under arrest and its supporters jailed, ending the 1981 protest before it had even begun.

{ 10 }

Throughout the tumultuous years that took Murtaza abroad, his studies at Oxford remained on his mind. The faculty and administration at Christ Church were sympathetic, having already educated a fair number of his family. After Murtaza moved from Oxford to London to work on the Save Bhutto Committee full-time, he received a letter from Professor Ian Stephens: 'I write to offer you sympathy, and support if needed. You must be having a horrible time.' Stephens remarks that a colleague saw Murtaza 'on the telly trying to persuade some absurd man that he was quite wrong in his amiable assertions about the vile conditions your father is at present jailed in'.[1]

The professor, an author who had just published a book on South Asia, went on, 'In or about 1931, your grandfather was kind to me at Delhi . . . And in 1973 your father, though appallingly busy, went out of his way to be kind to a Bengali lad – a Rhodes Scholar designate for Oxford, who found himself stranded in West Pakistan. On the strength of these items, I'd like, if there's any need, to be kind to yourself.'

It had been a struggle for Murtaza to be away from his tutors and classes, but he didn't shirk his studies. His supervisor was Hedley Bull, whose own work coincided with Murtaza's sphere of interest. Bull worked in international relations and had published his first work, *The Control of the Arms Race*, on the very topic Murtaza was researching. Bull's first supervisor's report, written in the Michaelmas term of 1977, noted that the student – who was still living at Oxford at the time – 'must have been under great strain, although as far as I can judge he is working satisfactorily'.[2] Bull went on to note that Murtaza's thesis, an expanded version of his Harvard dissertation on nuclear deterrence, needed more work on its case studies.

In the autumn of 1978, having submitted a draft of his thesis, Murtaza, who was in the midst of travelling and lobbying on his father's behalf, was told that Oxford had lost the draft. Murtaza hadn't made copies; nor, given all the movement and tumult surrounding the Save Bhutto Committee, had he organized his notes and index cards. He wrote to his supervisor, who in turn wrote to the college's steward, who sent out an internal SOS: 'I think you will have heard the sad story of Mir Bhutto's thesis . . . The loss is serious to him because he most improvidentially failed to keep a copy . . . I think it may ease Bhutto's mind if we could tell him another probe was afoot.'[3]

Another letter followed, still addressed to Murtaza in London, assuring him that 'no stone has been left unturned'[4] in the search for the missing thesis draft. Bull's supervisor's report for 1978 crisply noted that without the draft magically turning up Murtaza would have to start all over again. 'I have not heard from Mr Bhutto since the beginning of term. His father's affairs have of course reached a crisis. Mr Bhutto is involved in a crisis of his own furthermore since the copy of his thesis draft which I sent him back in July never reached him.'[5]

Murtaza changed flats at least three times during his stay in London, partially for security reasons and partially because the continuous coming and going of people caused a degree of panic in the central London neighbourhoods he lived in. Somewhere along the way, the draft, caught up in the confusion and chaos, got lost.

By the time the missing draft was found, Murtaza's life had been uprooted. Bull's supervisor's report for the following year noted, in the same scratchy handwriting, that 'Mr Bhutto has not been in Oxford this term but rang me up from Afghanistan for an extension of his thesis, which has now been found.'[6] An extension of three additional terms was given. The drama of the thesis continued, now played out over the smoky city of Kabul.

At the start of 1980 Bull wrote an unscheduled report, this time typed in harsh black ink, recording the fact that he hadn't heard from his pupil since shortly before the Soviet invasion of Afghanistan. There was no way for student and supervisor to work together normally given that the Russians were cutting the phone lines and the Afghan postal service was totally unreliable. But somehow, in spite of the maelstrom of activity and resettlement, not to mention the liberation movement he was setting up, in the summer of 1980 Murtaza sent in a complete draft. Bull received the effort well. 'It is clear that despite his distractions and political involvements, Mr Bhutto is still seriously pursuing his work.'[7]

But it wasn't enough. The thesis, though completed, was not in a good state. Professor Bull wrote that 'while Mr Bhutto worked hard under difficult conditions', for his thesis to be successful he would have no choice but to 'return here to his studies on a full-time basis'.[8] That was not going to happen. Murtaza never replied to Bull; the case of the Oxford thesis was over.

———◆◆◆◆———

At the start of 1981, Della, who remained in Athens, was hopeful of better times to come. She and Murtaza had weathered many storms together – the campaigns for their loved ones in jail, Zulfikar's execution and the move to Kabul. She opened her purple Asprey's diary and wrote at the top of the page some thoughts for the times ahead. 'Don't give any information out. Improve economics. Have own house by end of the year. Learn Urdu and Spanish.'[9] She had been thinking of leaving her husband, General Roufogalis, who had now been in prison for eight years. He had been arrested only three months into their marriage and Della had spent enough years waiting for him to be released to know that it wasn't a possibility worth holding on to. Plus, she had fallen in love with Murtaza.

Murtaza had often asked Della to marry him, but she couldn't desert Roufogalis while he was in prison. But Murtaza persisted, telling her of the mountainous areas in Pakistan that Alexander the Great had passed through with his troops, of the snow leopards in the Himalayas, of the land in Sindh where he had grown up, promising that together they could build a new life. Murtaza told Della that they would have children together, he told her they would make angels. 'Fix and clear my tubes,' she wrote in the list, ending her thoughts with 'Always love Mir'.

When Della received a letter from Murtaza on 26 January, she tore it open excitedly. He had written it twelve days earlier.

> Ever since I have been here we have seen less of each other. And then, naturally, we have travelled less together. I get confused each time I think of all the promises I made: if nothing else one promise I will fulfil at all costs is your trip to Sindh and to the snow leopards.

Della read on happily, the snow leopards reminding her of their future, a little code they shared together.

> My job is a far more difficult job than I thought it was. It is far more complicated than an outsider can imagine. It keeps me busier than I have ever been before in my life, but I am sure of success. Because the people are with us; the dynamics of history are with us. But in spite of all this I always think of you and I will always continue to think of you.

If Della had not sensed the tone of the letter till then, it now hit her like a slap in the face.

> But you, young and beautiful as you are, will have to seriously think about your own future. Don't worry about me, my destiny will be decided through the barrel of a gun . . . I have got involved in a job and a lifestyle that is not of my own making. You must not destroy your life for my sake.

Murtaza tells Della that he will always say, till his dying day, that she was the true and only love of his life. Think of yourself, of your future. I'm lost in my work for the next two or three years. He asks this much of her, for his sake. There is so much more he wants to write but cannot. It was the last thing Murtaza wrote before ending their relationship.

◆◆◆●◆

'We were the only organization at the time in which there was no free entry,' Suhail tells me about Al Zulfikar, the new name of the organization founded by the Bhutto brothers, a play on their father's name and the famous sword of Imam Ali. 'We contacted people, never accepting those who came to us because we were wary of infiltration.' He shakes his head and looks down. 'But it still happened, even though we were careful.'[10]

At the start of 1981 the organization was finally taking shape. Party workers who had been active from 1977 to 1979, the time of Zulfikar's trial and imprisonment, were the ideal candidates to join the liberation movement and they came to Kabul from all across Pakistan's four provinces. 'Because of the persecution in Pakistan,' Suhail explains, 'many loyal party workers and activists were compelled to migrate. It was too dangerous for them to stay on in Pakistan, they were being beaten, tortured and arrested. We were under a strict dictatorship. Party workers, those who had the most sincere records, were largely poor, had neither the resources nor the means to migrate to Europe or the West. They would come to us. Our base in Kabul was basically a refuge for them where they could be safe and carry on the struggle against the junta.'[11]

Suhail is a trim man, tallish. His hair has thinned on top and has greyed over the passage of time, turning even the light hairs on his moustache a cloudy white. He smokes cigarettes, like my father did, slowly and as if they require his consideration and attention. When we speak about the old days, the Kabul days, he wavers between laughing and joking about the memories of these three young men – all from privileged families – sitting in Afghanistan and plotting to overthrow a dictatorship and complete seriousness when we talk about the actual work they had sacrificed their lives to undertake.

217

'A few women did come from Punjab to join the movement,' he says, recalling every detail as if it was yesterday. 'We were certainly open to it, we didn't want to close any doors to those who had a sincere belief in our cause, but keeping in mind the terrain – having to cross through our Tribal Belt to reach Afghanistan – it didn't work out.' They did try though. It makes me happy, this small thought – that my father was progressive enough to recognize that men alone do not make revolutions, even at his young age of twenty-seven. As I linger on the thought, Suhail continues, describing the day-to-day life they led in Kabul – a period I've often heard him refer to as 'the best times'.

'There were about a hundred people who joined us at the end. We had a separate compound where we worked and housed everyone and had divided the movement into three parts – there was a political wing, a military wing and a security wing. Mir was the Secretary-General of Al Zulfikar and Shah initially headed the security wing and then later the military wing.'

Al Zulfikar, which we call AZO, adding the O for organization, was never completely real to me. I was very young when it was disbanded. I only heard about it in passing, saw its logo on stationery kept in a dusty unused drawer. I saw its members, like Suhail, as family friends, as uncles who would take us out to eat ice-cream and whose children I grew up playing with. The notion that it existed in a different context is a strange one, like someone telling me about a foreign film that I'd watched but never read the subtitles of. But now I can finally understand the danger that followed my father and Uncle Shah for most of my childhood; it suddenly all makes sense and while his are not the choices I would make now, I feel secretly proud of my father for abandoning the offer of a bland but comfortable exile in London to fight what he believed was an unjust system.

'The daily routine started in the early morning with physical exercises, which Shah would lead,' Suhail says, toying with his packet of local cigarettes. 'Then we'd have a political lecture – different people who worked in the political wing would come and talk on a number of issues, the floor was always open. We'd hear lectures on the history of the military in Pakistan, the growth of the People's Party, histories of democratic struggles in other nations – it was always varied.

'Then there would be a period of physical training, shortly before lunch. When the time to eat came, Shah would eat with everyone – he'd made a lot of friends among the recruits by that point and was very jovial and jolly during his break time with the men. And then we would have political discussions, group talks about our aims, what we were fighting for and general debates. Shah was very popular with the people who joined us; he was young and fun and had a real sense of the physical dynamics of fighting an armed struggle. Murtaza would visit the compound every day, but he was more concerned with the diplomatic and political side of things. He would meet with political groups that sent delegations or members from Pakistan, he would spend hours collecting news about the situation in the country, scouring the press and speaking to journalists, preparing political statements and so on – it was Murtaza's job as the Secretary-General.' Their separate roles – Shah as the more militant commander of the organization and Murtaza as the political leader – would become more defined as time went on and would mark their lives in very different ways.

Meanwhile, in Athens, Della was furious. She hadn't bargained for an easy life when she began to see Murtaza and she wasn't going to let him slip away into the ether of his political life.

She wrote an angry letter back to Kabul, her tears smudging the blue ink of her writing. 'You crazy fool,' Della began. 'Who asked your opinion about my future? My future belongs to me and I will do what I want with it . . . I too have a destiny, a duty that I am trying to fulfil and a big, deep love for you. When I read your letter I thought that the skies had opened up, that all the snow of the Afghan mountains was falling on my head.'[12] She made a copy of the letter, the one she gives me twenty-seven years later. She sent the original, crossed out 'Always love Mir' in her purple Asprey's diary, and waited.

A week later a postcard from Mutaza arrived, sent from Libya and postmarked 29 January. Della took the postcard to the Libyan embassy in Athens, showed it to the man seated behind a desk and demanded answers. She told him she was looking for the sender of the postcard.

The embassy official looked at the card carefully, wondering if the tall blonde woman was playing at something and told her to come back in a few days. When Della returned she was told that no such person was living in Libya and that she must have been deluded to think that the embassy could help her on such a wild goose chase. Storming out, Della grabbed an armful of tourist brochures on Tripoli. As soon as she got home Della called all the hotels explaining that she was looking for a certain man. But she couldn't find Murtaza. He had already left.

Undaunted, she eventually reached Shah by phone. He was surprised. If Della could find him by blind-calling hotels in random countries, their secretive lifestyle wasn't so secretive after all. Murtaza wasn't with him, but Shah told Della he'd relay the message. A few days later Shah called her back and told her Murtaza had called him from Abu Dhabi, asked Shah to speak to Della and assure her that he was fine, asked her to be patient and promised that he would write soon and explain everything.

On 24 February there was a serious earthquake in Greece. A lot of damage had been caused and Greeks sat in front of their TV screens watching the news of the disaster unfold. As Della watched, another headline caught her attention. A PIA aeroplane had been hijacked. The hijackers were claiming that they were part of a militant movement based in Afghanistan, to where the plane was being diverted. Della listened carefully, making sure she heard everything the newsreader was saying. It couldn't be, she thought. It can't be. Murtaza and Shahnawaz Bhutto, the news said, had ordered the Pakistani plane to be hijacked; the men on board claimed they were acting on the orders of Al Zulfikar.

The phone rang in Palace Number 2 sometime in the early evening, around 5.30. Murtaza picked up the phone and the caller asked to speak to Mir Murtaza Bhutto. It was a somewhat strange call, as their number wasn't public – it wasn't in the Kabul phone book and most of the government officials who called Murtaza were friendly enough with him for him to know their secretaries by name. However, he still assumed the call was from some government office or other. 'Salamullah Tipu wants to speak to you,' said the caller. The name was familiar, but not especially so. 'Who is Salamullah Tipu?' Murtaza, now annoyed, asked as politely as he could. 'He's hijacked a plane. I'm calling from the Kabul airport control tower. He's in the aeroplane now and asked to be put through to you.'

That was how Murtaza came to know that a plane had been hijacked in his name. But it was not the first time he had heard of Tipu.

None of the interviews I did on the hijacking were easy to arrange. Suhail and I tried to speak in 70 Clifton, but I think the chandeliers still have ears there. I moved us to the garden, where we sat under a *champa* tree speaking in whispers, hunched over our chairs under the watchful gaze of our neighbours, the Russian consul's residence and the Iranian consulate. It still didn't feel safe enough, even in such friendly company. The hijacking had been a sword hanging over my father's head, ready to drop at any time. It was important for me to get as much information as I could on the incident. The official case against my father and uncle, absolving them of any involvement, was quietly concluded in 2003 and has left, for me at least, a gaping hole of unanswered questions. Who had arranged the hijacking? Who pulled the plane out of the sky? It was too easy to end the case once the Bhutto brothers had been taken care of and removed from the picture. I took Suhail to a trendy coffee shop in Karachi's busy Zamzama shopping area. Here again we adopted our hunched poses and whispered over overpriced hot lattes. I thought it absurd that we were sitting among teenagers comparing mobile phones and *desi* yuppies gossiping in corporate-speak, discussing the details of a junta-backed hijacking. Suhail was indulgent with me and my constantly paranoid shifting; he's always been a surrogate father of sorts. He was present at my birth and at my brother Zulfi's, and was there when as a family we adopted Mir Ali, a month-old baby boy from a Karachi orphanage. Suhail travels to Karachi for all our birthdays, even mine and I'm nearing thirty.

A group of men had come to Kabul from Karachi three months earlier. Salamullah Tipu was one of them. He had a reputation in Karachi, known among students for his violence in university politics. He had fought with the student wing of the religious Jamaat Islami party and had been involved in a shooting incident at Karachi University as a result of a power struggle within the party.

Tipu was a good-looking man, Suhail remembers. He had been in the army once, briefly. It had been his childhood dream to join up and he had been selected by the armed forces as soon as he was old enough. But Tipu left claiming that he had been shunted out during training for personal reasons he would never go into. 'The story was unclear, a little foggy, that and the fact that he had come to us – it cancelled him out for us,'[13] says Suhail, struggling to put the pieces of that first meeting together.

'He wasn't a member of our organization, he didn't come through the PPP cadres; he'd come to Kabul through common contacts. Our headquarters were visited by many Pakistani activists, tribal leaders, nationalists, leftists – they'd often call on Murtaza to discuss the situation in Pakistan or to bring news from home.' Tipu seemed smart, he was aware of the problems the people were facing under Zia's regime, but something about him didn't click. There was something edgy about him, something rough. He'd come from a violent background within both his family and his community. 'But he came to us,' Suhail repeats, 'and that aroused our suspicion.'

The visiting group consisted of two men besides Tipu; one was his cousin and the other was his friend. It was the age of hijackings – made famous by the Palestinians, desperate to call attention to their plight. Leila Khalid, who proudly proclaimed hijacking as her occupation, became a guerrilla symbol of Palestinian frustration overnight. Hijackings, then seen as media-savvy operations, had captured the world's notice.

Tipu suggested to Murtaza that the newly formed Al Zulfikar follow the lead of other liberation groups and hijack a Pakistani airliner. Suhail remembers his pitch. 'You know, there was tyranny in Pakistan. There was no judicial remedy to the excesses of the junta. Tipu really caught on to that and talked about how people there were bubbling with fear. He talked about the fact that so many political workers were in prisons and that they had no recourse to the courts. He was right; the lawyers were divided between supporting and aiding the regime and those who were cracked down upon because they were vocally opposed to it. He spoke about hijacking an aeroplane to negotiate the release of prisoners.'

Murtaza turned him down. It was not the first time that someone had suggested hijacking an airliner, imagining it would strike a blow at the military regime in Pakistan. A month before Tipu and his friends turned up in Kabul, a group of young men from Rawalpindi had come and said the same thing. Murtaza had turned them down too.

He rejected Tipu's offer, remembers Suhail, on the grounds that 'we were fighting a military coterie which had usurped power from the people. Our fight was not against national institutions, like PIA, or against civilians.' But Tipu was disappointed his passionate pleas had been refused. After that first encounter, he got in touch again and tried once more to push his idea. Tipu was refused, more sternly this time. 'Mir was taken completely off guard when he got the call that night,' says Suhail, shaking his head and toying with his unlit cigarette.

The PIA plane was scheduled to fly from Karachi to Peshawar and had been taken over in mid-air by three men. Tipu led the group and ordered the pilot to divert the plane to the Middle East, not taking into consideration that it was only prepared for a short-haul flight. There wasn't enough fuel to take them that far. The hijackers then demanded that the plane be flown to Kabul; it was the closest landing point – a brief journey by air over the border from Peshawar. The Afghan authorities saw the hijacking as a rare opportunity to improve their relations with Pakistan and, strangely enough, the Bhutto brothers. As soon as the plane landed, the Afghan authorities called Palace Number 2 and asked Murtaza to intercede.

'We were going through a rough patch in our relationship with the Afghans at the time,' Suhail recalls. 'They had started trying to interfere with Murtaza's running of the organization, basically trying to work on the Pakistanis who were coming over to join us in the hopes of having some insider information on what we were getting up to. Murtaza was very upset; he was on the verge of leaving Kabul.

He wasn't willing to be compromised. And then this hijacking happened.' The call came from Dr Najibullah, the notorious head of the Intelligence services. He told Suhail he was coming over to the house to talk about the situation. The PIA station chief in Kabul also called Murtaza. 'He knew us, and he called and said you people should help solve this stand-off – there are women and children on board the aircraft.'

Dr Najibullah turned up at the house, aware of the tension between his government and their guests. 'He spoke English and Urdu perfectly,' Suhail says, laughing, 'but that night he insisted on speaking in Pushto and having me translate for Mir. Mir's initial impulse was to help end the hostage crisis so he put aside the friction between us and the government and said he was ready to do whatever was necessary to solve the issue peacefully.'

Together, Murtaza and Suhail were taken to Kabul airport, driven there by Captain Baba, the oddly named head of the national Ariana Airlines. When they reached the airport the authorities gave them two blue coats to put on, the sort worn by airport engineers, then drove them towards the tarmac where the plane was standing. 'Talk to them,' pleaded Captain Baba, 'tell them to end this, they'll listen to you.'

'It was late at night by the time we reached the tarmac,' says Suhail, 'two or three in the morning at least.' At that point, no harm had been done to any of the passengers and everyone was anxious that the hijacking crisis be settled quickly and peacefully. Captain Baba dropped the two men off right in front of the airliner and a message was sent asking the hijacker in charge to come down to the tarmac.

The meeting between the three men was short, no longer than fifteen minutes. Murtaza asked Tipu to release the women and children on board. He asked that the hijackers not harm any of the passengers. 'Mir was angry,' Suhail recalls, 'but he remained calm, aware of the danger everyone was in – our situation with the government, the passengers and the fallout from Zia's thugs in Pakistan. He asked Tipu to end it. Tipu refused.' The hijackers had already given a list of fifty-five prisoners in Zia's jails that they were demanding be released in return for the safety of the passengers on board. 'We can't stop now,' Tipu told Murtaza and Suhail. 'The government will butcher the prisoners, whom we've already identified to them.' The fifty-five prisoners were mostly PPP activists, but included known leftist activists and workers imprisoned across the country, mainly in the Punjab. While Tipu agreed to Murtaza's demand that the women and children be freed, he told them that without any concessions from the government it would be suicide for them to end the hijacking.

The meeting was over, Murtaza had asked for the end of the impasse and for the safety of those held hostage. There was no further discussion, no time to waste. After fifteen minutes Murtaza and Suhail left Kabul airport and Salamullah Tipu returned to the aeroplane. Several hours later, in the early hours of the morning, the women and children on board were released and taken to the Kabul Intercontinental Hotel.

'The government of Pakistan sent a negotiating team to Kabul soon after we'd left to deal with the hijackers and end the siege,' Suhail says. He sounds angry, even now, at the events that led to us, twenty-seven years later, sitting in a noisy and smoke-filled coffee shop in Karachi discussing the hijacking. 'Watching their negotiations play out you got the feeling that the junta was perfectly OK dragging the drama of the hijacking on. They didn't seem serious about ending the stand-off, almost as if they were stalling, as if they were trying to agitate the hijackers into a reaction so that the military government would be justified in responding to them with force.'

During the time the junta's negotiation team was dealing with the hijackers, still grounded in Kabul, a passenger was killed. Major Tariq Rahim was shot by the hijackers. Rahim had once been Zulfikar's aide-de-camp and was, since Zulfikar's execution, a serving diplomat in Iran. As the hijacking unfolded, culminating with the death of Major Rahim, the junta's public insistence that the Bhutto brothers and PPP stalwarts were behind the operation began to be questioned. Why would the brothers kill their father's ADC?

Zia's prisons were full of political prisoners and his reluctant international allies began to squirm at the clear evidence of the junta's human rights abuses. There had to be some change, some shift in the dictator's unrepentant violence – the prisons had to be emptied of democratic activists. But for Zia to simply release those detainees who had actively opposed him would have caused a huge loss of face, a sign of weakness in a country where weakness is not tolerated, least of all by the armed forces.

The hijacking would prove politically expedient for the junta – political prisoners would be released and offered as proof of the regime's clemency. All at once, the hijacking and its consequences would be a means of discrediting the popular resistance against the junta, thus providing a legitimate excuse to clamp down further on their opposition, notably the MRD movement. The Bhutto brothers would be branded terrorists, ending their ability to travel freely, and numerous charges of treason – complete with death sentences – would be brought against them. It would be a sword hanging over their heads for a very long time indeed.

The hijacking stand-off in Kabul lasted seven days, until the Afghan government came to the conclusion that Zia's regime wasn't serious about negotiating an end. At that point, fearful that the Pakistanis were holding out for a serious mishap to happen in Kabul so that they could forcefully intervene, the Afghan authorities requested the hijacked plane be moved elsewhere. The hijackers asked to be flown to Syria, another country they knew had ties to the Bhutto brothers, expecting a sympathetic landing place. President Hafez al Assad of Syria, however, refused permission for the hijacked plane to land on Syrian soil. He held out until an official request came from the Pakistani government asking the Syrian government to allow the plane to land and to give safe passage to the people on board the flight.

Once it reached Syria, the hijacked plane sat on the Damascus airport tarmac for another few days. The whole crisis lasted around twelve days. 'It was one of the longest hijacking crises in history, I think,' Suhail tells me carefully. Eventually fifty-four out of the original list of fifty-five prisoners were released in Pakistan and flown to Syria according to the hijackers' demands and the passengers and airliner were finally released. The prisoners and three hijackers were kept at the Damascus Airport Hotel and allowed to apply for asylum, facilitated by the United Nations. Dr Ghulam Hussain was one of the released prisoners. He had been the Secretary-General of the PPP and had refused to leave the party and join Zia's cabinet. For his defiance, he was charged with more than a dozen murders and thrown in jail. Dr Hussain is an elderly man; he looks like Santa Claus, with his clipped white beard and glowing white hair, and is a prolific poet and writer.

'The hijackers weren't PPP people,' Dr Hussain told me in his home in Islamabad. 'The whole thing was manoeuvred by General Zia! He wanted an explosion in front of the world that would destroy the Bhutto boys.'[14]

Dr Hussain is a gregarious man, he laughs loudly and talks in a melodic lilt. He wears thin glasses with gold frames and orthopaedic footwear. He has a strong, deep voice that's interrupted with shrill giggles at memories past. He is also a passionate orator. I've seen him at political rallies, watched how the crowd listens to him in silence, hanging on his every word. He calls me *sahiba*, or madam, but calls my father and uncle 'boys'.

Talking to him now, listening to his exuberant manner of answering a question with riddles and poems and laughter, I wonder how he survived Zia's jails; he was held in eight prisons, regularly shifted and threatened with torture. 'Every time they shifted me,' Dr Hussain tells me proudly, 'I would shout loudly *jiye Bhutto*, long live Bhutto!' In jail he was deprived of newspapers and books, but was allowed to keep his medical equipment and paper to write on. Dr Hussain had a routine; each time they moved him, he would create a garden in the small patch of dirt outside his cell. He learned how to cook 'very well actually' and wrote two diaries for his children, hoping they would be a substitute for his fatherly advice which was being missed at home.

'The brain is an organ, na?' he says in a jolly tone. 'You have to use it or lose it!'

Dr Hussain spent his time at the Damascus Airport Hotel, which lasted almost a year, writing poetry, a habit he had picked up in jail.

'The regime was going to use it, the violence of the hijacking, to balance the violence they had committed against Zulfikar Ali Bhutto. But unfortunately for them President Carter had another hostage crisis, in Iran, to deal with and Zia's attempt was pushed to one side.' Eventually Dr Hussain was granted asylum in Sweden.

Undaunted, the junta went into overdrive, using any angle it could to pin responsibility for the hijacking on Murtaza and Shahnawaz. Benazir made the mistake of making jubilant phone calls, excited by the prospect of a blow against the junta. 'We did it!' she bragged to friends and colleagues alike 'We finally got them!' Almost immediately, the police turned up and arrested her and Nusrat on charges of orchestrating the hijacking. Benazir hadn't spoken to her brothers, she had no idea of the danger they were in. Her phone call compromised her and Nusrat, but it sealed her brothers' fate. 'Sessions judge's report on hijacking concluding it was an individual act,' Benazir wrote in an undated entry in one of her large dusty registers. 'Regime calls it PPP hijacking before hijackers even reveal details – March 2 or 3 '81 . . . PCO order passed so that constitutional justice not available to us for fabricated case. Zia admits PCO passed to "eliminate" elements responsible for hijacking.' Benazir displays a surprising knowledge of the law as she weighs up the danger against the family caused by her spontaneous braggadocio and the aftermath of their arrest. 'Broadcast by BBC that *Begum Sahiba* and myself to be tried for hijacking. This is before any charges have been made against us formally and before we have even been questioned by relevant agencies to see if their investigation shows a prima facie case or not.' In the end, no case was filed against Benazir; only her brothers were indicted.

'What?' yelped one of my aunt's friends in Islamabad when I brought up the question of Benazir's exultation over the hijacking. 'No, no, no. Benazir was very opposed to her brothers' terrorism,' the friend, who repeatedly asked not to be named, insisted. Through gritted teeth I reminded the friend that they were honourably acquitted in the same courts that accused them of committing said terrorist acts.

It was a nightmare trying to interview my aunt's friends. They responded to my questions with a Stasi-like façade of revised, state-approved truths. 'What was Benazir like before she came to power?' I asked the friend, a woman who made a career of her friendship, even serving in parliament during Benazir's first term in power ('We were like children, the experience was so new to us!' she exclaimed, adding quickly, 'But we learned fast . . .') 'What do you mean?' she baulked, eyes aflutter. 'I mean, before she was Prime Minister, what was she like?' I clarified slowly. 'Oh, she was always the same person.' The friend's eyes glazed over. 'Generous, deeply concerned with her country – you could even say obsessed!' – pause for hearty laughter – 'Loving, nurturing, she never really changed.'

With others, it was like speaking to a brick wall. Benazir's role could not be questioned. She made no mistakes. Any suggestion that she might have was denounced as propaganda, vicious lies spread by anti-Bhutto enemies, malicious claims made by the undemocratic army, or misogynists' vendettas against the Islamic world's first woman prime minister.

But back to the hijacking. The friend organised Benazir's defence, to little avail since it was openly recognized that Benazir was arrested, along with her mother, for gloating about 'our people' doing the job. Only when she realized that she was playing into the regime's hands did Benazir begin to see what those around her understood as soon as news of the hijacking was released. Benazir began to backtrack; it wasn't 'our people' who carried out the hijacking. She was opposed to violence, of all kinds. Benazir was the innocent. It was her brothers who had become terrorists. Indeed, she had become a Muslim Aung San Suu Kyi, a Pakistani Gandhi, if you will.

A case was filed in Zia's courts against the two brothers and Suhail, carrying with it the death penalty. In fact, all three men were honourably acquitted of the hijacking charges in 2003 – the case had never been quashed, the charges never investigated beyond Zia's dogged insistence that the hijacking was part of a Bhutto plot to wreak havoc. It is, to this day, a stain on the Bhutto brothers. After they were acquitted, posthumously, by the same courts that had brought the charges against them, the file on the hijacking was put in a bottom drawer somewhere. It was as if it had never happened.

Salamullah Tipu, in time, began working openly for the Pakistan government. His role in leading the hijacking operation didn't seem to stand in his way at all.

------◆••◆------

Della hadn't heard from Murtaza for several months. On 20 April she called him at the Kabul number, but he'd long since stopped picking up the phone. Days later, she received a letter from him postmarked 25 April 1981 and handwritten on his personal stationery. 'Maybe it has now become clear to you why I was forced to write that letter,' he said. 'I am now hunted down not only by the Pakistani police and the Afghan rebels, but also by Interpol. It has become virtually impossible to travel. My lifestyle is no longer what you knew it to be. I am literally a fugitive and a person wanted dead or alive. I am forced to live in secrecy and under heavy protection . . . I believe you have tried to phone here. It is useless. They will never connect it.'[15] He ended the letter by saying that he hoped they would always be friends and that in time Della would understand why he had to make the decisions he did; they were, he insisted, in her best interests.

{ II }

By May of that year, Della and Murtaza were no longer in touch. They had separated and Della reacted angrily. She chopped off her long blonde hair, dyed it dark brown and did her best to move on with her life. At the end of the summer, she happened to be in London and ran into an old friend of Murtaza's. She asked him, after they had danced around the subject, about Mir and the friend told her he was fine. She asked if he had met someone; she always suspected that another woman had diverted his attention, causing him to end things with her so abruptly. The friend answered that he had. Is he happy? Della remembers asking. Yes he is, the friend answered. She knew it. She always had, she supposed.

When Della and I met years later in Greece, she told me that she felt Papa had been with someone else by the time he ended their relationship. Instinctively, I jumped to defend my father's honour, but then Della mentioned the dates. Counting backwards in my head, it was hard not to notice that Della and my father broke up a year, to the month, before I was born. By the time she found out my father was seeing someone else, I had already been conceived.

My father met my biological mother, Fowzia, by chance. She used to walk her dog, a rarity in Kabul in those days, around the neighbourhood and Papa noticed her. Murtaza began to join Fowzia on her daily dog walks, taking Wolf 2 along for the ride. Kabul was a lonely place, caught in between a civil war and foreign occupation; there was not much for young people to do. Eventually, Suhail, Shah and Murtaza befriended the young Afghani woman, who came from a diplomatic family and wore her long brown hair in a plait that ran the length of her back. They spent evenings together at her house with her family and, in time, Shah became besotted by her youngest sister, Raehana. Unlike her siblings, Raehana was shy and introverted. She and Shahnawaz, both youngest children, began to see each other and had a wildly tempestuous courtship. Raehana was a mujahideen supporter and Shah was benefiting from communist hospitality, so they fought and joked and pushed the universe around them to breaking point until it was decided that they would marry. Raehana married Shah first; her sister and Murtaza's nuptials came later; by that time Fowzia was already pregnant with me.

'There wasn't a large gap between their marriages,' Suhail remembers. 'They had a joint reception where they wore their khaki uniforms and *keffiyehs*, Mir's red and Shahnawaz's black, and Mir asked all of us to wear ours too for the party.' He laughs softly, almost to himself, and then switches gear, becoming more serious. 'You know, when I went to invite Dr Najibullah to the wedding reception, he pulled out a file in front of me.' Most ominous stories seem to start this way, furtively and with the presence of some file or another. Dr Najibullah, the head of Intelligence, member of the governing politburo and future President of Afghanistan, was a difficult man to read. He had a reputation for brutality and there had been ups and downs in his relationship with the Bhutto brothers since their move to Kabul, but he had always ensured their safety and had granted them every protection while maintaining a distance, for most of the time, that allowed them to operate freely.

Suhail wasn't sure what was about to be revealed in the file, but like the patient messenger and emissary that he had become, he waited to hear the worst. Dr Najibullah asked Suhail why he hadn't come to him with the news of the brothers' relationships before, as if their private lives were a matter of consequence to the state. He opened the file and said that the girls' family, the Zias (a macabre irony), had contacts with the mujahideen. Their father had worked in the foreign service, often travelling abroad to countries like Indonesia. Najibullah paused and reminded Suhail that General Zia's regime was supporting the mujahideen through Pakistan's Inter-Service

Intelligence and supplying them with arms and funds funnelled through the CIA.

It wasn't out of turn for Dr Najibullah's attention to be piqued by the brothers' romantic affairs. When Murtaza had been with Della the Afghan Intelligence service had been convinced that Della was a CIA agent. In his last letter to Della, Murtaza wrote:

I think Shah has explained to you our position here. Though I know it is not true, our friends are absolutely convinced that you are working for the Americans. I explained to them the factual position, but they were not convinced. They are conducting a complete and thorough investigation into you, your background, friends, travels, contacts etc etc.

Murtaza added that he was convinced the letter would be censored before it reached Della, though in fact it seems to have been left untouched.

Now Najibullah was making the same insinuation about the Zia sisters. Suhail wearily repeated what had become a standard response: 'You're welcome to come to the house any time and present this to the boys.'[1] When he came to the house though, Dr Najibullah saw that Murtaza, already married by this point, was wearing a wedding ring. He didn't bring up the file. As he left, Suhail walked him to the door and asked: 'Dr *sahib*, why didn't you say anything?' 'What can I say now?' Dr Najibullah replied, disappointed.

⬥•••⬥

I was born in Kabul under curfew around 3.45 on the morning of 29 May 1982. Labour started around seven or eight in the evening and Fowzia was taken into a government hospital under heavy protection. The mujahideen insurgency in Kabul was at its peak and there were constant attacks all around the city, necessitating lock-downs at curfew time. The government, under Dr Najibullah's orders, placed special troops around the hospital in anticipation of my birth, worried that the hospital might become a mujahideen target, allowing them to hit the Bhutto family and the regime in one go. Fatan, Dr Najibullah's wife, was there at the hospital to look after the arrangements. Ehsan Bhatti, a member of the Al Zulfikar Organization and a dear friend of Murtaza and Shahnawaz, was placed outside the delivery room in his khaki uniform and Palestinian *keffiyeh*, which he was asked to remove by Fatan on the grounds that it was 'too conspicuous'.

'Mir was so anxious,' Suhail told me, 'so Dr Najibullah's number two, Jamil Nooristani, who had become a friend of ours, took us and Shah back to his house to wait till the news of your birth came.'[2] Nooristani, I remember my father teasing me, had tried to distract him from his jitters by suggesting traditional Pashtun names for his future child, names like Gulabo or Gulrukh, all starting with the prefix Gul.

At four in the morning, Papa received the news that I had been born. It was not an easy birth and eventually the doctors were forced to resort to forceps. Papa celebrated with a toast and an earnest discussion began about my name. 'The first names that came to him were your paternal great-grandmothers' names,' Suhail recalled, recounting a story I have heard my father tell many times before, 'Fatima and Khurshid.' Thankfully, Papa went with the former and I was named after my Iranian great-grandmother. Suhail always clucks his tongue at me when I register horror at the possibility that I might have been called Khurshid. 'It means sun in Urdu, you know,' he always tells me.

'Mir was really happy,' Suhail says, smiling. 'He took to you immediately, like you were put on earth for him.' There is a black-and-white photograph of me soon after my birth, my little mouth is open as if I'm talking. 'About four weeks old,' my father has written in blue on the back of the photograph. 'Tall like me.' I was tall, until the age of twelve when my growth curiously slowed and then stopped, leaving me for ever at 5'3", a full foot shorter than my father.

Three months later, almost to the day, Shahnawaz became a father too. He also had a daughter and named her Sassi, after the tragic heroine of a popular Sindhi folktale. Two brothers married two sisters and both had daughters. It almost seemed as though life was turning around for the Bhutto brothers.

In fact it carried on as dangerously as before. After the hijacking, Al Zulfikar made its most daring attempt at confronting the regime. A group of three people attacked Zia's plane as it took off from Chaklala air base in Rawalpindi. They were armed with a Samsix heat-seeking missile and narrowly missed hitting the aircraft as it gained height. On board the plane, the pilot and passengers were aware of the attempt on their lives. Sharing the flight with General Zia was Ghulam Ishaq Khan, the then chairman of the senate – and the man from whom Benazir would take her oath as Prime Minister to his presidency in 1988 – and Mahmood Haroon, whose signature featured prominently on Zulfikar's death warrant, and who in another absurd placing would be appointed by Benazir as the governor of Sindh under her first government. It seems unthinkable that of the three junta leaders on board the aeroplane, Benazir would work with two of them, negotiating with but narrowly missing her chance to work with the third. The three men managed to escape, but the Samsix attack intensified the regime's fury towards the Bhutto brothers and their Kabul-based organization. 'It was the most daring, direct attempt we made,' Suhail tells me.[3]

But it was irresponsible nonetheless. The attempt on Zia's life, carried out soon after the PIA hijacking, only created a space, and a legitimate one at that, for Zia and the junta to react against the Bhuttos. Suhail says that eighty-four charges of treason were made against Murtaza and Shahnawaz by the junta, all carrying the death penalty. (I remember the number of charges being higher, in the nineties somewhere. Other people place them in the mid-hundreds.)

The junta didn't just bring charges against the Bhutto brothers. It began to actively fight them. I ask Suhail if there were direct attempts on their lives while they lived in Kabul. He begins and ends a sentence several times. He smokes and drinks his tea; he tries to change the subject. Finally, he tells me that there were. Tribals from Pakistan's lawless tribal belt were sent to Kabul to assassinate the brothers. He doesn't want to talk about it, not with me. But I know something of the matter. I remember marks on my father's body and on his face.

I remember scars on his back, near his heart, and on his nose. I remember that he couldn't talk about them easily and that when, as a little girl, I asked what they were from, he would only tell me that they were from people who had tried to hurt him.

It's a difficult history to contend with. Murtaza and Shahnawaz were young men, they were following their father's dying wishes, but it was that wish that eventually cost them their lives. For Zulfikar to have placed his sons, his heirs, in direct danger was maddeningly irresponsible. For him to have ended his children's chance of a peaceful, safe, ordinary life was vengeful; it would destroy his sons. Zulfikar should have known that. But they were wrong to have followed him too. There are signs, a changing of course over time, that suggest they understood that.

In 1982, around the time they were both due to become fathers, Murtaza and Shahnawaz re-evaluated the activities of their organization. 'Most of our work from then on,' Suhail confirms, 'was centred around helping to foment resistance to the regime within Pakistan. We had become a sort of headquarters for those disaffected with the regime, a refuge or gathering place for Pakistan's poor political activists who suffered the lion's share of the junta's political brutality.'[4]

Murtaza was working at the time on transmitting radio programmes into Pakistan from Kabul. He had been gathering accounts of life under the dictatorship, of human rights abuses and political malfeasance, and was putting together a series of programmes while trying to sort out the logistics of broadcasting across the border. Increasingly, the brothers had different roles. Murtaza, it seemed, was eager to get back to fighting the regime through diplomatic means. Shahnawaz, meanwhile, spent most of his time with the organization's cadres, focusing on security and military training. He was still angry and wanted to inflict the maximum damage on the dictatorship. 'After their father was murdered, Shah looked to his older brother as a father figure,' Suhail says, trying to explain their dynamic. 'They complemented each other, they really did. You have to give credit to Shah – he opted for this life. He gave up everything to come to Kabul, to work in the organization, he felt duty-bound to help his brother in this insurmountable struggle.'[5]

Back home in Pakistan, the movement to unseat Zia ul Haq was faltering. The MRD launched a campaign of civil disobedience in 1983, which was strong in Sindh but failed to take root in other provinces, except perhaps Balochistan. Unlike Gandhi's acts of civil disobedience, the MRD drive in 1983 was not entirely peaceful. There were strikes and shut-downs, but they were accompanied by significant acts of violence. Agitation in Larkana, Sukkar, Jacobabad and Khairpur in Sindh was so fierce that the Governor of Sindh was forced to admit that in the first three weeks of the unrest the government had 1,999 people arrested, 189 killed and 126 injured.[6]

But cracks surfaced fairly soon within the movement itself. The Sindh leadership of the MRD felt that their provincial counterparts didn't do enough to fight the regime, even though thousands of Punjabis had been jailed by the junta, while the Punjabi leadership felt that Zulfikar's young and inexperienced daughter Benazir had hijacked the movement as a personal vehicle for her political ambition. The MRD was not strong enough to overcome its internal strife. The movement backfired, destroying the resistance movement at large, in two crucial ways.

The success of the civil disobedience movement in Sindh but not in the Punjab enhanced the politics of regionalism and 'deepened the cleavage between the two provinces'[7], a dangerous harbinger of provincial discord that would last for many years to come. More importantly, by agitating solely about democracy and the necessity of elections, but not addressing the ethics of military rule and the political oppression and human rights violations of the regime, by 1983 the MRD had convinced General Zia that steps had to be taken to publicly legitimize his rule once and for all.

In December 1984, Zia held a referendum on his Islamization programme, linking the referendum to his right to remain in power. The question placed before the voters was insideously worded: 'If you agree that Islamic laws be brought in in conformity with the Koran, then say YES. If the results of the referendum are positive it will mean that you approve of General Zia ul Haq continuing as President for another five years.'[8] The referendum produced a ludicrously inflated 98 per cent[9] approval rating for the President and his policies. The MRD, afraid of upsetting the religious parties, did not campaign against the Islamization programme but decided simply to boycott the vote, a pointless exercise.

With the 'support' of the people behind him, Zia called for elections in early 1985, which in turn created the plausible façade of a new civilian order and effectively legitimized the General's rule. The MRD boycotted the elections and put itself out of the running. It had failed to dislodge the dictator and had pushed Zia in the right direction – he had taken it up on its suggestion and had begun to 'democratize'.

By the time the new government took power, Zia allowed the head of the MRD and newly appointed chairperson of the PPP, Benazir, to return to Pakistan from self-imposed exile in the UK. Benazir had taken a leave of absence from Pakistan. Her brothers, living in Kabul, disagreed with her choice. They weren't given the option of taking sabbaticals and re-energizing, but she had taken their father's death badly and had suffered ear infections under house arrest so they acquiesced and said nothing when she went to London. There was, however, a tremendous amount of friction over Benazir and her position at the centre of the MRD's and PPP's politics. Her takeover of her father's party was not subject to a party vote but was carried out unilaterally by Benazir herself, with her bereaved mother Nusrat as the symbolic head of the party. Nana, Della's sister, told me over dinner in Mykonos that she understood there was tension over Benazir's ambition, even at this early stage. 'There was friction between Mir and her. He loved her; he stepped aside for her. He said to us once, "She wants to be the political heir, so OK, I'll move aside."'[10]

The advisors to the new Prime Minister, Junejo, had in fact, pushed him to allow Benazir back into the country telling him and General Zia that 'Benazir was more a threat to the MRD than to the government'.[11] The advisors proved to be right. By 1985 the MRD was politically deflated; not only had it failed to unify the varied resistance movements, but it had broken them. Unwittingly, by constantly insisting on the importance of democratic government, but not tackling the abuses of the military regime or the incompatibility of the armed forces and an egalitarian system of rule, the MRD had given Zia the tools to strengthen his hold on power and neutralise the opposition to his junta. Democracy, after all, has always just been a word, a catch-phrase or election slogan – not a style of governance – in Pakistan.

By the time I was born, my father and uncle had decided to leave Kabul and the process of packing up had started. In the summer of 1982 it had become clear that the Bhutto brothers could no longer remain in Afghanistan. The fallout from the hijacking and the independence Murtaza and Shahnawaz exercised in marrying locals and expanding their activities meant that they lost the support of their hosts.

'We noticed that the Afghan authorities had started hindering our communications with Pakistan,' Suhail concludes, 'which was the very reason we were in Afghanistan to begin with – to be close to Pakistan. Our travel papers were being held up by official delays, we were living in an official government residence, being guarded by their security, using their driver, and things had become tense. We told them, "Your own situation has become difficult, so we'll go and return when things settle down." They were upset because we were choosing to leave and they understood that we were doing so on a protest note.'[12] But there was no animosity in their farewell. Nooristani, who had chiefly dealt with Murtaza, was sad to see him and Shah go but didn't try to stop them.

The hundred or so people who had joined the brothers in Kabul began to pack up their lives and prepare to be resettled under the protection of a new state. It was decided that Libya would be the next port of call. 'In those days, Libya was a hub for political dissidents,' Suhail remembers. 'Palestinians, Bangladeshis, Filipinos, you name it

– any spot in the world that suffered some kind of conflict or the other had nationals living in Tripoli.'¹³ Murtaza travelled first to Libya to speak with President Gaddafi, who had been an ally to the Bhutto family during Zulfikar's arrest. Suhail accompanied him on the trip and together they decided that while Murtaza and his family would settle in Damascus, Suhail and Shahnawaz would look after the organization in Tripoli.

Shahnawaz would look after the base as he had done in Afghanistan; he had become the most comfortable with the work. He had built a rapport with the many men who came to find a place in the struggle against the dictatorship back home and busied himself training the young cadres in military and security techniques. Murtaza, as the elder brother and the head of the organization, was the diplomat. He had spent his years writing, negotiating and trying to influence Pakistan's standing in the world through various projects – including the documentary that he had started while living in London. Suhail opted to stay with Shahnawaz, who moved to Tripoli with his wife shortly after their daughter Sassi was born. By January 1983, Suhail's wife Kamar and two sons, Bilal and Ali, had joined him in Libya. They would, however, barely last three months in northern Africa.

'It was the worst experience,' Suhail says. 'Kabul was a lively city, frankly speaking, but everything in Libya was upside down.'¹⁴ He wobbles his hand as if to illuminate how topsy-turvy life in Libya felt. 'The leadership, Gaddafi, was very sympathetic to us, very kind and very welcoming, but there was no structure in place, it was too sensitive.' With their families, Shah and Suhail lived in separate villas at the Shati Andalous Hotel near the sea. When I tell Suhail that their new digs sound picturesque, imagining the Libya I've seen in travel magazines, he sighs and smiles. 'Communication with the outside world was completely cut off, there were no newspapers because of the government's strict censorship, we couldn't understand anything on TV since it was all in Arabic. We were totally in the dark, we felt stranded. It was too bureaucratic.' He pauses and then adds, as an afterthought, 'It was also a *dry* country.'

It's strange to me that Libya would seem such an unattractive choice after living in war-torn Kabul, but Shah and Suhail couldn't stand living there. 'They ran a strange economy,' Suhail continued, keen to convince me how miserable they had been in Tripoli. 'You couldn't always find staples like eggs or cigarettes in the market. When, once in a blue moon, they'd turn up at the supermarket you'd see people walking out with eight or ten cartons of eggs at a time. It was really strange.' But they had changed too, these young men. They had seen their dreams of a Che Guevara-style resistance movement fail, they had seen their efforts, romantic but misguided, used against them. They had been swallowed up by negative public opinion. Years earlier they had been lauded as heroic young men trying to fight the abrogation of a constitution and now they had become simplified – they were called terrorists, derided as landless fighters. 'We don't want a medal for what we did,' Suhail says, 'but we were at the frontline of resistance to Zia. We weren't lobbying State Department officials in Washington or attending luncheons in London. We spent our lives struggling.'[15]

Eventually, it was decided that Shah and Suhail would join Murtaza in Syria. All three men had families now. They were no longer rebels alone in the hills. They had schools to consider and nappies to change. They spent a sleepy two years in Syria attending to the banalities of family life. The fuel that ran the resistance movement in Pakistan had run out, compromised by the political incompetence of the MRD. Journalists were tired of fighting a regime that showed no signs of weakening, aided as it was by American money and support. Students gave up their stone throwing and went back to classes, eager to earn degrees that would get them out of Pakistan. Writers who had made their names through subversive plays and articles had bills to pay. The same was true for Al Zulfikar. It existed, but only in spirit.

The brothers raised their families and did their best to pursue normal lives as the guests of President Hafez al Assad, the lion of Damascus. But, towards the end of 1984, the tedium of life as a wandering exile began to affect Shahnawaz. He started to feel frustrated. He was only twenty-six years old and had a young wife and a two-year-old daughter. He had always been the most free-spirited member of the family. It couldn't have been easy for Shah to adapt to living as a political refugee in a claustrophobic South Asian enclave, three families stuck on top of one another. It probably wasn't fair to him either. He considered the idea of moving, of settling in Europe for a while and giving his family a small chance of freedom. It was to France, near where Shah had studied as a college student, that he wanted to go.

'When it came to Shah,' Suhail says, 'Murtaza always treated him like his beloved younger brother. He adored him. So when Shah spoke about leaving, Mir must have put his feelings aside about the danger of being in Europe to allow Shah to make the move.'[16] Suhail's voice is tight and he drags hard on his cigarette. I sense that he might not be talking for Murtaza when he speaks, obviously upset about Shah's decision to move to France. I push. Why was it a bad choice? Why was France more dangerous than the other countries the brothers had been living in? Suhail puts out his cigarette, and looks straight at me. 'The mistake was moving to France. Absolutely. In Afghanistan the brothers were guarded, they were protected. In Damascus too. But in France Shah was living out in the open. He was exposed. Once the brothers had made the decision to fight the junta, once they went to Afghanistan to struggle against the dictatorship, they were marked men.'[17]

{ 12 }

What happened next is still a mystery. What we do know is this: in October of 1984, Shah and his wife Raehana and daughter Sassi left Damascus and moved to the south of France. The move was a welcome change of pace for the young couple. In Kabul Raehana had been a young student from a diplomatic family with ties to the ancien régime. Her husband was a guest of the Soviet-backed communist government. They were in their early twenties, younger than I am now writing this. They had married against the wishes of Shah's family, who were not happy that their son rush into a union so soon after his engagement to Nurseli, whom they had known and happily approved of, had been broken off. They had, by all accounts, a passionate and intense marriage. They were hindered not only by their families, but also by politics. Raehana had been a vocal mujahideen supporter, Shah an opponent. Fully ensconced in their anti-imperialist ideology, Shah and his brother believed that the United States not only had a hand in their father's execution, but was still propping up Zia's military junta.

France gave the couple their first opportunity to experience life on their own, away from divisive politics and away from their families. They settled into an apartment in Nice, a pleasant flat on the second floor of a building on the Avenue de Roi Albert. Shah travelled often to Syria to meet Murtaza, but kept his visits short and returned eagerly to France, where the family led as normal a life as their situation allowed.

In the summer of 1985, we met for a family reunion in Nice. It was the first time for years that the family had all been together at the same time. Nusrat came from Geneva, where she had been living in exile, Murtaza travelled from Damascus, and Benazir – along with Sanam – came from London.

The brothers were overjoyed to see each other – they had been virtually inseparable since their father was executed and they relished the opportunity to be together again. Murtaza and Shah shared jokes from their childhood, a popular tease being Shah's insistence during the family's state visit to China on posing with his arm bent at the elbow and folded across his midriff, imitating Chou En-lai, who was forced to hold his arm that way due to an old war wound. We moved into Shah's flat and planned to be in Nice for the month of July.

When we arrived, Murtaza noticed that Shah had put his name outside the building, on the intercom board. It troubled him that Shah had used his real name and he reproached him for it – you mustn't advertise your location, this is France, Murtaza told his brother. There was no protection provided by the government in Nice, no local officials were charged with minding the safety of the Bhutto brothers. But it seemed a small lapse and the summer began happily.

Our families spent afternoons on the beach, lounging in the sun. Shah, ever the athlete, would go jet-skiing or waterskiing, waving to us on the shore and fooling around with funny gestures – he could do anything. He was twenty-six years old and at the peak of his physical strength. I remember him waterskiing behind a perilously fast boat, lifting one hand behind his head and giggling when everyone gasped, but keeping his balance. He was the life of the family, the cherished youngest child and second son. He had a spirit that was upbeat, no matter the situation, a personality that always managed to shine in company.

Sassi and I were both three years old, I the elder by three months. We took particular delight in standing on the balcony of Shah's second-floor flat and pouring cartons of juice into the ground-floor flat's swimming pool, running away in hysterics when its owner came blazing out of the apartment, cursing us in French for having turned her pool into a cocktail of orange and apple juice. The balcony was our territory, it was where we often sat, on a small rocking horse that had been put out there, presumably to distract us from the pool. We wore 1980s sunglasses in neon colours that made us feel like rock stars and we shared a bracelet, a pink and white bangle, that we passed back and forth depending on whose turn it was to wear. We looked, double cousins as we were, strangely similar. We both wore our hair in shoulder-length bobs, heavily fringed. My hair was dark brown, Sassi's light brown. But we were almost twins, as we saw it anyway.

I used to grab on to Uncle Shah's leg when he passed by, to annoy Sassi, and scream, '*My* Papa,' knowing that she was too gentle to claw at my father and do the same. When Sassi would sniffle I would run back to my father's leg, hang on to it and declare, '*My* Papa *too*.' Sassi claims I used to bite her cheeks, but I don't remember that. I adored her and thought of her as my own. We were surrounded by grown-ups and were aware, with whatever limited understanding we possessed as children, that things around us were dangerous. We knew we had a grandfather who had been killed. We knew we didn't live in our own country, a far-away place we only heard the adults talk about. We knew that things weren't as they should be and so we stuck together and created a small make-believe world that entertained and fascinated us.

In the evenings, the family would eat out at restaurants, pulling tables together to accommodate our numbers, and the conversation and food would roll on late into the night. Inevitably, Murtaza and Shah would steal away and go for a drink at the Carlton Hotel, taking advantage of the freedom that the south of France afforded them, coming home in the small hours of the morning.

On 17 July, we spent the day swimming at the Port La Galère. A barbecue was planned for the evening and Shah and Raehana stayed at the flat getting food ready for dinner. Papa took Sassi and me to the beach and we spent most of the day splashing around in the water and enjoying ourselves. At the flat, Raehana sent Shah to the grocery to pick up some basics; we were going to eat out on the beach and there were going to be a lot of mouths to feed. He returned with drinks and disposable cutlery, then watched TV and smoked a cigar while we got ready for the night ahead.

There were several of us there that night on the beach at La Napoule. Shah and Murtaza drove around town picking up various members of the family and dropping them off at the beach. By 9.30 the party was complete and the revelry began. Joonam, as I now called my grandmother Nusrat, brought salad and yoghurt and cucumbers in the Iranian style. Someone else brought ice-cream for dessert. The grill was fired up and Shah began to cook the chops and meat brochettes over the open fire. I remember him squeezing lemon onto the meat and laughing when the juice got in his eye. He continued to cook, wary of the flying lemon juice, squinting theatrically for the pictures someone took as he barbecued. I remember the beach was empty that night, except for our rowdy family. I also remember that there was graffiti spray-painted on the wall near the cars. Papa told me later that Joonam had been lively that night, bringing herself out of the depression she had suffered from ever since Zulfikar was killed. She spoke in Farsi to her relatives and in English to the rest of the family and, at some point out of nowhere, said that she hoped she would die before her children; she couldn't imagine the pain of losing one more loved one.

The barbeque lasted till around 11 p.m., when Murtaza and Shahnawaz got into separate cars to drive their relatives home. I was with my father. I don't know where Sassi was. When Shahnawaz and Raehana reached Avenue de Roi Albert they were both angry; they'd had an argument on the way. Shah wanted to carry on to the casino in town and Raehana didn't, she wanted to go to the Whiskey a Go Go nightclub.

By the time they reached the lobby of the apartment block, things had become ugly. Papa asked what was going on and Raehana told him to mind his own business. He reacted angrily and expected Shah to step in to calm his wife down. But by then words were being exchanged between my father and Raehana and Shah was caught in the middle. Raehana asked my father and her sister to pack their bags and get out of her house. Papa swore angrily, he had been insulted.

He stormed into the apartment to pack our things. I remember the row. I remember wishing that everyone would stop screaming, I remember being scared and tired. Within a few minutes our clothes had been thrown into our suitcases and we drove over to Joonam's flat in a nearby neighbourhood.

Shah took his wife and daughter into their apartment and tried to calm the situation down. Raehana and Sassi went to their bedroom and Shah brought his young daughter a bottle of milk. He settled them to sleep and moved to the living room. Meanwhile Papa and some other family members left for the casino and spent the rest of the evening there together, leaving at five in the morning – closing time – and going to the nearby Manhattan restaurant before driving home. Papa reached us around 6.30 in the morning and went to sleep. What happened next is a mystery.

On the morning of the 18th, Papa got up and ran some errands in town. He picked up a copy of the *Herald Tribune* and returned to his mother's flat. At a quarter to two in the afternoon Raehana rang the doorbell. She was very distressed, and initially Papa was not in the mood to receive her. Joonam saw that something was amiss and asked Murtaza to come and talk to her. 'Something is wrong,' Raehana told them. 'At that moment, I thought Shah must have hurt himself doing something in the house,' Murtaza would later tell the police. No one will remember later on if the word 'overdose' was used or if it was not. Joonam immediately called the police and gave them Shah's address.

Papa got into Shah's metallic green Mercedes that Raehana had driven over with Sassi at her side and took them back to Shah's flat. On the way, another family member who was with them in the car asked how Shah was. Everyone remembers Raehana saying he was blue. Murtaza would recall being frightened and asked her angrily if he was dead or alive. The thought hadn't occurred to him until then. She replied that she didn't know, she had been too scared to look.

They entered the apartment and found Shah's body lying face down on the living-room floor, between the sofa and the coffee table. 'When I saw him,' Murtaza would later say, 'I knew he was dead.'

Shah had blue marks on his chest and his face had already begun to turn a blue-ish black. He was wearing the trousers he had on from the previous evening, but no shirt. He was dead.

When Murtaza saw the blue marks on his brother's body, he knew something unnatural had happened. He suspected poison. He directed someone to go downstairs to see if the police had arrived, and began to search the apartment. A year earlier, the brothers had been given small vials of poison to take if they were ever apprehended by Zia's authorities. Nobody knows where they got the poison from; they kept that to themselves. The small bottles were sealed with metal and contained a colourless liquid. If mixed with another liquid, they were told, the poison would be undetectable. If taken, they were warned, the toxins would work quickly and they would be dead within minutes.

The police arrived and immediately began to inspect the flat. Murtaza looked for the poison in all the rooms, but found nothing. He searched the kitchen cupboards, careful not to move anything. A doctor, who came hours too late to save Shah, was standing in the kitchen when Murtaza opened the rubbish bin and found under several tissues a small glass bottle labelled 'PENTREXIDE'. He gave the bottle to the doctor and informed the police of what he had found. Murtaza told the police that Shah had already survived four attempts on his life. He told them that they had enemies. He asked them if it was possible that the flat had been broken into. He told them that he didn't believe, not even for a second, that Shah had committed suicide.

Before Shah's body could be taken away, Murtaza had one more thing to do. He had to tell their mother. He got back into the car and drove to Nusrat's apartment. She had been calling and asking what had happened, and had been told repeatedly, 'Mir will tell you, he'll come and tell you himself.' Mir reached his mother's flat alone. She opened the door, hysterical with worry. He held her by the arms and told her that Shah was dead. 'Mummy, Gogi's gone,' he said, using the family's childhood nickname for Shah. Nusrat fell weeping into his arms and demanded he take her to see him. We all went back to the apartment, even me. There was no one to look after Sassi and me, so we were taken back to the crime scene with the rest of the family.

Sassi had been the one to find her father that afternoon. 'I've been haunted by flashbacks of discovering my father's lifeless body,' she told me twenty-four years later. 'It is the only clear memory I possess of him. It was so long ago, but I remember it vividly, staring at him lying there, waiting for him to wake. It was my duty to wake him up every morning. But this particular morning was far from routine, because my father wouldn't wake up and grab me and kiss me or toss me in the air as he usually did.'[1] Raehana later said that it had been her daughter's frightened voice that woke her up that day. She heard Sassi in the living room calling, 'Papa, Papa,' over and over again. When she found her, Sassi was sitting next to her father's lifeless body trying to wake him up.

The initial investigation found specks of vomit on the floor of the bathroom attached to the couple's bedroom. The police confirmed that they had found poison in Shah's system, that it was strong and that it was designed to leave a residue in the victim's nostrils, not in the blood or internal organs. But who administered the poison, no one can tell me.

Theories circulated quickly. There was the obvious – General Zia had ordered the hit on Shah's life. Though Murtaza was the elder brother and technically in charge of the organization leading the attacks on the military regime, he was regarded as the diplomat. There was a strong perception that Shah was the more aggressive of the two brothers; he was, after all, in charge of security and training. Murtaza always believed Zia's government had ordered the assassination. But how they carried it out was harder to explain.

Of course others assumed that he had committed suicide, a claim furiously denied by Murtaza. He told reporters and policemen that Shah 'had a very courageous character. He knew how to face life. He was never scared and always moved without a bodyguard. He knew how to face all types of situations.' He told the investigators that his brother was happy, successful and financially settled, and had never at any point in their lives together mentioned the notion of killing himself. There was no suicide note, no indication from the previous night or recent past that he had even contemplated the idea. Nusrat also denied the possibility of suicide. It was a sin in Islam to take one's own life. She never believed Shah, who had faced his father's death so bravely, would reach a point so far beyond hope that he would kill himself. But others felt differently. Fowzia told the police that she felt Shah had killed himself and that the Bhutto family was too proud to ever admit it. It was an assumption that hurt the family gravely.

And then, there was another theory, the main one. I have spent my life believing that Shah's wife, Raehana, had something to do with her husband's death. The autopsy placed the time of Shah's death in the early hours of the morning, approximately nine hours passed before the family and police were called to the scene. It didn't escape anyone's attention that Raehana had not raised the alarm until well past the time of death. This is where things get tricky. The police statements that Raehana made still exist and her testimony shakes everything up. It is rambling and incoherent. I have read the statements, both in French and in English. I have had them translated and retranslated. I have read them backwards and forwards and I still don't know what to make of them.

My own experience with the police leaves me with little trust in confessions obtained under detention. I don't believe that there are truths only the police can beat out of us. I cannot use Rachana's statements for this reason. I cannot say with any certainty that I know those police files to be an honest indication of the facts.

I grew up with my family's belief that Raehana had been involved in some way. She hadn't called for help in time. She hadn't reacted fast enough. She had a rocky relationship with her husband. She'd thrown Murtaza out of the apartment the night before. There had always been distrust and dislike. In Raehana's police testimony, there is a suggestion that she did not help Shah as he lay dying, but a clear assertion that she did not kill him.

Raehana was detained and spent time in jail in Nice. She was questioned over a period of several months and then released. She then left

France and flew to California to be with her family who were already looking after Sassi. It was the last time any of us saw her.

It was on the basis of Raehana's statements to the police that Murtaza and Benazir filed a case against her in France, on behalf of the Bhutto family, citing the country's Good Samaritan law. Jacques Vergès, the controversial French lawyer, would be the family's advocate in the case and he would secure a conviction passed in absentia against Raehana for not coming to the aid of a dying man.

I remember my father's growing doubts over the years as to what had happened that night in Nice. He was often silent when my aunts would be screaming blue murder in reference to Raehana. I remember that Papa was always unsure of what had really happened. But by then it was too late. Too much time, too much anger, too much sadness had passed. He blamed himself for not being there that night to protect his younger brother. That always stayed with him. Papa lost weight. He lost his smile and his ability to joke and laugh. Joonam too, I remember, took the death like a weight upon her heart. She was never the same again.

Sassi and I would not see each other for another twenty-three years. As children, we exchanged occasional letters and spoke on the phone once in a while but our contact was minimal. We both dreamed of meeting again one day, of our fathers' joy at knowing we would be reunited someday, but it never seemed very likely. Then, on the night of my twenty-sixth birthday, a month after I had started work on this book, I got an email from her. It turned my night upside down. It had been many years since we had been in touch, at least eleven, and I didn't know what to expect. I wrote back and asked for her phone number. We spoke several days later. We were adults now. We had graduated from high school, had gone to college and had embarked on postgraduate studies. We were no longer children. We spoke and eased ourselves into knowing each other again.

Sassi wanted to come to Pakistan. She wanted to pray at her father's grave. She had never been here before, never seen an inch of her father's country. We started planning immediately. We would have to get her to Karachi clandestinely, as there were many on our aunt's side of the family who would not like the idea of us finally getting together and trading stories. We had been kept apart during Benazir's lifetime and it wasn't going to be easy to bypass what remained of her legacy. We planned to meet in Abu Dhabi, at the airport. I would fly to London first, pretending I was on an ordinary trip. Sassi would book a flight from New York, where she was studying, to the Gulf, a move that would avoid any suspicion should Pakistani officials be on the lookout for a Bhutto entering Pakistan. I would book our onward flights and bring her home. No one knew Sassi was coming to Karachi except for Mummy and Zulfi. She hadn't told anyone and neither had I.

We had planned to meet at a specific point in Abu Dhabi's tiny airport, but bumped into each other before we reached it. We recognized each other instantly though we had grown to look like different people. My hair was curly and medium-length and hers was wavy and long. She brought a bracelet for us to share. As soon as we were on our flight to Karachi we began to compare notes and found too many unsettling similarities.

The next two weeks were a blur of travel between Karachi and Larkana. We visited Shah's grave and Sassi was overwhelmed by the emotion of finally being next to her father again. We took her to her father's house, the one in Naudero that Zufikar had hoped Shah would live in and contest elections from. It was occupied by Benazir's widower now and had been by her before him. The seat had been contested by Benazir in 1988. It was the seat from which she ascended to the office of the Prime Minister. We couldn't enter the house. We were enemies to those inside. Later, sitting in the room that our fathers once shared as they did everything else, we broached the topic of her mother. I told her what little I had heard growing up, that the family blamed Raehana for Shah's death. Sassi wasn't surprised to hear that. She had grown up under the weight of those accusations. But what she had to say had never occurred to me before. It was then, for the first time in my short life, that I heard the other side.

'The version of events commonly accepted about my father's death angered and frustrated me,' Sassi said. 'I knew the truth and I wanted it to be known that my mother was in no way responsible for my father's death. But I also knew that there was too much power, too many other forces that would prevent this from coming out early on.' I hadn't ever considered that there might be something else to the story; it wasn't what I was expecting to hear. 'She was an easy target,' Sassi said, speaking of her mother. 'If she were truly culpable, why did they let her go? And why were no other suspicions investigated? We certainly did not benefit from his death in any form.'

They were all good points. Why had Raehana been let go if she was involved? By all accounts she was not kept long as a suspect. She had been released and allowed to leave the country, surely not standard procedure for a murder suspect. But then who was responsible? I asked. And the answer, the possibility of who was to blame, at least indirectly in terms of benefiting from Shah's death, was nothing I had ever imagined before. It was scandalous, mind-blowing. But I knew, from experience, that anything is possible in the Bhutto family.

━━━━━◆••◆━━━━━

Sassi and I spent several months together after that. She took time off school and we travelled and spent time in Karachi together, living as our fathers once did in their annexed bachelor pad. We talked about Sassi's parents often and sat until late at night trying to understand what had happened to her father. 'My feelings concerning my father's death?' Sassi responded when I put the question to her in an email. 'I am angry, hurt, saddened. I regret not having been able to form more memories with him. I am angry that his life was taken from him, my mother, and me at such a young age. I am hurt that my mother had to endure so much pain. At a time when everyone should have formed a cohesive union, divisions were created instead. I am perplexed that there was no formal investigation into his death in Pakistan. It seems quite strange and convenient.'

I flew to Paris in the spring of 2009 on my quest to find someone who could tell me what happened that night in France, and finally made contact with Jacques Vergès. I had set up an appointment to meet in his office on a nondescript road in the heart of the capital. I had met Vergès before. I was maybe four years old and had sat in his office while my father and he discussed Shah's case. I remember he had small boxes on his desk that I busied myself opening and closing while they spoke of the case against Raehana. So it was that I found myself being received again, this time in a different office, by the man who might – I imagined – be my best bet for some definitive answers.

Except for his deafness, Vergès, now in his eighties, showed no sign of his age. He looked just as I remembered him, a slight man with thinning grey hair, dapperly dressed. He ushered me into his office. 'I was a good friend of Mir's,' he said to me in his thick French accent. 'I was very sorry to hear when he was killed.' I thanked him quietly, trembling and trying to appear at least nominally professional. 'And Benazir,' Vergès said and my heart thumped. People did this to me all the time. 'What a shame about your father, but Benazir oh what a tragedy *her* loss has been.' I imagined that Vergès was about to launch into a eulogy I had heard many times before. But he didn't. He shook his head and muttered an expletive. He had known her well and his disparaging remark caught me slightly off guard. He patted my shoulder and directed me towards two chairs. I laughed nervously and followed Vergès into his office.

We sat facing each other in front of his beautifully elaborate desk and spoke for a minute or two about my father and mother and his memories of them both. Finally, I plucked up the courage to ask about the case. 'I wanted to make a big scandal about Shah's murder,' Vergès said, 'but Benazir was against it. She didn't want to fight the CIA and the Pakistani Intelligence service, who your father was always convinced were behind his brother's death.'[2] Why not? I asked, genuinely curious. Vergès laughed again and made a face at me that I understood. Because she worked with them. Because her power was always based on their approval. Months before her death, reports now claim, Benazir contacted Blackwater, America's mercenary contractors, to provide the security for what would be her last election campaign. They declined. But my father, I asked, what did he think? 'He was convinced and was prepared to make a stir, but his sister, she stopped it.' Nobody believed it was suicide, Vergès confirmed, it just wasn't a possibility.

Gathering my strength, I asked about Raehana. Was there a chance she wasn't involved? 'The case against Raehana was difficult,' Vergès said, pausing as he spoke, speaking in English for my benefit. 'There was no concrete proof, only suspicions.' I mentioned what I had read in the police files, mentioning that as far as I understood it she had raised the red flag herself in her testimony. Is there a chance that there was something else at play? That Raehana, a young twenty-three year old widow could have been coerced into making statements that would ultimately backfire against her? Again, Vergès shrugged his shoulders. My head was spinning. I hadn't expected this. I had expected that Vergès would say to me in all certainty that X is the guilty party and Y is not. But he wasn't saying that to me. He wasn't at all. I was sitting on the edge of my finely woven antique chair so Vergès could hear me clearly and I lowered my voice, uselessly, to ask the unthinkable, remembering what Sassi had told me months before: why did Benazir leave the case so skewed by refusing to fight it all the way? Did she have something to gain by not pursuing it? My hands were shaking so hard I could barely write. 'It's not impossible,' Vergès replied cautiously.

Why? I asked, edging closer towards him and willing myself not to whisper. It was like blasphemy, this idea, how was it possible? Why was it not unthinkable? 'It's clear that when Mir and Shah decided to take this action,' Vergès said, referring to AZO, 'that Benazir would not approve. She was on another track – one with Western cooperation, especially with the USA. They were both against it, fighting it openly. I am not surprised that it would benefit her for one brother to be disposed of before the other.' Vergès's words hung in the air between us. I felt nauseous. Why was everything in this family so complicated? Why was it so ugly, so violent? Earlier, when he had spoken about my father, Vergès asked me about our situation in Pakistan. I told him life was difficult there, but that we remained. 'Imagine, to be killed by your own sister,' he muttered and I felt that I might cry. I nodded and told him that we had been heartbroken by my father's murder. But when we began to discuss Shahnawaz and Benazir's name came up I had asked what role she had played, if she even had a role ... We spoke about how she did not do right by Shah's family, how she had usurped his rights. And there was that word again. It stung in my ears. But why Shah first? He wasn't in charge, my father was. 'In her mind, what her two brothers were doing wasn't helping her,' Vergès calmly speculated. 'Among the two brothers, the strongest brother was Mir. Perhaps it was necessary to get Shah out of the way because he was the weaker one.'

I sat quietly in front of Vergès. I had planned to meet friends after my appointment with him, expecting that I might need some comforting. I was going to cancel now. I couldn't see anyone. Vergès watched me for a moment or two. 'You look like Mir,' he said and I thought I saw tears in his eyes. I smiled. But my heart was thumping. 'When did Benazir become Prime Minister?' Vergès asked, returning to our topic. 'Three years later,' I replied. He nodded his head and said nothing. 'She never opened an investigation into her brother's murder,' I said out loud, thinking back to what Sassi had told me earlier. 'Ahh well,' Vergès sighed, leaning back in his chair, 'perhaps she already knew.'

{ 13 }

Back in Damascus, our permanent home after Shah's murder, Murtaza was lost in grief. 'I saw Mir after the summer we lost Shah,' Suhail remembers, having witnessed the death from afar. 'He had lost so much weight. I hadn't seen him so skinny since we were kids in the seventies. It was a huge blow to him.'[1] Our two-bedroom apartment had once been a home full of people. Shah and his family lived on the floor above us, Suhail, Kamar and their two sons were permanent features in both flats. And all of a sudden, there was no one. Shah was gone, Raehana and Sassi were absent, and then the Sethis moved. It was just my parents and me. Papa and I lived alone in the Mezzeh building like lost people, like vagabonds.

By the time summer was spent, taking Shah with it, and autumn grew near, Papa and Fowzia began to fight. They couldn't live with each other any more, it had become too complicated. Murtaza had lost too much, and his wife was a reminder of what he had lost. When Papa decided that we would leave, that he would file for divorce, he sat me down and explained things to me. I was only three years old at the time, but I knew what had happened had to do with Uncle Shah. I knew it wasn't fixable. But I also knew that my father was the centre of my little world and I remember taking the news of divorce with as little fuss as possible.

Later on, I was told, I sometimes sidled up to women with long dark hair in railway stations and bookstores, thinking they were Fowzia. I got confused at times and would follow women with long plaits. I don't remember that; I only remember my father telling me about the divorce. I remember wearing a woolly coat in those days, and learning new words. I learned the word divorce early; I knew what it meant and it sounded very grown-up to me.

It is hard for me to disconnect my feelings about Fowzia from the woman I encountered as a teenager and adult. I am scared, frightened even, of my biological mother. As a child I remember her moods, her unpredictable temperament, how beautiful she was and how much care she took of her hair, the dark kohl she would line her eyes with, how aware she was of her beauty. She would let me drink tea with her, sugary and diluted with milk, in the afternoons – I think that was our time together. But that's it. That's as far as my memories extend. Papa gave me my baths, read my bedtime stories, cut my hair, dressed me, and bought me boots that looked like his own polished shoes. I was a tomboy, as if to distance myself from Fowzia (I used to cut her lipsticks with scissors to trim their pointy, pyramid-like tips), and was a walking, talking devotee of my father.

Maybe it is my fault. Maybe my heart was too full and I never cleared it to make space for Fowzia. But even as a child, I think I tried. I remember one afternoon, it may have been morning, when Fowzia called me to her as she lay on the bed in our Damascus flat moaning loudly and tossing and turning. 'Tell your father to buy watermelon,' she slurred sleepily.

I left the room and and told him. Fowzia called me again, more loudly this time, yelling my name. Watermelons, she kept groaning, I need Mir to bring me watermelons. She seemed confused, in pain; she frightened me. I couldn't do anything about the watermelons she wanted so badly. I was only three years old at the time. I felt her getting angry at me. I didn't know how to control a situation I had no way of understanding and started to cry. Papa rushed into the room when he heard me sobbing. He came in and saw Fowzia sprawled on the bed. She'd taken something, too much of something, she was hurting. I was made to leave the room.

Fowzia didn't possess the strength that Papa radiated, which as a child I selfishly depended on. Our lives were too heightened, too fragile, for me to have consciously accepted otherwise. Fowzia was, I confess, always somewhat of a mystery to me when I was younger.

I didn't get her. She didn't get me. She was erratic. I found her exotic and dainty, but not strong, not calm.

When I was older, after my father had been killed, Fowzia turned up at my high school in Karachi and demanded to be let in. Mr Dewolf, the principal, pulled me out of my biology class and explained what was happening. A woman claiming to be my mother was in the main office insisting I be brought to her. I felt sick. Mr Dewolf took me to the guidance counsellor's office, where I called Mummy, who was on her way to Larkana. I don't want to see her, I said on the phone. 'See her,' Mummy replied. Papa had wanted to throw out the photographs of Fowzia in our family albums after the divorce; it was Mummy who persuaded him not to. She convinced Papa to keep the pictures, for me. 'See her,' Mummy said gently on the phone. I told her that I would only see Fowzia if she postponed her trip to Larkana and came to be with me. 'I'll be there in half an hour,' she said.

Mr Dewolf, whose soft-spoken wife was my French teacher, sent me to the nurse's office to wait for Mummy. 'We'll do whatever you want,' he assured me. 'Don't worry.' It had been Mr Dewolf who helped Mummy and me tell Zulfi that Papa had been killed the morning after the assassination. He understood what this surprise visit meant. In the nurse's office, patients were quietly returned to class and the beds emptied. I was brought into the infirmary's bathroom and the doors were doubly locked, as per my panicked suggestion. Mrs Ali, the school nurse and my friend, stood in the bathroom with me, coaching me to take deep breaths as she sent for my friends to come and help me get through the next half an hour.

When I finally saw Fowzia in Mr Dewolf's office, I wasn't comforted. 'Your father kidnapped you,' she snarled once she had given me a huge cellophane-wrapped gift basket. It was less than six months after his murder. 'I could have taken you back, you know?'

The drama of a ten-year-old divorce was being played out in front of Mr Dewolf, whom I had asked to stay in the meeting room with us. 'I knew people in the American military. They offered to bring you back for me, by helicopter. Your father could have done nothing to stop them,' Fowzia continued. 'But I didn't, for your sake.'

Thank you? I didn't know what to say. I was shocked, scared, and so, so angry.

Call me Mom, Fowzia kept insisting. I said I didn't want to see her. Mummy nudged me under the table. I said I had lots of homework now that I was at high school and looked to Mr Dewolf for support. Mummy said I could do it at night. I relented, on the condition that Fowzia ('Call me Mom!' she bellowed, aggravated by my stubbornness) kept our relationship private and out of the media. She agreed.

That week, after I baulked and refused to see her, Fowzia gave press conferences about my 'kidnapping' and my brainwashing at the hands of my evil 'stepmother' from Bilawal House, Benazir and Zardari's Karachi home. She called Mummy a maid whom Papa hadn't loved but had married to take care of his child. She called Zulfi my 'half-brother', and said I was just like her. Fowzia wrote open letters to me in all the English language newspapers and filed a case for my custody in the Pakistani courts. The school librarian, a kind British woman, took the newspapers off their racks every morning and hid them from me so I wouldn't see Fowzia's latest salvo as I did my home-work in the library. I employed a lawyer and told Fowzia that I didn't want to be with her, that I would never leave my family for her, a virtual stranger. 'You'll forget about them in two weeks,' she assured me and gave me on bottle of vanilla-scented nailpolish. I am, I suppose, in some recesses of my 27-year-old being, still afraid of Fowzia.

———◆◆◆◆———

But the divorce was not the largest part of my small life; larger than everything else was the gap that Shah's absence created.

I had seen Uncle Shah's body. I don't remember it. But after Papa had told his mother that her son was dead, he took her back to the apartment. There was no one to look after us, so and Sassi and I went too.

'It stayed with you for a long time,' Mummy tells me twenty-three years later while we move around in the kitchen late at night one evening looking for something to eat. 'You remembered seeing your uncle face down on the carpet and nobody imagined how much it had affected you, but one afternoon, months later, you found your father napping in the bedroom in Damascus and he was lying down like Shah had been, on his stomach, his face covered, and you shook him awake, crying and screaming at him to get up. That's how we knew. You thought he was dead, like Shah.' I have no memory of seeing my uncle's body, none at all. But for years, sleeping in the same bed as my father, I would wake up at night to check on him and to make sure he was breathing.

Papa was consumed by sorrow. He lived for a while, it seemed, only for me, to feed me and bathe me and put me to sleep. But once in a while I caught him absorbed, unable to break through to the idea of life. One night, he was sitting in what would become his office in the apartment, a small room with a glass bookshelf covering the windows with white curtains behind them. Papa was sitting quietly, running his hands through his hair as he did whenever he was nervous or upset. I could tell something was wrong. I brought him a toy, a small Fisher Price computer set that had hologrammed images of fish and birds and turtles that would change every time you pushed one of the clunky computer keys. I showed Papa a few images, thinking it would cheer him up, but it didn't. I tiptoed closer to him and put my head on his lap. Papa, what's wrong? I asked him. He tried hard to smile at me and find a place from which to begin. Without Shah, Murtaza was all alone.

They had been closer to each other than to any of their other siblings. Shah possessed a lightness of spirit that came with his age and Murtaza was constantly taken by his younger brother's effervescent personality. Shah's joy was contagious. They were so different, but direct complements of each other. Where Shah was spontaneous, Murtaza was patient; when Shah was melancholy, Murtaza was hopeful. They were more than just brothers, tied by blood, they were comrades. Companions.

Shah's death extinguished the incandescence that filtered through his family at a time when they had little else to be happy about. Papa was totally distraught. I had never seen him so overwhelmed by sadness before and would never again, not like this.

Life in exile was bearable when Murtaza had Shahnawaz to commiserate with. His company made the long nights in strange lands pass easily. Together, they returned home often, in their jokes, their language, their memories of their father and his world. They shared that same exile's dream – the dream of returning home, one day, one day . . .

Papa's eyes welled with tears. There was nothing to break the silence, no one to explain for him. The holographic fish were swimming across the screen as I waited. I'm sad, he said to me as I shifted uncomfortably next to him. Why? I asked, knowing the answer. I miss Uncle Shah, Papa said and I saw my father cry for the first time. He told me it was Shah's birthday. It was November. He would have been twenty-seven that night.

⬥⬥⬥

Life in Damascus passed easily. I was enrolled at a new American school, Damascus Community School, that had only recently opened and occupied the basement in a large building on the main Mezzeh road. Our apartment, in the older section of Mezzeh, was near a large mosque, the Jamia al Akram, and a sports centre. We were a building of refugees. With Shah and Suhail gone from the floor above us, Omar arrived, our new neighbour whose family had fallen foul of Saddam's Baathist Iraq. Omar became a friend; he was roughly Papa's age and they'd sometimes play squash together and spend time talking about their countries and what had happened to turn them into exiles. There were rarely people living in the garden flat at the bottom of the building, they came and went leaving us Pakistanis and Iraqis to rule the roost.

Benazir, who travelled between her frantic political life in Pakistan and downtime with Sanam in London, spent some time with us in Syria. I called her *Wadi bua* and she called me *Fah-tee* with an elongated *ah* sound. Wadi would come to stay and move into our spare bedroom. I always cried when she left and she would hug me, her hair smelling powdery soft and her skin moist and dewy, and promise she would come back soon. I used to sit on her lap and stare at the mole she had somewhere between the nape of her neck and her shoulders and sniffle quietly until she kissed me and lifted me off her. Wadi introduced me to Beatrix Potter and read me *Jemima Puddleduck* as I begged her to, over and over again.

Sometimes, I could sense the tension between Papa and Wadi. It was subtle, but it was there. Papa would speak to Wadi and she would just ignore him, turning cross when he continued. Or else he would talk to her in an exasperated tone and roll his eyes at me when he thought something she said queer. But I had my own relationship with my aunt; I was too domineering not to. As the family's firstborn grandchild, a girl with a precocious attitude and a mouth that never stopped running, I reminded Wadi of herself. I reminded other people of her too. 'You're just like your aunt,' was often used as both a compliment and an admonishment.

Wadi travelled to spend my birthday with me whenever she could, coming to Geneva and Damascus for important birthday celebrations when I was very young. We were both Geminis, though her birthday was later than mine. (It is a strange coincidence that the three women my father had serious relationships with, as well as his pushy eldest sister and his pushy daughter, were all Geminis. I'm not sure what that says about him. Or us.)

We were friends, Wadi and I. We liked all the same revolting sweets – mint chocolate chip ice-cream, candied apple skins, and marron glacé; I have never, till this day, met anyone else who likes the sugared chestnuts. We complained of the same problems, earaches mainly, and shared an eldest child's self-importance.

As a young insomniac, something of a Bhutto family curse, I would be scared to sleep by Papa with my very own personalised bogeyman. Dr Alfonso was a dentist with a large moustache and gelled black hair who came to naughty sleepless children and pulled out all their teeth. He had a nasal voice and would ring the doorbell and ask for me when I refused to go to bed. Within minutes of hearing Dr Alfonso's creepy voice I'd be out like a light. One morning after a midnight visit from the bogey doctor, I asked Wadi if she'd seen Dr Alfonso. What did he really look like? Was he carrying pliers?

Was she more scared of him than of Zia? 'What are you talking about Fah-tee?' she returned. The dentist, I pushed, I was asking about the evil dentist who rang our doorbell at night looking to pull out all my milk teeth. 'There's no Dr Alfonso!' Wadi said, laughing loudly. 'That was just your father standing outside in his pyjamas ringing the doorbell like a mad person.'

I didn't confront Papa until the next time he threatened me with Dr Alfonso. I was half sure Wadi had been joking.

I began pre-nursery school and made friends easily. My first friend was a boy named Ali who would come over at weekends and ask Papa to fry him eggs. His parents become good friends of our family and we built a small circle around us.

We lived as guests of President Hafez al Assad and were given a large white Chevrolet to drive around Damascus in. Papa would put Elvis Presley or Motown tapes on and we would drive to the Noura Supermarket in Abu Roumaneh singing along with the songs. We made special trips to Apollo's, near the Cham Hotel, to eat fresh pistachio and strawberry ice-cream and my father would always correct my pronunciation of the berry. It's stro-beh-ree, he would say, not strah-bry. I had an American accent that my grammar-school-educated father would try, somewhat unsuccessfully, to jerk out of me. It was also lih-bree not li-berry. Foh-tee not fortee. In the summer months, we'd go to Damascus's old city and buy cactus fruit, *sabarra* in Arabic, which Uncle Shah had introduced us to. We would keep them chilled in a bowl in the fridge until they were sufficiently cold for us to eat.

Sometimes, Papa would draw pictures of Zia and his Prime Minister on pieces of paper as he spoke to me about Pakistan. They would have hollow eyes and pointy moustaches. He would explain what had happened, first to my grandfather, then to my uncle. I would ask if we were safe and he would kiss me and tell me that we were safe here. At night, before we slept, Papa would kneel down and search under the bed. I asked him once what he was looking for and he told me he was just checking, making sure there was nothing that might hurt us under there. I assumed he meant a bomb. Or a man with a weapon.

I never felt brave enough to look, but always felt a wave of relief once Papa had completed the routine search.

It was a strange, beautiful childhood. In between the real-life games of hide and seek, the fear of being found, the danger of Shah's fate following us, and the various other threats that had become regular features in our lives, I almost wouldn't have known we were different, my father and I. We watched James Bond movies (Sean Connery was our favourite) and we ate chocolates in between meals. Sometimes as I slept, Papa would draw a moustache on me with green Magic Marker and I would wake up for school with a smudged swirly moustache that we would frantically rub off with hot water before my first bell rang. Papa read to me at bedtime, creating funny accents for each story character, and I used to interview him, using a toy microphone. I wanted to be a journalist then, I loved to write and read. He answered all my questions most seriously, taking the time to think between answers and pausing earnestly to watch me form my questions.

Once, watching television and seeing the news of the first Palestinian *intifada*, I studied my father's face and watched his expressions change. I asked him what was happening on the screen. Papa picked me up and put me on his lap. He called me Fatushki when he was being funny and joking around, Fati when we were being intellectual and serious and Fatima when he was angry at me. He told me that the people on TV, wearing black and white chequered cloths around their faces to protect them from the smoke that surrounded them, were like us. 'They don't have a home any more and they're living like refugees. Fati, you have to include them in your prayers when you talk to God and ask him to help them home, like us.' I thought about it for a minute and then asked, 'But if I tell God about the Palestinians and ask him to send them home, what if he forgets about us?'

I knew we were landless; I knew I came from somewhere else, somewhere I had never seen. Papa played old Sindhi folk songs, '*Ho Jamalo*' usually, when he felt like remembering the sounds of his home. He used *ajraks*, the traditional Sindhi block-printed shawls, as tablecloths and he cooked *achar gosht* much too spicily. We ate every meal,

271

whether it was *hummous* or pizza with a dish of *Sikharpuri achars*, pickles sent from Sindh, at the table. He didn't speak to me in Urdu all the time; we shared our lives and thoughts in English, but when he was excited about something he would lift his voice a pitch and the sound of another man would come out. He would call me a *drama-bazee*, tell me I was jumping around like a *junglee*. He taught me to walk on his back before his afternoon nap and then returned the favour with *thadara*, running his fingers up and down my back to put me to sleep.

In the mornings as he shaved I would beg to be included in the process. So Papa would lather up my face with a dollop of foam and he would take out a plastic Gillette razor for me, without a blade, and we'd stand in front of the bathroom sink shaving our faces together. We did this till I was six years old at least. I walked around in my father's boots and dressed in his shirts while picking out his ties and cufflinks for him in the morning. I even shined his shoes. Papa was a meticulous dresser and secretly found the act of shoe polishing boring though he considered it a necessary part of his routine, getting 'suited and booted' as he would say, borrowing the phrase from a childhood shared with Shah when valets would press their suits and prepare their evening clothes. And there I was, eager to do anything and everything for my father. I polished his boots with relish and took the time to make sure they gleamed just like he wanted them to. He was the soul of my world. Every night, before I slept, Papa would tell me he loved me and that he'd die if something happened to me. He'd kill himself, he'd say. I would too, I'd reply, and roll over to sleep.

{ 14 }

My father fell in love with my mother in an elevator. Every day we would decamp to the Cham Hotel next to Damascus's Central Bank and go swimming at the pool. We would be the last ones there, deep into autumn when it was still just warm enough to go for a dip. Papa first taught me how to swim when I was two years old, and every summer I would forget and have to be retaught. On the days when there was more sun and we would be assured of quality swimming time, Papa would play squash in the courts next to the pool while I waded in the water. The same courts were used for weekly aerobic sessions and my mother was a regular attendee.

On 15 November 1986 we were at the Cham swimming pool. I was in yellow bikini bottoms and Papa in red swimming trunks. Ghinwa Itaoui was twenty-four years old and in exile from Lebanon. She had grown up during the Lebanese civil war, stopping school to live in the basement of her parents' apartment on the Green Line, caught in between East and West Beirut, when the shelling and sniper fire became too much. By the time she was twenty the Israelis had invaded and Beirut was no longer a battleground the locals felt familiar with.

Ghinwa left Beirut and came to Damascus, where she worked as a receptionist and taught ballet classes to young girls in the basement of a Catholic church in Abu Roumaneh. On that November afternoon, she noticed a man swimming with his young child. It was his salt-and-pepper hair, she says, that caught her attention and made her notice this tall tanned man. As we left the swimming pool, Ghinwa was leaving her twice-weekly aerobic classes in the squash courts. Murtaza was wearing a pin-striped navy blue suit with a pink shirt underneath and the scent of his Grey Flannel cologne filled the small elevator. Suhail was visiting us and stood in the elevator patiently while I spoke to my father. Ghinwa noticed how kindly the salt-and-pepper man answered his child and how attentive he was when she replied. 'He spoke in beautiful English; there was no accent at all. It wasn't fully British sounding; I couldn't place where he was from.'[1]

'It must have been Thursday when I saw him next, two days later.' They had a common friend, a dentist with a raucous personality named Mazen Aloush. Mazen was an old family friend of Ghinwa's – he knew her parents and various other relatives back in Lebanon – and a new friend of Murtaza's, who had been referred to him when experiencing some pain in his molars. 'As I was going into my aerobics class I saw Mazen walking over to me. He'd come to say hello and he teased me like he always did and asked me to introduce him to some of my friends walking into the class. I told him to shut up. He was married and I knew he was just wasting my time. But he leaned over and said, "Listen, you introduce me and I'll introduce you to a friend of mine." I played along; Mazen was teasing, as usual. "Who?" I asked and he pointed over at the man with the salt-and-pepper hair. Mir was walking by the pool and you were running along beside him in your swimsuit bottoms. I told Mazen, I don't go out with married men. He's not married, he said, he's divorced. Mazen was smiling from ear to ear. I left and went to my class.'

After aerobics had ended, Mazen took Ghinwa over to a table where Murtaza and some friends were sitting. He introduced everyone around the table to her as Doctor, an Arabism that Mazen was flying with, since he was the only actual Doctor there. Ghinwa sat down at the table. She was tall, over five feet eight, and had jet-black hair wound in tight curls. She was beautiful.

'Doctor in what?' Ghinwa asked Murtaza, breaking the silence between them. He smiled and answered back, 'Economics.' He was shy, but debonair. Ghinwa burst out laughing. What bullshit, she thought, what would an economist be doing in socialist Syria? He told her he was from Afghanistan. She bought that fib more easily. They chatted and Ghinwa asked Murtaza what his daughter's name was. 'Fah-tima,' he replied. 'Oh, Fa-ti-ma,' Ghinwa sing-songed back, pronouncing my name with an Arabic lilt. Just as she turned to look for me around the table, she felt my hand behind her back. I had sneaked up behind her chair and wedged my small hands under her back cushion. I was protective of my father; it had always been just him and me in my mind, and I'd come to take a closer look at the beautiful woman he was talking to. 'Hello Fa-ti-ma,' Ghinwa said softly. I ducked my chin to my chest and looked at her sideways for the rest of the lunch.

Hours later, Mazen and Ghinwa sat in a taxi together as he offered to drop her off at her flat in Muhajirin, a Damascene neighbourhood tucked under the Qasiyoon mountains. 'I said to him in the car, Mazen what nonsense,' referring to Murtaza claiming to be an economist. 'Who is he really?' OK, he replied, it is nonsense, but why did you have to ask so many questions?' Mummy laughs. I live to hear her laugh. She laughs with her ribs, from deep inside and her whole face crinkles with pleasure.

Mazen had been kicking Ghinwa under the table to shut her up when she persisted with her questions about Murtaza's economics doctorate. In the taxi Mazen told her who Murtaza really was, that he wasn't an economics expert, but a Pakistani exile, the son of the murdered Prime Minister. 'To me, Zulfikar Ali Bhutto was a hero,' Mummy says as we sit in Zulfikar's old dressing room, a space we've converted over time into a small family sitting room. 'If heroism had a face, it was Zulfikar Ali Bhutto's. I used to watch him on TV as a young girl. I was maybe twelve years old the first time I saw him. The whole Arab world was nauseated watching Zia ul Haq send him to his death, and we watched him die so bravely, like a man.' Ghinwa's parents were Marxists; her mother Kafia, the daughter of a respected religious sheikh, was a poet and a teacher and her father Abboud an engineer who had fought alongside the Lebanese nationalists in expelling the French colonialists from the country in the 1940s. They knew their history. Mazen swore Ghinwa to secrecy; she wasn't to tell Murtaza that she knew who he was. She was an exile too; she understood that he had been forced away from his home because of violence, and it was not a topic she wanted to discuss. She didn't bring it up with Mazen again.

The next time Ghinwa went to her aerobics class, Murtaza was at the pool alone. When she finished her class he invited her to sit with him and share a drink. They spoke for a while and he asked her about the ballet class she was running. 'What age do you start taking girls?' he asked. Ghinwa had resolutely decided she wouldn't take students younger than five, but she knew Murtaza's daughter would miss the mark by just six months. 'Four and a half,' she replied, and I was ceremoniously enrolled into the ballet class.

I called her 'Aunty Ghinwa' and we became fast friends. 'The next time Mir invited me for lunch, we came to pick you up from the house where you had stayed because you were ill. You were in these girly pyjamas making butterfly paintings with tubes of paint smeared across white paper that you folded and then spread out across the living room floor. You had covered the entire floor and I looked at the sheets of paper and asked you if you had painted them. You nodded, you were proud that your work had been noticed, though it was impossible to ignore it – it was everywhere! Your father took you to change and dressed you in a navy blue cardigan and we went to the Sheraton for lunch.'

The Sheraton was the only serious hotel in town. The Cham kept its pool open for longer, but you couldn't beat the Sheraton for quality in those days. The hotel was tiled in beige and black and boasted the best food in town, for us foreigners at least. But that day I was determined not to eat a bite of my lunch, taking refuge in my illness. I was always ill as a young child, suffering fevers and flus all the time; I caught any bug that was going around. I was a terrible eater anyway, and picked at my food if it wasn't dessert. It annoyed my father and the only time he became cross with me was when it came to food. I would refuse to eat and he would force-feed me. That didn't work for long because I would always manage to throw up the meal. I couldn't be goaded into eating, and tricks and games never worked – I saw through them. That day, Papa threatened to send me to Fowzia if I didn't eat. Ghinwa heard him and thought the threat was mean. I was obviously afraid, but held my ground by snarling at him as I gave in

and I in Geneva. He had broken his arm and I insisted on being
fitted with a cast too, which I wore until his came off

Our own informal portraits with Papa joking around
while I posed stiffly and seriously

Murtaza and Della in Greece
at the start of their relationship
in the late 1970s

Mummy and I
outside my school
in Damascus

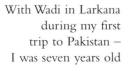

With Wadi in Larkana
during my first
trip to Pakistan –
I was seven years old

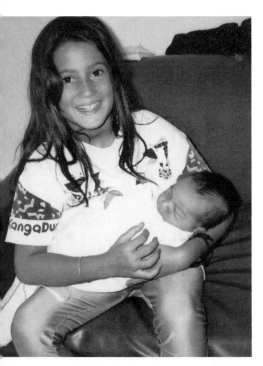

Ghinwa and Murtaza before they were married. I was the photographer

Holding my newborn baby brother, Zulfikar Ali Bhutto jr, in Damascus

a wedding during my first trip to Larkana I was ceremoniously seated on Ameer Begum's my grandfather's first wife, who was chatting away pleasantly with my Joonam. Surprisingly, n the only one who looks uncomfortable

Murtaza and Zulfi, also photograph[
during a court recess

A portrait of Ghinwa and
Murtaza taken in court

Asif and Benazir at their Mendh
wedding celebration held at
70 Clifton, 1987

Murtaza speaking to a gathering in the North West Frontier Province in 1994

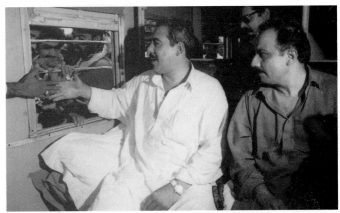

Murtaza on a train journey from Karachi to the interior f Sindh after his release from jail, 1994. Suhail Sethi sits next to him

urtaza's train journey to rkana was met with crowds nearly every station. He oke at each and every stop

Nusrat and Ghinwa visiting the hospital bed of Shahid Rind at Larkana Civil hospital 6 January, 1994. Rind was shot by the police in the 5 January police attack on Al Murtaza and later died from his injuries

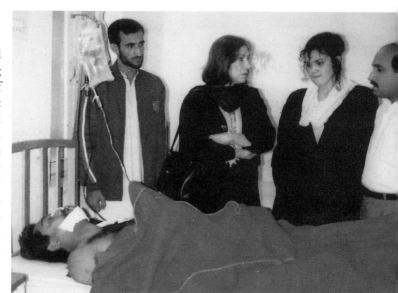

The six men who were killed alongside Murtaza:
Sattar Rajpar, Rahim Brohi, Sajjad Haider with his son Shahnawaz, Wajahat Jokhio, Ashiq Jatoi with his daughter Sabeen and Yar Mohammed Baloch

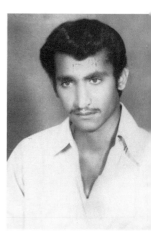

One of the accused
[poli]cemen, Wajid Durrani,
saluting Benazir as
she arrives at Mideast
on the night of
20 September, 1996

GULF NEWS

AL NISR PUBLISHING

Murtaza's death fuels family feud

[M]other points finger at Benazir

[By] Ahmed Rashid
[Spec]ial to GN

Islamabad

[The] bloody history of the warring [Bhu]tto dynasty took a dramatic [turn] last night when the grieving [moth]er of Murtaza Bhutto [accu]sed her own daughter, the [Prim]e Minister of Pakistan, of [cons]piring to kill him.

[Mu]rtaza, latterly his sister [Bena]zir's fiercest political rival, [died] in a hail of police bullets in [Kara]chi on Friday night. Six of his [suppor]ters also were killed.

"I could get justice I will reg[iste]r a case of murder against [Bena]zir Bhutto and her husband [Asif] Ali Zardari," Begum Nusrat [Bhut]to told stunned reporters fol[lowin]g her son's funeral. "They [are] responsible for killing him." [The] accusation was made at the [Bhut]to's ancestral home in the [town] of Larkana, as a 5,000-[stron]g crowd chanted "Benazir is [a kil]ler."

[Mu]rtaza was buried between [the g]raves of his father, Zulfikar [Ali B]hutto, executed by the mili[tary r]egime that deposed him as a [prime] minister, and his younger [broth]er Shahnawaz, who died in [suspi]cious circumstances in [Franc]e a decade ago. The suspect-

ed victim of assassination by poisoning.

Benazir, however, was making it clear last night that she utterly rejected the charges.

Supporters of the prime minister, who has ordered an inquiry into the shooting, dismissed her mother's claims as the over-emotional outpourings of an ailing and grief-stricken mother.

A Sindh province government notice said provincial high court judge Ali Mohammad Baluch would head an inquiry tribunal which would submit its report within a month.

Sindh Chief Minister Abdullah Shah said that the police officers involved in the shooting had been suspended from duty. He also appealed for calm.

Just 24 hours earlier, Benazir sat barefoot and weeping for two hours beside the body of her brother in a Karachi hospital, asking hopelessly: "What has happened?"

But early yesterday morning at a Karachi helicopter-pad, as their leader's body was flown north, stone-throwing activists from Murtaza's breakaway faction of the Pakistan People's Party chanted "Hang Benazir" and "They have killed our leader".

One of the many allegations being made is that Murtaza, who was hit by eight bullets outside his home, was allowed to bleed to death in the gutter.

Militant supporters have vowed to take revenge.

Close friends of the family also dismissed the idea that Benazir was involved in the killing. Instead, they suggested that the death was the result of repeated clashes with local police that spiralled out of control.

When the three days of mourning declared by Benazir's ruling Pakistan People's Party (PPP) end tomorrow night, Benazir will face the most serious political challenge to her thaky three-year-old government.

Her administration is already dealing with an acute economic crisis, a powerful opposition movement determined to oust her from power, and an increasingly truculent military.

In recent months, Benazir's

political survival has become ever more at risk.

There have been increasing calls from the opposition and business for President Laghan to use his constitutional powers to dismiss her before the economic crisis worsens. The task of holding it together looks daunting. If the government's official verdict this week is that Murtaza died "accidentally", the family feud could go into meltdown.

©The Telegraph plc, London

Our Correspondent Salahuddin Haider adds: More than 10,000 people turned up at the graveyard amid rice fields and several fainted in sweltering heat as the temperature soared to 37 degrees C.

Murtaza's sobbing widow, Ghinwa, appeared briefly in the crowd before her husband's bullet-ridden body was lowered into the grave.

Benazir and her mother Nusrat also arrived in Larkana but did

not attend the burial because of the crowds.

Earlier, Benazir wailed and prayed over Murtaza's body at a Karachi hospital.

In a mark of deep mourning, she went barefoot to the Karachi hospital where Murtaza died.

She flew overnight from Islamabad to Karachi after hearing of the death of the brother.

Editorial comment – Page 6
See also Pages 7 & 18

Pakistanis cling to a helicopter carrying the body of Murtaza Bhutto from Karachi to his hometown Larkana for burial. – Picture: Reuter

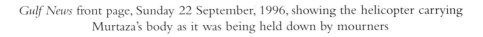

Gulf News front page, Sunday 22 September, 1996, showing the helicopter carrying
Murtaza's body as it was being held down by mourners

Ghinwa leaving Mideast
after Murtaza's murder

The last Bhuttos:
me, Sassi and Zulfi in
Garhi Khuda Bux in 2008
as Sassi visits her father
Shahnawaz's grave for the
first time. Mir Ali, our
brother, is to the left of us.

to his threat. I shovelled some morsels into my mouth, frowning at my father, angry that he had embarrassed me in front of my new friend.

After lunch, Papa had to take me to my doctor, a jolly woman with a white hijab called Dr Lemia Nabulsi. As we sat in the car, Aunty Ghinwa began to sing the letters of the ABC and I joined in. By the time we had reached Jisr al Abiad, or the White Bridge area in central Damascus where the paediatrician was located, I was holding Aunty Ghinwa's hand. Murtaza and Ghinwa stopped to part at a crossing; she was going to visit Mazan at his office and we were going to the doctor. I held on to Aunty Ghinwa and made to walk away with her. 'OK, Fati, see you later,' Papa said, and I realized I had gone the wrong way. I quickly ran over to him and took his hand in mine. 'I don't know who I fell in love with first, your father or you,' Mummy says to me twenty-three years later in Grandpapa's old closet/living room. 'It was a love triangle.'

Ghinwa and Murtaza courted for some time, cooking each other dinners, with Murtaza attempting to make Pakistani *chapli kebabs* with ingredients bought in a Syrian supermarket (and not grinding the pomegranate seeds and coriander, thus giving his date an instant stomach ache) and Ghinwa making him overly salty Lebanese food. I was the third wheel on most, if not all, of their dates. After several weeks of seeing each other, Murtaza asked if he could meet Ghinwa's parents. 'He was so decent,' my mother says, remembering how he came to their Muhajirin apartment, which was simply furnished with small mementoes from their house in Beirut. 'He brought you with him and I introduced him to my parents as Dr Khalid, his Damascene *nom de guerre*. Mir let me finish and then said no, that's not really my name. I am Mir Murtaza Bhutto, the son of Zulfikar Ali Bhutto, and told them that I was in safe hands.' Jiddo, as I called my grandfather in Arabic, was terribly impressed. He was the lone man in a house of five women – all daughters, all loud and difficult. Teta, my grandmother, was more wary. 'She pretended she couldn't speak English the first time she met Mir,' Mummy says, laughing. 'She was trying to suss him out.' But they liked me and instantly we formed a bond.

When Papa had to travel I began to stay with Teta Kafia and Jiddo Abboud. I'm not sure what I called them then, before they were formally my grandparents, but they always embodied some sort of familial warmth. Mummy says I knew just how to catch their attention without calling them anything formalized, but the truth is I've always thought of them as my grandparents, never as anything else. Aunty Ghinwa would move my colour TV into the apartment – because they only had a small black and white set – and bring my clothes over along with a certain kind of strawberry milk I drank, as I was such a fussy eater. I'd come straight to the apartment from school and spend the afternoon with Teta eating *zaatar*, the crushed thyme powder and olive oil that always sat on their breakfast table in small glass bowls. I busied myself by helping Teta with the laundry, which only created more work for her to take care of. Once, when Papa was away, I fell ill. I had to have blood tests and take antibiotics to bring my fever down. Exhausted, I started to cry. 'I want to go home,' I sobbed to Aunty Ghinwa, who was confused because we had decided to spend the night at our flat since I was ill and wanted my things around me. 'But you are home,' she said softly, because she always spoke to me in whispers at night. 'This isn't my home. Pakistan is my home,' I wailed back. I had never even been there.

Pakistan was an ever-present ghost in our house. As was Zia. And Zulfikar. And Shahnawaz. My father and I carried invisible baggage with us, both loved and feared. 'When we first met, Shah's death kept cropping up. I didn't know how much it affected Mir though, till a year later when Sassi's name came up and I saw your father cry. It was one of the only two times I saw him cry. He told me after that that he didn't want me to think he was taking me for granted, that he hadn't asked me to marry him because it was too soon after his brother's death – two years later by then – and that when the time was right we'd get married.'

On 17 August 1988, General Zia ul Haq, accompanied by five generals, including General Akhtar Abdur Rehman, the Chairman of the Joint

Chiefs of Staff and the former head of the ISI Intelligence agency that fought the Afghan war for the CIA, the American ambassador Arnold Raphel and General Herbert M. Wassom, the head of the US military aid mission to Pakistan, arrived at the Tamewali firing range to watch American MI Abrams tank trials.[2] The trials, however, were 'a fiasco' with the supertanks missing their targets ten out of ten times.[3] There was little to celebrate and the VIP guests were in a grumpy mood. They ate lunch in the officers' mess and had ice-cream for dessert. General Zia excused himself to say his prayers, which he never missed, and then summoned his companions back to Pak One, the presidential plane that was to fly them back to Islamabad.

Pak One was the aircraft that Al Zulfikar had narrowly missed hitting in 1982, and it had increased its security since then. The American-built Hercules C-130 had a sealed VIP cabin – air-conditioned, no less – to protect its most powerful passenger from assassination attempts.[4] In the cockpit was a four-man crew led by Wing Commander Mashood Hassan, along with a co-pilot, navigator and engineer all personally selected by Zia. The crew had flown the plane on exactly the same route the day before to ensure that there would be no hiccoughs on their flight with the President on board.

At 3.46 p.m. Pak One took off from Bahawalpur on schedule. The flight to Islamabad was expected to be smooth and trouble-free. Minutes after take-off, however, Pak One failed to respond to the Bahawalpur Tower Control. 'At a river eighteen miles from the airport, villagers looking into the sky saw Pak One lurching up and down as if it were on an invisible roller coaster,' wrote Edward Jay Epstein in his article for *Vanity Fair* a year later. 'After its third loop it plunged directly towards the desert, burying itself in the soil. Then it exploded and, as the fuel burned, became a ball of fire. All thirty-one persons on board were dead. It was 3.51 p.m.'[5]

All that was left of General Zia, who had left no section of Pakistani society free from his tyrannical grip on power for ten years, was his jawbone. There were no other remains found at the crash site.

The daytime weather was perfectly clear and sunny and pilot error was quickly ruled out. The rumour circulating at the time was that a box of mangoes had been packed with explosives and placed on board Pak One. People whispered that it was fruit that had finally taken the dictator down.

There were, according to Epstein, 'no outcries for vengeance, no efforts at counter coups, no real effort to find the assassins. In Pakistan, Zia and Rehman's names disappeared within days from television, newspapers and other media.'[6] The Pakistan Air Force Board of Inquiry said the 'most probable cause' of the crash was 'sabotage' but stopped short of taking the investigation further.[7] In fact a thorough investigation was never carried out. It was standard procedure; once the assassination had been carried out, no records were kept, no archives made. Nothing. Violence was the easiest means of disposing of yet another Pakistani politician, however odious he may have been. The United States National Archives has some 250 pages of documents on the incident, but they remain classified to this day.[8] Officially, Al Zulfikar, inactive in the years since Shahnawaz's murder, was disbanded. I know my father would have loved knowing that AZO was among the many groups whose names popped up in regard to General Zia's plane crash, but their symbolic resistance to the dictator's tyranny had ended. Hope, as usual, did not prevail for long.

The General had taken the step of announcing elections for 1988, fully emboldened in his new role as the seemingly 'democratic' head of an authoritarian government. He had even begun to conduct second-party negotiations with Benazir, who was not going to be left out of the power stakes by boycotting the elections like she had done in 1985. It was Benazir's tremendous luck, something she had always benefited from, that Zia was killed before the elections took place. She had been preparing to be Prime Minister to his President.

Murtaza had spoken to his sister about the party's decision to engage in power-sharing negotiations with the junta. He had disagreed with her fundamentally on this issue. I remember the conversation. 'What do you mean "take part"?' Papa said, almost shouting. 'You're willing to be Zia's Prime Minister?'

I was young, only six years old. We were in Geneva, spending time together as a family early in the summer. Papa was a passionate man, but he was always in control of his emotions. He never yelled, never swore, never overreacted. He always displayed the cool assurance of someone used to winning the argument in the end. We were at lunch eating pizza. The atmosphere grew dark and tense very quickly. Benazir was less calm, but she too had the air of someone used to beating her opponents. 'I have a plan,' she said. Papa was enraged. I got worried, I had never seen my father so upset. He started speaking angrily, talking about the dead, about their father, their brother, the many who lost their lives under Zia and the many more who were still suffering. I began to close my eyes and to block out what Papa was saying. I heard him speak of himself as dead. I heard him and shut him out. I stood behind his chair, holding on to the frame, and tried to hug him.

I could never bear to hear my father speak of not being there. Sometimes he would say, 'When I die . . .' and I would get angry and fight with him. 'But everyone dies at some point!' he would say, laughing to make the issue sound uncomplicated and natural, but I always hated hearing him talk like that. Papa was angry now and he was fighting with the sister he called Pinky, who was about to capitulate to power for the first of many times. 'I can't keep sitting on the outside,' she said. 'We have to be in government. It's my chance. I'm not losing it. We can't keep living like this.' She mentioned money, making it, and Papa exploded.

He refused to have anything to do with the party's election campaign. He didn't advise his mother or sister, he didn't put forward any candidates, didn't pledge his support. They spoke once more, Murtaza and Benazir, about the 1988 elections. He was upset that she had given her new husband, Asif Zardari, the party ticket to stand from Lyari, the heart of the People's Party Power base in Karachi. 'It's for the workers, it's their area, Pinky, how can you put him there?' he asked her. She became cross and the conversation was over.

To say Asif Zardari had a chequered past is something of a polite understatement. Benazir was in her early thirties before she began to consider marriage proposals, the first woman in her family to opt for a traditional arranged marriage. She didn't think it proper that she, who worked daily with men and was about to ascend to the land's highest post, remain single. And it might be damaging for her reputation. Mummy remembers one conversation in Damascus when Benazir was bemoaning her lack of options – who would marry her, a strong, powerful woman, and agree to take the back seat in the Prime Minister's busy public life? Alternatively, who was strong enough to hold their own next to her? 'She considered Yasser Arafat,' Mummy recalls, unable to stop a smile from spreading across her face. 'She thought he might be a suitable match.'[9] Karachi folklore says that it was Zia's secretary, Roedad Khan, who suggested to Asif's mother that he send a proposal to Benazir the year she was arranging her marriage and that Asif's mother took the idea to Manna, Zulfikar's sister and only living sibling, who did the rest of the damage. Dr Sikandar Jatoi of Larkana, the Bhuttos' hometown, snarls at the mention of Zardari's name, 'He was a vulgar street boy. Before marriage, who knew him? No one.'[10]

Suhail is more diplomatic. 'His father, Hakim Zardari, contested the 1970 elections from Nawabshah' – a centuries-old town since renamed Shaheed Mohtarma Benazir Bhutto by order of President Zardari – 'and joined the PPP. There are rumours, stories that Mr Bhutto didn't like the man – that he humiliated him and even had him thrashed on occasion – I won't go into them, but they exist. In Mr Bhutto's lifetime Hakim left the PPP – or was thrown out, depending on who you believe – and switched sides, joining the National Awami Party, an anti-Bhutto party at the time, as head of the Sindh chapter.' Suhail, a deliberate and cautious man, clears his throat before continuing. 'The NAP was part of the alliance that hounded your grandfather and supported the Zia coup by publicly chanting slogans like "Hang Bhutto not once but a hundred times" and "Double the noose around Bhutto's neck."' Hakim was with the NAP at that time and in a prominent position in Sindh. Did he take part in those chants and protests against Zulfikar? I don't know. The 'Hang Bhutto a hundred times' is attributed to him, Suhail reckoned.

'Of course!' screamed Dr Sikandar. 'Hakim was famous for such slogans.' Mumtaz Bhutto, Zulfikar's cousin and Chief Minister of Sindh, and keeper of all stories Sindhi, told me he didn't know which story was true and which wasn't, 'but the fact of the matter is, Zulfi certainly didn't like him. He had no time whatsoever for Zardari.'[11] In any case, Hakim Zardari later switched parties again, becoming what is called a *lota* in derogatory politicese. I remember Papa used to call him 'Hakoo the *Dacu*' – thief – in his public meetings, a taunt that riled Zardari to no end. But what about Asif, I asked Suhail, what was he known for in the days before he became Mr Benazir Bhutto? 'Oh, he was unknown,' Suhail replied casually, 'though he did have a reputation in Karachi circles as a gatecrasher.'[12]

━━━◆••◆━━━

That summer, I remember my father saying something to me about returning to Pakistan. He always spoke of home, always spoke of the return, but this time he added, almost as an afterthought, 'Don't tell Wadi, OK?' I promised Papa I wouldn't say a word. The chasm had already opened.

When the news came that Zia had died in a plane crash, Papa and I were at a family friend's house. My grandmother, Joonam, called our apartment and Aunty Ghinwa picked up the phone. Joonam was hysterical and had barely asked for her son before blurting out, 'He's dead, my God, Zia's dead.' Ghinwa frantically dialled Murtaza's friend's number and shrieked into the receiver that she had to speak to Mir. When his friends passed him the phone he listened quietly. His friends watched him, saw his neck turn red and worried that something awful had happened, that some other misfortune had befallen the family. Then Murtaza screamed. Ghinwa heard him drop the phone.

He rushed back home, me rushing along with him, all of us ecstatic that it was over. Eleven years of fear and violence were over. Zia was dead.

{ 15 }

The run-up to the 1988 elections started on the wrong foot. Benazir chose not to enter into electoral alliances with the other parties that made up the MRD – a mistake that resulted in her having to cope with a hostile coalition once in government – because she wanted to be free of the MRD's 1986 Declaration of Provincial Autonomy. The declaration called for limits to be placed on the centre's power in four areas: currency, communications, defence and foreign policy.[1] The declaration went a step further towards democratizing politics by placing 'strict limits on the dissolution of provincial governments by the centre'.[2]

Benazir might have been furthering her political career by championing a personal image of democratic leadership, but according to the historian Ian Talbot she 'displayed little interest in strengthening and democratizing her own party, while simultaneously leading the national crusade for the democratization of Pakistan's politics'.[3]

As a result, she alienated many of the Pakistan People's Party's inner circle. Founding members and old guard, including her uncle, Mumtaz Bhutto, and Hafeez Pirzada, the author of the 1973 constitution, were among many who left the party under Benazir's leadership. A core of personal business contacts and establishment politicians who trimmed their sails to the prevailing political wind and who would soon become the new party's power brokers swiftly replaced them. Benazir's new husband, Asif Zardari, was key in the shaping of this new coterie through his role in giving out election tickets for the 1988 elections. He allocated these tickets to his school friends and loyal sidekicks or as Talbot puts it 'opportunist entrants to the party', effectively sidelining old party loyalists.[4]

Dr Ghulam Hussain, a founding member, and one of the prisoners released in the aftermath of the PIA hijacking, found no place for himself under the new Benazir/Zardari reshaping of the PPP. Hussain had served as the party's Secretary-General under Zulfikar, a role that cost him five years in jail during martial law. 'Zia sent three generals to me in jail,' Dr Hussain tells me at his house in Islamabad, 'and they asked me to resign from my Secretary-General position in writing, offering me a ministership in the new regime. Otherwise, should I refuse, they warned, they would prosecute me for treason. They accused me of leading a shooting at Liaqat Bagh in Rawalpindi. Imagine! There was no trial, no conviction, I was simply arrested and put in jail. I told them, I'll stay with Bhutto come what may. They made good their threats once we were brought before a judge, to scare us into understanding our position as prisoners without rights and I caused a scene. I said to the judge, "You are scared of Zia. I am scared of God, not this small man." I was led out of the courtroom shouting *Zia hatao!*' – Remove Zia!'

'Benazir, who couldn't read Urdu – she had to write her speeches in English – bypassed me and gave the PPP ticket in Jhelum to Chaudry Aftaf, who was from the Pakistan Muslim League – Zia's party! – because he was a *jagirdar*, a man so powerful as a feudal master that he owned serfs. This same man, who violated all the party's principles ideologically, had also sat in Zia's *Majlis e Shoora*! I didn't even learn about my demotion from Benazir. I read about it in the press the next day.'[5] The PPP's current Prime Minister, Yousef Raza Gilani, was also a trusted member of Zia's religious council, which rivalled parliament in its power, during the days of the Junta, Dr Hussain reminds me.

While veteran party members were swept aside, it was the workers who felt the most betrayed. Maulabux is a stout *Sheedi* man, of African, Sindhi and Baloch ethnic heritage. He and his wife live in Lyari, the beating heart of the PPP in Karachi and a Bhutto stronghold for decades. '*Dil se*, from our hearts, we were with Zulfikar Ali Bhutto',[6] begins Maulabux, whose friends and comrades call him Mauli, meaning 'white radish' in Urdu, a nickname so widespread that even he uses it now.

'Our work, our sacrifices, were because of the love we had for him. Our thought, after his execution, was that no compromise with the killers of Bhutto was acceptable. The road was very difficult, of course, but we weren't afraid of paying with arrest and with our lives.' It's an emotional subject for Maulabux, who reminds me as we're speaking that we met once long ago – in Kabul when I was a baby. 'Those of us who worked for the party during the dictatorship, we were political workers. It was a big struggle, but we were a family. If one of us was stopped, was harmed, we all rallied round. We learned politics from the senior founding members of the party. We were young then, we considered ourselves their students and we fell in love with the socialism, the egalitarianism, the principles of the PPP.'

And they suffered. They risked arrest and flogging to pass out pamphlets for the MRD and to stage women's meetings and protest rallies in public roundabouts and parks. When things became too difficult, they would take the bus from Karachi to Gwadar in Balochistan then sneak across the border to Iran. The Iranians, ethnically Baloch on the border, would let them through without visas and they would lie low with friends and family in Irani Balochistan. The process of going underground was expensive, and they paid out of their own pockets. 'Mir *baba* thanked so many of our families and relatives across the border, personally reaching out to them by letters and phone calls, he thanked them for protecting us workers during a time of need. All of us joined Mir *baba* when he returned to Pakistan, there was no doubt that we would.' Why? I asked. 'Because,' Mauli said, uncharacteristically growing quiet, 'because we were still struggling.'

Shahnawaz Baloch, a thinner, taller replica of Maulabux, steps in to speak. The mood of our conversation has changed. There is a reckoning that someone has to make. 'By 1985 we had grown disillusioned with Benazir', he starts, speaking to me in a mixture of Urdu and English. 'The party had been taken over. A part of it by capitalist rich industrialists with zero political understanding, another part of it by friends of the Chairperson and her husband, another by *jagirdar*, another by feudals or *zamindar,* and those workers who had merited leadership positions because of their understanding of the party's ideology, because of their sacrifices, their loyalty, their immersion in the communities they represented – we were pushed out. Benazir was catering to those other factions for power. We lost our right to speak.'[7]

Aftab Sherpao, who was elected a vice-president of the PPP in 1976, was yet another of the party elite who lost his voice as the party regrouped in preparation for the 1988 elections. 'There was a vast difference between those two PPPs,' he says. Sherpao is the consummate statesman. When we met, he had just left General Musharraf's cabinet – he had been Pakistan's Interior Minister during the country's fight alongside the United States in the War on Terror, a role that placed Sherpao in danger as suicide bombers attacked him and his family, narrowly missing him several times. Some years earlier, Sherpao had founded a splinter group of the PPP, one that was openly critical of the PPP under Benazir and her husband. 'Mr Zulfikar Bhutto was a good listener. I was a provincial minister in the NWFP at the time and used to watch him as he sat for hours and hours listening to everyone around the table before taking a final decision on any matter, regardless how large or small. She, his daughter, if she didn't like something you said, she would cut you off. As far as political brilliance is concerned, there was no match. Yes, she had acumen, but not to the extent her father had. She got her momentum from *him*.'[8]

The party's decision to negotiate with the army and to work with Zia's protégés in the lead-up to the elections carried with it the end of the PPP as its workers knew it. 'The differences between Mr Bhutto's party and Benazir's only grew,' Shahnawaz continued. 'It became like a war – us old workers against these businessmen who had erased the party's founding ideology. It was a war about *soch,* about thought.' Mauli agrees. 'She was the opposite of what Zulfikar Ali Bhutto had been. He made the party what it was by giving tickets to the small, the poor. But working with Benazir, we were thrown aside and watched *waderas*' – a mixture of the land-cultivating *zamindar* and peasant-exploiting *jagirdar* – 'receive ticket after ticket. It was no longer about merit, it had become about power and favours.'

Why didn't they see it coming? Why had they been taken in by Benazir's politics, opportunistic at best? Mauli thinks for a moment. He nods, he knows what I'm asking. 'When Benazir came back from self-imposed exile in 1986 after her brother's murder we joined her because she promised to take Zulfikar Ali Bhutto's programmes forward. We stayed with her because she promised us no more Bhuttos would be killed, that they would be protected by the strength of the party. Even then, however, people asked us, "Why are you struggling for her?" and our answer was always the same. Our struggle didn't begin with her, it started a long time ago.'

———◆◆◆◆———

The deal Benazir brokered with the military elite sealed her fate, even after Zia was removed from the equation. The army ensured that the PPP would not sweep the 1988 polls, keeping Benazir on a tight leash. The party took ninety-two out of 207 national assembly seats – numbers which meant Benazir would have no power in parliament to roll back or reverse any of Zia's laws, leaving the dictator's legacy firmly in place.[9]

Benazir accepted the army's conditions. The defence budget was to remain 'sacrosanct', the army was to hold the ultimate veto in security and foreign policy matters, and IMF loan conditions and stipulations were to be reaffirmed and left untouched.[10] Zia's Foreign Minister, Yakub Ali Khan, remained in place to deal with the army's special spots like Afghanistan and Kashmir, and Zia's one-time favourite and Chairman of the Senate, Ghulam Ishaq Khan, was promoted to serve as Benazir's President.[11]

On 2 December 1988, Benazir Bhutto took her oath and at thirty-five years old became the youngest Prime Minister in Pakistan's history. In Damascus, Murtaza was anxiously watching the votes come in. The Pakistani embassy was calling our house with up-to-the-minute results.

When the polls had closed, Murtaza was furious. 'These elections are rigged,' Ghinwa remembers him saying to her. 'These aren't the numbers the PPP should be getting after eleven years of martial law.'

The PPP had won with only a slight majority. Murtaza called his sister and pleaded with her, 'Pinky, don't accept these results.' She ignored him, overjoyed that she was so close to power, close enough to touch it. Nusrat also advised her daughter to reject the results. It will make you stronger, she told her. Benazir made a public show of her irritation at the suggestion by leaving her mother in Islamabad and travelling to Larkana by herself, remaining there until her decision had been announced. She said yes to all the army's conditions.

'That day,' remembers Ghinwa, 'the phone was ringing off the hook with people calling to offer Mir *mabruk*, congratulations. He was gracious on the phone, but he was so disheartened. He was supposed to pick you up from school – you were in first grade – and he came to me and said, "Will you go pick Fati up instead?" I asked him why and he replied, "People are going to be coming up and congratulating me. This isn't a victory. I don't want to go."'

Papa and I had grown with my school, the Damascus Community School. We had followed it from a basement in Mezzeh to its refurbished campus in Abu Roumaneh. Papa had come to read to my class every year from pre-nursery onwards; he was the funniest storyteller and would make faces and voices to match every character in whatever book he was assigned to read that year. The teachers enjoyed his performances as much as we children did. The teachers and parents had become a proxy family for us, especially before Ghinwa came into our lives. But Murtaza couldn't face them that day.

It took Zia's number two, President Ghulam Ishaq Khan, a week to invite Benazir to become Prime Minister. The insult infuriated Murtaza even more. The army's conditions, the stalling, the rigging, it was too much. He called his sister again. 'They're tying your hands,' he told her. 'You're going to be weak. Refuse their conditions, Don't take the government, sit in the opposition, Pinky. You'll be in a phenomenal position. Don't bow down to these bastards.' But those around the future Prime Minister told her not to listen. 'We can't afford to sit in the opposition, Mir,' she told her brother on the phone. 'If people don't feel they're getting something from the party they'll leave us.' It was untrue. The party had nothing but loyal workers. It was the interlopers, the new moneyed recruits, who would have fled but they were a gamble Benazir was already unwilling to risk.

━◆••◆━

In the summer of 1988 Murtaza asked Ghinwa to marry him. We had both fallen in love with her. I put aside my normally controlling possessiveness about Papa to let Aunty Ghinwa in, setting forth some conditions. Papa was very considerate, buying us both Valentine's Day presents and bringing me a small bouquet of flowers for every large one he gave Ghinwa, but I had an issue with semantics that had to be urgently rectified. Driving along Mezzeh one afternoon, I asked Papa why he called her 'Darling'. I didn't appreciate not being included in this strange affection he was showing to someone besides me. 'It's because I love her,' he said, realizing at once that he'd put his foot in it. 'What about *me*?' I asked. We reached a compromise. He could call Aunty Ghinwa 'Darling' if he called me 'Dear' in the same sentence. As soon as Papa signed on to my terms I forgot all about it.

'It was my twenty-sixth birthday,' Mummy tells me. 'I knew Mir was going to give me an engagement ring. We'd talked about marriage and settling down and I just felt he was going to ask me to marry him on my birthday. He wanted to keep it a surprise, I thought, so I waited patiently for the day to come. That day we were at the Sheraton having lunch with some friends and in the middle of a conversation, Mir turned to me and said, very casually, 'By the way, what do you want for your birthday?" I wanted to burst into tears then and there. But he just stared at me with a poker face and said, "What? What did I say?" He didn't even laugh! I felt my face turning red.'

Mummy wears her engagement ring sporadically now. She wears it when she can bear the memories it brings; today she doesn't have it on. Her fingers are bare and she wrings them as she talks. 'I think he was

295

afraid I wouldn't say yes. He had to hear it directly from me, so I told him I thought he was going to propose to me. And he let out a gale of laughter and said, "Well, why didn't you just say so?"' The next day they returned to the Sheraton and picked out rings together at Muwafak's jewellery store, which also doubled as my post box since security precautions didn't allow me to use our home address for my mail.

A word should be said about the Sheraton Hotel, base of operations for my family during our lives in Damascus. We ate there; in the summer we swam in the pool from sunrise till sunset; I had my birthday parties, lavishly planned and orchestrated by my father, in the hotel ballroom – though my friends and I would always end up playing in the basement bathroom, leaving the adults upstairs. When the Sheraton opened a pizzeria, Luigi's, Papa insisted on taking me to pick up pizzas in my pyjamas and slippers when he got cravings late at night. It was, for lack of other public spaces, our own little world. After he had been killed, I went to Luigi's for lunch. The waiters gathered around my table and cried. Papa had been their friend and there are memories of him all over that hotel.

Murtaza and Ghinwa came home to tell me the news of their engagement and found me bored, jumping on my bed. With each jump I made a noise, a monotonous yea yeaa yeaa sound, seeing how far my voice travelled with every bounce. Papa couldn't hold the news in; he blurted it out in one breath 'Fatiauntyghinwaandiaregettingmarried.' I heard him and bounced harder, turning my bored yeas into loud and shrill yays. I was thrilled. I missed her whenever she wasn't with us. I knew Papa did too.

They married, on 21 March 1989. The preparations for the wedding went off without a hitch, except for one. Two weeks before the big day Aunty Ghinwa went to her hairdresser, at the Sheraton it goes without saying, and chopped off her beautiful long hair. Her hair was now the same length as Murtaza's. When Papa saw her for the first time after the cut, unveiled over lunch at the Sheraton the same day, he almost didn't recognize her. The wedding was going to be a small affair; Joonam came from Karachi and Teta Kafia and Jiddo Abboud represented Aunty Ghinwa's family, along with Kholoud, one of her three older sisters, whom I called Aunty Lulu. I was the unofficial matron of honour. 'You thought it was your wedding,' Mummy says, telling me what I already knew. 'We both got new dresses, mine was white and yours light blue with lace. I took you to buy gloves and pretty clips for your hair. And you wouldn't let us sit together. You were always in between us in every photograph.' They signed their marriage papers, according to Islamic custom, in our dining room. I carried a camera in one hand and my diary, a pink journal with Minnie Mouse on the cover holding a sign that read, 'I love you', a gift from Papa, as if it were a bouquet.

I had titled each page with some sort of first grade code – I had just learned how to write – and occasionally invited Papa to contribute thoughts to my diary. Under the page quizzically headed E.M. he had drawn a picture in pencil of a mouse and me. 'It was the night before Christmas,' Papa wrote, 'not a creature was stirring, not even a Fatima or a mouse. Anyway, what is the difference?' On the day of the wedding I wrote two entries. The first read, 'Papa is good, he loves me a lot oh and he loves you to.' There followed some drawings of hearts and horses and then, 'Today Papa and Ghinwa got married and it is a Special Day For me. Now I call Ghinwa MoM and I still call Papa Papa.' I was seven years old.

After the mullah approved the marriage papers, Joonam sat me down and explained to me that now Aunty Ghinwa was my mother and that I should stop calling her aunty. I mulled over whether to go with 'mother', which was new and exciting to me since I'd never really bonded with my biological mother (too old-fashioned, said Joonam) or to go with 'mom,' which is what my friends all called their mothers, but finally decided to go with 'mummy', which sounded the nicest. It was also what Papa called Joonam. 'Since then it's been an unending call,' my mother says, imitating me, 'Mummymummymummmy . . .' This, embarrassingly, is true.

Because is was a special occasion, Mummy was allowed to have a page in my diary too, which she filled in several days later, writing, 'Now I am a very happy person because I am a mother of a beautiful child called Fatima. Fatima, my child, is very sweet and very cute. It is true. Sometimes she doesn't listen but this is only because she still doesn't know and doesn't mean to be mean.' I don't remember what she was referring to, I must have been ignoring her at the time.

Ten days later, my parents hosted a wedding reception for thirty friends at the Sheraton. Mummy wore an off-white sari that Papa had given her as a wedding present. I had just had my tonsils removed and sat grumbling at home with Aunty Lulu, missing the party.

At the end of August that year, Mummy and I travelled to Pakistan together. It was her first visit and my second. Coming back to Karachi with Mummy made it feel more like home, but it was a difficult trip for her. 'Mir never thought he'd live in exile, no, never,' Mummy says, shaking her head adamantly. 'He always thought of going back, though to me it didn't seem possible. Every time I wanted to change something in the flat, Mir would say, "No, don't do it, it's not ours. We'll be going back home soon." He was always preparing to return.'

Murtaza had spoken to his mother about the idea of coming home, to end the exile that started with Zia and should have ended with his death. Joonam was always supportive, but there was one family member who wasn't. Benazir baulked at the idea when Murtaza suggested coming back to Pakistan, ready to face the multitude of cases of treason Zia's junta had brought against him and Shahnawaz. 'Please don't come back now, Mir,' she had begged him, 'it's too hard on me.' Benazir told her brother that Pakistan's Intelligence, the ISI, had 'lost his file', that no one knew the exact number of charges the dictator had brought against him. She told her brother that her hands were tied.

'After the first PPP government was formed in 1988 a lot of political dissidents who had gone abroad came back to Pakistan,' Suhail tells me. 'Many Sindhis who suffered persecution under Zia, Baloch too – even Khair Bux Marri returned from Afghanistan – so it was expected that Murtaza and his followers would be afforded the same treatment. We had fought for democracy too, we had struggled against Zia and yet we were singled out and not included in this process of return.'[12] Suhail, along with Murtaza, had to stay abroad, in limbo. Why didn't Papa go back? I asked him. Why didn't you just ignore the Prime Minister's objections and return? 'The strength of Murtaza's cadres were in Pakistan. He was away from them, but he didn't want to create problems for his sister by pushing his return, he didn't want to be blamed for rocking her boat, because he knew how much she wanted it, and I suppose, ultimately, he felt it was a weak government and it would eventually be removed.'

When asked, in an interview with the BBC, why he hadn't immediately returned with the advent of so-called democracy in Pakistan, Murtaza replied candidly. 'I'm staying away. I couldn't live with the idea that I'd be the cause of my sister losing her government.' She would in fact do that very ably on her own.

In Karachi, on that first trip, my mother gave her first press conference. Papa had trusted Ghinwa to speak for him. A journalist asked the question on everyone's mind that winter of 1989: why hadn't Murtaza returned to participate in his country's turn towards democracy? Mummy answered honestly: 'He wants to. But his sister has asked him not to come back now.' Benazir would not forget her sister-in-law's frank remark.

It was shortly after our return to Damascus that Mummy found out she was pregnant. My parents told me together. They seemed nervous, again. I had been an only child, and a pushy one at that, for so long. 'Fati,' Papa started, gulping air, before launching into his single breath breaking news style, 'Mummyandiaregoingtohaveababy.' I was thrilled. I started screaming and jumping up and down, this time on the marble floor. I just hoped it wouldn't be a girl.

Zulfikar Ali Bhutto junior was born on 1 August 1990, ten days late. I was at my friend Paula's house when Papa raced over to pick me up and take me to the hospital. Papa was early and I was annoyed. I had two more hours left of playtime and he didn't say why he had come early to pick me up. Papa honked from the car downstairs like a madman. When I didn't respond, he ran to the intercom, calling that I should get my things and come down. Papa wasn't normally so anxious; I thought he was playing a trick on me.

A few weeks earlier he had burst into my bedroom on a Saturday morning shouting for me to get up. 'Fati! Fati! *Fati!*' he yelled '*Come quickly!*' I rubbed my eyes and looked at the clock on my bedside table. It was only 7.30 in the morning. 'What is it?' I asked, sitting up groggily. '*Hurry up, Get up. Get up!*' he yelled and ran out the door. I slung my legs out of bed and dragged myself out of my room. The minute I went through the door Papa dumped a bucket of water on me. He had a laugh that sounded so mischievous when he was playing pranks it was hard not to laugh along. I burst into fits of giggles and we stood there in the wet hallway, me drenched in water and him holding an empty red bucket.

But this time there was no prank. I sat in the car, having taken my time to get downstairs, and we zoomed off to the Chami Hospital in the centre of town. We saw Zulfi for the first time together. He was dry and scaly, from having hung around in the womb well past his due date, and bright pink. Joonam came to Damascus to be with us for the birth. Benazir, in an attempt to patch things up with her mother and keep her in the right sphere of influence, so to speak, made Nusrat a federal minister. Joonam didn't sacrifice her life for the job, understanding perhaps why it had been given to her, and left her post to spend a month with us in Syria. Joonam was with us in Damascus when Benazir's government fell. Our new life as a family was blissfully complete.

Benazir's government ended with a whimper, not a bang. The ethnic and sectarian violence that would cloud her second term in power, with allegations of widespread human rights abuses, had its roots in her party's first term in office. 1989 saw tensions between ethnic Muhajirs, those who had crossed over from India at the time of Partition, and Sindhis come to a head with 'an escalation of unexplained shooting incidents in Karachi'.[13] Even the Sindhi Prime Minister herself was forced to admit that the spiralling violence in her home province was out of control, calling it a 'mini-insurgency'.[14]

In a letter to his mother, Murtaza raised the concerns that had been creating ripples of anger in the party. 'On the telephone I threatened to write a long letter,' Murtaza started. 'However, I will try my best to keep it short. I am sorry that the content is a bit grim, but I believe it is at least worth a mention. In Clifton recently two dedicated PSF [Pakistan Students Federation, the student wing of the PPP] boys were killed by police under the guise of 'anti dacoit operations'. Other staunch party loyalists who were active and/or imprisoned during Zia's years are now back in prison. We are receiving word that many are now being tortured again.' Murtaza spends the next page listing the names of those suffering at the hands of Benazir's police system; the list goes from Hyderabad to Thatta to Karachi and onto various other cities in the province. The grievances then continued: 'Kausar Ali Shah [not yet a PPP parliamentarian] who in Kabul conspired with the Afghan rebels to have Shah and me killed, has been made Managing Director of the National Construction Company. Saifullah Khalid meanwhile continues to face abuse and humiliation because despite having his body and mind broken in torture camps, he refused to implicate you or Pinky in Zia's false cases. I hear Pinky says he is "burnt" and "must be disposed of", at least agree to see his father and try to help his brothers.'

Murtaza's letter is written in red ink, not the kind he used normally but it adds a measure of urgency.

> Two other boys, from Punjab, Javed Iqbal[15] and Mohd Yousef were horribly tortured during Zia's years. Till the end they said 'We are Bhuttoists and will remain so no matter what you do to us.' In 1983 a team of army psychologists interviewed them to determine how the PPP could so effectively 'brainwash' its cadres that under the severest torture they did not break. These two 'case studies' of loyalty to Bhutto Shaheed are still in prison in Lahore. Isn't that a shame? I am sure you have many other problems to confront but I also believe we have a moral obligation to redress these ones too.[16]

Murtaza ended the letter with love to his mother and sister and on the back of the page he taped a clipping from a Pakistani newspaper reporting on the silencing of the independent press by Benazir's government's, adding, 'P.S. I thought you may like to see this.'

Meanwhile Benazir and the coterie that surrounded her were busy making as much out of Pakistan as they could. There was no room for matters of domestic politics. The PPP had been fully opened to the remnants of Zia's regime. Mahmood Haroon, whose signature was on Zulfikar Ali Bhutto's death warrant, was appointed the Governor of Sindh; Nisar Khuro, who publicly demanded that Zulfikar be 'hanged first and tried later', was made the head of the party in Sindh, and various other floaters from Zia's cabinet and inner circle had been given party tickets.

Benazir reversed many of her father's programmes, easily and openly. She asked the Commonwealth to allow Pakistan back, oblivious to Zulfikar's principled decision in leaving the British-run organization; she scrapped the ceilings on land holdings set in place by Zulfikar's land reforms, thereby safeguarding the feudal system her father had been taking steps to roll back; and she began the process of privatizing the industries that her father had nationalized and made sure that the lion's share was never far from her hands. The Naudero sugar mill built by Zulfikar for the people was privatized by Benazir and bought by Anwar Majid, a businessman and Zardari's frontman for many years. The Shadadkot textile mill, also part of Zulfikar's people-owned Sindh-based industries, was snapped up by Nadir Magsi, a member of Benazir's PPP, the party that had built and nationalized these very mills for the province's poor. The list of mills bought by the first couple's stand-ins is long and embarrassing; suffice it to say the list continues to grow to this very day. Zardari's crooked business chums along with petty small-time thieves he happened to know also found space for themselves within the inner sanctum of the PPP. It was said that they made millions, money taken under the table, and that kickbacks were ceremoniously given back to the first couple, earning Zardari the nickname Mr Ten Per Cent.

Internationally, the government carried on Zia's policies unamended.

The Afghan adventure continued, aided and abetted by the Intelligence agencies, as did Pakistan's nuclear programme. Iqbal Akhund, one of Benazir's foreign affairs advisors and a career diplomat who watched Benazir's government first hand, summed up the PPP's foreign policy perfectly: 'On Afghanistan, Kashmir and India the government was faced with very complex and thorny issues but the decision making in all these had been taken over by the army and the intelligence agencies in Zia's time, and there, in the ultimate analysis, it remained.'[17]

As Prime Minister, Benazir made the decision to cover her head with a white *dupatta*. She was the first member of our family to wear a *hijab*. Her father, so progressive that he shunned traditional Sindhi dictates of *purdah*, the system of keeping one's womenfolk at home and behind closed doors so no unrelated male might eye them, and broke barriers by taking his wife and daughters to public gatherings along with his sons, never considered the headscarf necessary for public approval. Fatima Jinnah, the sister and companion of the nation's founder, fought elections against General Ayub Khan in the 1960s and she, an unmarried woman, never covered her hair. Benazir's choice was the first of its kind; not even her mother Nusrat covered her hair; it was a choice designed to keep the Islamic parties and leaders, like Maulana Fazlul Rehman's Jamiat e Ulema Islami – a constant election ally – on her side. Islam was an accessory at times and at others, it seems, an ideology. Benazir did not suspend the Hudood Ordinances, that called for women who commit adultery or engage in premarital sex to be put to death; nor did she enhance women's rights in any official way. In a two-year period, the Pakistan People's Party government led by Benazir did not introduce any meaningful legislation. Nothing was changed, no institutions strengthened. At the start of August 1990, in the days of Zulfikar's birth, Benazir Bhutto was sacked by President Ghulam Ishaq Khan on the grounds of massive corruption and the failure to control ethnic violence in Sindh.[18] According to the historian Ian Talbot, 'The Bhutto government had comprehensively failed to live up to expectations during its twenty months in office.'[19]

{ 16 }

Murtaza was overjoyed at the birth of a son. He called him Zulfi, borrowing his father's nickname, and privately fretted over what he'd call him when he wanted to scold him – how could he yell his father's name? In the family we called him Junior. He was a gorgeous baby. He never cried, never made a fuss, ate plenty and was exactly the companion I had been longing for. Zulfi would follow me around the house, copying me and acting like I had split the atom. As he got older, and I sterner, Mummy would intervene when I reprimanded him, only to be told, quite seriously, by Zulfi, 'Mummy, let Fati be. She's doing it for my own good.' I'd never felt so protective of anyone, not even Papa, until we had Zulfi.

Papa was nostalgic and uninspired when he imagined his life for ever caught in the comfortable malaise of the Middle East. One afternoon, we drove a short way outside the city limits to eat lunch at the Ebla Hotel, for once cheating on the Sheraton. It was early spring. The weather was warm, but not yet dry and arid as the summers in Damascus become. On our way to our table in the garden, we walked past the Ebla's large swimming pool and I saw a mischievous look in Papa's eyes. I could feel his excitement as we rounded the corner of the pool; he wanted to push me in. I had been dressed up by Mummy, wearing nice shoes and little earrings that I was quite proud of. Papa was looking elegant, as always. My friend Nora was with us and I wasn't in the mood for Papa's jolly hysterics. 'Don't,' I warned him as we made our way to lunch. He held himself back, but only just, and we enjoyed a perfectly forgettable lunch.

As we walked back towards the car park and passed by the pool, I was lost in earnest discussion with Nora. '*Fati!* Look!' Papa yelled, confusing me long enough for him to pick me up and hurl me into the water. I hit the ice-cold spring water with a loud splash and almost scraped my chin on the side of the pool in an attempt to avoid being totally subermerged. After touching the bottom of the deep end with my toes I swam back up and angrily pulled myself out of the pool. Papa was bent over in laughter. Mummy was shaking her head at his shenanigans, thankful that he had spared her. Nora was giggling along with Papa. I was on the verge of tears. 'You can't do that to me again!' I shouted through clenched teeth, 'Not ever again!' Papa was still laughing his whispery *khe khe khe* laugh and stopped only to say, 'Oh come on!' and wave his hand at me. 'No!' I yelled 'You can't.' I thought for a minute, aware that this was what Papa and I did – we joked around, we pulled pranks, we were the only ones who enjoyed these silly sorts of games. 'You can't, not until I'm fourteen at least. Then you can throw me in a pool again. But not until then.' I was nine years old. Fourteen seemed like a lifetime away. Papa's laughter petered out and he surprised me by saying softly, 'But Fatushki, what if I'm not alive then?'

I burst into tears. Here I was trying to reach a compromise, banning pool dunkings till the reasonable age of fourteen, and there was Papa talking about his death. I bawled and bawled. He sat me down on his lap, soaking wet and ruining his silk suit, hugging me and rocking me back and forth. He didn't take it back. He didn't say he was just kidding. He just wiped my eyes.

In between my tears, I shouted at my father. 'Fourteen isn't far. Of course you'll be alive. You have to live till I'm a hundred!' I wiped my nose on his shoulder. Papa kissed me and continued to rock me. 'I hope so,' he said.

———◆•••◆———

Back in Pakistan, Benazir was now in opposition. She reprinted her stationery to signal her new posting as head of the largest party opposed to the government and set about planning her political return. Dr Ghulam Hussain was summoned to meet his former political student, who was, in late 1990, in a good mood.

'She asked me what I thought the difference had been between her government and Zulfikar Ali Bhutto's,' he says. 'I told her, "Leave it." But she insisted, she was feeling quite jolly. So I told her. "In front of Zulfikar Ali Bhutto we party workers were afraid to lie – we were punished for it greatly. In front of you," I said, "we are afraid to tell the truth."'[1]

Dr Hussain is an emotional man. His eyes welled up as he spoke to me in the living room of his Islamabad home. 'I was called to the party's Central Committee meeting once, as the ex-Secretary-General, and I saw all these new sycophants there around the table. I told her, in front of them, "Benazir *sahiba*, your people are selling employment tenders, are you aware of that?" And she replied, "Oh doctor, you're from an old time. This is a new age, we have to keep up with Nawaz Sharif"' – Benazir's one-time arch enemy/soon to be best friend, and Zia's protégé who led the Pakistan Muslim League. '"He has tons of money,"' she helpfully added, by way of explaining her party's dubious financial tactics.

'"But Benazir *sahiba*," I told her,' Dr Hussain says, having now forgone his tears for anger, his voice rising, '"You think you can buy credibility? You can't! How much will it cost?"' Dr Hussain doesn't mince his words, but still, I'm amazed that he spoke to her like that. That she tolerated his questioning of her leadership. It was never easy to do, but Dr Hussain's seniority afforded him his right to speak, and he continued, before the doors were closed on him for good. '"In my village,"' Dr Hussain shouts, as if with my notebook and pen before him I suddenly represent Benazir, '"there used to be no electricity, no schools." I told her, "If you were born in my village, you wouldn't have got past primary school. We earned this right to criticize and we fought to speak openly. You only inherited it."'

Suhail, like all the others who spent their lives under the powerful shadow of the PPP, was disappointed by the party's short turn in government. 'When I met Mir in the run-up to the '88 elections he was conscious that the coming time was going to be difficult – it wasn't just time to celebrate. Now Zia was gone, the party had to deliver.'[2] When the party left office leaving nothing concrete in its wake, people snapped out of the reverie that they'd built around Benazir and her promise of democracy. It had been a government manufactured entirely around promise, not principles. A state founded on the slippery premise of potential and legacy but nothing tangible in terms of grassroots work or ideology. Benazir was out of power and her husband, Asif Zardari, began his first stint in jail for the millions he'd taken while his wife was Prime Minister. It was rumoured that Zardari, who fancied himself a polo player, had built air-conditioned stables for his ponies – all imported, of course – in a country where Karachi, the commercial capital, often went without electricity for days (and still does). The ponies were pampered and fed almonds and milk daily. Zulfikar's cousin, Mumtaz Bhutto, the head of the Bhutto tribe, who was a founding member of the PPP, and Benazir's paternal uncle, spoke out openly against Zardari: a criminal who has made his way to power, he called him in the press. (Within three months of Zardari ascending to the presidency in 2008, Mumtaz was arrested. 'He steals our name and our history and then he thinks he can eliminate us one by one,' local newspapers quoted Mumtaz as saying.)

'It was after Benazir and then Nawaz Sharif's governments fell that there was immense pressure on Murtaza from his people in Pakistan. He was a political figure, he always had been, and he had political cadres behind him,' Suhail says. 'And they felt that the time for Murtaza had come and that he should participate in the next elections and play his due role in Pakistan's politics.'

Maulabux, one of those political workers, speaks forcefully when I mention this idea of the prodigal son returning home. 'In our culture, the *asl waris*, or true heir, was Mir *baba*.'[3] The assumption was that Benazir's brothers were not in Pakistan during the time that Benazir built her political career under Zia because it was too dangerous for them to remain in their country. Zulfikar had sent his sons out of the country specifically because he saw them as the inheritors of his throne. 'The unsaid understanding,' Mauli continues, 'was that whatever Benazir did at that time she did as a representative of her family, not as Benazir the individual, but as Benazir the child of Bhuttos.'

Mauli understands how this must sound, this trying to explain to me that we are our families, nothing more defined, nothing more unique than that. He's also talking to another eldest child, a daughter ironically. 'Look,' he starts again, measuring his words, 'it's the same in Baloch culture, in Pathan culture – even in Western cultures, isn't it? – it's the eldest son's role, duty even, to take over the father's work whether it is farming, business or politics.' Mauli stops. '*Bibi*,' he says, 'Bhutto *ka waris* Bhutto *hai*.' 'Bhutto's heir is a Bhutto'. Benazir had become a Zardari. It's a not so subtle reminder to me too, though Mauli is taking pains to make sure I don't take his explanation to heart – I'm single after all; there's no reason to take it personally, not yet at least.

'It's not about heirs or patriarchy,' Suhail corrects me when I put the idea to him. 'Mir had the same background as Benazir – he was a Bhutto, had a strong relationship with his father too, and also struggled against a dictator. But that's all Benazir had. Murtaza had the clean hands, the corruption- and compromise-free record, and the ideological understanding of socialist politics. *That's* what threatened his sister.'

The PPP worker cadres, almost uniformly made up of men in their early thirties who had come of age under the Zia dictatorship, seemed to agree. Hameed Baloch, from the opposite end of Karachi, in Malir, had worked under Benazir during the MRD period and as an office bearer in her first government. 'The youth elements of the party, the frontline workers in the Zia period were supporters of Murtaza and they wanted him back.' His disillusionment with Benazir was for the same reason as most of the old-school supporters who had started to leave the party under the new leadership. 'It had been taken over by Zardari and his corruption – there was no history to the party any more, no ideology, it had become a money-making operation.'[4]

'In the twenty months of his sister's rule, Mir maintained his silence' Suhail reminds me. 'Even though he saw and disagreed with what was going on. He took a very political and democratic path: he decided to contest elections. He didn't return and demand his title. He set himself up for a fight. How many people, you tell me, have

311

contested elections from abroad and won?' Suhail asks, raising his eyebrows. He's right, I only know of one.

In the summer of 1993, Murtaza made up his mind. He was going home. He called Ghinwa, who had taken Zulfi to Oklahoma for the summer to visit her elder sister, Racha, and told her to come back home; he was going to contest the election. Ghinwa cut her trip short and flew home. I was away with my grandmother, Joonam, and was also put on a flight and bundled home. Murtaza spoke to his mother, who still held – and not for much longer – an honorary chairpersonship in the party. Murtaza asked Nusrat for the application forms to file for election tickets. But it was Benazir, the active Chairperson, who along with her husband had the task of choosing the party's candidates.

Benazir spoke to her brother directly. She refused him a ticket straight out and offered him some advice: if he was serious about coming back to Pakistan then he ought to leave Syria, a rogue state in her estimation, and settle in London for a few years, long enough to expunge any taint of socialism, and then they could talk about him running on a party ticket, maybe in an election or two. Benazir was a consummate bully; she had got her own way for too long.

Murtaza had been a card-carrying member of the People's Party since it was founded. He had paid his dues and had given the party his life, as he saw it. No, he finally insisted to his sister, I'll contest *this* election. Murtaza asked for nine tickets – all of which were eventually handed out to Zardari and his cronies. Benazir pushed back and rejected his request. 'I can't give you and your people nine seats,' she said and offered him a provincial seat in some backwoods constituency. None of us at the time could imagine why Benazir was so frightened of her younger brother.

Explaining Benazir's trepidation, Aftab Sherpao, a former vice-president of the PPP and the leader of his own faction now, puts it frankly. 'She was vindictive. She got the feel for power and didn't want to let go. She removed Begum Bhutto from the party because she was afraid of your father. She was on the weaker wicket; the Bhutto legacy was his, not hers, and this was always at the back of her mind.'[5] It was at the end of 1993 that Benazir ousted her mother, who had spent the better part of the year campaigning for Murtaza, from her largely ceremonial post as honorary Chairperson and installed herself as Chairperson for Life, an actual title.

Sherpao had once been a trusted colleague of Benazir's in the party. He would even deputize for her when she travelled, albeit watched carefully by two Benazir loyalists, who ensured he didn't deviate from any key agenda points. It was her political insecurity, culminating in the imposition of her chairpersonship in perpetuity, that Sherpao saw as the cause of their break. 'I even said in the press,' he says, using the dirty P word, one Benazir never liked (especially if it was preceded by the even dirtier F word – foreign), 'that if we had elections for party chairperson, no one would have opposed her! What's the fear? Instead she had some mock election where the Central Committee members were asked if they opposed her life chairpersonship and the results were never shown to the party workers. The sacrifices made by the party – everyone has a limited share in them.' Sherpao, whose brother Hayat was assassinated early in the party's history, eventually left Benazir and formed his own PPP. 'Whether you've been lashed, jailed, cast a vote, you are an asset of the party,' he tells me over cardamom-scented tea at his home in Islamabad. 'We've all contributed – my brother did, I did. This isn't anyone's personal fiefdom – it belongs to us all.'

But the party had become feudal turf; there wasn't room for charismatic leaders from across the party, or indeed, the family. All the old guard of the party made allusions to Benazir's treatment of her mother during party meetings. It was embarrassing, they would murmur, eyes downcast.

'Nine seats in all of Pakistan,' my mother says to me later as we stand in our kitchen and discuss our past and the book I'm writing that is making us relive it chapter by chapter. 'It is how she sidelined him since taking over the party. She virtually eliminated Murtaza – he had become a burden to her. There was simply no space for him.' Eventually, the seat that Murtaza had asked for as his first choice – PS 204, the Bhutto home seat of Larkana, where Zulfikar built the family home that would become Murtaza's residence – was given to a newcomer called Munawar Abbassi. Locals knew him as the landlord who had bestowed an *ajrak,* a Sindhi sign of hospitality, around General Zia's neck the first time he visited Larkana.

Murtaza decided to run as an independent and began to prepare for the race of his life. It must be said, because it cannot be left out, that nothing in Pakistan moves without the pull and sway of the Intelligence service. While Benazir corralled family members like Sanam, and distant friends and acquaintances, to dissuade Murtaza from returning home, the Intelligence – it's easy to see now, in hindsight – made some calls of its own to assess how serious the rift in the Bhutto family was. How far they reached and what influence they sought to have, I don't know, but a public feud opened a space for those who wished to work against the family. In Benazir's mind, her decisions always had the blessing of the all-powerful political establishment; this case was no different. In any event, the political establishment couldn't have influenced Murtaza either way; that was their fundamental misunderstanding. If Papa won a seat in parliament, we were packing our bags. If he didn't, we were staying put in our Damascus home. That was our family deal.

In August 1993, Ghinwa travelled to Pakistan with Zulfi to file Murtaza's election papers as an independent candidate. Papa and I dropped them at Damascus International Airport to catch the midnight flight to Karachi. We sat in the departure lounge, eating stale mortadella and cheese sandwiches while Papa went over the process with Mummy. He told her what her schedule would be like, how to deal with the press, and mentioned the name Ali Hingoro to her – an old party worker who had once served as one of the inner core of Benazir's security detail and had been shunted out in her post-power shake-down. Stay with Ali, Papa told Mummy, he'll protect you. I remembered the name because it sounded incongruous, Italian almost. 'Ali is a diehard worker,' Papa said. Diehard.

By morning Mummy had touched down at Jinnah Airport and was met by thousands of people who had come to welcome her. 'Zulfi got scared because of all the shouting and the slogans,' she remembered. 'We walked off the tarmac into Joonam's car and went straight to Lyari to condole with some workers' families – it was my first introduction to Pakistan's condolence culture . . .' (There is a bitter laugh and a pause. We would all become very well acquainted with our country's condolence culture.) They filed Papa's papers first in Lyari and were mobbed by throngs of the neighbourhood women who came out to dance and celebrate the occasion. From there Mummy travelled by road to the poorest parts of Sindh, to Dadu, Badin and Thatta, and presented her husband's candidacy. The usual six-hour drive from Karachi to Larkana took their convoy of cars an agonizing eighteen hours because of all the crowds along the way.

After a strenuous two weeks, Mummy and Zulfi returned to Damascus. I was waiting for them. We had fifteen days to regroup and then go out for the second campaign push. It was an exciting time. Papa asked me to take his photograph for the various posters that were going to be plastered across Sindh. We took sombre and serious pictures – nothing flashy, him wearing an *ajrak*, him sitting on a chair. Basic stuff, really, but I felt proud of my role as Papa's official portrait photographer. I told my friends that I was going to Pakistan for two weeks to campaign for my father. If he won, we'd be leaving. No one took me very seriously. We always spoke of going home to this Pakistan place (Bakistan in the Syrian accent), but everyone thought of me as Syrian ultimately.

In Pakistan we hit the road running. We drove for twenty-one hours a day, stopping at small towns and villages along the way to speak at neighbourhood markets and canvass for Papa among local merchants and traders. I had, up until that point, only visited the chic suburbs of Karachi and our ancestral homeland of Larkana. I'd never been into the interior. It was a shock. We climbed the roofs of mud houses to stand on barely cemented tiles to speak to crowds; we commiserated with families who had lost children to suicide because of the lack of employment opportunities; we went to weddings at night that were punctuated not by music or dancing but by rifle fire; we ate all our meals from communal plates crawling with flies.

At one resthouse, in Thatta, we found our bedroom ceiling covered with lizards. Mummy and I slept with *ajraks* over our faces to protect ourselves from any untimely falls. In the bathroom of another resthouse, I went to brush my teeth in the morning only to find that the bucket of water that served as our sink was also home to a family of tadpoles. I ran next door to warn Joonam that the water was contaminated only to find her washing her face. 'There are tadpoles in the water!' I shrieked, trying to stop her. 'Thank God there's water, Fati,' Joonam responded nonchalantly and carried on washing.

At the daily public meetings and rallies we attended, Joonam would speak in Urdu to the crowds who screamed and clapped for her. Mummy would be asked to read a speech too, one that she had written in Urdu, no different from the Arabic script, but that she pronounced gingerly because the language was alien to her. She was brave and spoke at each meeting, directly after her mother-in-law, stopping every once in a while to tweak the speech and add thoughts of her own. Inevitably, I would be encouraged by some member of our campaign group to speak too. They would whisper a slogan or two in my ear and have me hold my brother while I trembled in front of the microphone. I hated the sound of my squeaky adolescent voice and would make myself sick with worry in the short walk from my chair to the podium. I pretended to have a sore throat, a fever, anything to stop me having to speak to the crowds. Until one day I stood up there, faced with thousands of eager faces, trying to summon the courage to parrot the three phrases I'd been given when Zulfi, only three years old, grabbed the mike and repeated what he'd heard for the last two weeks: '*Ji-ye Bhuttooooo,*' he cooed, 'Long live Bhutto,' and the crowd went wild. I laughed and turned around to look at Mummy, who was just as shocked as I was that our little boy had been listening and waiting for his chance. From then on, I became Zulfi's delighted crutch; I would walk him to the microphone, lift him above the podium and patiently hold him while he wowed the crowd with his baby Urdu and mature showmanship. I had been saved.

On the road, we memorized the campaign songs – Sindhi folk music but with new words about Papa. On those long road trips we all slept bundled together, legs sprawled out over each other's laps, our heads contorted and cramped and lost all sense of privacy. But there were moments of worry and anger too.

In Larkana, the base of operations for Papa's campaign, we were in the car driving to a series of rallies when Joonam noticed an election banner and ordered the driver to hit the brakes. She stormed out of the car and walked straight up to the shopkeeper whose store was displaying the dark-blue banner. 'What is this?' Joonam yelled, her hands shaking with anger. The banner had been put up by Munawar Abbassi, Benazir's candidate against her brother. 'Vote for Munawar,' the banner read, 'Zulfikar Ali Bhutto's *sepah*' – '[soldier]'. 'He's running against Bhutto's son and he calls himself his soldier?' Joonam was livid, she was screaming at the storeowner. I thought she might hit him. The shopkeeper froze. It wasn't his banner. He wasn't to blame for the sign, but he kept his mouth shut and let Joonam scream. She was furious, at her daughter, at the party, at how hard she had to work to bring back her only remaining son.

There had been a creatively vicious slander campaign carried out, unsurprisingly, by the PPP. It attacked Murtaza's candidacy by calling him a terrorist, by claiming that he had been living abroad in the lap of luxury; it promised, through Chinese whispers, that he would not return, even if he won.

But our campaign continued undaunted; the excitement over the return of the prodigal son was infectious, remembers Maulabux, even though the divide between the party and family was turning ugly. 'Before Mir *baba* returned,' he tells me over biscuits and cooled Pakcola bottles at a party worker's house in Malir, 'we made T-shirts with his face on them. They were simple white shirts with a photograph in the centre. As we were going to a PPP rally in Nishtar Park in Karachi one day, people stopped me and said, "Mauli are you looking to get beaten?" Why? "Why should we get beaten?" I asked – "We're only showing his face, we're remembering him here today, letting the media see Murtaza has the support of the ordinary workers." So, we went on to the rally. We were stopped at the entrance of the park by the police – they told us we couldn't go in, that we were "Murtaza's boys," "*Al Zulfikaris*". We thought, straight away, that this must be the police, the establishment, trying to make trouble for BB and create bad press for the party. So we waited for her outside the park. When we saw her car approaching I went to meet it and told her, through her window, "*Sahiba* they're not letting us in." She looked at me, coolly, and said, "If you're going to wear these pictures, then go and make your own rally, don't come to ours."' Maulabux shakes his head. 'I'll never forget that she said that to me, never.'[6]

On election day in October, Papa sat in his office in the Damascus flat with the doors uncharacteristically shut. He made forms on plain white paper to tally the incoming votes and was sitting quietly in front of two phones. He was tense. We weren't allowed to make the smallest of noises; if Papa heard any of us outside talking or larking around in the hallways he'd slowly come out of his office and with his face looking quite red and tired ask us to be quiet.

Papa had no polling agents on the ground in any of the constituencies he was contesting; no first defence against vote-rigging, no workers filing complaints of irregularities, no monitors. Joonam had spent the last three days in Larkana knocking on hundreds of doors asking people to vote to bring her son back to his country. The disinformation campaign put out by Benazir's party had reached fever pitch in the weeks before election day and Joonam worked tirelessly to turn back the tide.

In the early evening Mummy and I were in the kitchen, getting food ready for the friends who would be joining us for dinner, regardless of the outcome. We weren't preparing for a celebration, but we weren't going to face defeat hungry either. Mummy was leaning over the oven and I was standing next to the door when we heard a scream. I had only heard a noise like that once before – the night Zia's plane had crashed. It was so loud I thought the oven had exploded. My heart leapt into my throat and lodged itself there and before I could figure out what was happening, Papa ran into the kitchen. He had won from Larkana, from his father's home constituency, from his independent, hotly contested seat.

We hugged each other and tried to take in what this meant. We were going home. People started coming over shortly afterwards. The house, our small two-bedroom flat, was full of music and friends. He had won.

{ 17 }

After sixteen years of exile, of being kept quiet, Murtaza had been propelled into the limelight as the heir apparent of the PPP. He had been giving interviews to Pakistani newspapers throughout the summer, meeting journalists who flew to Syria to write about his decision to contest the elections, speaking to press clubs on the telephone, and sending statements from his black fax machine that hadn't stopped whirring for months. In the beginning it was Al Zulfikar and the Bhutto brothers' militant activities that fuelled much of the media interest. It was like a ball and chain, holding Murtaza, his name and his reputation firmly in their place lest he ever got out of hand. He countered the allegations that he was an anti-democratic vigilante with candour.

'If force comes by force, against the will of the people and breaks the constitution of the country, imprisons members of the parliament, kills representatives of the people . . . then the people must resist. It is their moral and national duty. It is their constitutional duty to resist the force that broke their will,' Murtaza said in an oft-quoted interview.

I am prepared to speak on every subject. I have never betrayed my people. I would like to live with my people. My brother died for the cause. I will live and die in Syria but I will never compromise. I am not ashamed. The hijacking of the PIA plane was an act of three people to secure the release of political prisoners. In Kabul the plane was wired from the cockpit to the tail with 100 small explosive devices. They threatened to blow up the plane . . .

I am against hijacking, hostage taking. I saved the lives of over 100 people by intervening. Why don't you give me credit for that? It is said Mir Murtaza hijacked the plane, but who saved the lives of over 100 innocent people on board the plane?[1]

The flurry of negative press attention in Pakistan, no doubt spurred on by the political establishment, could not damage the momentum that had started with Murtaza contesting the elections and climaxed with his win in Larkana.

On 12 August he had told the *Pakistani Daily News*, 'My decision to return and contest elections is final . . . If the Pakistani establishment want, they can hang another Bhutto – but will they hang my son, Zulfikar Ali Bhutto? And hundreds of other Zulfikar Ali Bhuttos across the country?'[2]

I hated it when he spoke like that. It seemed like tempting fate, especially with a family history such as ours. The article noted that Murtaza's voice was 'choked with emotion'. He was so close to his dream of going home, he couldn't see beyond it.

Another story two weeks later quoted Murtaza declaring he would return to Karachi 'come what may', followed by his scathing criticism of Benazir's first government. 'The deserving, honest and underprivileged people of Sindh should sit in parliament as opposed to the corrupt, wealthy, power-seekers who have thronged the assemblies in the past.'[3] His interviews were dangerous – they pitted Murtaza firmly against his sister, whose party members constituted the bulk of those corrupt power-seekers that were returning to government for a second term. 'I am incorruptible, with a clean heart,' Murtaza continued, prompting the interviewer to ask if they might call him Mr Clean, a pun on Benazir's husband, Mr Ten Per Cent – which would inflate to Mr Fifty Per Cent in the coming second term. The paper noted that Murtaza laughed and answered, 'Yes, you may.'

The press played on both sides; one day writing that Murtaza was returning to Pakistan to bring militancy and terrorism back into Pakistani politics and the next day editorializing that he was a representative of the lost dreams of the PPP and reminding readers that he had been a 'four *anna* paying member of the PPP since he was a thirteen-year-old boy'.

Papa was set to leave Syria on 3 November and we were to follow him a month later, when the school term had ended. Suhail, who had been widowed during the long years of exile, came to Damascus with his two sons, Bilal and Ali, to prepare for the return home with us. Everyone was caught up in a frenzy of excitement. We had been preparing to leave almost since we had first settled in Damascus. Mummy gave me a suitcase one evening and asked me to start gathering my things and sorting out what I was taking and what I would leave behind. I filled the case with my books, Nancy Drew and Hardy Boys mysteries, and when it was full went to my mother and asked if I might have another case for my clothes. I began telling all my friends I was leaving for good, and acted casual when they reacted sadly. I was going home too. Papa's enthusiasm was contagious.

Several days before his departure, Murtaza went to see President Hafez al Assad to thank him for his country's hospitality. *Al Qa'ed*, the leader, had been a gracious host to us for many years and a constant friend of the Bhutto family. When Benazir came to Damascus on a state visit during her first term, she was received with great ceremony and honours. Papa made me miss my annual spring concert to receive Wadi and though I was a little annoyed to miss my class's performance, I was excited to see my aunt. This time, though, she wasn't staying at our small flat but at the presidential guesthouse on the top of a hill overlooking the city.

Upon her arrival I glued myself to my aunt, sitting on her lap and nuzzling her shoulder with my nose, looking for the mole between the nape of her neck and where her shoulders began, my navigation now stunted by the new obstacle of her prime ministerial *hijab*.

Wadi brought me a set of encyclopedias, the most perfect present. Asif, on the other hand, gave me twenty-four Barbie dolls, that year's entire series, along with a gargantuan Barbie doll's house that seemed larger than I was. Papa didn't care for Zardari's overly generous gift. 'Is he trying to buy my family?' Papa complained to Mummy when we got home. I was allowed to keep one Barbie and the rest were donated to a local orphanage. I don't know where the doll's house went; I didn't get to keep it either. Papa had only met Zardari once or twice before, the first time in Paris, where we met Wadi when she had flown in to celebrate the 200th anniversary of the storming of the Bastille, but it was in Syria that Papa first experienced Asif's reprobate nature first-hand.

At the state dinner President Hafez al Assad held for Benazir, I slipped away from my seat as soon as dinner was served and climbed on to my aunt's lap as she sat next to President Assad. The President smiled at my breach of protocol and patted my head. He turned to the official interpreter to relay a question about what grade I was in school and whether I liked it.

Mummy had insisted that my American school place me in classical Arabic classes with the native speakers. 'Leave her in the colloquial class,' Papa suggested. 'She'll be with the other foreigners, we're going home soon anyway, why does she need Arabic?' (The Bhuttos seem to have a personal distaste for all languages other than English. Even though Papa spoke beautiful Sindhi and Urdu, he never taught me a word of either. My aunts would speak to each other exclusively in English and Joonam had managed to pass on to her children only the most basic understanding of Farsi, though she spoke it beautifully herself. But Mummy, wary of my fate as part of this monolingual lot, persisted and I was placed in the advanced Arabic classes in school.)

I understood the President's question before the interpreter translated it into English and answered him directly. Assad's official aides seemed to be flustered, strutting and fidgeting around us like peacocks, and my aunt's people were positively unhinged at my breach of diplomatic etiquette. My parents, initially amused by my precociousness, had since been trying to lure me back to my seat, but I ignored them. I was chatting to the President and nuzzling my nose into Wadi's powdery scented neck. I remember President Assad as very kind and informal that night. Wadi too. She was in a loving and relaxed mood and let me sit on her lap all evening.

———◆◆◆◆►———

'Have we not treated you well?' President Assad asked Murtaza. At their farewell meeting he assured him gratefully that he had protected him and his family at their time of need. 'Then why must you leave?' replied Assad, who always treated Murtaza with a fatherly affection and ease. Murtaza said that he had a duty to return home now. 'Why are you in a hurry?' Assad asked. It was a good question. Murtaza replied that he had to return to his country. In that case, answered the President, if we cannot convince you to stay, please accept my help in your return. He offered Murtaza the use of his presidential aeroplane, knowing that Murtaza's security was going to be an issue in the days to come.

Papa was excited and nervous. I don't remember him sitting still in those heady days. All those years of 'one day' were finally over. Suhail was going to fly back to Karachi with his comrade and old friend, but the day before the departure, plans were changed and Suhail was to stay behind in Damascus with us. 'Just in case,' Papa said, and left it at that.

On the night of 2 November our small flat was full of friends coming to bid Murtaza farewell. It wasn't a sad goodbye, but one filled with laughter and music and joy. After all the farewells were said and done, Frank Sinatra was playing on the stereo, and Ghinwa and Murtaza were alone together at last; it was the end of a long, emotional night. Ghinwa turned to her husband and said, 'So, you did it your way finally?' But Murtaza didn't laugh. He smiled softly and shook his head 'No. I did nothing my way. If I had, things would have been very different today.'

The next morning I woke up crying. I was so attached to my father, I felt sad every time he travelled, and this time my emotions were multiplied a hundredfold. I was scared for him. And I didn't want to go to school. I wanted to be at home with Mummy and Uncle Suhail, listening to the news so that I knew Papa was OK. In the hallway, bright and early, my father, who hadn't slept a minute all night, hugged me and wiped away my tears with his thumbs. 'Be brave,' he told me. 'But you're going to be arrested,' I wailed. The newspapers and reports from Pakistan would not let us forget it.

A story three days earlier had claimed that Benazir's government was holding 'in readiness non-bailable warrants of arrest for Murtaza on arrival',[4] while another article helpfully pointed out that a seasoned criminal like Murtaza was still legally entitled to seek 'protective bail before arrest' since he was a member of parliament, if the notion of jail didn't tickle his fancy.[5]

That Papa would be arrested was something we took for granted. He had packed several magazines – *Newsweek* and *The Economist* and *Vanity Fair*, his favourite – to read in jail. He had pen and paper to write letters – which he promised he would have someone fax across to me – and books to keep him company. He was so relaxed about jail, for my sake I'm sure, he made it seem like nothing more frightening than a spa weekend away and even joked that he planned to lose a few pounds while incarcerated.

I left for school shortly after Papa set off for the airport. We were having a soccer tournament for the regional American schools at DCS and we had the morning off to cheer on our home team. I saw Nora, my best friend, as soon as I walked into the campus gates. She was quiet. 'May he come back to you exactly as he left you,' she said, uncharacteristically stoic. Nora is half Armenian and half Syrian; she said it was a traditional saying. I was miserable and moped around school for much of the day, quietly wondering where my father's plane had got to and trying not to worry. 'Your father's making history, you know,' a teacher who had heard about Papa's return on the BBC World Service said to me as I stood with Nora by the football field. I felt uneasy all day.

Hafez al Assad's presidential plane had received clearance from all the countries it had to fly over, except one – Pakistan. The Syrian Ambassador in Islamabad was dispatched to the Foreign Office to facilitate the landing of the presidential plane and was rudely rebuffed. The government would not allow the plane to land, a move that would have caused a diplomatic incident had Assad not anticipated Benazir's actions. She was petty, this he knew; it was partly why he had offered Murtaza his plane in the first place. Eventually the aeroplane landed at Dubai International Airport, where Murtaza was received by senior UAE officials, arranged by President Assad, and continued his journey home on board an Ethiopian Airways flight.

'It was such a complex operation,' Suhail remembers. 'I was on the phone for twenty-four hours that day – hectic efforts were being made to get Murtaza on a connecting flight to Karachi. We were anxious to get him there on the third as crowds had been gathering at Jinnah Airport. They had been waiting for him since the morning.'[6] Hameed Baloch, who had once been an office bearer in the party under Benazir's leadership, was in Karachi that day and out on the roads outside the airport since the morning. 'There were Rangers, police vans, we even saw some military vehicles – there were thousands of us workers at the airport to receive Mir *baba* and it seemed that the job of all the officials there that day was to keep us away. Every couple of hours they would try to confuse us by saying that his flight was landing at the old Karachi airport terminal, fifteen minutes away, and once we had walked there we would be told the flight was landing at the new terminal that we had just left.'[7]

In Damascus, we heard the news of the police contingents at the airport. No one had expected the state to put on such a show of force. Murtaza was a Pakistani citizen, he was on board a commercial airliner, and he had said, repeatedly, that he was prepared to face the charges against him. 'We weren't worried about his travelling from Damascus to Karachi,' Suhail says, 'but we were worried about his security on the ground once he reached Karachi.' To make sure things were under control, Murtaza's mother Nusrat was at the airport throughout the day. But she too was being shunted back and forth between terminals along with the rest of the workers who had flocked to see Zulfikar's eldest son return home. And after four hours of being held at bay, she snapped. Nusrat presented herself at the new airport terminal after having wasted the morning and afternoon driving back and forth between terminals being harangued by officials. Unfortunately, the police officer who made the last feeble attempt to restrict her entry received a smart slap on the face.

Nusrat was a tough woman who had faced Zia's military and had been violently attacked in a Lahore stadium during the dark days of the dictatorship. She strode into the airport and waited for her son to arrive, leaving the police officer stinging from the slap but unable to stop her going forward. 'When we heard that the police were mis-behaving with *Begum Sahiba*,' Hameed says, 'we were prepared to storm the gates of the airport, but the police began to beat us with *lathis* and lobbed tear gas grenades into the crowds – they were trying to disperse us, to make us leave so Mir *baba* would return to Pakistan without any support. But we stayed, just so we could be there, just so we could see him.'

It was night-time when Murtaza finally landed. The police had become more aggressive after dark, taking several workers into custody and facing down the crowds with riot gear, but the crowds resisted, hurling rocks at the police vans as they stopped them from making their way towards the airport. Murtaza walked down the steps alone, seeing Karachi for the first time under cover of night. He knelt on the tarmac and kissed the ground. Nusrat was there, emotional, crying. He embraced his mother and was led away by the police and taken to Landhi Jail in North Karachi. It would be his home for the next eight months.

None of the workers who had waited under the Karachi sun saw Murtaza that night; he was taken to jail from a side exit. But there was jubilation in the air. He was home, finally.

Benazir was in power once again and this time she was faced with a different opponent, her brother. He wasn't some ordinary member of a vague opposition party; he was popularly recognized in patriar-chal Pakistan as the heir to the Bhutto throne. She was liable to be replaced and the threat came from within her own family.

Maulabux found himself in jail too. 'A number of Murtaza Bhutto's supporters were jailed during Benazir's second government. They were afraid of us politically. We had been fighting for the party all our lives, they knew our strength. And we had left them; they had become so corrupt by then, there was nothing left to defend about them.'[8]

Over the years I've always seen Maulabux and Shahnawaz together. They're both highly energetic men, even after years spent in jail, and when they speak, their stories often slide into each others. They are both tall, proud-looking men of Sheedi origin; Shahnawaz is the slimmer, quieter, of the two. He had been doing his master's in public administration at Karachi University when Benazir's police, around the time of Murtaza's return, arrested him. 'In jail there were no criminal cases against Murtaza Bhutto's people,' he says, echoing Mauli. 'It was purely political – they held us on charges of treason, anti-state activities, those sorts of things.'[9] Shahnawaz hired a private lawyer; since he had left Benazir's PPP he no longer benefited from the party's legal aid schemes, which he bitterly notes were being put to use defending the new party members who were serving time in jail for corruption, narcotics and extortion.

Most of those men who had formed a loyal core around Benazir in the days before she came to power had abandoned the party after her first government and had begun to work for Murtaza. They were punished for their desertion with prison sentences. 'I used to meet Ali Sonara in the Karachi Central Jail dispensary,' Shahnawaz says. 'They always kept us in separate cells so we used to meet there to relay messages and keep each other informed of what was going on. The word on the block was that that those who the government managed to flip against Mir *baba* were being released then badly beaten by the police and then held up at press conferences as examples of what Murtaza Bhutto did to people who deserted him. It was standard procedure for the government. Once, in the dispensary, Ali – who had been in charge of Benazir's security – told me that Ghous Ali Shah, the advisor to the Chief Minister of Sindh, had offered him a position in the Minister's office if he would come out and publicly denounce Murtaza Bhutto.'

The offers were not unattractive, especially considering how Murtaza's workers were being kept in jail. 'When I was arrested in 1993,' Shannawaz goes on, 'I was kept in illegal custody – there was no warrant for my arrest, no charges were made clear to me. The police used to torture me by putting cigarettes out all over my body.' I notice the marks on his arms as he speaks. They're small and dark, angry patches of skin pinched together. What Shahnawaz describes, the warrantless arrests, the lack of judicial procedure, were hallmarks of Benazir's second regime. The police were empowered to act as a mercenary force, with no regard for law and order or justice. I know this now, but at the time we learned about the human rights abuses as they unfolded, as neighbours were picked up and failed to return, and from the whispered stories about the police torture cells.

'When the police finally took me before a magistrate, I was blindfolded and chained – my hands in one pair of shackles and my legs in another set. They started to throw questions at me and I refused to answer. "Remove my blindfold first," I demanded and they did and I saw the judge before me was a fellow with such a big beard and the *nishan*, the sign from daily prayers, etched on his forehead. My arms hurt so much from the torture, I could barely move. I thought he'd help me, being a religious man, and I told him how the police had tortured me for days – I didn't know how many, I had lost count. I opened my shirt to show him the scars on my chest. And this magistrate, this devout judge, you know what he told me? He said that the police could continue to hold me illegally without warrant or charges for two more days. He sent me away and told the police to bring me back then. Of course, they never did.'[10]

It is peculiar to hear these stories, to feel so helpless in hindsight and to know that these men before me suffered at the hands of my aunt, for my father, in ways that I cannot bear to imagine. I sometimes wondered, as a maudlin teenager, how I would hold up under torture. It seemed to be a reasonable thing to ponder, given the stories I grew up hearing, but I've never had to find out. I haven't escaped the question though; it is answered for me by others all too frequently, their scars and their families' pain the evidence of how they fared under torture.

Maulabux was also sent to jail in the first month of Benazir's new government. I ask him why he was imprisoned, and he thinks back to those years and laughs. 'The case against me in '93 was made by a local superintendent of police who claims that I was seen planning a murder in Lyari, our area, at midnight one evening. The man I'm meant to have killed dies the same night, at 12.15, fifteen minutes later, in Malir – two hours away. What am I? Superman? How am I supposed to have managed that?' I laugh along with him. I don't know what else to do.

'We weren't with Mir *baba* for the money,' Mauli continues. 'We were in jail, in chains, and we didn't leave him. We were there for love – this scared Benazir's people a lot. We couldn't be bought. One day in jail, Nabeel Gabol came to see me.' (I know Nabeel Gabol. When I was writing a weekly column for Pakistan's largest Urdu news-paper I attacked him in several articles over the lack of potable water in Lyari and the electricity power cuts that lasted whole summers. He's a feckless man who was elected to parliament from Lyari and made a hefty amount of money in Benazir's first government. He made enough to move out of the area, which is desperately poor, and into the plush suburb of Defence. In her second government, Gabol was elevated to deputy speaker of the Sindh Assembly. The very mention of his name makes me cringe.) Maulabux continued, smiling at the look on my face. 'He stood in front of me and said, "Mauli, give a press conference and say Murtaza Bhutto's policies are bad and that you're leaving him." I looked at him and asked, "Nabeel, what door did you come in from?" He turned around and pointed – there was only one door in the room – "OK," I said, "now leave through it."' Mauli wheezes into laughter. I like him very much. He's brave. He radiates courage. He and his wife, also Sheedi, run a free tuition centre on the roof of their apartment building designed to keep Lyari's poor children off the gang-infested streets.

'They offered money, lots of it, to our friends, other workers, in jail. Some were tortured very badly and gave in, but our feeling was, if we die, then we die, but we're living for Murtaza. The jailers used to abuse us regularly. They called us "Al Zulfikar boys", terrorists. They would taunt us as they beat us, saying, "What is your leader Murtaza Bhutto doing for you now?" It was us experienced workers who were on their hit list. When they saw that we didn't respond to their blows, they would cut us and rub *masala* into our wounds.'

I know it's painful for Mauli to tell me these things and for him and Shahnawaz to admit this humiliation and vulnerability. As we speak, I focus hard on my notebook, on getting their words down, so I don't have to look at them. Pakistani society is too traditional, too patriarchal for these grown men to share stories of their pain with a young woman half their age. I always imagined I had a high tolerance for disturbing truths and frightening stories, but I'm unable to be professional at moments like these, wanting to apologize instead of just nodding along seriously. As if noticing my unease, Mauli, always jovial, breaks the tempo of the interview and tells me about his encounters with Papa in jail.

They were both held in Landhi Jail, some two hours away from 70 Clifton. Papa was kept in solitary confinement, removed from the other prisoners lest he launch an in-house recruitment drive. He asked repeatedly to be moved to the common cells and was routinely refused. 'We were in B class cells and Mir *baba* was in solitary. One day he sent the warden, a man called Durrani who was charged with guarding him, to our block to ask if Mauli was getting food and if I was eating properly or not. There were many Sindhis in our cells, belonging to other parties, and when they saw that they said, "*Vah!* We want to join Murtaza Bhutto too." "*Bismillah!*" I said. Mir *baba* always looked after me and once he sent me clothes from 70 Clifton along with some *shalwar kameez* that were being brought for him. "These are for Mauli *sahib*," I was told. People were shocked that not only was I getting clothes and food sent to me on Murtaza Bhutto's behalf, but here I was being called *sahib*! They thought I was a religious leader or something – they couldn't understand why Murtaza Bhutto would treat a worker with such affection!' Mauli laughs and for once I can look at him and smile too.

Benazir, eager to show that she had no animosity towards her brother, even as he sat in solitary confinement in Landhi Jail, and that the stories of a political falling-out were *noorah kushti*, pretend feuds, offered Papa Eid parole. The government declared 70 Clifton a 'sub-jail' for the duration of the holiday. Papa refused his sister's charitable invitation. 'I will only accept the Prime Minister's offer if all political prisoners are awarded the same parole for Eid and are allowed to be with their families too.' Of course, Benazir said no. We, Mummy,

Zulfi, Joonam and I were kept – somewhat comically and somewhat frighteningly – under 'sub-jail' status for the first day of Eid. A special treat, I suppose, freed from the bizarre house arrest after twenty-four hours.

————•••••————

We reached Karachi from Damascus in mid-December, arriving at 70 Clifton at night. We were worried about Papa being in jail and wondered all the time what his conditions were like. Though he was kept in solitary confinement, in a cell with only a small cot and a urinal and sink in the corner, Papa downplayed the spartan conditions. He joked that he had made friends with the lizards who lived on his ceiling and the cockroaches that crept out of the drains at night. He told a magazine that it was a great feeling to be back home after exile, but pointed out that he was unsure of the government and his sister's hostility towards him when he landed.

> I was saying I hope they don't torture me now when I am so sleepy. When I wake up they can do whatever they want. It took me sometime to adjust . . . They took me straight to jail. Sometimes I was awakened and there were guards outside speaking in Urdu. It had been so many years, I would say to myself, 'Oh, there are Pakistanis outside.' I thought I was still in Syria or some place. Then I would remember I'm in Pakistan. Of course, there are Pakistanis in Pakistan![11]

The house at 70 Clifton felt empty when we arrived. Joonam had been its sole occupant for some time and she travelled frequently and didn't have the energy to run the huge house in the manner that it had been accustomed to during the days it hosted state dinners and functioned as a Prime Minister's residence. Mummy moved her and Papa's things into the guest room downstairs, and I raced up the stairs desperate to claim my father's old room. Sensing my eagerness, Joonam put her foot down and declared that I had to move into the old girls'

333

room. I didn't want to live in Benazir's old room. It was painted black. The bookshelves – only three – were full of her Mills and Boon romance novels and there was no space for my things. In my annoyance at having to move into the one room I didn't want, I asked Joonam if my aunt could come and take her things. I didn't want to keep them.

I enrolled at the Karachi American School, starting in the second semester of sixth grade. Unlike in Damascus, everyone knew who I was. My aunt was Prime Minister and my father was in jail. I wasn't anonymous any more. The school was enormous, with a swimming pool and tennis courts and a football field the size of my old school. I missed Damascus and my friends more than I thought possible. I spent all my free time on the telephone to my friends in Syria, racking up huge bills.

A few days after reaching Karachi, we finally saw Papa, in court. He was being brought to the High Court near the American consulate and we went with Joonam to see him for the first time since he'd left that early November morning. We were all so excited, Mummy dressed up and I imagined a family reunion with Joonam at our side. But the minute we reached the courts, I felt out of my depth. There were reporters everywhere and hundreds of men who had come to meet Papa and shake his hand and have a picture taken with him. There was almost no space for us. We sat behind him in court and I leaned forward, not understanding a word of the court proceedings. Papa was wearing a starched white *shalwar kameez*, which I'd rarely seen him in. He was seated at a bench with his lawyers but his co-accuseds in the case, young men, were standing in the dock, their arms and feet shackled in large rusty chains. I'd never seen anything like it. Papa leaned over to talk to them in between proceedings and joked and laughed with them, his way of reaching out and breaking the barriers that kept him seated on a bench and them standing in chains.

Shahnawaz Baloch told me later that the first time he met Papa after his return was in court. He was in custody too at the time, jailed by Benazir without warrant, and appearing as one of the co-accused in

Zia's ninety or so cases against the Bhutto brothers. 'He hugged me', Shahnawaz said, 'like a bear. He told me, "Shahnawaz, don't worry. Now I'm back, everything will be fine."'[12]

Everyone flocked to see Murtaza in court – it was the only glimpse of him that they could get: parliament was too secure and the gates guarded against citizens coming in. Hameed remembers how after not being able to see Murtaza land at Jinnah Airport, he and some fellow workers prepared to receive him on his first showing in court. 'We were in our area, Malir, and we had gone and bought rose petals. We parked on a street that we knew the police car carrying him to court would pass through, and sat there right in the middle of the road! We didn't want to miss Mir *baba* this time. We covered the flowers in the back seat with fabric so that the police wouldn't stop us, and got out of the car and waited. We showered the street with rose petals when Mir *baba* passed, we shouted *Jiye* Bhutto, and he saw us. He raised a fist to us, we knew the signal. Be strong. Then when we got to court, he hugged me and said, "Hameed *bhai*, what name are you using here?"' Hameed laughs, expecting me to understand the Kabul connection, but I don't. He has to explain it to me. I am learning the codes of this language, it has taken time but after enough *nom de guerres* are bandied about you eventually start to think in double identities.

We had to share Papa in court that day. I wanted to have him all to myself and I kept trying to squeeze my way closer to him. Finally the court broke for a recess and we went into a side room for Papa to smoke and for us to finally be alone. We hugged and I cried. He seemed larger, taller, stronger here. He was more formal. He told us, when everyone had left, that we had brought too much luggage from Damascus, which rather annoyed Mummy and me. After all the trauma we'd been through that's the first thing he thought to say to us? But we didn't dwell on it. We were so happy to see Papa and to know that he was OK. We had all felt so stranded in 70 Clifton without him, as if we were in a waiting room, in transit, living unofficially until he returned. We spent a lot of strange moments in courtrooms while Papa was imprisoned. Mummy and I both spent birthdays in court, watching bail hearings being postponed. We had our first – our only – family portrait taken in a Karachi courtroom. We experienced Papa in public, as a politician, in those rooms for the first time.

$\left\{ 18 \right\}$

In an interview with the local *Weekend Post*, Murtaza was asked what had become a frequent question. His sister, the Prime Minister, insisted there were no problems between the two siblings. Everything was fine. He's in jail, yes, I had him arrested, but aside from my brother being a terrorist we have no problems, only personal ones here and there. She projected their differences as trivial, familial ones. 'There is no personal conflict between me and Benazir,' Murtaza answered – sometimes he called her Mrs Zardari, because he said she had long since stopped behaving like a Bhutto. I'm a feminist, I kept my name, Benazir would return, infuriated at being called by her husband's name. If the Prime Minister is a feminist, it prompts the question as to why she hasn't repealed the Hudood Ordinances, Papa would retort. The argument usually met its end at this point – 'There, however, exist differences in political perceptions, concepts and method.'

The question that followed was, again, typical; was this all a show then? Some sort of inter-family drama being played out on the national stage? And Murtaza answered as clearly as he always did.

As far as the 'drama' is concerned, I can assure you that . . . had it been a drama, my plane would not have been turned back. I would not have been arrested without a warrant, locked in jail without formal charges, wouldn't have been brought to the court until after a lapse of seventy hours. I should have met my lawyers the next day and not after twenty days. We should have got all the papers pertaining to my cases immediately. At the time of writing this, my lawyers still do not have them. If all this had been a drama, the champions of justice who believe that 'the law should take its own course' would have not arrested thousands of my supporters, my reception camps (at the airport) would not have been uprooted, my supporters' houses would not have been bulldozed. I would not be sitting and writing these answers to you from solitary confinement in the former punishment ward of Landhi District East Prison.[1]

Murtaza was taken to the Sindh Assembly to swear his oath and when he rose to speak for the first time in parliament, the *Daily Nation* newspaper noted that 'the hall of the Sindh Assembly was in a state of pin-drop silence when a new voice intended to introduce itself in the House for the first time, the voice of Mir Murtaza Bhutto, jailed brother of the Prime Minister.'[2]

I was at school that day. I wasn't allowed to miss any of my classes. Papa was strict about only one thing – my education – and when I returned home I saw my grandmother crying. 'He sounded just like his father,' Joonam said. It was true; they shared the same hoarse almost high-pitched voice when they were speaking publicly and the same deep tone in conversation. 'It was people from her party, from what was supposed to be the opposition to Mir, who had tears in their eyes when he spoke that day,' Suhail tells me. 'Some of them broke party lines and came and kissed your father's hand after he spoke, it was such a strange thing to do, but they were moved. You see, that's what really threatened Pinky. The challenge to her and the support for Mir came from within the workers in her own party, from inside not outside.'[3]

Though Murtaza was essentially received as the heralded elder son of his father when he returned to Pakistan, he had a lot to prove. He was keenly aware of this. It informed his decision to contest a provincial seat, as opposed to a national one; he wanted to start from the bottom. Murtaza was different from his family. He didn't believe in the feudal entitlement that came with the name; he had seen his sister go from gainfully unemployed to Prime Minister at the age of thirty-five and then back out of a job two years later. Murtaza made it clear that he would start from the bottom and work his way up. People had to learn about him, they had to discover who he was – he had to prove himself. And slowly, he did.

Speaking to a *Dawn* journalist during a court recess Murtaza addressed the negative campaign the PPP was launching against him, 'It has become a favourite pastime for certain opportunist elements in the party to harp on the theme that Murtaza Bhutto is living in a time warp,' he said.

> This presumes that when I speak of the crippling poverty around us, I am living in the past because there is supposed to be no poverty in Pakistan. When I speak of the poor, of the shirtless, the homeless, and the hungry, of the need for clean water, rural dispensaries, schools, the crying need to eradicate corruption, rape, drugs and so on, I am supposed to be living in the past. The presumption being that these are not the urgent tasks facing us as a nation about to enter the twenty-first century. If I'm living in a time warp, where are these jokers living? In Switzerland?[4]

Papa was a sharp and sarcastic breath of fresh air. He said that the PPP had become a party of 'robber barons' and called for a 'system of progressive taxation on all sectors of a certain income bracket, including agrarian land owners' to be strictly implemented, no small suggestion coming from a man with a rich feudal background. He said the country would need 'open heart surgery' to treat corruption. The newspaper noted that he also 'favoured party elections'. Murtaza had become the anti-Benazir in the media. He was, by virtue of his ideology, the antithesis of what Benazir had become in power. And this did not please her.

I still spoke to my aunt, somewhat awkwardly. We had been very close when I was younger. I was the first child born into the family and she was my *Wadi bua*. I loved her deeply and used to ask to spend time with her whenever I could. I was present at her engagement to the man who would take over her life and party. I was a chaperone on their dates, including the one – at an amusement park outside London – where she decided to marry Zardari. Her hand had been stung by a bee and Asif asked an amusement park stall holder for some ice to put on it. She said later that that's when she knew he was 'the one'. But since we returned to Pakistan I had seen a different, ugly side to my aunt.

I called her one afternoon and in a fit of childish hope asked her why she was being so vicious to my father. Wadi was conciliatory, as she usually was when backed against a wall. You don't know what's happening, I'm not doing anything. You've misunderstood the situation, etc. etc. Finally, I had her where I wanted her. 'Well, if you're being honest and you have nothing to do with his bad treatment,' I said, 'come and see him with us in jail tomorrow.' She froze. I was eleven years old. I pushed again. We have to be there at four. She was in Karachi. I had waited for Wadi to be in the city before making the call. She mumbled something about speaking to the head of some department for permission to visit the prison and promised she would call me back to confirm. I was elated. 'She's coming!' I told Mummy and Joonam. 'Wadi said she would – she just needs to confirm.' They both looked at me a little sadly. 'No, no,' I assured them, 'she's coming.' I knew what they were thinking. I was naïve; she was engaged in a political war against her brother. But I thought that if she'd only come and meet him face to face, alone, she'd realize that she was wrong; that they were strongest together, not apart; that she'd been led astray, that his politics were the ones their father built a nation on years ago and were the beliefs Wadi had held as her own before power happened to her. I thought these things could be true, could happen. She didn't call me back. I called her in the evening, several times, starting from 6 p.m. Finally, somewhere around dinner time Wadi took my call and said, 'Sorry, Fati, I can't come.' 'Why?' I asked. I had started to cry, but was biting my lip, hoping she wouldn't hear. 'I couldn't get permission from the jail to come' was Wadi's reply. *'But you're the Prime Minister,'* I shouted. 'Yes, well. They didn't give me permission.' And with that, the conversation was over. I couldn't shift the blame from her any more. She was involved. She was running the show.

We made the trip to Landhi Jail to see Papa once a week. I remember it being midweek, Wednesday or Thursday. It took us forty-five minutes to get to Landhi from our school, which was near Karachi's Jinnah Airport. Our visits began at 4 p.m. sharp; if we were held up in traffic or for some reason delayed, the time started without us. We couldn't have a minute longer than the forty-five given to us once a week.

During the first few trips, I'd ask, beg, for a few more minutes with Papa. He wouldn't ask. He knew that his warden, Durrani, who was kind and accommodating, would lose his job if it was discovered that he was treating Murtaza Bhutto too well. So *I* would ask. Could we have one more minute, please? The warden would bow his head, unable to grant my request, and shake his face from side to side without looking at me. It wasn't his fault, I knew that, but I had to ask. What damage would an additional sixty seconds do? I remembered, in those minutes, those head-shaking minutes, Wadi's descriptions in her book of how she was torn from her father, from Zulfikar, when he was spending his last days in Rawalpindi Jail. Why didn't she remember that? I used to stay up late at night thinking. Why was she punishing us the way she had been punished herself?

It bore away at my heart to have only forty-five minutes a week with my father. Mummy assures me we only had forty minutes a week with Papa, I don't remember. Five minutes extra seems generous to me now, 300 glorious seconds, so I add them on. We couldn't speak on the telephone – there were no mobile phones around then, and even if there had been, Papa would not have been allowed to keep one. I had grown up with my father being my sole property until the age of seven, I couldn't handle not sharing my day with him, not having him nearby to listen to jokes or check my homework. It was too much for the eleven-year-old me to handle.

So I wrote Papa a letter on my adolescent stationery, the kind printed on Day-Glo paper and covered with unicorns and rainbows. 'For Papa: FOR YOUR EYES ONLY,' I wrote on the envelope. I spent two pages wailing and moaning. It wasn't fair that Mummy got to see him in court when I was at school, I whinged. I offered, quite magnanimously, to miss school on the days when Papa had court appearances or Sindh Assembly meetings, which always met in the mornings and during the week. He wrote back and marked his own plain white envelope: 'To Papy from Papa'. The top right hand corner had '<u>PRIVATE AND CONFIDENTIAL</u>' underlined in all capitals and on the bottom left '<u>FOR YOUR EYES ONLY</u>, also underlined.

'Dear Fatima (frustrated) Bhutto' he wrote, instantly making me laugh.

My little darling, I read your letter and sympathize with your complaint. You have every right to see me and be with me as much as possible. And you know that nothing gives me greater pleasure than to see you, be next to you and to hold you in my arms. But, because I love you so much I want to make sure that you get your full education. You are a brilliant child and will one day become famous in your own right. But that won't be possible without a complete education. Grandpapa used to say that you can take everything away from a person – homes, money, jewellery – but you cannot take away what is in the mind. That is the safest treasure . . . If my court meets on Saturday then I would be more than happy if you came. When I am free from this jail where Wadi has put me then we will again be virtually inseparable. Until then, and for ever, I love you and adore you more than you can imagine. Love Papa. P.S Papy, you know when you were much younger you already had a natural talent for poetry. I still have in Damascus one lovely (and funny) poem you wrote about Mummy about 2 or 3 years ago. And the poem you read me recently (during your last exclusive visit) was beautiful. Here is a small one on Wadi and Slippery Joe:

Inky, Pinky, Ponky
Her husband is a donkey
Both loot the country
Her husband is a monkey
Inky, Pinky, Ponky

From then on, buoyed by my father's letter and his efforts to make me laugh and look on the bright side of our strange life, I reconciled myself to counting the minutes until Papa was released from jail, but resolved to make the most of our miserly time together.

Soon, the jail visits became a normal part of our bizarre lives. We would always arrive full of jitters and sit in the empty cement room, which was unpainted and grim but at least cool in Karachi's repressive heat and open the tiffin boxes we'd packed with food to share with Papa. Mummy and Zulfi both ate earlier in the day, small meals so they'd have room for another later, but I'd starve in school so I could have lunch with Papa at 4 p.m.

We sat on wooden chairs that would have seemed uncomfortable if we weren't so thrilled to be there and put the food and plates out on the rectangular table covered with a gingham plastic tablecloth, waiting anxiously to see Papa. Zulfi and I would stand at the window until we could make out Papa being escorted across the dusty prison yard, at which point we'd bolt out of the room to run to him. The warden would always smile when he saw us and would pat Zulfi's head affectionately.

Zulfi would often sit on Papa's lap during our visits and would get his father's undivided attention whenever he spoke; he was going to be four years old and was already a chatty and clever young boy. Sometimes Papa would ask us to bring Kashmiri tea. He never drank tea or coffee, but he liked Kashmiri *chai*, a strange drink of coagulated pink tea, flavoured with spices and pistachios. I never cared for it much then, but I always had a cup. Now I can't drink it. It reminds me too much of those forty-five minutes. Forty-five minutes I would kill for now.

———◆◆◆———

Zulfikar Ali Bhutto's birthday falls on 5 January and has been celebrated, since his death, at the family's ancestral graveyard at Garhi Khuda Bux, near Larkana. In 1994, 5 January coincided with Murtaza's second month in jail. He had last seen Zulfikar in 1977 when he and Shahnawaz were sent into exile by their father. Murtaza had never been to his father's grave to offer the customary prayers of Muslim mourning. He wrote a letter to the Sindh Home Ministry asking to be paroled for three days so that he could travel to Larkana to mark his father's birthday and pray at his grave. His request was swiftly turned down. The Eid parole was one thing, everyone in the country celebrated Eid. But there were only two Bhutto heirs in Pakistan for 5 January.

Mummy and Joonam and many of Murtaza's supporters travelled to Larkana to stand in his place and it soon became apparent that Benazir's government was going to make use of Murtaza's absence by putting on a large show of their government's strength. Some 10,000 plainclothes policemen had been deployed to Larkana for the occasion.

Murtaza reacted with unmeasured anger. 'We will not allow the killers of Zulfikar Ali Bhutto to come to *mazaar*,' he said. That ruled out virtually the entire top echelon of Benazir's PPP, all but five of her Central Committee members, and most of her closest advisors. 'Do not enter Larkana,' Murtaza warned, further adding that any attempts by the government to threaten or impede his workers' movements on the day would be noted and not forgotten. Already, Larkana was being swept by the police and many of Murtaza's most vocal workers, old Bhutto activists among them, were being detained on flimsy pretexts to keep them off the streets on the big day.

'There were so many of us in Al Murtaza, the family home. Ten people were staying in one of the guest rooms, many of the workers from across Sindh and Punjab were with us, staying in the house wherever we could find room, and Joonam was quite ill, she had a fever and a bad flu,' Mummy remembers of the lead-up to the 5th. 'Everyone was agitated about the hostile reaction from the government and was pushing for us to go to the *mazaar* early the next morning. "We have to go," they kept saying and I thought we shouldn't. Look, I said, we've come. We're here. We made our point. But no one registered me.'[5] No one could have expected what happened next.

On the morning of 5 January 1994, the police, led by a Karachi-based officer named Wajid Durrani, and acting under the orders of the Prime Minister, cordoned off our Al Murtaza house. The Bhutto house was locked down. The state was determined that no one should leave the house, not even Zulfikar's widow, the Prime Minister's own mother, who had never been stopped from travelling to her husband's grave, not even under General Zia's junta. The police were also charged with ensuring that no one should enter the house. Mummy exhales deeply before continuing. 'There was a big crowd of workers coming towards the house to join the convoy that was supposed to take us to the *mazaar*. They were stopped by the police. Inside the gates of the house, the workers who had been barricaded in began to shout slogans. The police were in the middle of these two crowds. At around eleven in the morning, the police fired into both groups.'

Mummy was inside the house when she heard the gunfire. One of Murtaza's paternal cousins, who goes by the nickname Poncho, was with the family at Al Murtaza. Joonam, who was in her bedroom resting, ran out of the room in a hurry and went through the gates to try and stop the police. The police were unprovoked. They had barricaded and isolated the house. The crowds of workers trying to reach Al Murtaza were stuck in limbo on the streets. No one in the crowds had any weapons – they were armed only with banners and posters, slogans and pictures. No reason for the police siege was ever given.

Joonam was outside the house, screaming, trying to stop the police from firing into the crowds, but the officers didn't put down their guns. They kept shooting, and then turned their guns towards Joonam and the open gates of the house and fired. 'They barely missed her,' Mummy says to me, shaken still by the memory of it all, 'two young boys, workers, were shot and killed that morning. One of them because he had stood in front of Joonam to protect her and he was hit by gunfire . . . It was meant for her . . .' Mummy's voice trails off.

Several young men were wounded. The police, led by Wajid Durrani, refused to open the cordon for the wounded to be taken to hospital. An Edhi Trust helicopter, privately owned by one of Pakistan's largest charitable foundations, came to airlift the wounded to safety – Larkana's local hospital is only a five-minute drive from our house – but was denied permission to land. The man who protected Joonam died on the road in front of Al Murtaza. He could have been saved had he been treated in time.

Joonam was distraught. No one had ever fired upon Bhutto's house. Not under Ayub Khan's dictatorship, not under Yahya Khan's martial law, not under Zia ul Haq's repression. She had been imprisoned, denied the right to trial and had even been beaten, but Nusrat Bhutto had never been shot at before. She spoke to the media, to the BBC, to Indian and Pakistani journalists who were at the scene. She said to the *New York Times* that only two days earlier Benazir had offered to drive her mother to the *mazaar* on the 5th, so desperate was she that Nusrat be seen with her and not with Murtaza's workers. 'Instead, she sent people to tear-gas and to shoot.'[6] Joonam continued angrily, 'She talks a lot about democracy, but she's become a little dictator. I can't forgive her.'[7]

'Night came and the house was still surrounded,' Mummy remembers, coming back to me. 'Our electricity was cut off. We knew that they were listening to everything we were saying so we spoke to each other in whispers the whole night. They had heard us talking about going to the *mazaar* early in the morning the night before the 5th, and when we woke up we had been encircled by the police. There were no phones, no lights, we didn't have enough food to feed everyone who was trapped inside and outside the gates and it was a cold night in the middle of Larkana's winter.'

Across the road at Larkana's sports stadium, the PPP celebrated the birth of Zulfikar Ali Bhutto. Music blared, people danced, and dinner was freely served. Benazir was there celebrating the show of strength she'd arranged, even after two men – two more men died of their injuries later – had lost their lives across the street. Many more were wounded. 'There was a total lack of decency,' Mummy says sadly when I ask her about Benazir's celebrations. 'She displayed a total lack of sympathy, of political maturity, of compassion. They were celebrating when just a few hours earlier a massacre had taken place.'

Zulfi and I were in Karachi. We couldn't reach either of our parents or our grandmother. We had stayed back to attend a cousin's birthday party. We refused to go. Our cousins were annoyed with me that day; I was spoiling the party, I was self-righteous, I was no fun. Go without us, I said, still not knowing the full extent of what had happened. People were being killed and my father was in jail. I refused to go to whatever hotel they were having the festivities at and didn't send Zulfi. We wore black armbands that day. Zulfi was still little and I carried him most of the day as we sat in the office waiting for news.

Mummy woke up in Larkana the next morning to find that the cordons hadn't been lifted. 'Joonam called Benazir, who was in Naudero,' she recalls, 'and she asked her daughter, "When are you going to stop killing people?" She was so angry. And Benazir told her mother that the 'crowds were shooting at *us*', meaning at the police. It was simply untrue. "They're RAW agents," she hissed at her mother before slamming the phone down.' The notion that RAW agents – or members of India's Research and Analysis Wing Intelligence agency – had infiltrated Al Murtaza sounded delusional to everyone but the Prime Minister, who made sure that the press picked up her conspiracy theory. Police were forced to fire at Murtaza Bhutto's house, mother, and supporters because they were all protecting/aiding/working as secret RAW agents. 'Mir found his sister's allegations, which were divorced from any logic or rationality, totally incredible,' Mummy remembers. 'He responded by saying, "Really? RAW agents? How did they get past the Prime Minister's stellar security and into the country? How did Indian spies manage to bypass her obscene security in Larkana?" It was too absurd.'

Speaking to the *New York Times* after the attacks, Joonam raged further, 'She tells a lot of lies, this daughter of mine . . . She has become paranoid about her brother.'[8]

{19}

The spring of 1994 passed slowly. We continued to visit Papa once a week in Landhi Jail and carried on building a life for ourselves in our new home. 70 Clifton felt like a house that hadn't been lived in for years; the rooms were musty and used more for storage than for living: albums and political gifts from random governmental functions spanning generations of political Bhuttos cluttered most cupboards and drawers, the furniture was frayed from lack of care, and it felt as if we were guests in our own house.

Mummy and I, both summer-born Geminis, spent our birthdays in courtrooms hearing Papa's bail hearings being postponed or put off because the prosecution had failed to show up. My school term had ended for the summer and we were alone at home, all of us moping around with nothing to do and nowhere to go. So when Mummy burst into my room one June morning, I assumed that she must be upset about something. Or that the house was on fire.

She turned on all the lights – there were no windows in my aunt's old room, they had all been boarded up. 'Get up! Getupgetup!' Mummy screamed. I sat upright in bed, unsure of how scared I should be and sleepily confused over what was happening. 'He's being released!' Mummy yelled. Only then did I realize that her voice was happy and excited. 'Papa's got bail – he's coming home!'

Papa was being tried in six major cases – all charges involving treason and sedition and all carrying the death penalty. There was confusion, even in Karachi, over just how many cases Zia's regime had brought against the Bhutto brothers. It was even said in the press that the total number of charges against Murtaza and Shahnawaz was higher than the ninety-odd that we knew of, that the junta had placed a total of 178 charges against the two men.

Although Murtaza had been awarded bail in many of the cases against him, there was one last case that was keeping him in jail. An application for bail had recently been put forward by his lawyers and the presiding judge, Ali Ahmed Junejo, had been overtly pressured by the Sindh government to deny the application and keep Murtaza in jail. 'I'm going to make history with this case,' Junejo declared. The proclamation sounded ominous to me. I remember Papa recounting to me what the judge had said and thinking that he was threatening to convict Papa, to send him to the gallows. It sounded to my twelve-year-old ears like a warning.

Rumour has it that on the day that he was preparing to read the bail decision to the court, 5 June, Junejo was interrupted several times by a court clerk who kept handing him slips of paper informing him that an urgent phone call was waiting for him in his chambers. He ignored the messages and continued with his proceedings, reading the order pronouncing Murtaza's bail.

What is certainly not rumour, however, is that the very next day Justice Ali Ahmed Junejo was sacked from his job by the government. Later, Junejo spoke openly of his belief that it was his decision to grant Murtaza Bhutto bail that cost him his job but that he felt he had done his legal duty and that justice had been served.

But Papa didn't come home that day. We waited all day, but there was no sign of him being released from Landhi Jail. Something was wrong; his release papers should have been processed in an hour – two at the most – but we had no information over what was causing the delay. Eventually, Joonam picked up the phone and called Benazir. Mummy and I sat in Joonam's bedroom as she made the call. 'Why aren't you releasing Mir?' Joonam asked, her voice tight and strained with nerves. 'We have more cases against him, Mummy,' the Prime Minister replied. She was not feeling chatty. She didn't elaborate on where these cases came from, how the 'missing' ISI file against Murtaza had suddenly reappeared, and didn't sound terribly aggrieved at the prospect of keeping her only brother in jail.

It was petty, it was so petty what Wadi was doing. My stomach hurt. I couldn't believe – even after the 5 January shooting – that she could be so cruel, so consumed by the myopic maintence of her power.

When Papa's release orders were finally signed the next day, close to twenty-fours hours after his bail had been granted, we heard that Benazir had been rung up by the army, by someone with enough epalettes to order the Prime Minister around. 'Stop making a hero out of him,' the army man reprimanded Benazir. 'Let him go, quickly.' Whatever else he said, it shook the Prime Minister. Papa received his release papers on 6 June.

———— ••••• ————

We busied ourselves getting dressed and tidying up the house. Papa hadn't been home to 70 Clifton in seventeen years. It was the home he was born into; they were the same age. I remember coming back from winter breaks in Karachi and Papa would pick us up at the airport and interrogate me about the house all the way back to Mezzeh. 'Was this painting still looking scary?' (The modern art piece of a crucified Jesus in Zulfikar's library and yes, it was.) Was that Chinese carpet still in the sitting room? How did the garden look? What shade of purple were the bougainvilleas? Everything had to look perfect for their reunion.

We watched the news of Papa's release on the BBC. The broadcast showed women in Lyari dancing and celebrating the court's verdict. It was confirmed. He was free. No calls of congratulation, however, came from the Prime Minister's house. Some time after lunch we received news that Papa had left Landhi. Joonam had already gone to bring him home. Throngs of supporters joined Murtaza on the journey out of jail and to his father's home. It should have taken Papa around two hours to reach us. But he didn't get home till after midnight.

Mummy, Zulfi and I stood at the doors of 70 Clifton when we heard the chanting, joyous crowds approaching. Mummy and I were holding on to each other, Zulfi in Mummy's arms. It was the homecoming we had been dreaming of since arriving in Karachi.

Papa was carried through the gates by the crowds who raised slogans and wept with the significance of what they were witnessing – Zulfikar's surviving son, finally free and making his emotional journey to his father's home. Papa was wearing a white *shalwar kameez* that was wrinkled and blotted with stains of Karachi's summer heat. His hair was flecked with deep pink rose petals. He was tired, but radiant. We hugged him at the door and I stood on my tiptoes to kiss his face. He smelt beautiful, as always, Gray Flannel cologne lingering on his brown skin.

Papa walked into the home he'd left as a young man of twenty-three. He was almost forty when he finally returned. Mummy, Joonam and I let Papa walk through the corridor of the house alone – we imagined that his heart must have been so heavy with nostalgia and all sorts of emotions, he would need his space. He was returning to a life that had been so violently changed, but whose scenery looked the same. Well, sort of. Papa walked as far as the ugly glass sliding doors that Joonam and Benazir had erected between the corridor and the downstairs lobby during their time under house arrest in the 1980s.

'What's this doing here?' Papa said, turning around, his face contorted with horror. The glass doors were removed the very next morning.

<hr />

The first trip Papa took, several days after being released, was to Larkana so that he could pray at his father and brother's graves. He planned to drive the 300 kilometres, stopping at some forty towns and villages on the way to meet and speak to people. It was a long and arduous journey, but an emotional one, marred only by the government's constant attempts to delay and harass him and his workers as they travelled across the interior of Sindh.

'All along the Super Highway from Karachi to Jamshoro people waited in the scorching heat of June to catch a glimpse of Mir Murtaza Bhutto,' a local magazine reported. 'From the Jamshoro toll plaza to the city's railway crossing, the road was so jam-packed that it took his motorcade a couple of hours to cross that distance of five minutes.'[1]

In Jamshoro, Murtaza was audacious, upping the ante in his criticisms of the government. 'My sister Benazir and the party of *Shaheed* (martyr) Bhutto are besieged by a mafia of thugs, thieves, and Zia's agents. We'll boot them out of the party,' he promised. 'We are the real party of the *shaheed*.'[2] Papa's convoy drove through cities large and small, pulling crowds along the way. 'I was surprised when in a small village like Kakar, in district Dadu, which has a total population of 2,000, he was received by a crowd of at least 10,000,' a Sindhi journalist covering the journey was quoted as saying.[3]

But Larkana's homecoming, that was something special. 'It was a prince's welcome,' reported the press. Murtaza's constituency was alive with the news of his imminent arrival. 'Normally the people of the town go to sleep by 9 or 10, especially in this sweltering heat,' a journalist commented. 'It has been like this only twice before – once when Bhutto's body came to Garhi Khuda Bux after his execution and the second time when Benazir returned from London in 1986.'[4]

As Murtaza's convoy reached the city limits, crossing the dusty roads of interior Sindh into Larkana's lush agricultural land, chants of '*Chamki haider ji talwar, aayo Bhutto jo pagdar.*' 'The sword of Hazrat (saint) Ali shines, the successor of Bhutto has arrived'[5] and men and women cried, '*Aya, Aya Murtaza Aya*' ('he's come, Murtaza has come'), while throwing flower petals on the passing cars.

Suhail, finally back in Pakistan and fighting the cases that Zia's dictatorship had made sure to lodge against him too for his loyalty to the Bhutto brothers, accompanied Murtaza on the trip to the family graveyard at Garhi Khuda Bux. 'Mir went first to Grandpapa's grave and did the *fateha* prayer there. He laid rose petals on the tomb and spent some time standing over his father's grave. It was very emotional for him. Then he went to pray at Shah's grave and was visibly shocked and hurt to see how his brother had been buried. The grave, unlike their father's, which had been encased in marble, was flat on the ground. It was untidy, there was dust and dirt around it, and it was circled by bricks that hadn't been properly fitted. The stage outside the *mazaar* that Benazir built for her rallies and public speeches was properly constructed, it was quite sophisticated. Papa was horrified.

'It was such a shame to see him at Shah's grave. His eyes welled with tears and he had to hold himself back from weeping.' Suhail knew both the brothers well. He was Murtaza's friend, closer to his age, but he too had regarded Shah as a younger brother. Angrily, which is not an emotion that comes easily to Suhail, he continued, 'She usurped Shah's land, took his Naudero house as her own, not leaving it for his daughter Sassi, and stood for elections on the NA 207 seat that their father had wanted for Shah.' Was it not convenient then, I asked, for her to tend to his burial site? Suhail shrugged. 'Papa called the manager of the *mazaar* then and there – he was an old man who took care of basic things. He told him to fix the *shaheed*'s grave properly and expected that when he next returned Shah would have a decent resting place.' And it was done, finally, nine years after Shah had been interred in Garhi Khuda Bux.

After the emotional visit to the family *mazaar* Murtaza spent several days receiving condolences for his father and brother at Al Murtaza. In Sindh, condolences are paid religiously, no matter how many years since the bereavement has passed, and with Murtaza finally home, people flocked from across the province and beyond – from Quetta in Balochistan, from Gujranwala in Punjab, and Gilgit in the Frontier to meet Murtaza and offer their respects.

Benazir and her cronies were now backed against a wall. Murtaza's threat was manageable for them when he was behind bars and access to him and his ability to speak to the people were restricted. Now that he was free, he was unstoppable. They did their best to subvert him as much as they could. The courts were ordered to hold his passport so that he was forbidden from leaving the country, a sort of reverse punishment for his return. He was constantly made to travel across Pakistan to appear at court hearings that continued against him in the various provinces, and his workers were routinely rounded up, arrested and viciously beaten.

In Karachi, Papa's movements were watched by the Intelligence service, who parked outside 70 Clifton in a dilapidated beige car with brown leather interior and followed him everywhere he went. But even they were no match for Papa's sense of humour. Once, en route to a wedding, we got lost on the road. Papa stopped the Intelligence vehicle and asked them for directions.

Murtaza continued to travel across Pakistan. People wanted to meet him, to hear him speak, to see if they was any hope to be placed in this newcomer or whether he was another elite feudal landowner who had no political connection with the ordinary masses. Murtaza spoke bravely and openly against the government and their dismal economic record and violent stance on law and order. And people were listening. It seemed as if Murtaza was the only politician speaking against the status quo instead of lining up to join it.

Unable to answer Murtaza's political criticisms of her regime, Benazir played the gender/sibling card, turning the political into the personal and the principled into the trivial. Speaking to the *New York Times* in the aftermath of the shooting at her brother's house in Larkana and responding to the allegations that her police force had illegally barricaded the house and shot at her mother, Benazir sniffed, 'Once my father died, I knew the day would come when, like all feudal families, they'd lock up the daughter so that the son takes over.'[6] She sulked further, saying that it was the 'fear of male prejudice that prompted her marriage. She married "for a home" she said.'[7] It should be noted that feudal families intent on locking up their daughters don't send them to Radcliffe and Oxford.

When questioned about the gender card, Murtaza answered directly. 'I have never asked to be the chairman of the party. I neither wanted to be the chairman of the party nor the Chief Minister of Sindh (as constantly alleged by Benazir). I have simply demanded elections in the party at all levels. Is that an unreasonable demand?'[8]

There is a lot of pain for me when I write about my aunt during this period. I stopped seeing her after the 5 January shootings. I wanted nothing to do with her; I was so shaken and completely horrified by what she had done. I lived in a city with crumbling roads, flooded with filthy rainwater during monsoon season because there was not even a rudimentary sewage system. Her corruption was evident, it was all around us. I was disappointed. I was taken to see her, forcibly, once or twice. Inevitably they were photo opportunities. I would be made to have lunch with my aunt at the Sheraton Hotel, taken by my grandmother Joonam, who was somewhat stuck in between her two children, where there would be a contingent of cameramen to take our pictures. 'Bhutto family feud a sham,' the papers would scream, and my photograph with my aunt would be the proof.

I had gone with Joonam to Wadi's house in Karachi in the first few months after our arrival, when everyone seemed intent on pretending that things were normal and there there was nothing strange about visiting your aunt who has just chucked your father in jail. We were sitting in Wadi's bedroom, her on the bed and us all around her. Joonam was uneasy. She was doing her best to pretend too, but she was distressed over the way Papa's return had been handled by the government. Joonam didn't like the way her children were so easily pitted against each other. 'I don't like the way you're fighting,' she said to Wadi. 'It's bad for your father's legacy.' Zardari had been sitting in an armchair in the room, silently, until then. 'As if there was a legacy,' he sneered loudly, filling up the room all of a sudden.

Everyone went quiet, even Wadi. No one ever spoke about Zulfikar like that, dismissively, vulgarly. Not in the family, not ever. Joonam seemed shell-shocked, but more than that, she looked deeply pained.

At home, I told Mummy what I'd heard. She swore in Arabic. I didn't know how to tell Papa, so I didn't. He didn't need the extra ammo in any case.

When he gave speeches or interviews, Papa often called Zardari a *chor*, a thief. He coined the term '*Asif baba and the chalees chor*', 'Asif Baba and the forty thieves' which became an instant hit (it remains part of the popular parlance to this day, I'm proud to note). When Papa was out of jail and infinitely more exposed, Joonam would nudge him when he started on like that. 'Stop, please!' she'd beg him. 'They're tyrants, they'll hurt you.'

'There's no question, *Begum Sahiba* was firmly with Mir', Suhail says to me over dinner in Karachi. 'But you must remember, Nusrat was the spirit of the PPP after ZAB was arrested in '77. Zia wanted to split the party and your grandmother played a very large role in keeping it together initially. She stood on trucks to give speeches, led rallies across the country, was beaten by the police and arrested – she was the life force of the PPP in those dark days. But as soon as Mir came back, Benazir ousted her mother from her honorary party post. She was terrified that her mother might try to overturn her decisions and welcome Mir into the party fold.'

I don't understand my family, I tell Suhail. Are you sure they were Rajput warriors? They sound like wild beasts sometimes. Suhail clucks his tongue at me and laughs. 'Yes, it's strange,' he admits 'but your grandmother never gave up on one child for the other, she was genuinely stuck between them. She wanted Mir to have a chance to fulfil his role, as Benazir had, and that put her in a very difficult position when it came to her daughter.'[9]

When I stopped accepting her invitations and finagled ways out of being forced into seeing her, Wadi tried to bribe me. One day, towards the end of sixth grade, I returned home from school to be told the Prime Minister urgently needed to speak to me. 'Pack your bags, Fati,' Wadi said excitedly on the phone. 'I'm taking you to South Africa for Nelson Mandela's inauguration. We leave in an hour.' She knew Mandela was a hero of mine, she knew I was desperate to meet him. It wasn't lunch at the Sheraton, she figured, there was no way I could refuse. But I did, even though I badly wanted to go. My father was still in jail at the time. 'I'm not going with you while you're imprisoning my father,' I said. She was furious. I was the family's first grandchild and my father treated me like a little grown-up. I got away with a lot and felt I had the right to speak my mind. I often did and it further distanced me from my aunt. The more I write, the more time that passes, the more my aunt becomes unrecognizable to me.

{ 20 }

My father spent the rest of 1994 touring Pakistan. He travelled to the mountains of Balochistan, to Waziristan and Swat, across the Punjab and through the heartland of Sindh. In Lahore in August he spoke against the government's attempts to subvert the judiciary by sacking judges who had ruled against the state and the shifting of qualified judges to lower courts to create vacancies for PPP loyalists and political appointees. Murtaza spoke about the government's curtailing of press freedoms; printing presses belonging to newspapers, especially to the more widely read vernacular papers, were shut down if their articles came out too harshly against the government. In Lahore Murtaza spoke of the case of Amir Mateen, a journalist from a local paper, who had been attacked by 'unknown assailants' and beaten in response to his reporting.

In Karachi Murtaza addressed the Federation of Chambers of Commerce and Industry and spoke sternly about the government's corruption. 'Economic crimes have to be checked effectively and tackled with an iron hand . . . loot and plunder is the order of the day and yet no one is brought to book.'[1] Again in the Punjab several months later, having travelled to attend a court hearing in one of the ongoing cases the government was pursuing against him, Murtaza lambasted the foreign deals the government was engaging in as fraudulent schemes based around huge kickbacks. The *Frontier Post* newspaper recorded Murtaza as frustratedly explaining that in spite of a 4-billion-dollar investment from the US and 7 billion dollars coming from Hong Kong to the Pakistani energy sector, the cost per unit to Pakistani consumers would be '6 to 6.5 cents, whereas the international rate was 3 to 3.5 cents per unit. Electricity would be sold to consumers around double the international rates.'[2]

By December the gluttonous corruption of the state gave way to another crisis; Sindh was being engulfed in ethnic violence. The ethnic Muhajir population, Urdu-speaking as opposed to the rest of the province's Sindhi speakers, were the target of political violence. The Muhajir Quami Movement (MQM), a quasi ethno-fascist party at the time, began to riot and incite violence as a reaction to the government's treatment of the Urdu-speaking population, who were a majority in Karachi. It was an ugly conflict that had its roots in Benazir's first government.

In the Sindh Assembly, Murtaza, a Sindhi, raised the issue of Karachi's increasing ethnic strife. 'In one breath, the Prime Minister says that the disturbances are in only 11 of our 80 police stations and in the next she comes out with "there is a mini-insurgency and guerrilla warfare in Karachi". The government is confused and unaware of the situation. The husband of the Prime Minister referred to the killing of persons as if they were not human beings when he said "during one month only 150 persons have been killed".' Murtaza went on to say that providing protection to the life and property of citizens was the basic responsibility of the government.

> How can law and order be restored when postgraduate youths are begging for even menial jobs. Without eliminating the curse of unemployment how can there be peace? When there is an abnormal increase in the prices of rice, flour, *ghee*, sugar and other commodities up to 150 per cent, how can you expect restoration of normality . . . the salaries of the President and the Prime Minister have been increased at the cost of facilities for the labourers who have been left groaning under the unprecedented price hike.[3]

Papa gave his monthly MPA salary to the Edhi Foundation every month. We didn't know this until after his assassination.

After Murtaza began to speak against the government's attacks on the ethnic Muhajirs and the escalating law and order problem in Karachi, the government saw another chance to portray Murtaza as a 'terrorist'. It did its best to spread paranoia, claiming that Murtaza was planning a partnership with Altaf Hussain, the leader of the MQM who had fled Karachi when his infamous gang-style brutality looked likely to land him in jail for the rest of his life. Hussain lives in England now, as a UK citizen, and plays a very active role in Pakistani politics.

Murtaza had no affinity for the MQM. He deplored their use of sectarian scare tactics and abhorred their violent behaviour. He had raised his voice not because he was enamoured of the MQM, but to speak out for the Urdu-speaking Muhajir community, which was an ethnic and linguistic grouping and distinct from the MQM, a political party.

After the government released a barrage of stories in the press attempting to discredit Murtaza by calling him a terrorist sympathizer, he responded with characteristic satire. He wrote to the Lahore-based weekly, the *Friday Times*:

Sir, It is not my habit to comment on news reports through 'letters to the editor', nor is it my responsibility to speak on behalf of the MQM. However, I am compelled to make an exception with regards to Adnan Adil's article 'Altaf's Cobras strike in Liaqatabad'. I have met Adnan Adil once and I mistook him for a normal, reasonable human being. But I have developed serious doubts on this score after reading his 'Cobra' story ('story' being a polite word). I quote from the article: 'It is said that they (Altaf's MQM) also possess a small tank – it is learnt that the MQM has obtained the support of Murtaza Bhutto's Al Zulfikar Organization which is providing it with weapons. Official sources say that wagons loaded with weapons have recently reached 70 Clifton.'

It is normal practice for Chief Minister Abdullah Shah's dogs to kidnap visitors coming to, or going from, 70 Clifton and subject them to vicious torture in undisclosed locations (eight days ago my private secretary was kidnapped, along with my driver and car, from outside my house. Only yesterday we were able to trace them to the CIA[4] centre in Saddar. Both the driver and secretary were barely alive).

How wagons loaded with weapons can get past the combined dragnet of a dozen federal and provincial agencies that have laid permanent siege to 70 Clifton is best left to Mr Adil's galloping imagination. But let me here, for the sake of posterity, set the record straight. Actually, one summer's evening Altaf Hussain and I met at the edge of a forest and sat down under the shade of a large banyan tree. We, both Mir and Pir [a religious mystic in Urdu and used here as a sign of the MQM's devotion to their leader], were in a melancholy mood. The following conversation transpired:

Altaf: You speak of the rights of Sindh and I of the rights of Muhajirs. Why don't we cooperate?

Murtaza: No problem. I can see your logic.

A: You know, things are getting hot in District Central. RPGs just won't do any more. We need tanks.

M: You are talking to the right man. I have several of them in my basement at 70 Clifton. They are the latest in high-tech and are left-hand drive. When can I gift-wrap them for you so that you can escalate your chauvinist Muhajir agenda effectively?

A: No, no. I don't want those kinds of tanks. You Sindhi feudals live in large houses that have big basements. I am from the middle class and have a modest house. I want a small tank.

M: Think small, want small. Look, I am sorry I can't help you there. I don't deal in Suzuki-class tanks. I only have Main Battle Tanks.

A: All right, forget the small tank. You got any fighter aircraft?

M: You pressed the right button again, Altaf (no wonder they call you Pir). I have a dozen F-16s parked in my garage. They are yours for the asking.

A: I don't know why they call you a terrorist. You don't seem to have a clue as to what this business is all about. F-16s are ineffective in urban areas. What I need are B52s capable of saturation bombing.

M: Er, actually yes I do have one B52 parked on 70 Clifton's roof. But it's the only one I have so I cannot give it to you for good. However, I can lend it to you for a couple of months provided you promise not to wipe out Larkana with it.

A: Promise. Scout's honour.

M: Another thing, for God's sake don't go telling Adnan Adil about all this.

A: You bet. But on one condition: you promise to let me test-drive your nuclear-powered submarine parked in front of your Hawksbay beach hut and I won't tell a soul anything. Cross my heart.

Yours,

Mir Murtaza Bhutto

Karachi

As the year came to a close, however, the government's violence against the Muhajirs would become increasingly aggressive and Karachi would become the centre of the state's bloody war against their political opponents, the MQM. The violence that Benazir's government would unleash on Karachi during her second term had its roots in her first stint in power. The MQM was first pushed into existence in the 1980s by General Zia's dictatorship in an attempt to break the PPP's strength in Sindh. The party's dubious origins aside, it grew into a political reality strengthened by the strong support of Karachi's middle class, who rallied around the MQM's secular, ethnic, anti-feudal (but very pro-industrialist and oligarchy friendly) leanings.

In 1988 Benazir entered into a coalition with her former enemies and formed her first government with the help of the MQM. Her '88 alliance with the MQM was an uneasy one and was continually rocked by Muhajir–Sindhi violence in Karachi. Benazir's inability to quell the violence and her refusal to admit any responsibility resulted in the MQM quitting the coalition.

Benazir was dismissed shortly after the MQM walked out of the alliance. The MQM, she believed, had sold her out. She may have been right. The 1990 elections that brought Benazir's then nemesis Sharif to power saw the MQM appearing on the side of the new victors and ready to perform their role as willing allies once more.

In 1993, however, the MQM was without establishment strength. It was the second-largest party seated in the Sindh Assembly but had lost its power to 'make or break' governments on account of its lack of ministries and national clout.[5] The MQM, desperate not to be deprived of its strength, turned into a militant street party and launched an armed movement in Karachi to wrest back its grassroots power and maintain its grip on the city. Benazir, already antagonized by the MQM, seized the opportunity to fight the party that had betrayed her. And she was prepared to fight dirty.

Instead of entrusting the judiciary to tackle the criminal and political thuggery of MQM, she bypassed the courts and directed her Interior Minister, General Naserullah Babar, to teach the MQM a lesson. General Babar, a cruel man with shady Afghan connections said to be so strong that he often publicly referred to the Taliban as 'my boys', launched an attack on the MQM and Karachi's Muhajirs so brutal that even its name, 'Operation Clean-Up', does not do justice to the level of violence the state employed.

Karachi's security forces, largely the police and the elite Ranger squads, became an uncontrollable force. Anyone who didn't fall into line with the Sindh government led by the PPP was declared a 'terrorist' or a criminal. The MQM became known simply as a party of terrorists and all Muhajirs as 'supporters of Altaf'. Altaf Hussain is undoubtedly a man with a criminal past, but he is not the sole – or most credible – representative of the Muhajir community by any means. The most infamous of the methods employed by Operation Clean-Up was the notorious 'police encounter', extrajudicial killings disguised as shoot-outs. Assassinations, torture, mutilation and blackmail were also popular with Karachi's security forces charged with 'cleaning up' the city.

The violence of Operation Clean-Up was so extreme it paralysed the city for the two years that it was officially in force. Schools shut down, certain neighbourhoods became out of bounds, and the economy shrank to such an extent that the 'flight of domestic capital due to the violence was Rs. 102 billion in the first three months of 1995 alone.'[6] Karachi had never before, and has never since, been so crippled by random and arbitrary displays of violence or so ably brought to its knees by the unchecked powers of the state and the police.

I remember weeks would pass when Zulfi and I would be stuck at home, school shut owing to the violence in the city. When things quietened down again we'd return to our classes, making up for lost time with lessons on Saturdays and Sundays and extra minutes added to our regular school time.

Once, as I rushed to my eighth-grade French class with Madame Hadi, a Francophile who had taught at the school for years, wondering how I was going to explain my incomplete homework assignment that had completely slipped my mind the night before, the sound of gunshots rang out. The slap of sneakers on KAS's cement floors, the hum of students going to class, the sound of lockers opening and closing – all disappeared around us, penetrated by the burst of gunfire.

KAS was an open-plan campus-style school. The shooting could have come from anywhere. Everyone, all of us middle- and high-school students, froze. Finally, a tenth-grader, a tall and lanky boy I quite liked at the time, yelled at us. 'Get down!' he screamed. 'Everybody get down now!'

I didn't want to seem afraid, not in front of the tenth-grader, so I took my time crouching down outside Madame Hadi's classroom. The shooting sounded as though it was coming from outside the school's main gate and the shots were sporadic. We lay on the cold floor for some fifteen minutes before the sound of shooting receded. I finished my French homework on the floor, trying stupidly to appear nonchalant and unaffected by the shooting, even though my hands were shaking.

That afternoon as we ate lunch on the long dining table in 70 Clifton, I told Papa what had happened at school. He was not at all entertained by my story of (a) not having finished my French homework as assigned and (b) my feigned coolness at the shooting.

School wasn't safe, but at least it was open and functioning again. I remember a three-week period earlier in the year when I was kept at home because of the shooting and rioting in the city. I was not missing more school, I warned Papa sternly; I had been bored to death sitting at home during those earlier three weeks. He had already sent Mummy, Zulfi and me to Damascus for a quarter of the school term (which I secretly delighted in, meeting up again with my old school friends) because Karachi had become too dangerous. OK, Papa said, you don't want to miss school? Don't worry, I'll figure something out.

The next morning our car had bulletproof vests taped to the back windows. Papa had turned Joonam's old brown Mercedes into a makeshift bulletproof vehicle. I had a fit. 'How can I go to school like that?' I moaned. 'People will laugh at me!' I had no real conception of just how dangerous our lives were. They couldn't be real, all those threats. Nothing was that bad, was it? Papa said he'd only move the vests from the windows if I wore them instead. 'But my head will be exposed!' I complained. I may have been a self-conscious brat but I didn't want to die, myths or no myths. We reached a weird settlement. Sometimes I wore the vests, sometimes they hung over the windows. Nobody laughed me. Boys ran to ask me just how much Kevlar was in the vests and to ask what sort of impact my bulletproof windows could withstand.

A year into Operation Clean-Up, *Herald Magazine*, a local publication that was printed in English and thus less censored than the more widely read Urdu magazines, launched a thorough and hard-hitting investigation into the Prime Minister's programme of genocidal violence in Karachi. The *Herald* report is thirteen pages long, filled with specific police encounters that a distinguished and respected investigative journalist, Ghulam Hasnain, helped by Hasan Zaidi, examined, taking apart the official version of events carefully and thoroughly.

The issue, whose cover featured a grisly photograph of the supposed MQM terrorist Naeem Sharri, who had been killed by the police, concentrated on the operation as it moved into its second year.

Herald Magazine revealed that Benazir had attended a political seminar in Karachi and had been angrily questioned over the 'government's apparent policy of eliminating suspected "terrorists" by summarily executing them'. In response, the Prime Minister 'praised the heroic efforts of the security forces and countered the allegations of extrajudicial killings by claiming that out of the more than 2,000 people killed last year [1995] only 55 were "terrorists" of the "Altaf Group" and that all of them were killed in real gun battles with the Rangers or the police'. 'She could not have been more wrong,' the article stated.[7] The Prime Minister's fuzzy logic and her fervent praise for the operation make clear her role; she was aware of what was happening on the ground. She was aware that Babar had turned Karachi into a killing field.

In 1994, 1,113 people were killed in what *Herald Magazine* called a 'bloody trail' that had turned Karachi into a 'virtual city of death'.[8] The city was on fire. The police acted with impunity and brazenly killed those who got in their way. No arrests were made – not legally at least; warrants were not produced in the event of detentions, those who were seized by the security forces were hardly ever taken before the courts.

Top-level officials in the government spoke anonymously to the *Herald* about the state's decision to target their enemies by assassination rather than through legal action and parroted the government's official line. 'Look at what happened when we tried to seek justice through the courts,' a senior police official told Hasnain and Zaidi. 'We used to arrest these terrorists but the courts let them go.' Another well-placed policeman defended Operation Clean-Up by insisting that the extrajudicial murders were actually 'the most cost-effective way of tackling crime'.[9]

Publicly, of course, 'there is an outright denial of any such policy, since it amounts to premeditated murder by the state'.[10] Furthermore, to admit that gunning their enemies down was their modus operandi would openly 'express the executive's ultimate contempt for the judiciary, which in theory at least, is supposed to balance the powers of the state'.[11]

Naserullah Babar, the retired army general who ran the operation, spoke to the *Herald*, attacking it for its coverage. 'I don't know why you should talk all the time about people who in any case have a large number of killings to their name,' General Babar said. 'Every man killed in an encounter had a record of murder.'[12]

'Encounters' were elaborate police set-ups that always followed the same pattern. The police or Rangers would claim to turn up at location X with the intent of arresting terrorist Y who would inevitably 'fire' at the police and so had to be killed on the spot rather than be taken in. It bears noting that the dead terrorist was usually shot very precisely, often in the head or the chest. They were never shot in the back, for example, which might have given credence to the claim that they were running away or trying to evade arrest. Their bodies often bore countless bullet wounds, evidence of torture, broken bones and other signs that their attackers had mutilated them. Witnesses, other than those within the police contingent, could never be found to testify that an actual gun battle had taken place. The police officers involved in 'encounters' were rarely investigated, internally or otherwise, for their excessive use of force – only twenty cases of internal investigation into encounters and deaths in police custody were opened and the results were never made public[13] – and none were ever punished for their actions.[14]

In 1995, Karachi's death toll rose considerably: 2,095 people were killed under Operation Clean-Up.[15] The *Herald* published a list of people killed by the law enforcement agencies from the official start of the operation in July 1995 to March 1996. The tally is disconcerting. Executions take place almost daily, several murders per day. The victims, all men, are described by name when known or by epithets such as 'unknown (alleged bandit)' or 'so and so (MQM)'.[16] Except for a few cases of alleged carjackers or thieves, the official list confirmed by the police is *exclusively* MQM victims. As always, the numbers on the police list and the number of actual dead bodies varied hugely.

The Prime Minister and General Babar, who both played for sympathy by dredging up stories of how nasty the dead men had been and how much better the city was now that they were gone, rejected the moral ambiguity of the state. 'We are all idealists when it doesn't hurt us,' General Babar explained in his interview, 'but when it directly affects us, we have totally different values.'[17]

Hasnain and Zaidi went so far as to visit mortuaries to see the victims for themselves. They discovered that 'extreme forms of torture' had been used on many of the victims, 'with detainees being burnt with cigarettes and iron rods, beaten, cut with razors, having their flesh gouged out and their bones broken'. The mutilated bodies were, they said, 'the norm rather than the exception'.[18] The investigation detailed how thoroughly outside the parameters of the law the police were operating. Operation Clean-Up was murder sanctioned by the state. Now any and all acts of police brutality and illegality could be condoned as 'politically necessary'.

Karachi's police were getting away with murder. The elite Rangers squads had even more freedom, fearing no repercussions from the law. When Rangers picked someone up, since they were not registered to specific stations or neighbourhoods as the police were, there was virtually no record. 'While the police also regularly detain people illegally,' the *Herald* team wrote, 'the mere fact that a *thana* [police station] is a public place makes it nominally easier to trace those arrested and usually – unless they are killed immediately – their arrest is admitted by the police in three or four days. Rangers' premises, on the other hand, are considered to be "security" establishments and are barred to the public.'[19]

Legally, Rangers were not empowered to perform arrests – only to maintain order. Tasleemul Hasan Farooqui, a former MQM councillor, was – according to the *Herald* investigation – 'one of the lucky ones' who left the Rangers custody alive. 'He was dumped in a shopping area in Buffer Zone after being tortured, during which hot iron rods were inserted into his ear and he was slashed by knives on his back and on his inner leg.'[20] Farooqui had no criminal background; no allegations of 'terrorism' were levelled against him. He was a

375

political worker. After he was released, Farooqui moved his family out of Karachi. No Rangers were questioned for their role in his detention and torture.

Hasnain and Zaidi witnessed a doctor at Jinnah Hospital, one of Karachi's two main emergency hospitals known for dealing with police cases, conduct four autopsies in twenty-five minutes.[21] Post-mortems of police victims were conducted 'with scant regard for the facts'. Often, victims' bodies were not brought to medical facilities until hours after their murder, allowing the corpses to decompose and forensic evidence to be destroyed. There was often no effort to conduct proper medical examinations on the victims; 'the MLOs (Medical Legal Officers) usually just make an incision on the chest and then sew it up to give the impression that a post-mortem has been done.'[22] A gruesome photograph accompanies the authors' assertions.

The *Herald* journalists, digging further into the role of the medical community, uncovered more distressing facts: out of the fifty-five MLOs and eight assistant police surgeons in Karachi at the time of Operation Clean-Up, not a single one was trained in forensic pathology – a basic requirement of doctors performing post-mortems.[23] The nine doctors in the Sindh Health Department with forensic training, and therefore qualified to conduct autopsies in Karachi's bloody 1990s, did not have sufficient *safarish* or political connections to land themselves a well-paid MLO posting. In addition, Karachi's only forensic laboratory at the time – with a staff of over a hundred people – did not have a single forensics expert on its staff.[24]

Close to 3,000 people would be killed on the streets of Karachi before Operation Clean-Up was declared successfully completed. These are, of course, the official numbers – they are the numbers of the body bags that had names on them, of the corpses who had relatives to identify and retrieve them for burial. There must be others, unnamed and unclaimed victims of the state's war on their citizens. People told me there were parts of Karachi, in Korangi and places like it, where bodies were left to rot out in the open, serving as gruesome warnings.

Naeem Sharri's bloodied face appears on the cover of the *Herald*'s issue on Operation Clean-Up. He was, at the time the magazine went to print, the state's latest and most notorious victim. Sharri was a wanted man, one of MQM's most feared figures; he was accused of numerous counts of murder among many other crimes and had a price of 5 million rupees on his head. On 11 March 1996 Sharri and a companion were killed in a police encounter. The Rangers at the helm of the operation claimed that the two men had resisted arrest and fired at them – a standard excuse – and that the Rangers had to fire back to protect themselves, resulting in a deadly gun battle during which four Rangers were injured. However, in the course of their investigation the *Herald* journalists uncovered a more sinister reality. The Rangers, alleged Hasnain and Zaidi, were hit by 'their own high-powered bullets ricocheting off surrounding walls' while Sharri and his companion were killed in a premeditated manner.[25] No evidence matched the Rangers claim of crossfire and photographs of Sharri's body, showed that the skin on his torso and arms had been scorched off, with the flesh on the left side of his body torn off his bones. He had not died as a result of a simple gun battle.

Sharri and his associate were, by all accounts, hardened thugs and ruthless criminals. That is not in dispute. But even hardened thugs have the basic right to a trial, and deserve the right to defend themselves before a court of law. Friends of my aunt and her supporters in general attacked me when I wrote about Operation Clean-Up in Pakistani newspapers or brought up Benazir's dismal human rights record. 'You don't know,' they would say condescendingly, 'they were monsters.' 'This is what we should be doing in Swat now,' they would urge. 'We need more Clean-Ups.' The government is currently doing exactly that.

'A leading human rights watchdog says it has received "credible reports of numerous extrajudicial killings and reprisals carried out by security forces",' the BBC reported, noting that twenty-two bodies were discovered buried in the Surat valley, bringing the total of mysterious deaths in the month of August 2009 to 150.[26] Some were blindfolded, some were bound. The Human Rights Commission of Pakistan has demanded the state launch an inquiry into the killings in Swat, but so far nothing has been done.[27]

{ 21 }

This was the Karachi of my youth. This was the city we loved and feared. In the winter of 1994, we would experience the full brutality of Karachi's police force first-hand for the first, but not the last, time.

It happened out of the blue, towards the end of December 1994. Karachi's temperature had dropped a few degrees. A soft breeze was coming in from the Arabian Sea, the only sign of a change in seasons during an otherwise warm and temperate winter. Joonam was returning from the Karachi Special Courts where Murtaza's court cases continued to be heard. He often had to appear before the judge lest his bail be revoked, but sometimes it was sufficient for his lawyers to be present and Joonam often went along to make sure everything was in order. She was accompanied by Ali Hingoro, one of Papa's top workers who had been an important activist in the ranks of the PPP since Zulfikar's arrest. It was Ali who had taken charge of Papa's election campaign alongside Joonam and Mummy; he was a diehard PPP activist.

As they pulled out of the courts, turning on to the main road, Joonam's car was stopped by a police van. Policemen ran towards our car, opened the door of the old brown Mercedes, grabbed Ali by his arms and dragged him out of the car. They took him away without an arrest warrant and without informing him what charges they were acting upon. All that was said was that he was being detained on the orders of the Chief Minister, Abdullah Shah. This was not the first time that my father's workers had been harassed by the Chief Minister; he had made mention of several instances in his otherwise humorous letter to the *Friday Times* not long before.

Joonam got out of the car and tried to intercede. She placed herself between the officers holding Ali and their mobile unit and demanded to see the official papers ordering his arrest. There are no papers, the police said brusquely, we have orders. Ali was taken, illegally – without warrant – to Karachi's Central Jail. That was the last time Joonam saw him alive.

Ali Hingoro had been a life-long supporter of the PPP and the Bhutto family. Growing up in Sindh, he had been a sporty child, bringing home trophies from football matches. But soon politics consumed his life and he would bring home a different sort of accolade. He joined the MRD movement after Zulfikar's execution – by that time already fired up by the PPP manifesto and the politics of confronting the military junta, Ali became known as one of the MRD's most committed grassroots activists. Nusrat, his brother Usman remembers, used to keep the gates of 70 Clifton – as opposed to 71 Clifton, the family's office – open for Ali and would leave the door of the downstairs annexe unlocked, for Ali to use as an office.[1]

In 1986, when Benazir returned to Karachi, it was Ali who organized the massive reception that greeted her at Jinnah Airport. A sea of hundreds of thousands carried Benazir to Lyari, Ali's community, where she rode on top of the truck that Ali had arranged and built to her security specifications, standing alongside her the whole time to make sure no harm came to her. 'Yeh mera subse acha bhai hai,' she told the jubilant crowd that day. 'Yeh Ali bhai hai.' This is my favourite brother, she said. My favourite brother is Ali bhai (the honorific for brother).

◆•••▶

In jail, Ali's health began to deteriorate. His family believes he was tortured on a daily basis. He had been in fine health before his detention, they say, but within weeks of being imprisoned he began to waste away. Usman, Ali's brother, believes he was being poisoned; the superintendent of Karachi's Central Jail at the time was a close acquaintance of Asif Zardari. The Hingoro family has always held the current

President and the then first spouse responsible for what happened to Ali. Ali was being beaten, humiliated, given false confessions to sign implicating Murtaza in some terror plot or other, and pressured to hold a press conference and denounce Murtaza before publicly deserting him. He refused. He said no.

'Mir *baba* told him to do what they said,' Usman remembers. 'He sent Ali messages – do what they want. Denounce me, hold the press conference. Your life is too precious for us to lose.'[2] But still, Ali refused.

The then Chief Justice of Sindh, Justice Nasir Aslam Zahid, a respected judge who now works with the Women's and Juvenile's Jails in Karachi, ordered Ali Hingoro to be released when his case of illegal arrest and detention came before the courts. Justice Aslam Zahid concluded that Ali was *bekasool*, innocent. So naturally the case was shifted out of his court. A new judge took the case and sat on it. 'We kept fighting to have Ali released on medical grounds,' Usman says, adding quietly, 'but nothing.'[3]

Papa was frantic. He had been the only non-Muhajir politician to condemn the government's extrajudicial killings in Sindh. He knew what Ali was up against and it frightened him. He wrote urgently to several justices, asking them to consider the illegality of Ali's detention. He contacted Amnesty International and sent information to other human rights groups, including Ali's family's allegations of torture.

On 26 March Papa wrote Ali a letter. 'You are a brave and honourable young man. For me there is no difference between you and my brother Shahnawaz. Allah is the final judge and we seek justice from his court. Your tormentors too will have to face that court.' He signed the letter 'Your brother, Murtaza Bhutto'.[4] Before his death, Ali was sent to Jinnah Hospital's prisoners' wing. He was told that if Murtaza Bhutto came to see him, he'd be carted right back to jail and left to die there.

Eventually, Ali was shifted to Agha Khan Hospital, which had better medical facilities. He was near the end of his life and asked Murtaza to come and see him. Papa went under the cover of night on 27 April. Our car drove through one of the hospital's numerous gates, with Papa hidden from view crouching on the back seat. He entered the ward by the back doors and walked quietly up the stairs to reach Ali's deathbed. Usman was there at the time. 'We left them alone,' he recalls. 'Ali was in a near coma and it was very difficult for him to speak, but we could see from the window that he was trying to talk to Mir *baba*. Both of them cried.'[5] Papa was with Ali for more than an hour.

At 6.30 the next morning, Ali died. 'He was waiting for Mir *baba*,' Usman says. That day, we had plans to drive to Karachi's Hawksbay Beach, an hour from 70 Clifton. Mummy and Papa had arranged a lunch for some diplomats who had become new friends – including the Dutch and British consuls – and we were preparing our things in the morning when we got the news. Papa came into the bedroom, shaken. 'The bastards, they killed him,' he told Mummy. Ali's only crime had been his refusal to denounce Murtaza Bhutto. That was it; that was what his life had hinged on at the end.

We all got into the car, leaving Zulfi at home because he was too small to accompany us to the funeral, and drove straight to Ali's family home in Lyari. Papa went to the men's section and Mummy and I to the women's. Ali's mother, I remember, was on the floor next to a stretch of white fabric, weeping. 'They killed my child,' she kept saying, over and over again, her arms around the cloth. As we drew closer to her, I saw that it was Ali's body shrouded in his burial *kaffan* that she was holding on to. It was the first time I had been so close to a corpse. The second time would come soon.

Across Pakistan the tide was turning. Stories of the state's bloody Operation Clean-Up were spreading far beyond Karachi, creating fears of a civil war and of the secession of Karachi from Sindh. This was a menacing threat from the MQM and it would result in Pakistan being cut off from its economic and commercial lifeline. But it wasn't simply violence that had begun to rock the foundations of Benazir's second government; stories of the first couple's corruption had resurfaced.

Eventually, it would be estimated that during their second stint in power the couple stole somewhere between $2 billion and $3 billion from the Pakistani treasury.

In his seminal article 'House of Graft', the *New York Times* reporter John Burns exposed the Zardaris' corruption. They bought a huge estate in England, nicknamed Surrey Palace, for approximately $4 million. The couple later denied it was theirs, even though the British authorities returned to Pakistan various artefacts from the house such as plates bearing inscriptions that suggested that they had been gifts to the first couple.[6] When an English court issued a notice to sell the house and return the proceeds of the sale to the government of Pakistan, Zardari demanded that the proceeds be returned to him as the rightful owner.

In 1994 and 1995, Burns alleged, Zardari spent more than half a million dollars at Cartier and Bulgari jewellery stores.[7] But it wasn't just shopping; the couple were also embroiled in kickbacks and high-level government deals. In 1995, a French military contractor signed a deal to pay Zardari and a business associate $200 million for a billion-dollar fighter jet deal that never reached fruition.[8]

During a state trip to Syria during Benazir's first government and while we were still in exile there, Zardari had gone so far as to ask Papa to facilitate a deal he was considering in the Middle East, offering him a cut of the profits. Papa was sickened; he had never liked his sister's husband. His corruption and the stories of his excess reached Papa's ears often and it hurt him that such a man would use Zulfikar's name and memory to bilk investors the globe over of millions. He was further annoyed that Zardari, hapless when it came to any under-standing of what Zulfikar Ali Bhutto's legacy meant, would be so crooked as to assume that the son of a martyr, who had been strug-gling in exile for over a decade at that point and who had never compro-mised on his beliefs, would jump at the sound of a cut in a Zardari deal. 'We don't do that, Zardari,' Papa said furiously.

In another deal, made just weeks after Benazir took the oath as Prime Minister for the second time, her Swiss banker set up an offshore company called Capricorn Trading with Zardari as its principal owner.

'Nine months later,' according to the Burns article, 'an account was opened at the Dubai offices of Citibank in the name of Capricorn Trading. The same day, a Citibank deposit slip for the account shows a deposit of $5 million paid by ARY, a Pakistani bullion trading company based in Dubai.' Two weeks later, ARY, which at the time was known for producing gaudy gold necklace pendants in heart shapes, deposited another payment of $5 million into the account.[9]

The corruption allegations kept piling up. A deal for Polish tractors was made with considerable kickbacks and properties were bought in Spain. An Oil for Food deal was drawn up with Saddam Hussain's Iraq, in exchange for a $2 million payoff. According to a BBC investigation led by Owen Bennet Jones and aired in October 2007, a UAE-based front company called Petroline FZC – either listing Benazir as its chairman or including her as a director (along with one of her nephews and another close political advisor), depending on differing documents, including papers with Benazir's signature and a photocopy of her passport ('Occupation: former Prime Minister') which Bennet Jones claims to have seen during the course of the BBC investigation – was caught in the Oil for Food scandal. An independent inquiry committee established by the United Nations and chaired by the former head of the US Federal Reserves, Paul Volker, found that Petroline received a contract for $145 million worth of Iraqi oil after a $2 million kickback was paid to Saddam's regime.[10]

As Benazir's former press secretary, Hussain Haqqani said of his one-time boss, 'She no longer made the distinction between the Bhuttos and Pakistan . . . In her mind, she was Pakistan, so she could do as she pleased.'[11] Haqqani is now, in a typically ironic twist, Zardari's ambassador to Washington.

But the case that finally brought the couple down was the SGS/Cotecna case in which the Zardaris were convicted by Swiss courts of receiving an approximate $15 million pay-off in return for awarding a government customs contract to a Swiss company. The 2007 BBC investigation followed the trial that led to the damning Swiss conviction.

Sometime in the summer of 1997, while Zardari was in prison for a second time, jailed on a fresh round of corruption and murder cases, Benazir went shopping in London. At a jeweller's on Bond Street she bought a sapphire and diamond jewellery set costing $190,000. A year later the necklace – the most extravagant item of the set – was seized by a Swiss magistrate, Daniel Devaud. An investigation into the money that was used to pay for the jewellery was launched, involving thousands of pages of bank documents, receipts and paper trails. After six years and exhaustive research on the part of the Swiss magistrate, Benazir and her husband were found guilty of money laundering and receiving kickbacks while she was Prime Minister, a portion of which went towards the hefty price of the Bond Street jewellery. Devaud found that Benazir and Zardari were equally culpable of corruption; Benazir controlled the bank account used to buy the jewels and husband and wife shared fifty-fifty control over the bank account used to receive kickbacks. Devaud's 2003 verdict was scathing: 'Benazir Bhutto knew she was acting in a criminally reprehensible manner by abusing her role in order to obtain for herself and for her husband considerable sums in the interest of her family at the cost of the Islamic Republic of Pakistan.'[12] It was not just Benazir and Zardari who were convicted by the Swiss courts; various lawyers, random friends and relations, and most shockingly Nusrat, who shared bank accounts with her daughter from the days of Zia's dictatorship when they needed to hold each other's power of attorney, were also dragged into the fray. The former first couple were ordered to repay approximately $11.9 million in kickbacks to the Pakistani government, hand over the Bond Street necklace to the state, and spend 180 days in prison.

The couple launched an appeal against the conviction, but the damage to their reputation was done. Even though Benazir's 2007 negotiations with the dictator General Musharraf eventually resulted in the passing of a bill called the National Reconciliation Ordinance which wiped clean twenty years' worth of corruption cases against politicians, bureaucrats and bankers, and shelved the SGS/Cotecna case in the Swiss courts, she responded to the allegations by saying, 'I mean, what is poor and what is rich? If you mean, am I rich by European standards, do I have a billion dollars, or even a hundred million dollars, even half that, no, I do not. But if you mean that I'm ordinary rich, yes.'[13] In 2009, after becoming President, Zardari would publicly declare his personal fortune to be around $1.8 billion. A fraction of what he and his wife are reputed to have stolen from Pakistan.

Politically, Benazir's government had meddled with the judiciary, filling the courts with judges sympathetic to the party and sacking those who ruled unfavourably against the state. She had been exposed for her government's policy of creating 'ghost schools'. Schools were opened with funds provided by foreign NGOs or rich foreign governments, PPP officials would cut school ribbons to declare open the hundredth school in the scheme but would not bother to equip the schools with desks, books, teachers or, for that matter, students. Incompetence was rife and people in Pakistan were beginning to react.

After a year of travelling across Pakistan, speaking to local press clubs, answering his critics in parliament and writing regular articles in both Urdu and English newspapers, Murtaza had shown that he was a different breed of Pakistani politician. He had not returned to Pakistan with the assumption that after sixteen years of exile the Bhutto mantle was his for the taking. He had returned as a member of the provincial assembly, the first rung on the political ladder, aware that he had a lot to prove before he rose any further.

After Murtaza's hard work and the growing evidence that Benazir's second government was failing, people began to turn towards him – even those who had initially dismissed him as inexperienced and untested. Writing on the anniversary of Zulfikar's death, 4 April, a columnist wrote, 'To call Benazir the heir apparent of Bhutto is the height of absurdity. Mir Murtaza is without any doubt the only heir apparent . . . [but] it is she who inherited her father's legacy. The question really is: what has she made of that legacy?'[14] The conclusion was damning and it echoed the sentiments being voiced in newspapers and drawing rooms across the country.

Papa spent the winter of 1994 working on a paper that presented his political programme and included his remedy for the political ills which had destroyed the PPP. It became a family endeavour of sorts.

Having Papa finally at home with us for long stretches of time as he worked on the paper, we banded together as a family and relished our time alone. We would sit with Papa as he wrote in the downstairs drawing room. He would sit in his usual green armchair, writing by hand while four-year-old Zulfi, already a budding artist, sketched and I curled up on the long blue sofa reading. When the paper was ready, Mummy sat at the computer with Papa and they typed it up together. The paper, 'New Direction: Reforms in the PPP and Pakistani Society', was printed in 1994 and would serve as the manifesto for the political party he was preparing to launch.

The preface, written a month before the paper was printed, is passionate and heated.

Shaheed Bhutto's slogan was '*roti, kapra aur makan*' (food, clothing, and housing), but the slogan of the highly corrupt and disreputable coterie who have hijacked the party and are in full control of it seems to be 'loot, plunder, steal' . . . they use political power not in the service of the people but rather to dispense favours to a selected few, to enjoy the grandeur of the corridors of power at the taxpayers' expense, to use the police as a private army against opponents who dare to raise a voice of dissent and above all to feather their nests.

His hope, he wrote, was to:

realign the course of the People's Party with the salient features of the ideology of *Shaheed* Bhutto . . . Whereas the question of altering or diluting *Shaheed* Bhutto's ideology does not arise, there is need to bring his views into conformity with contemporary values and standards. It is entirely possible to work within a certain framework of ideas, while allowing for changing times, but remaining sincere to the spirit of the original concept. This shall be my endeavour.

'New Direction' touched upon all the issues that Murtaza had spoken about since returning to Pakistan – the redistribution of powers and decentralization of the state, the law and order situation in Sindh, agriculture, health, education, bilateral foreign policy, poverty alleviation and more.

When Papa received the first print run of the manifesto, he gave me a copy to read and asked me to put down my thoughts. I was six months away from my thirteenth birthday and had recently read about the American Supreme Court's landmark ruling in *Roe* v. *Wade* and felt that nothing was under more threat in the modern world than women's reproductive rights. I told Papa that I thought abortion freedoms as well as free access to contraceptives should feature somewhere in his manifesto.

I also suggested that a section be included on my other cause at the time, AIDS awareness and treatment programmes. I had just finished reading a cautionary novel for teenagers, the kind that starts with a young girl having fun at a rock concert and ends with her dying of AIDS, alone and afraid. Papa listened to my suggestions. We went over them one evening in the drawing room while we nibbled on salted carrots and cucumbers and he wrote my thoughts down in his copy of the manifesto. He was a progressive but still typical father in that he was very strict about the idea of his daughter having boyfriends or dating, but he listened to me thoughtfully, not freaking out over the apparent fact that his twelve-year-old daughter was obsessed by abortion and AIDS.

On 15 March 1995 the streets outside our house were opened to the public. People came from across the country – from Balochistan and the Frontier and from across the interiors of Sindh and the Punjab – for a two-day workers' convention. The topics covered in 'New Direction' were discussed and notes were made on what form the new party should take and what additions should be made to the draft manifesto. At the end of the convention, the Pakistan People's Party (Shaheed Bhutto) was launched. Papa was no longer an independent candidate.

He launched his party with great passion and continued travelling the country and speaking out against the excesses of the regime. In November 1995 Murtaza addressed a press conference in Larkana on the law and order situation in Karachi and spoke aggressively against Operation Clean-Up. 'The police have collapsed totally and become a part of the criminal underworld,' he said. 'How strange is it that in this modern world, the Frontier Constabulary [a branch of law enforcement] is cordoning off entire areas to catch terrorists – in this way the government is giving birth to more terrorists.'[15]

Joonam often accompanied Papa on his tours and she too spoke openly against her daughter's politics. With good reason; bank accounts in her name, that she had opened with Benazir years before, had been used to siphon money into and her name was being mentioned as one of the beneficiaries of the first couple's corruption. 'I fear that when her government ends,' Joonam said in a newspaper interview, 'she will be held accountable.' But she could not have foreseen her own name being dragged through the muck too, not until it was too late. She felt let down and betrayed by her daughter's graft at the nation's expense, but she was still her daughter. While Joonam criticized Benazir and Zardari's politics, she never closed the door on her eldest child.

Papa's career was on the up. He was no longer the inexperienced politician that people initially perceived him to be, justly or unjustly, when he returned to the country. He was now seen as a force to be reckoned with.

Mummy, Zulfi and I went away for the summer to visit friends and family in Damascus and Lebanon and Papa and I exchanged our usual letters. Because of the increased violence in Karachi, we spent extra time in Damascus. It was too volatile for us to be in Pakistan, he said, and asked us to remain in Damascus for a little while. In one of the last letters Papa sent me before we returned to Karachi in the winter of 1995 he wrote:

As you know, in our country's politics people love to introduce you to fortune tellers, 'holy men' and the like. I get to meet my share of such people. They then expect me to ask them about my political future, prospects of power, and so on. Being a firm believer in God, fate and my own abilities, I refuse to do so. I do, however, ask about you and Zulfi (not that I doubt your abilities). Recently I met one such 'holy man' and he advised me to always keep you beside me. He told me that even when I reach a position of power I should make sure you are always with me and that I should take your advice and listen to your views. I guess that means kissing university goodbye. I will have to chain you to my desk in whatever office I hold.

I had sent Papa some photographs I found of us during the old exile days and he responded to my excitement over the snapshots.

It was lovely to see the sweet pictures you sent me of when you were a little baby. I have always told you that for me you will always be my little baby. There is nobody more precious and dear for me in this life than you and Zulfi. May God look after you and may you live to be 150 years old. I adore you and love you both very much.

We returned to Karachi and spent the New Year together as a family. Papa harrumphed when I came into the drawing room wearing dark maroon lipstick. 'Aren't you a little young for that?' he asked. I was going to be fourteen that year. I was a grown-up now, I insisted.

1996 passed with Papa building up his party, speaking to young activists and old stalwarts from across the country in the hope of bringing them on board. He had been working night and day and finally, it seemed, things were looking hopeful.

{ 22 }

At around 7.30 in the evening on 20 September 1996, four cars left Surjani Town on the outskirts of Karachi and headed back towards Clifton. In front, leading the convoy, was a red double-cabin pick-up truck with four of Murtaza's guards in it, Mahmood, Qaisar, Rahim and Sattar. At twenty-three, Rahim was the youngest, though his rugged face and prominent moustache made him look older. He had always been politically committed. When I asked his cousin many years later about Rahim's life before politics, he seemed genuinely baffled at the notion. 'Before politics?' he asked. 'It was always politics.'[1] But he was, given his young age, also a warm and jovial man; those around him always found Rahim good company.

Sattar had excelled in his studies, graduating with an honours degree in engineering from college in Khairpur. Though he too had always been political, he'd never joined any parties or movements in his youth. The youngest child in his large family, he had grown up wanting to become a teacher. But though he worked for some time as a primary school teacher in his village, he was never to pursue the career he had always dreamed of. In 1995, Sattar was arrested by the police. He had been carrying copies of the PPP (SB) manifesto, along with posters and pamphlets. Sattar was taken to Hyderabad Central Jail – without a warrant, a registered police case or any prior offences to his name – where he was regularly beaten. He spent three months there, never signing any of the 'confessions' or repudiations of the new party that the police brought before him. He was, everybody concurred after his release, lucky to have made it out alive.

Qaisar, who sat in the back of the pick-up with Rahim, remembers the drive back from the rally towards Clifton. 'The police followed us from the *jalsa*,' he says, his voice deep and strong. 'When one police district came to an end, that police car would stop and be immediately replaced by the next one which was waiting for us. They followed us like this, in formation, the whole way.'[2] There had been a large police presence at Surjani Town that evening. 'There were so many police,' Qaisar says, nodding when Mahmood estimates that there were some thirty police cars stationed near the area where the public meeting was taking place. 'They were in the gulleys, behind the stage, ahead of us, on each side. There were, besides the police cars, large trucks and armoured cars but they didn't put their hands on us then.'

Earlier that day, before leaving for the *jalsa*, Murtaza had spoken to his guards and had been clear regarding the possibility of danger that lay ahead. 'He explained to us that we might be arrested,' Qaisar says, his voice unwavering. 'Don't resist, he told us. Don't be afraid, it will be fine. Let them take us in. I'm ready to go to jail.' Papa's black briefcase with his books, magazines and papers was in his bedroom. It had been ready for several days. 'We told Mir *baba* that we would do as he instructed,' Qaisar says and for the first time I sense a break in his strong, clear intonation. On the drive home, Qaisar and Rahim sat in the open back of the double cabin and watched my father in car behind. 'He was smiling and laughing,' Qaisar tells me. 'He was talking to Ashiq Jatoi the whole time. They looked very happy.'

The second car was Ashiq's blue Pajero jeep. It was the car he used to drive his children to school and that evening he sat at the wheel with Murtaza next to him. Ashiq too had packed a small bag just in case he was arrested. In the back seat of the Pajero, directly behind Murtaza, sat Yar Mohammad, Papa's personal bodyguard. Yar Mohammad was in charge of Murtaza's security, even though he had a master's degree in political science, it was a job that he did out of his devotion to Murtaza. Yar Mohammad, like Ashiq and many others in the party, had been active in the MRD movement in the 1980s and had spent time in Zia's prisons for his role in the pro-democracy agitations against the junta. At thirty-eight he was the oldest of Murtaza's security detail. Yar Mohammad was tall and distinguished; he often wore dark aviator-style sunglasses and had six children. He was fiercely protective of my father.

Along with Yar Mohammad was Asif Jatoi, Ashiq's family driver from their ancestral village of Beto in Dadu, and Asghar, a bearer from our house who often travelled with Papa to take care of the food arrangements. Papa would tease Asghar that no matter the weather or the transport, he would always bring Thermoses of hot tea along. Jokes aside, Papa earnestly appreciated Asghar's domestic arts and often brought him along on his political tours.

A small white Alto drove alongside Murtaza and Ashiq to protect the car. It was part of Yar Mohammad's security arrangements and carried several party members who had been in the audience at Surjani Town that evening along with Sajjad, another of Benazir's former MRD workers who had joined Murtaza upon his return to Pakistan. Sajjad was thirty-five years old and had, like Yar Mohammad, named one of his sons Shahnawaz after my uncle. He too had volunteered to be part of Papa's security detail even though he had recently been elected to the post of the party's finance secretary for Sindh.

The last car in the convoy was a white jeep belonging to another party member who had joined Murtaza that evening. It carried the last of Murtaza's five guards, Wajahat. He was thirty-five and single and had an MA in political science. Out of all of Papa's guards, Wajahat looked the least like a bodyguard. He had curly-ish hair and wore thick wire- and plastic-rimmed glasses. He, like many of the others there that night, came from a middle-class family and his brother remembers him as 'always being interested in social work'. Wajahat's brother pauses, then concedes, 'Though he had always been interested in politics too, we didn't know how political he had become until it was too late.'[3]

As the convoy of cars reached the *Do Talwar* or Two Swords roundabout that marks the main road leading to 70 Clifton, Murtaza noticed that Rangers were prominently stationed near the Caltex petrol station on the main Clifton road and around the roundabout itself.

The street lights had been turned off and Clifton was cloaked in a quiet darkness. The guards of the nearby embassies that lined Clifton road, including the Italian, Iranian and British high commissions, had been visited by the Rangers and police and told to go indoors; their guard posts were eerily empty.

To Murtaza and the men driving back to 70 Clifton with him, the number of police officers stationed in armoured vehicles and cars along the road became increasingly apparent. There were approximately seventy to a hundred policemen there that night: on the roads, blocking traffic, and in sniper positions in the trees. In front of Clifton Park, one house number away from ours, a police car drove in front of Papa's car and cut it off from the pick-up ahead of it. The police officers' club, directly across from the park, was surrounded by policemen. They were everywhere.

Asif Jatoi saw their car being separated from the others in the convoy. '*Raste band hogaya*,'[4] he told me – the path was blocked. Many of Karachi's most notorious police officers, high-level officials, were present at the scene that night. Shoaib Suddle, an expert in criminology known for his handiwork in Operation Clean-Up, was there, as was Zeeshan Kazmi, a notorious torturer within the Clean-Up team. Wajid Durrani, who led the shooting at Al Murtaza on 5 January, was stationed by the roundabout and his position would become significant as the night progressed. Rai Tahir, Shahid Hayat, Shakaib Qureshi, Masood Sharif – then head of the Federal Intelligence Bureau that reported directly to the Prime Minister's office – were all said by witnesses to have been on the cordoned-off road that night. Witnesses recalled their heavy-handed presence and survivors remembered their faces. The policemen have always denied any wrongdoing, painting themselves as the unfortunate victims of a law and order situation gone wrong. The police would claim later that they had come to arrest Murtaza. No warrants were ever produced to back up their claims. Fourteen years later and we've yet to see a warrant.

Murtaza realized what was happening and rolled down his front window to speak to the police. As he did so, Yar Mohammad opened his door and jumped out of the back seat and stood in front of

Murtaza's window, placing his body between Murtaza and the police. Murtaza turned his upper body to lean out of the window, holding his arm up. 'Don't shoot,' he said in Urdu to his guards. Yar Mohammad had only just repeated Murtaza's directive to the guards in Sindhi when a single shot struck him in the forehead. He fell to the ground and died instantly.

Murtaza opened the car door and got out. As he did so, a policeman – reports vary on who it was – yelled 'Fire!' and a burst of gunfire rang out in the night. The police were firing wildly from all directions. Ashiq was hit in the arm. From his vantage point in the driver's seat he could see that they were surrounded.

As soon as the firing started, Sajjad got out of the Alto and ran to cover Murtaza. As he tried to push Murtaza back into the car, he was shot. The bullet hit Sajjad squarely in the chest, in the heart, killing him instantly. Rahim, the youngest of the guards, jumped from the red pick-up which had been separated from Murtaza's car and ran to replace Sajjad by covering Murtaza with his body. He too was felled with a single sniper shot to the head, dying instantly.

'They were targeting us,' Qaisar tells me. 'Everyone who went to protect Mir *baba* was hit precisely.' Sattar, who had been in the pick-up with Rahim, had also been shot, but he was still alive. He'd been hit by a single shot to the torso and lay on the road bleeding. 'Sattar was alive,' Qaisar remembers. 'We saw the police kick him to check if he was dead or not. They put their shoes on him. We saw it.' There's no greater insult in our culture, being shown a shoe is tantamount to a slap in the face, and for Qaisar to tell me these things, these humiliations that no one had ever told me before, unsettled me and I felt my face flush with anger and my heartbeat quicken. How could I not know this? How were these details kept from me? Wajahat, the last of the guards in the fourth car, was shot in his back, also with a single shot. Three of Papa's guards were killed instantly, two lay bleeding in the road. Others in the convoy were injured, some badly so, the rest were unharmed but very shaken.

My father had been shot several times. His face had been hit, his beautiful smiling face, and he had superficial wounds on his chest and arms. None of the shots in the hail of gunfire hurt him seriously. He was still alive.

Ashiq was sitting in the front seat pressing his palms down on the car's horn. 'Call an ambulance!' witnesses heard him shout. He was yelling, screaming, 'Murtaza Bhutto is injured! Get help!' But none of the police responded.

Two of the police officers at the scene, Haq Nawaz Sial and Shahid Hayat, both shot themselves in the foot and leg respectively. The police were going to claim that there had been a shoot-out, but it wouldn't look right that seven men were killed – five of them on the spot and two murdered later, while no policemen had any injuries. Forensics later showed that both men's wounds were self-inflicted. Furthermore, the ballistics and forensic examination proved that there had been no crossfire. The only spent ammunition came from police-issued weapons. Haq Nawaz Sial later died mysteriously. The police insisted it was suicide, but those close to him insist that he had been killed. No investigation into his death was ever carried out. Shahid Hayat is currently still employed in the police force, as all the others are, in high-level, government-sanctioned posts.

All the wounded, Qaisar, Mahmood, Asif Jatoi and Asghar, who had been shot in the arm, were face down on the road. According to Asif Jatoi there were eight of them. 'We were made to lie on the foot-path,' he tells me. 'The police – there were so many of them and they were all armed – turned on the searchlights on one of their vehicles to scan the road and see who was dead and who was alive. A car drove over from *Do Talwar* and surveyed the area too. When they saw it was clear, they came on foot. Rai Tahir, Shukaib Qureshi and Shahid Hayat – still walking at the time – checked the bodies that lay on the street. They kicked the dead with their boots to see if they were moving.'

Asif Jatoi was uninjured at that point. He had been next to Asghar in the back of the blue Pajero, but was unharmed. Asghar says that he heard my father speaking after the shooting. He heard him say, 'They got us, Zardari and Abdullah Shah' – the Chief Minister of Sindh – 'finally got us . . .' Asif says he heard it too. I've never been able to concentrate on Papa's dying declaration. They weren't his last words, not for me at least, they meant something larger. That he was speaking at all meant, up until that point, that Papa was OK. He was alive.

Ashiq got out of the driver's seat and, holding his arm with his uninjured hand, tried again, in vain, to call for help. He called out for an ambulance to come and help the injured. After some time, sensing no one was going to alert the medics and that this was how the police intended it, Ashiq returned to the car to tend to Murtaza.

Qaisar and Asif Jatoi tell me separately they saw the police approach my father. 'We were lying on the road,' Qaisar tells me, confirming what other witnesses have testified in court, 'and we saw Mir *baba* being taken out of the car. I saw blood on his clothes, but he was strong. He got out of the car on his own and walked.'

Ghulam Hasnain, the investigative journalist who wrote the exposé on Operation Clean-Up, was at the scene of my father's murder. He had been at the Karachi Press Club when he heard of the shooting and rushed straight over to Clifton. 'We saw your father being led into the police car,' he told me when we met to discuss the murder twelve years later. 'There were two or three cops inside with him and he was sitting upright and holding on to the side of the car.'[5] Hasnain remembered seeing bodies lying all over the road. 'I used to carry a leather bag with notebooks and cameras,' he says. 'When the police saw us, they started snatching our bags.' Only one journalist who had come along with Hasnain managed to hide his camera and took furtive photographs when the police weren't looking. Hasnain, who is one of the most respected journalists in Karachi, tells me that the street lights had been turned off so the junior officers wouldn't know who they had been summoned to kill that night. I don't know if I believe that. 'Shoaib Suddle' – one of the police contingent – 'is a criminologist,' Hasnain says when I voice doubt about the street lights, 'everything has a reason.'

'Mir *baba* was fine at that point,' Asif Jatoi tells me later. 'He didn't even need to lean on anyone. The police' – Asif remembers the group including Rai Tahir, Shukaib Qureshi and Shahid Hayat – 'told Mir *baba* that they were going to take him to hospital and he walked over to the police car. He got into the open back section, where the policemen sit, and the APC drove off. As it neared *Do Talwar*, it stopped. We heard a single shot. Then it drove off again.'

It was the last shot that killed my father. He had been injured, but he would have survived. He was walking and talking. It would take more than one bullet to kill Papa and the policemen made sure that the last bullet did the job. The last shot, Papa's autopsy showed, was fired into his jaw at point-blank range. It was fired, forensics confirmed, by a gunman standing over him as he lay down in the police car.

Ashiq was still in the car after Papa had been taken away by the police. Asif Jatoi was lying down on the road when he heard Wajid Durrani and Shukaib Qureshi speaking. They were talking freely and openly. '*Isko khatam karna*,' one of them said. *Finish him off.* According to Asif, Shukaib Qureshi then walked to the car and opened the door to the driver's seat and took Ashiq out of the car.

Shukaib Qureshi, all the survivors tell me when I speak to them separately and over the course of a year, was wearing a helmet and a bulletproof vest. They tell me that he was the only one wearing such protective gear. He was prepared. It is a significant point. Besides Zardari, Shukaib Qureshi, who was an absconder from the courts for twelve years, is the only accused to have been acquitted in the middle of an ongoing trial. Qureshi fled Pakistan in the aftermath of the murder and moved to England, where he worked as a lawyer, first in a private law firm and later as in-house counsel for a multinational firm. He returned to Pakistan only after Zardari became President, entering the country as a fugitive and as an absconder from the law who was miraculously spared prison. He, of course, denies having anything to do with the assassination.

Ashiq was led away, no one can say where. No one knows. When he was next seen he was dead, killed with a shot to the back of the head.

At around 8.30, just before I would make my call to the Prime Minister's residence in Islamabad, both my father and Ashiq had been moved and killed and Rai Tahir had made a final sweep of the blood-stained road. The police, Asif Jatoi says, kicked Yar Mohammad's dead body in the face. They put their boots on his and Qaisar's faces, pressing down on them and rubbing their heels in their mouths. Approximately forty minutes had passed since the police had begun their operation.

'We heard a voice say, "*Auw jawano, kam hogaya,*"' Qaisar tells me. 'Come, boys, our work is done'. 'Then we were blindfolded and loaded into the police vans. We didn't know where we were being taken.' He pauses. 'I'll never get that voice out of my ears,' Qaisar says, dropping his head. 'We heard it again in the torture cells where the police kept us after the murder,' Mahmood adds. They were taken to Clifton police station. Outside the station, all the dead bodies had been lined up for identification. Qaisar was ordered to identify the bodies and says he saw Ashiq's body among the others. No one would see the body again till after two in the morning the next day, six hours later. It was standard Operation Clean-Up; keep the bodies, destroy the evidence.

The street outside our house was hosed clean; all the blood and glass was washed away. By the time Mummy and I left the house at around 8.45, some fifteen minutes later, the police had removed all the evidence.

———◆◆◆————

Ashiq's in-laws owned a medical centre in Clifton called Mideast and many well-known local doctors held their outpatient clinics there. My paediatrician used to practise at Mideast, as did many other doctors we knew. It was where we bought our Strepsils, Band-Aids and other first-aid necessities. Mideast was a fine establishment, but it was not an emergency hospital. A large sign on its glass doors, in capital letters, said as much. It was a clinic, a dispensary, a recovery centre. But it was not an emergency hospital.

Ashiq's only son, Aneed, had driven to Mideast to play computer games with his cousins. The offices there had faster internet connections than the rest of the city. Aneed was eighteen years old and about to go abroad to university. 'I heard the shots as we were walking into Mideast that night,' remembers Aneed, who at six feet tall is a striking copy of his father, even down to his heavy voice and patient manner. 'People came out from the hospital in a panic when they heard the gunfire. "What's all this firing?" someone said and I replied, casually, "It's Karachi, there's firing everywhere."'[6] Another half an hour would pass before Aneed had cause to worry.

After the police fired the fatal shot into my father's jaw, they drove the police car the few metres over to Mideast. Only two hospitals in Karachi, Jinnah and Civil, take gunshot victims because they are police cases and therefore require official paperwork. These are well-known facts. The police, however, took my father to Mideast. It was intentional. He was not going to get the care he needed there. They dropped Papa, his midnight-blue *shalwar kameez* covered in blood, outside the hospital and drove off.

Aneed heard a great deal of commotion and found out that Murtaza Bhutto had just been brought into Mideast in a critical condition. He raced down to the hospital's lobby just as my father was being put on a stretcher and moved inside by Mideast staff. Aneed never told me that he'd been at Mideast when my father was left there. I never knew. It's a shock to me when this comes up as we are speaking about the night of the murder thirteen years later and I feel my hands shake as he speaks. Aneed tells me that he was standing there in the lobby; he says my father's face and body were drenched in blood. 'He had one leg flat on the stretcher and one bent, he was trying to get up,' Aneed says, describing my Papa fighting for his life.

Aneed and I are similar in many ways. We're seen as the tough, domineering types in our families and when we all get together, our siblings often complain that we spend too much time talking about politics and mafia movies. I cannot cry in front of him. I do not want to cry in front of Aneed, whom I respect and admire, but I did not know that my father was conscious when he was brought into Mideast. If only Mummy and I had reached Mideast ten minutes sooner than we did, we would have seen Papa conscious. He would have seen us, he would have known we were there with him. 'He was conscious when he arrived,' Aneed continues. 'He looked at me, our eyes met. He was holding his jaw and his neck with his hand and he was trying to speak, but he couldn't. There was a lot of blood. It hit me, this was serious. You know that sense of worry you get? I got it then. To see Murtaza Bhutto, who was so large and strong physically, like that . . .' Aneed mentions that he remembers my father wearing cufflinks and I tell him, desperate to have a minute to breathe and collect my thoughts, that they were a gift from Mummy. 'People started asking me where my father was,' Aneed recalls. 'And I didn't know. I knew they had been together that evening, so I found a Mideast worker and asked him what he had heard about the shooting. At some point I asked him what car Baba had been in – I knew there was a convoy – I didn't know they had been in the same car. He looked worried when I asked and he told me, "Your father was driving Mir Murtaza. They were together." Still, I thought then that things would be OK, I thought somehow that they'd both survive.'

———◆•••◆———

Asif Zardari was on the phone. 'Don't you know?' he said casually to me. 'Your father's been shot.' I dropped the phone. My body went numb and cold and my heart beat so hard it drowned out everything around me. Mummy picked up the phone. She saw my face, I looked ashen. She must have known something was terribly wrong though I couldn't get the words out to say anything or even look at her. She screamed. I don't remember what she said. I was frozen to my chair, Papa's green armchair.

It must be the arm, I kept telling myself. He must be hit in the arm; it can't be serious, maybe the leg. Why would Zardari tell me, a fourteen-year-old girl, that my father had been shot if it had been serious? I couldn't breathe. Mummy must have called for the car. The next thing I knew she was running towards the door. I got up and ran after her. 'Stay here!' she yelled. 'No!' I screamed back. 'I'm coming with you!' Zulfi was sitting in the lobby now, with Sofi, his nanny from when he was a baby. Sofi watched Mummy and me yelling at each other in the corridor by the door. She held Zulfi close to her and tried to distract him from our screaming.

'Fati, it's dangerous!' Mummy shouted. But I wouldn't let her leave without me. 'He's my father!' I cried and grabbed her arm, pulling her with me to the car. She couldn't stop me. Mummy held on to me as we drove out of the house. The roads were clean, empty. I remember looking out, searching the dark streets for some sign and seeing nothing, calming myself into believing that whatever had happened wasn't serious. It must be the arm, I kept repeating to myself and to Mummy like a mantra I was desperate for us to believe.

————◆••◆————

Ashiq's wife Badrunnisa was at home with their three daughters. They lived far enough away for the sound of the gunfire not to have reached them. 'Phone calls kept coming from the Urdu media asking for my father,'[7] Sabeen, Ashiq and Badrunnissa's eldest child, remembers. 'When I would tell them that he's in Surjani Town with Murtaza Bhutto they would go silent.' A family friend called the Jatoi house with the news that there'd been firing outside 70 Clifton, but when speaking to Sabeen, then nineteen years old, he had downplayed the seriousness of the gunfire. Sabeen, who is by nature remarkably poised and composed, stayed calm. It wasn't until her aunt, whose husband owned Mideast and who was on his way there, having been called when Papa was brought in, phoned and told Sabeen that Murtaza Bhutto had been shot and was in a critical condition that Sabeen worried. 'We panicked,' Sabeen recalled. 'We knew Murtaza Bhutto always sat in front and that Baba always sat next to him in the driver's seat. If your father was in a critical condition then what had happened to Baba?'

Sabeen and her mother got into their car to go and look for Ashiq. Before leaving, Sabeen told her two younger sisters, Anushka and Maheen, to man the phones and to keep the news of what had happened away from their elderly grandparents – Ashiq's parents –

who were asleep upstairs. 'We went to Mideast first. Baba wasn't there. Then we went to Jinnah hospital, thinking that any police cases should have gone there. Amma was too shaky to get out of the car, so I went. I had to go to the morgue to ask if his body had been brought in. As I was walking towards it some Urdu journalists came up to me and told me that my father wasn't in the morgue. I was relieved. I trusted them. We got back in the car and continued searching.'

Sabeen is a very brave woman. She was the first woman in her family to be sent abroad to college. Ashiq supported her; he was wonderfully progressive and knew that his daughter was intelligent and that more than marriage proposals awaited her in life. Sabeen was home that September for the summer holidays and was preparing to go back to England to start her second year of studying law. She and I had met for the first time a few weeks earlier when we both attended a rally for the party in Lyari that our fathers were speaking at. By then I had spent some time with Sabeen's father and knew how besotted he was with her. I liked Sabeen. She had a warm and genuinely friendly manner and she immediately befriended Zulfi, who was only six years old then. I also knew that she was a rebel, a trailblazer, and that made me like her even more.

Sabeen's *chacha* Zahid, Ashiq's younger brother, had rushed over to join Aneed as soon as he heard the news about the firing. No one knew where Ashiq was or whether he'd been hurt. Ashiq's family were on their own, going from hospital to police station looking for him. Zahid's wife Nuzhat, a doctor like her husband, had also been searching for her brother-in-law. No one had any leads. 'At some point,' Nuzhat tells me, 'they told us at Jinnah that two seriously injured people had been brought to the hospital but had been taken back. They didn't give us any names or any information other than that.'[8]

'We went to the Agha Khan hospital – at the other end of town. It was far away but we were desperate,' Sabeen continues. 'Amma stayed in the car and I went into the emergency area and asked if Ashiq Jatoi had been brought in. There was a lot of confusion and the people behind the desk weren't giving me any clear answers. I described my father's build, his height, and his weight, told them that he had been wearing a black *shalwar kameez*, but they didn't seem to have a clear idea of anything. My aunt Nuzhat had joined us there and together we decided that we'd go back to Mideast to check if any of our relatives there had any news. As we were leaving and walking back to our cars I saw a police car parked near the emergency wing. I went up to one of the officers standing near the rear of the car – at that time we still had no idea that the police were involved – and I asked him if he knew where my father was. I told him my name and said I was looking for Ashiq Jatoi, who was with Mir Murtaza Bhutto. 'There's been an incident at 70 Clifton,' I said. 'Do you know where they've taken them?' I was polite, I had no reason not to be, I was so nervous and scared, I just wanted help. And this cop, he was young and he had a moustache, he turned to me and grunted, 'Huh, we've killed them already.' Sabeen started to scream. She totally lost the calm she'd been fighting to retain throughout the hour or so that she'd been out with her mother searching for Ashiq. 'I was yelling at the top of my lungs. "What are you saying?" I screamed "How dare you!" But he just stood there, unmoved. Another cop, he must have been more senior, got out of the front seat and came over to us. He asked me why I was creating a scene. I was in a total state of shock. Some of the drivers who were standing nearby and had witnessed what the policeman said to me came forward to defend me and told the second officer what his colleague had said.' Sabeen goes silent. She's breathing heavily and takes a minute to collect herself. We've spent the last thirteen years together, inseparable almost, and we've often spoken about that night. Sabeen is my best friend; we speak about our fathers all the time. But neither of us had ever shared the details of that night with each other; it is too painful. 'I know I'll see that policeman again some day,' Sabeen says, almost to herself. 'I remember his face so clearly.'

Eventually, Sabeen's aunt Nuzhat persuaded her to get back into the car. They were wasting time. Ashiq's whearabouts were still unknown and his family could not be sure that he'd already been killed. They drove back to Mideast with the nagging fear that something awful had happened, that the policeman hadn't been lying.

'If Murtaza Bhutto was critical, where was Baba?' Sabeen repeats. 'They were always together.'

<hr />

I don't remember how we got to Mideast or how we found ourselves in the large recovery room that Papa had been placed in. I remember walking in and seeing only my father's legs. I thought I would collapse. Mummy ran into the room and straight towards Papa, who was lying unconscious on a low hospital bed. I saw him and froze. I stood before my father, covered in blood, and wanted to scream but I couldn't open my mouth. I was paralysed with shock. I just stood there.

Mummy ran straight to Papa's side and began speaking to him, as if she hadn't registered how frightening he looked, how much blood covered his face and his chest. 'Wake up Mir! Wake up!' she yelled. I went closer to him and crouched beside the bed. I touched Papa's face but got blood on my fingers and got scared. His face was still warm, the blood dark and wet. I stood up quickly and walked to the end of the room and sat down on a white metal chair. I couldn't breathe.

Mummy sat with Papa as he was fitted with a heart monitor and as the hospital staff scrambled to find surgeons to operate on him – there were none on call, there never were at Mideast. People filtered into the room, coming in to watch, to have a look, to see Murtaza Bhutto die. I screamed at one of them, an odious magazine editor turned politician who behaved as if she had bought tickets to an event. 'Why are you here?' I screamed at her. 'This isn't a show! Get out!' She moved away from me, but she didn't leave. Others, friends and strangers, came. I couldn't focus long enough to understand how dire things were, how we ended up in a hospital with not one surgeon to save my father's life.

Dr Ghaffar Jatoi, Ashiq's brother-in-law and Mideast's principal owner, was there. He had come as soon as he was called by his staff. 'I had no driver,' Dr Ghaffar recalled as I spoke to him about that night for the first time. 'So I drove myself. The area was in total darkness. There were Rangers, police, I can't tell you how many, it was too dark to see – the road was lit only by my car's lights. They stopped me and said I couldn't pass. I told them I had an emergency, and they still refused to let me go through.'[9] Dr Ghaffar tried two or three other routes before finally reaching Mideast. It must have taken, he estimates, half an hour to make the two-minute drive from *Do Talwar* to Mideast.

'Your father, I was told, was very restless,' said Dr Ghaffar, who reached Mideast a few minutes before we did. 'He was trying feverishly to breathe, he was gasping for air, but he couldn't. The doctors couldn't put the endotrachic tube in properly, to give air to his lungs, because there was so much blood in his throat. I could see that his tongue had been lacerated. We had to do a tracheotomy to pass the tube in and bypass the blood blockage so he could breathe. While this was going on, he went into cardiac arrest. We had to resuscitate him.'

It was at this time that Mummy and I reached Mideast. Mummy positioned herself right by Papa's ear and curled herself into a ball, bending down so that she was small and not in the way of the doctors who were frantically moving around her. She didn't leave Papa's side, not for a second, and she spoke to him non-stop, begging him to pull through. I remember listening to Mummy and wanting to join her and talk to Papa too but I couldn't. I was in shock. I was frozen in fear. She yelled at Papa, 'Don't go, Mir! Don't die! Fati and Zulfi need you! Stay with us . . . please stay with us . . .'

Every time Mummy said my and Zulfi's names, Papa's heart monitor would react, lines jolting across the screen. 'Every time,' Mummy remembers. 'His heart was only beating for you and your brother.'

'Murtaza was losing a lot of blood,' Dr Ghaffar says. He checks every once in a while, as we speak in his living room, that I am all right. I am not. But I need him to tell me everything. I say I'm fine and ask him to continue. 'He was losing blood from his nose, his mouth, the side of his neck where he had been shot fatally. The major blood vessels going to the brain must have been ruptured, there was just too much blood leaving him. There was also blood in his mouth; he may have even inhaled blood into his lungs. I don't know how much blood he lost on the road that night, before he came to Mideast, we'll never know. He needed blood badly, fifteen units at least. I asked the staff to donate because we didn't have enough. Murtaza was losing blood faster than we were able to give it to him.'

I heard the commotion and understood that Papa needed blood. I had just asked him about our blood types. It was the only moment where things began to slow down for me. 'I'll give blood' I said to one of the doctors. He asked me what my blood type was and I repeated what Papa had told me: 'I don't know, but we're the same type.' They needed blood fast and I ran down the stairs after the doctor who was sprinting down the Mideast corridors to get us to the room where I'd be donating the blood. Running behind the doctor, I saw Sabeen out of the corner of my eye. 'What's she doing here?' I thought to myself. I had no idea that anyone besides Papa had been hurt.

'Fati!' Sabeen yelled, trying to stop me. 'Have you seen my father?' I didn't stop. I didn't know why she was asking about her father. I shook my head. I don't remember the rest of our conversation in the hallway but Sabeen tells me I told her 'We need blood for Papa.' 'I'll give blood,' she replied, 'I'll do it now but tell me, do you know where my father is?' I didn't answer her. I had already run into the room and sat down, rolling up my sleeve for the needle. It was the first time that night that I thought there was a chance we'd save Papa. For the first time, as the doctor filled clear donor bags of my blood, my head cleared and my spirits lifted. If they were taking blood, there was a chance. I was doing something, finally. I was doing something to help. I ran back upstairs after the doctor had taken as much as he thought I could handle and entered the room. Papa was no longer there. After various people placed calls to surgeons across the city, enough had come to operate with a fighting chance – Papa was being wheeled into the operating theatre just as I returned. Mummy and I were escorted into a waiting room. He was going to be OK. He was going to survive. I said it over and over again, to Mummy, to those who had joined us, to anyone who would listen. It was all going to be OK.

It was past eleven at night and we waited patiently for news. Many people had joined us; the small carpeted waiting room was crowded and impossibly full. Someone had taken out prayer beads, *tasbees*, and started to pray. Someone else ran back and forth bringing cups of water to Mummy and me. We were very lucky not to have been alone then. I focused all my thoughts on seeing Papa again. He was going to be fine. This was going to be a night we'd talk about for many years to come and I'd end up in school after the weekend with a harrowing story to tell but everything was going to be all right in the end. I didn't let any other thoughts, any negative ideas, enter my head. It was going to be fine.

One of Papa's cousins, a man nicknamed Pitu, whose brother had been with Mummy and Joonam in Al Murtaza on 5 January when the police fired on the house, had come to the hospital and ran between our waiting room and the doctors, bringing whatever news he could, keeping Mummy and me as informed as possible. Pitu made things seem manageable and I waited for his periodic updates, they seemed almost hopeful. Things were going to be OK after all, I received each of Pitu's updates with this silent mantra.

'Murtaza had another cardiac arrest in the operating theatre,' Dr Ghaffar Jatoi remembers. 'We had to open the chest to try and resuscitate him by massaging his heart, but we couldn't bring him back this time.'

Pitu came into the room; it was close to midnight. I don't know if he told Mummy first or if he told us together. 'I'm sorry,' he said. He was crying. 'Your father will make history,' he said to me. I couldn't understand what he was saying. I didn't want to understand what he was saying. 'He's going to be fine,' I said, not veering from my mantra. Pitu shook his head. 'He's going to survive, you said he was responding,' I continued. For a moment all the anger in my my heart, reaching breaking point, was directed at Pitu, he lied to me I remember thinking. I wanted to be distracted, I wanted to scream and shout and fight with Pitu, anything but receive the news he was trying to give me. No, he said. I'm sorry, Fati, he's gone.

I don't know how we made it from the waiting room to the operating theatre. I think I was being supported and held. I think Mummy was holding me. Papa lay in the middle of the room, a thin white sheet pulled up to his collarbone. His face had been bandaged with white gauze, holding his jaw shut. His eyes were closed. There was dried blood congealing on his face and flecks of blood in his hair. Papa's hair was always perfectly combed, the only time it ever looked that messy was when he woke up in the mornings. I kneeled on the floor next to his body. He wasn't dead, he couldn't be. There had to be some mistake. I kissed my father's face, his cheeks, his lips, his nose, his chin, over and over again. I didn't kiss his eyes; a Lebanese superstition says you will be separated from anyone whose eyelids your lips brush. I didn't want to be separated from Papa. I cried from the very rawest part of me, with my lungs and my soul fighting for air. I wanted to black out, to fall and awake when this was all over. I couldn't say goodbye to my father, I couldn't accept that he had left me. My throat burnt and my body shook. His face was cold. Why was his face already cold? The doctors and Mummy lifted me up from the floor and walked me out of the room. They couldn't say anything. Everyone around me was crying. There were no words of comfort that came easily to anyone, it was too large a shock.

Mummy was going to stay behind while the autopsy was being carried out. She would return home with Papa's body. She asked Pitu's wife to take me home.

As we left the hospital there were cameras everywhere; flashes went off in my face. I was wailing with pain, my eyes were sealed shut and my face wet with tears. My whole body ached as I cried. The cameras surrounded the car as we drove off and the cameramen got their pictures of me. Mir Murtaza Bhutto was dead. I left the hospital as walking proof of his passing.

There were still police everywhere. I saw officers lined along Clifton road as we reached home. Sofi had put Zulfi to sleep and had waited up for us in the lobby downstairs. She rushed to me as I entered the house, assuming that I had returned because everything was fine. How was Papa? Where was Papa? It took me a moment to understand that Sofi thought he was alive. They killed him. 'He's dead, they killed him Sofi,' I said. 'He's gone.' I felt like I had blood in my mouth.

I should have been with Papa. Why hadn't I gone with him to Surjani Town? Why did I listen when he told me I couldn't join him? I climbed the heavy wooden staircase and walked into Zulfi's bedroom. The lights were on but he was fast asleep in bed, he had no idea what had happened in the night as he slept. I lay down next to him, wanting to protect him. I knew I couldn't live without Papa. I finally understood all those bedtime whispers, finally knew what he meant when he said he'd die if anything happened to me. I had to die too. I felt that my soul had been ripped apart, like someone had taken my heart out of my body and emptied everything living inside me. I cried silently, not wanting to wake Zulfi, until I thought my throat would close. I got up and went into the living room and picked up the phone. I started to call those we knew around the world to tell them what had happened.

⟶◆•••◆⟵

Sabeen left Mideast after midnight when the news that Papa had died filtered out. 'We were afraid there would be mayhem,' she remembers. 'And so we returned home to gather our strength as the search for my father continued.'

Aneed was on the road when the news broke. 'After your father died,' he told me, 'and we still had no news about my father, everyone became more worried. The anxiety heightened. Uncle Ghaffar was asking us, "Where's Ashiq? Why can't we find him?" We just didn't know.'

At Jinnah hospital Zahid and Aneed saw Asghar, our bearer, who had been shot in the arm. 'He was crying and he said to me in Sindhi, "They killed my father and they've killed yours too." Aneed remembers clenching his teeth. 'I told him not to say things like that but Asghar said it again and told me he'd seen it all with his own eyes.

I raised my voice and told Asghar more strongly not to say that, but after Asghar and I spoke I knew my father was dead. As they were leaving Jinnah, without any new information on Ashiq's whereabouts, Aneed lashed out at some police officers stationed at the hospital. He grabbed one of them. 'You're murderers!' he screamed, close to tears, until his uncle Zahid pulled him away and calmed him down.

At the Jatoi home, family members were taking up positions in the living room, kitchen and garden comforting each other and trying to gather as much information as they could. Sabeen took out her father's diary in which he had written – on that very day – 'What happens to me doesn't matter, what matters is how I behave when it is happening to me. Cool mind, clean hands, warm heart.'

Sabeen paused after reading her father's ominous words and assured herself, like I had earlier, that everything was going to be OK. After finding the phone numbers of various friends and contacts, Sabeen started calling people in Ashiq's diary and asking them if they had any information about her father. 'One family friend called me back and told me he had heard through reliable sources that Ashiq Jatoi was alive but under arrest.' Sabeen put down the phone, joyously relieved, and ran to tell the family the good news. But the friend had been mistaken. He had been told that Asif Jatoi, the family driver, was alive and under arrest, and assuming that there had to have been only one Jatoi with Murtaza Bhutto that night reported the incorrect news to Sabeen. It was a cruel mistake. Sabeen's relief was short-lived.

Aneed and Zahid had returned to Mideast to make sure that their family had left and to make some phone calls before continuing with their search. Finding no new answers at Mideast, they were preparing to go back to Jinnah hospital one more time and sweep the emergency wing to see if Ashiq had been brought in. 'I sat in the back seat of the car,' Aneed says slowly. 'I don't even remember whose car it was. *Chacha* Zahid was next to me and a cousin of mine was in front. As the car pulled out of Mideast, my cousin turned to my uncle and me and said, "I'm sorry, he's gone."' The call that directed the Jatois back to Jinnah hospital had been taken by Aneed's cousin. They were going to search for Ashiq, but in the morgue, not the emergency room. After many hours of not knowing, the dreaded call had come. Ashiq was dead.

Aneed and Zahid reached Jinnah and found the hospital in pitch darkness. Karachi's Electrical Supply Company had shut off the electricity across parts of the city. They identified Ashiq's body in the darkness and waited as his post-mortem was carried out by candlelight. 'No one knew where Ashiq's body was until it reached the mortuary,'[10] Zahid tells me thirteen years later. It was two in the morning, six hours after Ashiq had been shot in the back of the head.

Zahid stayed back to take care of the arrangements necessary for Ashiq's body to be released and Aneed drove home alone. They reached the Jatoi house minutes short of each other and Sabeen heard the sound of the gate opening and cars entering the driveway. 'I was so happy – I ran to Aneed and *chacha* Zahid to tell them the good news. "He's alive! He's alive!" I said to them. "We got a call – he's only been arrested!" And then I saw *chacha* Zahid put his hands to his face. He was crying and shaking and he said, "I've just seen his body, he's dead *beta*. He's gone." Somebody held me. Everything afterwards is a blur.'

Somewhere around three in the morning, while Mummy was still at the hospital waiting for the autopsy to be completed and for Papa's body to be released so she could bring him home, the Prime Minister came to Mideast. Benazir flew from the Prime Minister's residence in Islamabad to Karachi. She stopped at her home and then came to the hospital barefeet – a sign, people assumed, of her grief. She was accompanied by Wajid Durrani, one of the shooters that night who is seen saluting her in many of photographs taken of her arrival, and by Shoaib Suddle, another of the men who participated in her brother's assassination. Abdullah Shah, the Chief Minister of Sindh, and another accused in the murder, would also be by Benazir's side at Mideast.

Benazir, my Wadi, would say, years later in an interview broadcast days before her own death, that it was Murtaza's own fault that he was killed. She changed the facts about his injuries, rambling incoherently, claiming he was shot in the back by his own guards, that his guards opened fire on the police, that Murtaza had a death wish. I did not see Benazir until after Papa's burial. Every time she tried to drive to Al Murtaza house where Papa's funeral was held her car was attacked by Larkana locals, who pelted her car with stones and shoes. In the days after we laid Papa to rest in Garhi Khuda Bux, Benazir brought a case against Mummy in the courts. Mummy had refused to go into *iddat,* an obscure Islamic prescription for widows, who must remain cloistered in their homes for forty days and forty nights, not meeting any outsiders or leaving the confines of their rooms. Mummy, who was only thirty-four then, was wasting away with her grief and loss. She lost a lot of weight and drove herself ragged making sure our police complaints and court cases were filed. 'You know why your aunt wants me to do *iddat?*' Mummy, in a rare livid moment, cried. 'So there's no one there to file the cases against the men who killed your father. So he disappears and his murderers disappear with him.' The *iddat* case against Mummy, accusing her of violating Islam, was filed by a Larkana ally of Benazir's. Many years later, some five at least, the man who filed the case – which was summarily thrown out by the courts – left Benazir's PPP and came to Mummy and apologized. But Benazir's war against my mother and my father's memory raged on. Towards the start of the New Year, after Mummy had joined Papa's fledgling party and began to consider the party pleas for her to run as chairperson of the party so that they might contest their first national election, we watched Benazir, since deposed from power and soon to be rejected by the 1997 electorate which brought in her then enemies the PML with a big majority, give an interview to the famous and respected Lebanese journalist Giselle Khoury. Wadi called Mummy a 'bellydancer' who came from the 'backwoods of Lebanon' and repeated the vulgar claims she had made in the first Sindh Council meeting after Papa's murder, wildly insisting that Murtaza hadn't been sleeping with his wife and had only married her as a maid to run his house and rear his children. Mummy, so similar to Papa in style and wit, kept her cool and responded, privately of course, 'If Benazir knew what was happening in Mir's bedroom, how come she claims not to know what was happening outside his house on the night of 20 September?' After Papa was killed, I never saw that old Wadi again. She was gone.

Sattar and Wajahat died in police custody, succumbing to their wounds after not being treated in time. All the survivors and witnesses to the murder were taken into police custody. 'We were taken to Clifton *thana* and questioned,' Asif Jatoi tells me. I ask him if they were shown arrest warrants or if they were taken for remand at any point in their detention, which lasted three months, exactly until Benazir's government was thrown out of power. He laughs bitterly. 'The government was theirs, what treatment do you think they gave us?'

The survivors and witnesses were arbitrarily held and moved from police station to police station. We did not know where they were. Our efforts to file a First Information Report, the most basic right given to all citizens in the event of a legal grievance, was blocked by Benazir's government, thus denying us our right before the law. We had to go to the high courts of Sindh for our right to file a police case.

Meanwhile, the police were not stopped from filing cases of their own and immediately filed a case against all the dead men and survivors claiming that they had initiated the gunfire and had attacked the police. It was standard Operation Clean-Up.

In jail, the survivors were taunted and tortured. 'In the *thana* that night,' Qaisar tells me, 'the police beat us and told us, "We've killed your leader, now we're your *sahibs*' – 'your bosses'. Asif was also told by Rai Tahir, one of the gunmen that night, 'We killed your leaders, what do you think we're going to do to you?' The police routinely carried out mock executions on the survivors, going so far as taking Asif Jatoi out of his cell in the Clifton *thana* at night in the days immediately after the murder and blindfolding him before putting him in an unmarked car. 'They covered my eyes and tied my hands and a *sepah*' – an officer – 'said to me, "Your time is up. We're going to kill you tonight."' They drove Asif around in circles for twenty minutes before laughing and throwing him back in his cell, still blindfolded and gagged.

The survivors often saw the policemen from that night in jail. Several of them told me, independently, that Rai Tahir, Wajid Durrani and Shukaib Qureshi were constant presences. They ran the questioning, supervised their torture – which included beatings with *sachoos*, a Sindhi term for the leather paddles with sharpened nails that tear out the skin and flesh – and carried out intense psychological tauntings, like the mock executions. Asif Jatoi told me how once a lower-level constable in charge of cell duty had ignored the policemen's instructions not to give the prisoners anything to eat or drink and had brought them water. 'Rai Tahir beat this *sepah*. He told him, "I don't care if they die from thirst, no water goes to these men." The constable was a kind man though, and he gave us water again, facing worse punishment from Tahir.'

Using the details that Asif Jatoi gave me, I managed to track down the constable. He was a Sindhi policeman who was posted to cell duty during the late hours of the night, often ending his shift between five and eight in the morning. When we began to speak, I asked the officer if he minded me using his real name. '*Aap ke marzi*,' he replied, it's up to you, I'm at your mercy. 'Whatever is best for your work,' he added. People in far less sensitive positions had asked me to treat them as anonymous sources, but this officer didn't. I will not name him. He is still a salaried employee of the police, and has been for the last twenty years. When we met, he was accompanied by his young son, who depends on his father's continued employment. When the wounded survivors, all blindfolded, were brought to the *thana*, he brought them some water, whatever small scraps of food he could find, and something to sleep on. 'Rai Tahir beat me first,' he says, wringing his hands in his lap as he speaks, 'and then Zeeshan Kazmi' – one of the most brutal policemen who served on the Operation Clean-Up taskforces and was later murdered in Karachi – 'found out that the witnesses were being given water. He went into a rage and beat up a Punjabi constable who told him that he had not been the one to give the water to the men, that it had been me. I was on a break, having some food at a small stall called Ali Baba near the station. Zeeshan Kazmi had me picked up, blindfolded, and brought back to the *thana*. He beat me, knocking out my front teeth, and asked me why I had helped them. "What are they, your fathers?" He took away my gun and suspended me without pay as further punishment.'[II]

None of the survivors were released until Benazir's government fell three months after Papa's assassination. In one of my last phone calls to her, I asked my aunt why her government had arrested all the survivors while the police were free – they had been honourably exonerated by an internal review of any wrong-doing and were back on their beats, not missing a day's pay. 'You're very young, Fati,' Wadi told me, bristling at the questioning. 'This isn't the movies, this is government and we have our own ways of doing things.' She never answered my question.

Several days after my father's assassination, Ali Sonara was shifted from his secret detention centre in Karachi to another police cell in Hyderabad, three hours away. No charges had been filed against him and they wouldn't be for several more weeks. Warrants for his arrest had not yet been produced and no judge had approved his illegal transfer out of Karachi. Sonara was kept a prisoner of the Karachi police till 2003. One year after his release, he was killed in Lyari.

Papa's body was taken to Larkana in an Edhi Foundation helicopter. As it tried to take off from an empty plot of land near the city's Jehangir Kothari Parade, several men attached themselves to the airborne helicopter, clinging on to the doors and landing gear as it struggled to lift off. The funeral in Larkana was intense and cities across the country marked a three-day mourning period in solidarity. Thousands of people, supporters and mourners alike, came to the gates of 70 Clifton to escort Mummy, Zulfi and me to an adjoining helicopter, shielding us from having to make our journey alone and unguarded. They stayed with us, keeping a protective eye on us, for weeks. We would have been so vulnerable, to Benazir, to the state, to the police, if it had not been for the strangers in those crowds who came to protect us. When we landed in Larkana, thousands more met us there and carried Papa to the grounds of Garhi Khuda Bux to lay him in his final resting place. Papa was buried in the original People's Party flag. I think he would have liked that.

Joonam arrived from a foreign trip that day to find her second son murdered. No one had told Joonam, who was beginning to suffer from Alzheimer's, that her beloved elder son had been killed. They told her only minutes before her car had pulled up at the 70 Clifton gates. In the helicopter ride to Larkana, Joonam beat her chest in the Shiia style of mourning and wailed uncontrollably. She never recovered. The day after the burial she walked up and down the corridors of Al Murtaza calling her son. 'Tell Mir he should change his *kaffan*, his burial shroud, it's full of blood.' On the third day of mourning, Benazir came to Al Murtaza under cover of darkness to evade the protestors who had been attacking her motorcade. She said she wanted her mother to be with her for a few days and swept Joonam out of our house. We never saw our grandmother again. Joonam is now held incommunicado by the Zardaris in a garish house in Dubai. Benazir never allowed us to see her again, save for a brief forty-minute visit in Islamabad six months after Papa had been killed. Joonam looked ghostly, pale and haggard. She was being given medicine, I didn't know what for. She cried when she saw Zulfi and me – Wadi said the meeting would be called off if Mummy came with us – and we clung to her when we were told our time with our father's only family member who truly loved and was loved by us was over. We are not permitted to speak to our ailing grandmother, not allowed to visit her and not allowed to care for her as she wastes away alone, minded by maids and strangers and various Zardari clan members. Sanam, my father's younger sister, entered the political fray after Papa's death when she filed a case against Zulfi, then nine years old, Mummy and me (I had just turned eighteen) for the ownership of 70 Clifton. She comes to Pakistan every once in a while for some official presidential function or other and gives interviews against Papa, Mummy, my brother and me. I miss the Aunty Sunny I used to know as a child, I haven't seen her in a long time either.

———— ⋅•⋅•⋅ ————

Having arrested the witnesses to Papa's murder, and not the perpetrators, Benazir's government prohibited us from filing a criminal case against the police officers involved and instead set up a tribunal – which would have no legal authority to pass sentence – to look into Murtaza's murder.

'It was not a court, it was just an inquiry' Justice Nasir Aslam Zahid, one of the judges and a former Chief Justice of Sindh selected to sit on the tribunal bench, tells me.[12] 'Our job was to find who was the aggressor and who a police case should be registered against. We made it clear in our report that the police were the aggressors.'

The tribunal, though not empowered to pass legal sentence, made several important rulings in its final report. It concluded first that Murtaza Bhutto's death was a premeditated assassination, and that there was no shoot-out and no crossfire. 'Who turned the lights off?' Justice Aslam Zahid asks. 'The police, Wajid Durrani in particular, claimed they didn't notice the street lamps were off! But we found that it was done on purpose, because only one street, yours, had been affected and once the firing was over, the lights were turned back on.'

Secondly, the tribunal ruled that the police used an excessive amount of force and left the injured men to die in the road. 'We named the police – Wajid Durrani, Suddle and their colleagues – as the aggressors,' Justice Aslam Zahid continues. 'When we compared the evidence of the injuries it is amazing that the police claim Murtaza Bhutto's men were the aggressors when all of them are dead and only one police officer, Shahid Hayat, is hurt from a self-inflicted wound to the thigh and the other officer, Sial, had a bullet in his foot. Then after the fact, they left your father at Mideast. Mideast was not a hospital where doctors sit. They brought him there and then just left him.'

Shahid Hayat has since arranged for a government medical legal board to examine the scars of his thigh wound and claim, by virtue of his stitches, that the wound was not self-inflicted. The bullet still happens to have been fired from a police weapon. When questioned, another private doctor who examined Hayat's leg said it was against doctor–patient privilege for him to talk about his patients.

Third, the tribunal ruled that the order to assassinate Murtaza Bhutto must have come from the highest level of government.

The criminal case against the police officers Asif Zardari and Abdullah Shah was launched in 1997. It is still in the courts today, though the notion that we will ever receive justice from the corrupt and now Zardari-managed courts of Pakistan is not one I place a lot of faith in. Judges have been constantly changed in our case – sixteen in total, one because she was a woman and the Chief Justice of Pakistan didn't think she could bear the stress of such a case – and the accused are currently being acquitted in the middle of the ongoing trial, before all the evidence has been heard, before all the witness testimonies have been recorded and before any attempt at presenting the facts has been completed.

Justice Wajihuddin Ahmed, a former Chief Justice of Sindh like Justice Aslam Zahid and the man who bravely contested General Pervez Musharraf's presidency in 2007, didn't take a moment to think when I asked him if there was any hope that we would get a free and fair trial. 'Certainly not now,' he replied.[13]

On 5 December 2009 Karachi's Session Courts acquitted all the policemen accused of the assassination of Mir Murtaza Bhutto and six of his companions. One month after the judgement was passed, former President Farooq Leghari – who sacked Benazir's second government in the winter of 1996 – came on national television and spoke of my father's murder. In the interview, aired on Duniya TV, a popular private channel, Leghari claimed that Zardari came to him in the late hours one night during his wife's term and insisted that Murtaza Bhutto be eliminated. 'It's either him or me' Zardari is alleged to have told the President. President Leghari, now looking frail and old beyond his years, said that both Benazir and her husband, whom he accused of gross corruption, were at the helm of the 'massive cover-up' after the murder. 'He has Murtaza's blood on his hands' the former President said 'and Allah knows how many others.'

Epilogue

April 2009

As I finish this book it feels as though the world around me is slowly collapsing. There is a peculiar sense of déjà vu as I write about the death of my father. There is a similar danger, a tangible feeling that we are not safe. Seven months ago, I packed my bags and flew to see my brother off in a foreign country.

Zulfi had enrolled for the start of his A-level year, twelfth grade, at a private school not far from our house in Karachi. Some of his friends had got into the same school. They had made plans for a more relaxed year in which they would be treated like college students. In the autumn of 2008 Zulfi had just turned eighteen and was aware how precarious our situation had become since Asif Zardari had acquitted himself in our father's murder case. He was aware that because of our history with the man now called President, we weren't safe in our country any longer. When Zardari announced himself as the PPP's unanimously chosen presidential candidate we knew he would stop at nothing to reach the pinnacle of power. There was no turning back for him. Against all odds, he was going to rule Pakistan. We made the decision to take Zulfi out of the country. It was a decision we had been avoiding, hoping it would not be necessary, since Benazir was killed in December 2007. But as Zulfi was the only surviving male heir of the Bhuttos, we couldn't take the risk of leaving him vulnerable. Besides Zulfi, the only Bhuttos remaining are Sassi and I. We don't live in a country with a free press, we don't live in a country with an independent judiciary – or any judiciary for that matter. We have no safeguards against a violent and vindictive government.

We went through the application process for boarding schools abroad. We dealt with new administrations, new fees and new time-tables. We would send him after the twelfth anniversary of our father's death. It was not going to be easy. Zulfi, eight years younger than me, had always been the glue that held our small family together. Mir Ali, our little brother whom Mummy adopted when he was one month old, was the boisterous one. A year after adopting Mir Ali from the Edhi Orphanage in Karachi, Mummy said that little Miroo was her idea of justice. Revenge was never how she saw it. After pure blood is spilt, Mummy said, you can't restore the balance by spilling dirty blood, that of the killers. You can only restore the balance of loss and justice by saving another pure life. Mir Ali is a hurricane; you get caught up in his movement. I am loud and opinionated. But Zulfi, he isn't as obvious as we are. Far more unassuming, he speaks in a gentle voice and carries a big stick. My mother and I spoke quietly about our relief that he would soon be away from Karachi, that he would be safe somewhere far away.

But we didn't imagine how devastated we'd be by the silence when that gentle voice left the house. We feel it every day when Mummy and I are having lunch and there's no one sitting across the table from us who finishes all the cucumbers and tomatoes before anyone else has got to the salad. We notice it when a friend comes over and asks where Zulfi is. 'Gone,' answers Mir Ali, tilting his head as he says the word. We didn't realize that a gulf caused by Zulfi's absence would grow between each one of us, that we would seek him in our conversations and, not finding him nearby, retreat.

<hr />

The closest we came to each other, Zardari and I, was at Benazir's funeral in December 2007.

It was election season, once again. I had been canvassing door-to-door in Larkana, where Mummy was running against the might of the PPP, trying to get women out to vote. At some point in the evening, Mummy called me. 'Benazir's been hurt. They're saying something happened at a rally,' she said. I felt my breath slow down. Not again. I asked if she was alive. I think so, Mummy replied. I carried on working. It was maybe forty minutes later when one of the men with me, one of Papa's old political workers, Qadir, entered the house I was visiting and whispered to me, 'I think we should go home.' No, I answered loudly, in a bit. Qadir tried again, '*Bibi*, I think it might be good if we went home.'

I got into the car and as soon as the doors shut, Qadir turned to me and said, 'Wadi has been killed.' I felt a portion of my brain register what he had said, *Wadi?* I hadn't heard anyone call her Wadi in a long time; it had been years since I used the name myself. Qadir made me sit in the middle of the car, with two other people on either side of me, next to the windows. I didn't realize initially what he was doing. I was stuck on Wadi. When I understood, I got up and squeezed over to return to my seat by the left-hand window. This was ridiculous, I told Qadir, they can't kill another Bhutto tonight.

But my words rang in my ears. I had heard my father say a variation of the same thought: *they* couldn't kill another Bhutto, they wouldn't dare. I tried calling Zulfi and Mummy, who were also on the road, their phones weren't responding. I called Sabeen, who was with us in Larkana, working around the clock as Mummy's election agent – a major domo on the day and something of a campaign manager until then. No line to her either. It hit me then, they could. They could kill more of us. Every decade someone in this family, in this immediate family of Zulfikar and Nusrat's children, is killed.

I was the last one to reach Al Murtaza. Mummy and Zulfi and Mir Ali and Sabeen were already there. Once I saw them I leapt out of the car and ran to hug them. It seemed strange. I was sad for my family. I was sad for my country. I was sad for Zulfikar. But the news of my aunt's death didn't fully hit me till two hours later. I was walking down the corridors of the house, cleaning up. A strange reaction for me in normal circumstances. I had tidied up my room, checked on Zulfi's and rearranged the clutter in the hallways. I could see Sabeen through the open door of the drawing room. She looked at me and furrowed her brow. What are you doing? I smiled and waved to her. I was cleaning up, for Papa. Then Zulfi, tall and sombre, walked towards me. 'What are you doing, Fati?' I hugged him and patted his shoulder. 'Don't worry,' I replied madly, 'everything is going to be OK now. Papa's coming back.' Once the words left my mouth and I saw my brother's face, I heard what I had said. He wasn't coming back. Nothing was ever going to bring my father back. I broke down. I cried for the next five days. By the time I had drained myself of tears I had cried for everyone. For Papa, for my grandfather, for Shah, for Joonam, for my Wadi whom I had lost long before that winter.

I saw Zardari the night Benazir's body was brought from Rawalpindi, where she was killed, to Garhi Khuda Bux. Mummy, Zulfi and I made the forty-minute drive from our house in Larkana to Naudero. The house had once belonged to Shahnawaz but Benazir took it over after his murder and used it as a base to build her political platform. I wondered if Asif would be there; if he'd have the courage to show his face at the funeral of another Bhutto. I reminded myself that he was her husband, he was sure to be present. I didn't think he'd be able to face us, and I didn't know how I would react to him. I felt as if my heart would explode in grief and anger – that I would break inside.

In the end, it was only a moment. We stood by the door, waiting for the coffin to arrive, and he walked in, agitated. Zardari was shorter than I remembered. Barely taller than me and I'm not tall. And he was shaking. Someone, it could have been anyone, there were so many people pushing in through the doors, brushed past him and he jerked, his whole body quivering. He's scared, I thought. He can't wait to get out of here. It gave me no solace.

Zulfi decided he would be present at Benazir's burial. He was a family member, the only male alive. Someone from the family should be there to bury her, he said. The other men around the funeral were all political assistants, enablers, criminals, petty distributors and thieves. She can't be buried by them, he reasoned. I cried and tried to threaten my brother. I didn't want him near her, I didn't want him standing in the six-foot-deep pit with Zardari, with the man many believe was responsible for my father's murder. People were saying the same sort of thing now, about this death. 'It's too dangerous, are you crazy?' I exploded. It would be insane, I whimpered.

In the end, Zulfi was more dignified, more gracious than I could ever have been. He placed Benazir's body in the ground, said the *fateha* prayers and walked to our father's grave. He bent down and kissed the cloth and old rose petals that covered Papa's grave. And then he left. Zulfi was alone that day. He was only seventeen then.

Two months later I had another encounter with Asif Zardari. It was after the February 2008 elections had been rigged and won, after he had given a press conference on the third day after his wife's death, the most important day in Muslim mourning, after he had farcically changed his children's last names from Zardari to Bhutto and announced his hostile takeover of Benazir's PPP and his intention to be the last 'Bhutto' left standing. It was longer than the first encounter and it burnt me; every fibre of my being and feeling was scorched by it.

A French film crew had come to Karachi to do a story on the family dynasty and in my new role as black sheep and naysayer to hereditary politics, I was to give them the opposing viewpoint. The crew, two women and their Pakistani fixer, asked me to take them to the spot where Papa had been killed. It's a ten-second walk from our front door and I'd done it in the past for journalists. I stood by the spot, directly in front of the police station, where my father was shot and as I spoke to the cameras I noticed a white Pajero jeep standing a few feet away from me. There were three men inside and Benazir stickers on the windows. I stopped talking. I was shaken. I went to Hameed, one of the men who guard Zulfi and me and asked him to go and find out who the car belonged to and why it was there. I asked the French women to give me a moment. I was upset. I didn't want to lose my composure, not with two journalists around, not with cameras and story-making potential present. Hameed spoke to the men and they got out of the car; that surprised me. Why hadn't they just left? They held their hands up, in some sort of placatory gesture, but stood their ground. It was taking more heat, this moment, than I had expected. After a few minutes the men drove away. 'What happened?

Who were they?' I asked Hameed in Urdu, hoping the journalists would not notice my voice shaking. 'It's Zardari,' came the reply. 'He's at the British consulate next door. They're his security.' They told Hameed that they weren't there to make trouble, hence the hands, but that they had to patrol the area for Zardari's safety. Hameed asked them to patrol elsewhere and they left. It was a Kafkaesque irony.

Here I was, standing where my father was murdered, and the man who I believe was in part responsible for the execution was across the road from me, being received diplomatically. I felt my knees buckle. I sat down on the kerb. 'What's wrong?' one of the French women asked me. 'Nothing,' I mumbled. I carried on from where I had left off, talking about my father's murder, taking them through it step by step. Then I noticed another car, a different one this time, but also white, across the street. Hameed stepped closer to me and bent down. 'Shahid Hayat is in the car. He's providing the police security for Asif's Karachi visit,' he whispered. Shahid Hayat was one of the policemen present that night, the one who shot himself in the thigh, another police officer we accused and who protested his innocence. And there they were, reunited. In broad daylight, driving up and down Clifton road in front of me. All of a sudden, those distant threats became very clear and very close. We were in danger. I stood up and continued talking. I spoke slowly, so we would have to stand there longer. I told the French filmmakers what was happening. I wasn't going to leave. Minutes passed, a quarter of an hour, then half an hour. I had nothing left to say. I walked back the few feet to my house, shaken.

The fear, the palpable, obvious fear remained with me. I thought of it when I returned to my room to write at night. I thought about it when my phone rang, when people emailed me. The feeling of being watched eventually settled down and I became used to the idea that things had changed. That we were on the defensive, that we had enemies in the highest places, once again.

In April, two months after that day, I was in Larkana to attend the twenty-ninth anniversary of my grandfather's death. Asif and Benazir's PPP had taken to marking the occasion not on the 4th, the correct date, but the night before. They would erect tents and bus people in. Their public meeting started shortly before midnight and they ensured their numbers, made up of strangers, not locals, were visible even in the dark. It was the night of the 2nd and we were at the dinner table: my family, our family friend and lawyer Omar, and Dr Jatoi, an old friend of Papa's and a loyal party worker. I made an off-the-cuff comment about not wanting to go to the *mazaar* at Garhi Khuda Bux. I hadn't been since Benazir's funeral and the cult of personality worship that had started then could only have spiralled. I wasn't prepared to see my father's graveyard turned into a fairground. Mummy nodded as I spoke and said, 'I think maybe you shouldn't come.' I stopped mid-rant. 'Why?' I asked, has it got worse, more kitschy? More hawkers selling food and snacks outside? 'No,' Mummy shook her head. Were there more posters of her put up? I had always taken them down; it was a graveyard not a shrine and some things, some places, are not campaign grounds. Mummy spoke. 'Yes, there are posters, but they're not of Benazir.' 'Who?' I asked, putting down my fork. 'They've put his posters up,' Mummy said, leaning towards me, taking my hand to soften the blow. I couldn't believe what I was hearing. His posters? Zardari's? 'Are they near my father's grave?' I asked, my voice trembling and tears running down my face. Mummy didn't answer. Omar got out of his chair and came over to mine. I didn't want to be steadied, didn't want to be hugged. I leapt out of my chair and went outside. 'Get the car,' I said, I don't remember to whom. I was crying, hard. Mummy and Omar were trying to convince me to go back inside the house. I was upset, they said, come back and we'll talk it about it. I didn't. I got into the car. Dr Jatoi and his twenty-year-old daughter Jia jumped in with me, unsure of what I was going to do. The *mazaar* was being prepared for the next day's PPP jamboree. Prime Minister Gilani was coming. Zardari was going to put in a rare public appearance; he saved most of his energy for foreign trips. A local pundit estimated, a year into Zardari's presidency, that Richard Holbrooke, the US special envoy to what is now lugubriously called 'Af-Pak', had spent more days in Pakistan than the President himself.

Thousands of security forces, policemen and Rangers had been brought into the city to protect the VIPs.

The driver drove towards Garhi. '*Bibi*,' he said to me, trying to be heard over my tears, 'why don't we go tomorrow, it's not a good idea to go now.' I was crying so hard I could barely speak. 'Take me or I'll walk,' I threatened. It works every time. I can't walk, the *mazaar* is too far, the roads unlit, and I have a useless sense of direction. But I was angry and my bluff held.

Mummy called Dr Jatoi. 'Come back or I'll get in a taxi and follow you,' Mummy bluffed back at me. 'Come then,' I replied. I wasn't turning back. They were afraid I was going to take down the posters, cause a scene, get people into trouble. But I wasn't going to do that. I just wanted to see what Larkana had been looking at, what people had been watching and allowing to happen in their fear and obsequious obedience to power. Jia was passing me tissues; she had given up trying to blow my nose for me, I kept swatting her hand away. I couldn't talk, I was gasping for air in between my howls. She patted my hands and tried to comfort me. When we got to the grave-yard we were stopped by a roadblock. There had never been a road-block at Garhi before, this was a sign of the new Zardari management. Two men, in plain clothes, came up to our window to ask who we were. 'I'm the *Shaheed's* daughter,' I replied, through my window. He recognized us and let us through. In front of the *mazaar*, there were metal detectors, for Asif's security. A ramp had been built so he could drive the car into the graveyard. It was too dangerous for him to alight from his car and walk. He was going to park at the graves and pray. I went to my father's grave. By now I had stopped crying. Everywhere around the dead were posters of Asif Zardari, his children and his sister, Benazir's *siasi waris* according to her 'will', her political heir. She has a pug nose and a headscarf, trying as much as possible to resemble Benazir. I asked for the doors to the *mazaar* to be closed. I removed the posters of the Zardaris that surrounded my father and uncle's graves. I apologised to Papa. I left. As I got back into my car, three police vans pulled up around us. A daughter of the Bhuttos, only one of two left, a child of the dead, had frightened them into arriving to assess the threat. Now, several months shy of the second anniversary of Benazir's death, the government of Asif Zardari, while begging international donors and rich nations for billions of dollars to aid Pakistan, has allocated some 400 million rupees to the Zardari-fication of Garhi Khuda Bux. Metal detectors, four at least, are oper-ated solely for the President's security, rules for visitors written in bad English have been nailed to the front entrance, and two hotels are reportedly being built nearby to handle all the devotees – both foreign and local – of the Bhutto cult that power is now based on.

This is the legacy Benazir has left behind for Pakistan. This is the saprophytic culture she created and thrived in. Bloodlines, genetics, a who's who of dynastic politics – this is all her. It is this corrupted and dangerously simple system that allows her husband to rule a country of 180 million people by virtue of having a close enough tie to the dead, to the corpses that demand – and receive – sympathy votes.

<hr />

One of the four murder cases pending against Zardari in the build-up to his bid for the nation's presidency was the case of Justice Nizam's killing. He had been president of the High Court Bar Association at the time of his death and was killed outside his home three months before Papa.

Justice Nizam had opened a case against a property deal that was being carried out in Zardari's name. A valuable plot of land was being sold through Zardari's frontmen, without auction. In the public interest, Justice Nizam got a stay order against the sale and readied himself for a fight in court; he was, his brother Noor Ahmed told me, ready to take the case against Zardari to the Supreme Court.[1]

On 10 June 1996, at around two in the afternoon, Justice Nizam was on his way home for lunch. His son, Nadeem, had picked him up from the office as he often did when the family's driver was unavail-able and they drove home together. Nadeem had only recently returned home to Karachi after graduating from college abroad. As they drove towards the gates of their home, two men on a scooter drew up alongside their car. One of the men gestured to Justice Nizam and his son. Nadeem, who was driving, stopped the car and wound down his window. The men fired into the car, killing both Justice Nizam and his young son.

The gunfire startled their family, who had been inside waiting for them before starting lunch. The justice's brother-in-law ran out of the house as soon as he heard the shots. By the time he reached the car, the scooter had driven off. Both men were dead. Nadeem was in his mid-twenties; he had got engaged to be married a month earlier.

When I meet Noor Ahmed, Justice Nizam's brother, the ball had already started rolling – Zardari had been magically acquitted in two of the four murder cases against him. The third, Justice Nizam's case, had just been thrown out of the courts and Zardari declared innocent. Our case, Papa's murder case, was next. Noor Ahmed is an elderly man. We met after Friday prayers and he wore the customary white *shalwar kameez* and white prayer cap. His wife brought us tea and cakes while we spoke. A photograph of Justice Nizam sat by his brother's armchair. The two brothers resembled each other, both with serious, heavy-set eyes and white hair. I asked Noor Ahmed if he thought he would ever get justice. Softly, he replied, 'I doubt it.' He had been very brave to meet me and speak so openly about his brother's case. I thanked Noor Ahmed for seeing me and in response he told me that he had met my father once, at the Karachi Boat Club, after Justice Nizam had been killed. 'Murtaza came to my table and shook my hand. He offered his condolences and said, "The same people are after me." Was he certain, I asked, that it was Zardari who was behind his brother's murder? 'I came to know only after his death,' Noor Ahmed responded, switching between English and Urdu, 'that every judge and every advocate knew that this had been done and planned by Asif Zardari.' When he said his name, Zardari, Noor Ahmed's body shook. 'Even housewives know Zardari was behind this,' he said, raising his voice. I couldn't help but worry for him. Worry what the consequences of his outspokenness would be in such a dangerous climate.

But he wasn't afraid to speak, not now and certainly not then. 'The only thing I did, on the second day after the murder,' Noor Ahmed says, his voice still calm, 'was this – Hakim Zardari, Asif's father, came to condole with me. He asked me, "How did this happen?" In my heart, which was hurting, I said everyone knows it's your *larka*, your boy, who did this. I said it to him. Did he answer? No. He just kept quiet. What could he say?' Noor Ahmed's wife, who is sitting quietly next to me, breaks the tension in the room. Both of us are getting emotional now, so she interjects. 'You look like Benazir,' she says to me. I laugh, not knowing what else to do. Sensing my discomfort, she adds, as if to console me, 'It's in God's hands.' Noor Ahmed, who had been sitting quietly with his hands folded in his lap, threw out a palm and swatted the air. 'What's all this *God-shod* business?' he says, almost to himself. 'Her whole family has been killed!' Before I leave, as I am thanking him for his time and for seeing me and talking to me at a time when most might find it sensible not to, Noor Ahmed smiles at me and asks, 'What's the *faida*, *beti*, of writing this book of yours?' What's the benefit, he asks, and calls me daughter. Memory, I tell him.

The day Zardari was acquitted of my father's murder, I was halfway around the world. I was on assignment in Cuba to cover the past and present of the revolution in the lead-up to the fiftieth anniversary of Castro's takeover. I knew it was coming. Even when he had been incarcerated for the murders and myriad cases against him, Zardari hardly spent time in jail – a serious, mortally ill heart patient at the time, he had himself transferred to a luxury suite at his friend's private hospital in Karachi. That doctor friend was rewarded with the cabinet post of Minister of Oil and Petroleum after his chum miraculously rid himself of his heart problems and ascended to the highest post in the land.

I had been visiting hospitals and schools, meeting officials and travelling the country. I was away from email. I had disconnected myself from Pakistan intentionally. I got a phone call one afternoon in Havana. It was April and the weather was tropical and humid. I was sitting on my hotel bed in front of a balcony overlooking Calle

Obispo trying to cool down from an afternoon spent walking between ministries on the Malecon. It was Hameed, calling from home. 'I'm sorry, *baba*,' he said. He didn't have to explain why. Zardari had bypassed the courts' standard procedures to have himself absolved of my father's murder. There was no point in appealing, he was going to be President legally or illegally. It was typical of the way he operated; justice was always the first casualty.

———— ◆•◆◆• ————

On 20 September 2008, on the twelfth anniversary of Papa's death, Asif Zardari took his oath as President of Pakistan. The ceremony had been scheduled for the day before, the 19th, but had been moved on the orders of the new President, who rescheduled his big day for Saturday, Papa's *barsi*. As he stood in front of parliament, which had voted him into the post almost unanimously (in the same highly democratic way that General Musharraf was 'elected' President), he paused in his speech and asked for a moment of silence to mark the occasion of his brother-in-law's death. My blood froze. It was as if he was taunting us. But that would be nothing compared to what would follow. On Zardari's first Pakistan Day as President he would honour Shoaib Suddle, one of the most senior police officers present at the scene when my father was killed. Suddle was awarded Hilal-e-Imtiaz, a national medal in recognition of his services to the people of Pakistan. Shoaib Suddle was then made the head of the Federal Investigation Bureau.

The MQM has forgotten Operation Clean-Up and is now an enthusiastic coalition partner in Zardari's government. Aftaf Hussain, still living in London, and Zardari have become firm friends and often pose menacingly for photographs holding hands and embracing each other for the cameras.

The Sindh Assembly, chaired by Nisar Khuro, in the middle of the state's war against Swat and the northern territories that had made close to 3 million Pakistanis homeless, marked the death of the pop star Michael Jackson in the summer of 2009 with a minute of silence.

Nothing was said (or not said with a moment of silence) for the many killed by American drones and the Pakistan Army's bombarment of the NWFP.

The National Assembly, meanwhile, used the summer to quietly pass the Cyber Crime bill which makes 'spoofing', 'satirizing' or 'character assassinating' the President a crime punishable by imprisonment – anywhere from six months to fourteen years (for the very funny spoofer, I suppose).

———————◆◆◆◆◆———————

It has been a trial writing this book about my family. Through letters and notebooks, photographs and interviews, it has opened them up to me and made them, all my ghosts, whole. But by virtue of what I now know about them, I must close them off. I must take my leave and remove myself from their shadows, their glories, their mistakes and their violent, extraordinary lives. There is just one member I cannot leave behind, Papa. I started this book with the intention of making my peace with my father, of finally honouring my last promise to him – to tell his story – and then, to finally say goodbye. But I can't. He especially became whole to me, flawed and ordinarily human, unlike the immortal being I revered as a child growing up. His choices, remarkable and dangerous, honourable and foolish, are not mine but I lived them. I have also lived, since his death, with an incomplete picture of my father as a murdered man – holding vigil for him daily in my thoughts, in my steps and travels, in my public moments and in my eyes blinking him in every morning and closing him off to sleep every night. I had forgotten, in these fourteen years, that he was once alive and, for a brief while, only mine. He seems very alive to me now. It is too sweet a thought to push aside, so I delay the thought of farewells, if only for a little while longer.

Amidst all this madness, all these ghosts and memories of times past, it feels like the world around me is crumbling, slowly flaking away. Sometimes, when it's this late at night, I feel my chest swell with a familiar anxiety. I think, at these times, that I have no more place in my heart for Pakistan. I cannot love it any more. I have to get away from it for anything to make sense; nothing here ever does. But then the hours pass, and as I ready myself for sleep as the light filters in through my windows, I hear the sound of those mynah birds. And I know I could never leave.

Acknowledgements

Many of the Pakistan People's Party's founding members and former cabinet members spoke openly and candidly with me. I am indebted to the following for their insights into Zulfikar Ali Bhutto's chairmanship and political career: Abdul Waheed Katpar, Miraj Mohammad Khan, Dr Ghulam Hussain, Aftab Sherpao and Dr Mubashir Hasan, a national treasure among men. Mumtaz Bhutto and Ashiq Bhutto were very helpful in constructing a time-line of the Bhutto family history; many thanks to them and their families. Ilahi Bux Soomro and Sherbaz Khan and Mrs Mazari spoke to me about Zulfikar Ali Bhutto's youth and Yousef Masti Khan and Khair Bux Marri, senior Baloch politicians, spoke to me about Balochistan. I am very grateful to them.

Three years ago I travelled to America to seek out my father's professors and college friends and I must thank Nancy Sinsabaugh and the Harvard Alumni Association for helping me track down so many helpful friends. Milbry Polk, Bobby Kennedy Jr, Magdalena Guernica Castleman, John Hess, Peter Santin, the late Samuel Huntington, William Graham, Robert Paarlberg, Gudu Shafi, and Bill and Andrea White opened their homes and their memories to me and I am grateful for all their help and kindness. Many friends helped me along the journey across America and I am thankful for all their help.

Tariq Ali, a friend and a forthcoming interviewee, was invaluable with his knowledge, encouragement and support. William Dalrymple suggested that I write this book on the eve of an election in Larkana and I thank him for his help and friendship.

In Karachi there were many who spoke to me with full knowledge of the danger that came with their participation in this book. I am grateful for their trust and their bravery: Bangul Channa, Hameed Baloch, Maulabux, Shahnawaz Baloch, the Hingoro family, Maqsood Billoo, Qaisar, Mahmood, Asif Jatoi, Ghulam Hasnain, Bashir Daood, Noor Ahmed Nizam, Malik Sarwar Bagh, Ayaz Dayo, Haji Khan Rajpar, Nisar Ahmed Ghakro, Amer Jokhio, Ramzan and Mushtaq Brohi, Abdul Majid Baloch, Siddiqueh Hidaytullah, Justice Nasir Aslam Zahid, Justice Wajihuddin Ahmed, and Dr Ghaffar Jatoi. There are many more I cannot name, but without whom I would not have been able to reconstruct the details of my father's murder.

Zahid and Nuzhat Jatoi, Badrunissa, Anushka, Maheen, Aneed and Sabeen Jatoi all spoke to me about Ashiq Jatoi and his murder. I am deeply appreciative for their recollections. Sassi Bhutto, my cousin, spoke to me about her father Shahnawaz and was instrumental in shedding light on her father's life and death. In Paris, Jacques Vergès and his staff were accommodating and gracious in my quest to uncover more about Shahnawaz's mysterious death.

In Greece, Della Rounick opened up a world of information I would never had access to without her. Thank you Della mou, for finding me, and for sharing your life with me. In Syria, Nashaat Sanadiki and his family were a great help and support, as always. Shoaib Billoo and RMZ in Pakistan, thank you for your assistance and support. Omar Sial, a great lawyer but a better friend, deserves many thanks for his assistance in fact-checking and sourcing information. Dennis Dalton, my teacher, mentor and beloved friend reminded me – in between chapter notes – of the importance of the journey. Thanks to Henry Porter for supporting the book and reading early drafts. And to Suhail Sethi, without whose love and support I could not have written this book, thank you.

Thank you Ellah Alfrey – a sensitive and intuitive editor. At Jonathan Cape, enormous appreciation and thanks must go to Dan Franklin, who protected my work, whose instinct was spot on, and whose enthusiasm carried me forward. Many thanks are also owed to Tom Avery and to Amanda Telfer.

At DGA, Charlotte Knight and Sophie Hoult were invaluable and let me bore them rigid with stray book thoughts during my office visits. Heather Godwin is owed many thanks for the great help and guidance she gave me. David Godwin, my agent and the most patient man I've ever tortured with questions and queries and drafts and concerns, deserves the largest thanks here. He should get a separate page of appreciation.

Allegra Donn and Sophie Hackford kept me sane, made me lalf, and universed when I needed it most. Lovie.

To my mother Ghinwa, Zulfi, Mir Ali, Teta, Lulu, Zeina and Racha. My family. I love and adore you all more than you will ever know and more than I will ever be able to say. I can't say thank you enough. But I'll keep trying.

Notes and References

Chapter 1

1. Pakistan's CIA has no relation to the nasty American CIA. Or so we're told. For some inexplicably bureaucratic reason, however, they share a name.
2. Interview with Malik Sarwar Bagh, Karachi, 14 May 2008.

Chapter 2

1. Interview with Ashiq Bhutto, Karachi, 6 June 2008.
2. Oriana Fallaci, *Interview with History*, p. 208.
3. Fallaci, p. 206.
4. Zulfikar Ali Bhutto, *My Dearest Daughter*, p. 8.
5. Fallaci, p. 208.
6. Fallaci, p. 206.
7. ZAB letter to Murtaza Bhutto. Camp Gilgit, 12 May 1976. Personal collection.
8. Ibid.
9. Interview with Illahi Bux Soomro, Karachi, 6 June 2008.
10. ZAB, *Treaties of Self-Defence and Regional Arrangement*, p. 47.
11. Ibid.
12. ZAB, *The Islamic Heritage*, p. 15.
13. ZAB, *One World*, p. 5.
14. ZAB, *The Islamic Heritage*, p. 8
15. Ibid., p. 7.
16. Ibid., p. 15.
17. ZAB, letter to Murtaza Bhutto. Rawalpindi, 8 May 1975. Personal collection.

18. ZAB letter to Murtaza Bhutto, Camp Gilgit, 12 May 1976. Personal collection.
19. Interview with Begum Mazari, Karachi, 5 June 2008.
20. Ahmed Shuja Pasha, *Pakistan: A Political Profile 1947–1988*, p. 181.
21. ZAB, *Reshaping Foreign Policy*, editors' note by Hamid Jalal and Khalid Hasan, p. 90.
22. ZAB, *Pakistan-Soviet Oil Agreement*, p. 131.
23. Ibid., p. 6.
24. ZAB, *The Indivisibility of the Human Race*, p. 23.
25. Sanghat Singh, *Pakistan's Foreign Policy: An Appraisal*, p. 91.
26. ZAB, *Regional Cooperation for Development*, p. 67.
27. ZAB, *Role of Political Parties*, p. 176.
28. Hugh Trevor-Roper, *Introduction to New Directions*, p. vi.
29. ZAB, *Phases of Foreign Policy*, p. 17.
30. Ibid., p. 15.
31. Mohammad Ehsan Chaudri, *Pakistan and the Great Powers*, p. 43.
32. China–Pakistan Boundary Agreement, signed at Peking, 2 March 1963.
33. Chaudri, p. 43.
34. Ibid., p. 91.
35. Ibid., p. 95.
36. *Dawn*, 26 March 1965.
37. Rafi Ullah Shehab, *50 Years of Pakistan*, p. 406.
38. Chaudri, p. 95.
39. Ibid., p. 38.
40. Ibid., p. 50.
41. *Daily Telegraph*, 13 September 1965.
42. Chaudri, p. 96.
43. Ibid.
44. Ibid., p. 97.
45. Ibid.
46. Tashkent Declaration, signed 4 January 1966.
47. Pasha, p. 209
48. Interview with Miraj Mohammad Khan, Karachi, 12 May 2008.

49. B. N Goswami, *Pakistan and China*, p. 128.

50. Interview with Abdul Waheed Katpar, Karachi, 4 June 2008.

51. Pakistan People's Party, *Foundation and Policy*, p. 4.

52. Ibid., p. 5.

53. Ibid., p. 4.

54. Ibid., p. 6.

55. Ibid., p. 7.

56. Ibid., p. 6.

57. Ibid., p. 14.

58. Ibid., p. 6.

59. Ibid., p. 15.

60. ZAB, Pakistan and the Alliances, p. 50

61. ZAB, *The Role of Muslim States*, p. 78

62. Ibid., p. 91

63. ZAB, *The Imperative of Unity*, p. 17.

64. Ibid., p. 22.

65. Ibid.

66. ZAB, *Regional Cooperation for Development*, p. 67.

Chapter 3

1. *Xtra* magazine, March 1996. Interview with Fifi Haroon.

2. Ibid.

3. Ibid.

4. Ibid.

5. Ibid.

6. Ibid.

7. Ibid.

8. Interview with Suhail Sethi, Karachi, 13 August 2009.

9. *Xtra* magazine, March 1996.

10. Ibid.

11. Interview with Gudu Shafi, Washington DC, 28 April 2006.

12. Khurshid Hyder, *The United States and the Indo-Pakistan War of 1971*, p. 10.

13. Ibid.

14. Richard F. Nyrop, Beryl Lieff Benderly, Cary Corwin Conn,

Wiliam W. Coer, Melissa J. Cuter and Newton B. Parker, *Area Handbook for Pakistan*, p 57.

15. Ibid.
16. Interview with Miraj Mohammad Khan, Karachi, 12 May 2008.
17. Election manifesto of the PPP, 1970, p. 12.
18. Ibid., p. 13.
19. Nyrop et al., p. 59.
20. Ibid.
21. Ibid.
22. Interview with Abdul Waheed Katpar, Karachi, June 4 2008.
23. Nyrop et al., p. 59.

Chapter 4
1. Anwar H. Syed, *The Discourse and Politics of Zulfikar Ali Bhutto*, p. 158.
2. Ibid.
3. Carnegie Endowment for International Peace and Non Proliferation, www.ceip.org/programmes/npp/China.htm.
4. Syed, p. 159.
5. Zulfikar Ali Bhutto, letter to Murtaza Bhutto. Rawalpindi, 25 October 1973.
6. Rafi Raza, *Zulfikar Ali Bhutto and Pakistan 1967–1977*, p. 207.
7. Ibid., p. 209.
8. Ibid., p. 229.
9. Ian Talbot, *Pakistan: A Modern History*, p. 237.
10. Raza, p. 235.
11. Ibid., p. 180.
12. Ibid.
13. Ibid., p. 185.
14. Ibid.
15. Interview with Khair Bux Marri, Karachi, 11 May 2008.
16. Interview with Yousef Masti Khan, Karachi, 7 May 2008.
17. Interview with Miraj Mohammad Khan, Karachi, 12 May 2008.

Chapter 5

1. Rafi Raza, *Zulfikar Ali Bhutto and Pakistan 1967–1977*, p. 187.
2. Interview with Abdul Waheed Katpar, Karachi, 4 June 2008.
3. Tariq Ali, *The Duel*, p. 106.
4. Interview with Katpar, Karachi, 4 June, 2008.
5. Ali, p. 109.
6. Interview with Mayor Bill White, Houston, Texas, 7 May 2006.
7. Interview with Milbry Polk, New York City, 19 April 2006.
8. Interview with Peter Santin, Phoenix, Arizona, 5 May 2006.
9. Interview with Madgalena Guernica Castleman, New York City, 18 May 2006.
10. Interview with Robert Paarlberg, Cambridge, Massachusetts, 26 April 2006.
11. Interview with William Graham, Cambridge, Massachusetts, 25 April 2006.
12. Interview with Samuel Huntington, Cambridge, Massachusetts, 25 April 2006.
13. Interview with Bobby Kennedy Jr, Mount Kisco, New York, 15 May 2006.
14. Nusrat Bhutto, letter to Mir Murtaza Bhutto, 18 October 1975.

Chapter 6

1. Tariq Ali, *The Duel*, p. 114.
2. Interview with Suhail Sethi, Karachi, 21 March 2008.
3. Zulfikar Ali Bhutto, *If I am Assassinated*, p. 25.
4. Interview with Della Rounick, Athens, 18 August 2008.
5. MMB, letter to Della Rounick, 6 June 1978.
6. MMB, letter to Della Rounick, undated, October 1978.
7. Interview with Robert Kennedy Jr, Mount Kisco, New York, 15 May 2006.
8. Ibid.
9. Ibid.
10. Ibid.
11. Interview with Milbry Polk, New York City, 19 April 2006.
12. Ibid.

Chapter 7

1. Interview with Suhail Sethi, Karachi, 21 March 2008.
2. Interview with Della Rounick, Athens, 18 August 2008.
3. Interview with Della Rounick, Mykonos, 22 August 2008.
4. Interview with Tariq Ali, Karachi, 26 March 2006.
5. Ibid.
6. Clips from the press conference can be seen at http://www.youtube.com/watch?v=AzetHoYI52Y
7. Ibid.
8. Interview with Tariq Ali, Karachi, 26 March 2006.
9. Interview with Della Rounick, Athens, 19 August 2008.
10. A clip of Murtaza speaking can be found at http://www.youtube.com/watch?v=jOg5zFyU4P4
11. Interview with Robert Kennedy Jr, Mount Kisco, New York, 15 May 2006.
12. Interview with Abdul Waheed Katpar, Karachi, 4 June 2008.
13. Ibid.
14. Interview with Tariq Ali, Karachi, 26 March 2006.
15. Ibid.
16. Ibid.
17. Interview with Suhail Sethi, Karachi, 21 March 2008.
18. Interview with Tariq Ali, Karachi, 26 March 2006.
19. Interview with Della Rounick, Mykonos, 22 August 2008.
20. Ibid.
21. Published in Greek – translated, unpublished version under the name 'A Crumb of God' given to me by Della Rounick.
22. MMB letter to Della Rounick, Kabul, 20 July 1979.
23. Interview with Della Rounick, Mykonos, 22 August 2008.
24. Interview with Milbry Polk, New York City, 19 April 2006.
25. Interview with Mayor Bill White, Houston, Texas, 7 May 2006.
26. Interview with Magdalena Guernica Castleman, New York City, 18 May 2006.
27. Interview with Mayor Bill White, Houston, Texas, 7 May 2006.

Chapter 8

1. Diary entry of 27 October 1979.
2. Diary entry of 2 November 1979.
3. Diary entry of 5 December 1979.
4. Diary entry of 28 March 1980.
5. Interview with Suhail Sethi, Karachi, 21 March 2008.
6. Ibid.
7. Ibid.
8. Ibid.
9. Ibid.
10. Published in Greek – translated, unpublished version under the name 'A Crumb of God', given to me by Della Rounick.
11. Ibid.
12. Interview with Suhail Sethi, Karachi, 8 March 2008.
13. MMB, undated letter to Della.

Chapter 9

1 A. Jilani, *Advance Towards Democracy: The Pakistani Experience*, p. 36.
2. Jilani, p. 36.
3. The Lawyers Committee for Human Rights, 1985, *Zia's Law: Human Rights under Military Rule in Pakistan*, p. 76.
4. Hassan Abbas, *Pakistan's Drift into Extremism: Allah, the Army and America's War on Terror*, p. 108.
5. Lawyers Committee for Human Rights, p. 77.
6. Z. Niazi, *Press in Chains*, Karachi Press Club Publication, p. 123.
7. Ibid., p. 178.
8. Interview with Siddiqueh Hidayatullah, Karachi, 8 August 2009.
9. Niazi, p. 178.
10. Ibid.
11. Ibid., p. 179.
12. *Dawn*, 8 July 1980.
13. Niazi, p. 179.

14. Ibid. p. 182.

15. Lahore Committee for Human Rights, p. 80.

16. Interview with Mazhar Abbas, Karachi, 11 September 2004.

17. Niazi, p. 185.

18. H. Askari Rizvi, *The Military and Politics in Pakistan*, p. 239.

19. E. Duncan, *Breaking the Curfew*, p. 70.

20. S. P Cohen, *The Idea of Pakistan*, p. 58.

21. S. Shafqat, *Civil–Military Relations in Pakistan: From Zulfikar Ali Bhutto to Benazir Bhutto*, p. 193.

22. Owen Bennet Jones, *Pakistan: Eye of the Storm*, pp. 16–17.

23. Ibid., p. 24.

24. Ibid., p. 26.

25. Ibid., pp. 31–5.

26. Ibid., pp. 35–8.

27. Ibid., p. 68.

28. Michel Foucault, *Discipline and Punish*, p. 49.

29. Ibid., p. 48.

30. I. H. Malik, *State and Civil Society in Pakistan*, p. 147.

31. Asma Jahangir and Hina Jilani, *The Hudood Ordinances – A Divine Sanction?*, p. 23.

32. Ibid., pp. 85–6.

33. A. M. Weiss, 'Pakistani Women in the 1980s and Beyond', in C. Baxter and S. R. Wasti (eds.), *Pakistani Authoritarianism in the 1980s*, p. 139.

34. Malik, p. 148.

35. Jahangir and Jilani, p. 68.

36. Weiss, p. 144.

37. Ibid.

38. M. Asghar Khan, *Generals in Politics: Pakistan 1958–1982*, p. 159.

39. R. LaPorte Jr, 'Urban Groups and the Zia Regime', in C. Baxter (ed.), *Zia's Pakistan: Politics and Stability in a Frontline State*, p. 18.

40. Ibid.

41. Ibid., p. 170.

42. Ibid.

43. Ibid.

44. Lawyers Committee for Human Rights, p. 61.

45. Ibid., pp. 59–62.

46. LaPorte Jr, p. 16.

47. Jahangir and Jilani, p. 67.

48. J. Dad Khan, *Pakistan's Leadership Challenges*, p. 173.

49. Askari Rizvi, p. 239.

50. Duncan, p. 70.

Chapter 10

1. Ian Stephens, letter to Murtaza Bhutto, 11 April 1978.

2. Hedley Bull's supervisor report, 17 December 1977.

3. Memorandum dated 12 October 1978.

4. Letter dated 28 November 1978.

5. Hedley Bull supervisor's report 17 December 1978.

6. Ibid., 17 December 1979.

7. Ibid., 6 July 1980.

8. Ibid., 17 December 1980.

9. Interview with Della Rounick, Mykonos, 22 August 2008.

10. Interview with Suhail Sethi, Karachi, 28 December 2008.

11. Ibid.

12. Published in Greek – translated unpublished version under the name 'A Crumb of God', given to me by Della Rounick.

13. Interview with Suhail Sethi, Karachi, 28 December 2008.

14. Interview with Ghulam Hussain, Islamabad, 21 May 2008.

15. MMB Letter to Della Rounick, postmarked Kabul, 25 April 1981.

Chapter 11

1. Interview with Suhail Sethi, Karachi, 21 March 2008.

2. Ibid.

3. Interview with Suhail Sethi, Karachi, 28 December 2008.

4. Ibid.

5. Interview with Suhail Sethi, Karachi, 29 December 2008.

6. Ian Talbot, *Pakistan: A Modern History*, p. 181.

7. S. Shafqat, *Civil–Military Relations in Pakistan: From Zulfikar Ali Bhutto to Benazir Bhutto*, p. 193.

8. J. Dad Khan, *Pakistan's Leadership Challenges*, p. 174.

9. B. Cloughly, *A History of the Pakistan Army: Wars and Insurrections*, p. 292.

10. Interview with Della Rounick, Mykonos, 20 August 2008.

11. Lawrence Ziring, *Pakistan in the 20th Century: A Political History*, p. 483.

12. Interview with Suhail Sethi, Karachi, 21 March 2008.

13. Ibid.

14. Ibid.

15. Interview with Suhail Sethi, Karachi, 28 December 2008.

16. Interview with Suhail Sethi, Karachi, 29 December 2008.

17. Ibid.

Chapter 12

1. Interview with Sassi Bhutto, 21 March 2009.

2. Interview with Jacques Vergès, Paris, 2 March 2009.

Chapter 13

1. Interview with Suhail Sethi, Karachi, 21 March 2008.

Chapter 14

1. Interview with Ghinwa Bhutto, Karachi, 11 February 2009.

2. Ian Talbot, *Pakistan: A Modern History*, p. 284.

3. Edward Jay Epstein, 'Who Killed Zia?', *Vanity Fair*, September 1989.

4. Ibid. and Tariq Ali, *The Duel*, p. 131.

5. Epstein.

6. Ibid.

7. Talbot, pp. 284.

8. Ali, pp. 131–2

9. Interview with Ghinwa Bhutto, Karachi, 22 August 2009.

10. Interview with Dr Sikandar Jatoi, Karachi, 5 August 2009.

11. Interview with Mumtaz Bhutto, Karachi, 4 September 2009.

12. Interview with Suhail Sethi, Karachi, 13 August 2009.

Chapter 15

1. Ian Talbot, *Pakistan: A Modern History*, p 297.

2. Ibid.

3. Talbot, pp. 297–8.

4. Ibid., p. 297.

5. Interview with Dr Ghulam Hussain, Islamabad, 21 May 2008.

6. Interview with Maulabux, Karachi, 10 May 2008.

7. Interview with Shahnawaz Baloch, Karachi, 10 May 2008.

8. Interview with Aftab Sherpao, Islamabad, 19 May 2008.

9. Talbot, p. 294.

10. Ibid., p. 292.

11. Ibid., p. 293.

12. Interview with Suhail Sethi, Karachi, 29 December 2008.

13. Talbot, p. 303.

14. Ibid., p. 305.

15. Javed Iqbal, one of Pakistan's longest-serving political prisoners and a member of the PPP, remained in jail until after the fall of Benazir's first government. Iqbal joined Murtaza when he returned to Pakistan in 1993 and played an active role in the founding of the party with Murtaza a year and a half before his murder.

16. Mir Murtaza Bhutto, letter to Nusrat Bhutto, 21 December 1989.

17. Owen Bennet Jones, *Pakistan: Eye of the Storm*, p. 237.

18. Ali, p. 135.

19. Talbot, p. 310.

Chapter 16

1. Interview with Dr Ghulam Hussain, Islamabad, 21 May 2008.

2. Interview with Suhail Sethi, Karachi 29 December 2008.

3. Interview with Maulabux, Karachi, 14 May 2008.

4. Interview with Hameed Baloch, Karachi, 14 May, 2008.

5. Interview with Aftab Sherpao, Islamabad, 19 May 2008.

6. Interview with Maulabux, Karachi, 10 May 2008.

Chapter 17

1. Interview in *The Nation*, 16 May 1991.

2. Interview in *Daily News*, 12 August 1993.

3. *Dawn*, 24 August 1993.

4. *Daily Mushriq*, 30 October 1993.

5. *The News*, 27 October 1993.

6. Interview with Suhail Sethi, Karachi, 29 December 2008.

7. Interview with Hameed Baloch, Karachi, 6, March 2009.

8. Interview with Maulabux Karachi, 14 May 2008.

9. Interview with Shahnawaz Baloch, Karachi, 14 May 2008.

10. Interview with Shahnwaz Baloch, Karachi, 10 May 2008.

11. 'The Lion King', *Vista* magazine, 1994, p. 67.

12. Interview with Shahnawaz Baloch, Karachi, 10 May 2008.

Chapter 18

1. Interview with the *Weekend Post*, 10 December 1993.

2. *Daily Nation*, 29 December 1993.

3. Interview with Suhail Sethi, Karachi, 13 August 2009.

4. *Dawn*, 15 December 1993.

5. Interview with Ghinwa Bhutto, Karachi, 14 February 2009.

6. Henry Kamm, 'Karachi Journal: With Blood Ties Surrendered, Blood Divides Bhuttos', *New York Times*, 12 January 1994.

7. Ibid.

8. Ibid.

Chapter 19

1. *Newsline Magazine*, Hasan Mujtaba, 'From Guns to Roses', June 1994, p. 49.

2. Ibid.

3. Ibid.

4. Ibid.

5. Ibid.

6. Henry Kamm, 'Bhutto fans the family feud, charging mother favours son', *New York Times*, 14 January 1994.
7. Ibid.
8. 'We can't talk with the murderers of Shaheed Bhutto', interview conducted by Massoud Ansari, *Newsline Magazine*, June 1994, p. 51.
9. Interview with Suhail Sethi, Karachi, 13 August 2009.

Chapter 20
1. *Dawn*, 12 August 1994.
2. *Frontier Post* newspaper, 18 October 1994.
3. *Dawn*, 27 December 1994.
4. Not the American CIA but the Pakistani Intelligence and security authorities, also unhelpfully called the CIA.
5. *Newsline Magazine* 'MQM: Road to Nowhere?', Ghulam Hasnain, May 1997, p. 21.
6. Talbot, *Pakistan: A Modern History*, p. 343.
7. Ghulam Hasnain and Hasan Zaidi, 'The Politics of Murder', *Herald Magazine*, March 1996, p. 25.
8. 'City of Death' special edn., *Herald Magazine*, January 1996.
9. Ibid., p. 26.
10. Ibid.
11. Ibid., p. 27.
12. Naserullah Babar interview with Idrees Bakhtiar, *Herald Magazine*, March 1996, p. 36.
13. Hasnain and Zaidi, p. 27.
14. Ibid.
15. 'City of Death'.
16. Ibid.
17. Bakhtiar, p. 37.
18. Hasnain and Zaidi, pp. 30–31.
19. Ibid., p. 33.
20. Ibid.
21. Ibid., p. 32.
22. Ibid.

23. Ibid., p. 33.
24. Ibid.
25. Ghulam Hasnain and Hasan Zaidi, 'Fact and Fiction,' *Herald Magazine*, March 1996, p. 38.
26. http://news.bbc.co.uk/2/hi/south_asia/8230267.stm
27. http://news.bbc.co.uk/2/hi/south_asia/8219814.stm

Chapter 21
1. Interview with Usman Hingoro, Karachi, 4 May 2008.
2. Ibid.
3. Ibid.
4. Mir Murtaza Bhutto, letter to Ali Hingoro, Karachi, 26 March 1995.
5. Interview with Usman Hingoro, Karachi, 4 May 2008.
6. Bennet Jones, *Pakistan: Eye of the Storm*, p. 233.
7. Ibid.
8. Ibid.
9. John F. Burns, 'House of Graft: Tracing the Bhutto Millions', *New York Times*, 9 January 1998.
10. *Benazir Bhutto: the investigation*, BBC, 30 October 2007.
11. Bennet Jones, p. 233.
12. *Benazir Bhutto: the investigation*.
13. Bennet Jones, p. 233.
14. Rao Rashid, 'Bhutto's Legacy: The Other Version', *The Nation*, 4 April 1995.
15. *The News* newspaper, 26 November 1995.

Chapter 22
1. Interview with Ramzan Brohi, Karachi, 14 March 2009.
2. Interview with Qaisar, Karachi, 15 March 2009.
3. Interview with Amer Jokhio, Karachi, 14 March 2009.
4. Interview with Asif Jatoi, Karachi, 6 June 2008.
5. Interview with Ghulam Hasnain, Karachi, 8 May 2008.
6. Interview with Aneed Jatoi, Karachi, 10 March 2009.
7. Interview with Sabeen Jatoi, Karachi 8 March 2009.

8. Interview with Dr Nuzhat Jatoi, Karachi, 9 March 2009.

9. Interview with Dr Ghaffar Jatoi, Karachi, 1 May 2008.

10. Interview with Dr Zahid Jatoi, Karachi, 9 March 2009.

11. Interview, Karachi, 14 May 2008.

12. Interview with Nasir Aslam Zahid, Karachi, 5 May 2008.

13. Interview with Justice Wajihuddin Ahmed, Karachi, 6 May 2008.

Epilogue

1. Interview with Noor Ahmed Nizam, Karachi, 9 May 2008.

Index

decides to contest elections, 311–12
Benazir rejects his request for election tickets, 312, 313
decides to run as an independent, 314
Ghinwa travels to Pakistan to file election papers for, 314–15
election campaign, 315–17
election result, 318
and the press, 321–3
thanks Assad for hospitality, 323
and Fatima's Arabic classes, 324
last evening in Damascus, 325
travels to Karachi, 326–7, 328
arrested, 328
in Landhi Jail, 328, 332, 333, 340, 343–5, 353, 354
supporters jailed, 328–32
refuses Benazir's offer of Eid parole, 332
in court, 334–6
interview with *Weekend Post*, 339–40
speaks in Sindh Assembly, 340
starts from the bottom in politics, 340–1
speaks to *Dawn* journalist, 341
Benazir refuses to visit in prison, 342
unable to attend celebration for his father's birthday, 345–6
and Benazir's allegations about RAW, 349
release, 353, 354–5
returns to 70 Clifton, 355–6
visits Larkana, 356–8
watched by Intelligence Service, 358–9
speaks openly against the government, 359, 365–7, 391
opinion of Zardari, 360, 385
Nusrat's support for, 360–1
government attempts to discredit, 367
satirical response to allegations, 367–9
makes vehicle bulletproof for Fatima, 372
and Ali Hingoro's detention and death, 383–4
people turn towards, 388
works on political programme, 388–9
'New Direction' printed as party manifesto, 389–90
launch of Pakistan People's Party (Shaheed Bhutto), 390
travels the country, 391–2
letter to Fatima, 391–2
in the days before his assassination, 13–15, 18–23
last day, 23–33
shooting and death, 33–6, 395–406, 409–14, 416
Benazir prevented from attending funeral of, 416–17
funeral, 420–1
tribunal to investigate death of, 422–3
murder case, 423, 435, 436
Bhutto, Mumtaz (daughter of Sir Shahnawaz), 43
Bhutto, Mumtaz (Zulfikar's cousin, and head of Bhutto tribe), 40–1, 48, 88, 285, 289, 310
Bhutto, Nabi Bux, 41
Bhutto, Nusrat ('Joonam'; author's grandmother)
meets and marries Zulfikar, 49–52
birth of children, 54–5, 81
and Zulfikar's entry into politics, 55–6
affectionate towards her children, 141
and Zulfikar's arrest, 148
travels in disguise, 151
Della's similarity to, 163, 177

Margaret Thatcher sends letter of condolence to, 174
Della's visit to, 177–8
in jail and under house arrest, 185
junta's smear campaign against, 194–5
attacked by police in Lahore, 209
arrested in connection with hijacking, 228
role in PPP, 240, 360–1
in Nice for family reunion, 248, 250
and death of Shahnawaz, 251, 252, 254, 255
and Zia's death, 285
advises Benazir to reject 1988 election results, 294
at wedding of Murtaza and Ghinwa, 296, 297
supports Murtaza's idea of returning to Pakistan, 298
in Damascus for birth of her grandson Zulfi, 300
Murtaza voices his concerns in letter to, 301–2
ousted as PPP chairperson by Benazir, 312–13, 361
and Murtaza's election campaign, 316, 317, 318
at Jinnah airport for Murtaza's arrival, 327–8
and 70 Clifton, 333–4
attends court proceedings, 334, 381
moved by Murtaza's speech in Sindh Assembly, 340
and events on Zulfikar's birthday, 346, 347, 348, 349
and Murtaza's release, 354, 355, 356
and arrest of Ali Hingoro, 381–2
and corruption charges, 387, 391
criticizes Benazir's politics, 391
after death of Murtaza, 421
brief references, 82, 84–5, 303, 324
Bhutto, Pir Bux, 41
Bhutto, Raehana (author's aunt), 234, 247, 249, 250, 251, 253, 254–5, 256, 257, 259, 263
Bhutto, Rasool Bux, 41–2, 45
Bhutto, Sanam (author's aunt), 55, 81, 82, 85, 89, 134, 136, 145, 186–7, 248, 268, 314, 421
Bhutto, Sardar Wahid Bux, 41
Bhutto, Sassi (author's cousin), 236, 247, 248–9, 251, 252–3, 255–7, 263, 266, 425
Bhutto, Shanawaz ('Shah'; author's uncle)
birth of, 55
childhood, 81–2, 86, 87, 88–9, 92
close relationship with Murtaza, 87, 88–9, 267, 268
joins Murtaza in Larkana, 146–7
leaves Pakistan, 148
campaigns with Murtaza to save his father's life, 148, 149
studies in Switzerland, 150
at press conference in London, 170
and his father's death, 173, 174
and idea of armed struggle, 175–6, 178
and formation of People's Liberation Army, 178
meeting with Gadaffi, 180
meeting with Arafat, 180–1
relationship with Nurseli, 187–8
joins Murtaza in Kabul, 188
in Kabul, 193, 194, 218, 219, 220, 233–4, 236, 238–9
portrayed as terrorist, 195
accused of hijacking, 220, 228, 229

464

467